International Travel and Tourism

Online Services

Delmar Online
To access a wide variety of Delmar products and services on the World Wide Web, point your browser to:
    http://www.delmar.com/delmar.html
    or email: info@delmar.com

thomson.com
To access International Thomson Publishing's home site for information on more than 34 publishers and 20,000 products, point your browser to:
    http://www.thomson.com
    or email: findit@kiosk.thomson.com

A service of I(T)P®

International Travel and Tourism

Helle Sorensen

Delmar Publishers

an International Thomson Publishing company I(T)P

Albany • Bonn • Boston • Cincinnati • Detroit • London • Madrid
Melbourne • Mexico City • New York • Pacific Grove • Paris • San Francisco
Singapore • Tokyo • Toronto • Washington

NOTICE TO THE READER

Publisher does not warrant or guarantee any of the products described herein or perform any independent analysis in connection with any of the product information contained herein. Publisher does not assume, and expressly disclaims, any obligation to obtain and include information other than that provided to it by the manufacturer.

The reader is expressly warned to consider and adopt all safety precautions that might be indicated by the activities herein and to avoid all potential hazards. By following the instructions contained herein, the reader willingly assumes all risks in connection with such instructions.

The publisher makes no representation or warranties of any kind, including but not limited to, the warranties of fitness for particular purpose or merchantability, nor are any such representations implied with respect to the material set forth herein, and the publisher takes no responsibility with respect to such material. The publisher shall not be liable for any special, consequential, or examplary damages resulting, in whole or part, from the readers' use of, or reliance upon, this material.

Illustration: Alex Piejko
Design by Bob Clarke

Delmar Staff
Acquisitions Editor: Christopher Anzalone
Editorial Assistant: Judy A. Roberts
Developmental Editor: Jeffrey D. Litton
Project Editor: Eugenia L. Orlandi
Production Coordinator: Linda J. Helfrich
Art & Design Coordinator: Douglas J. Hyldelund

COPYRIGHT © 1997
By Delmar Publishers Inc.
an International Thomson Publishing Company

The ITP logo is a trademark under license.

Printed in the United States of America

For more information, contact:

Delmar Publishers
3 Columbia Circle, Box 15015
Albany, New York 12212-5015

International Thomson Publishing—Europe
Berkshire House
168-173 High Holborn
London, WC1V 7AA
England

Thomas Nelson Australia
102 Dodds Street
South Melbourne, 3205
Victoria, Australia

Nelson Canada
1120 Birchmount Road
Scarborough, Ontario
Canada, M1K 5G4

International Thomson Editores
Campos Eliseos 385, Piso 7
Col Polanco
11560 Mexico D F Mexico

International Thomson Publishing GmbH
Konigswinterer Strasse 418
53227 Bonn
Germany

International Thomson Publishing—Asia
221 Henderson Road
#05-10 Henderson Building
Singapore 0315

International Thomson Publishing—Japan
Hirakawacho Kyowa Building, 3F
2-2-1 Hirakawacho
Chiyoda-ku, Tokyo 102
Japan

All rights reserved. No part of this work covered by the copyright hereon may be reproduced or used in any form or by any means—graphic, electronic, or mechanical, including photocopying, recording, taping, or information storage and retrieval systems—without the written permission of the publisher.

1 2 3 4 5 6 7 8 9 10 XXX 03 02 01 00 99 98 97

Library of Congress Cataloging-in-Publication Data

Sorensen, Helle.
    International travel and tourism / Helle Sorensen.
      p.   cm.
    Includes index.
    ISBN 0-8273-7448-8
    1. Tourist trade.   I. Title.
G155.A1S595   1997
338.4′791—dc20
                        96-34466
                          CIP

Contents

Preface xiii

Acknowledgments xv

About the Author xvii

Chapter 1 Introduction to International Travel and Tourism 1

Learning the Travel Profession   2
Historical Reasons for Travel   3
Growth of International Tourism   4
   Emerging Nations   4
   Reasons for International Travel   5
The World Tourism Organization   6
Trends in Travel and Tourism   6
   Trends in Regional International Tourist Arrivals   7
      Trends in the Middle East   7
      Trends in East Asia and the Pacific Region   7
      Trends in South Asia   8
      Trends in the Americas   8
      Trends in Europe   8
      Trends in Africa   10
   Trends in International Tourism Income   10
The World Travel & Tourism Council   12
Travel Employment   12

The World's Top Tourism Destinations   13
Health Issues when Traveling   16
   Jet Lag   17
   Altitude and Motion Sickness   18
   Food and Water   18
   Yellow Fever   19
   Cholera   19
   Typhoid Fever   22
   Hepatitis   22
   Tetanus   22
   Meningitis   26
   Malaria   26

Chapter 2   Air Travel Geography   33

Eight Freedoms of the Air   34
The International Air Transport Association   41
   The Roles of the IATA   41
   IATA Membership and Accreditation   42
The International Airlines Travel Agency Network   43
   Travel Agent Identification Cards   43
Interline Travel   44
IATA Geography   45
   IATA Areas   45
City, Airport, and Airline Codes   47
Air Routes   50
International Time   52
   The 24-Hour Clock   52
   Time Zones   54
      Calculating Time Zone Differences   55
   The International Date Line   57
      Calculating Time Differences across the Date Line   57
   Elapsed Flying Time   58

Chapter 3   Travel Requirements   67

Travel Documents   68
   The Passport   68
   The Visa   71
   The Tourist Card   76
   Proof of Citizenship   76
Customs and Immigration   77
   Customs Inspection   77

    Immigration Procedures   78
    Customs Procedures   79
    Duty-Free Shopping   81
    Restricted Items   81
Money Matters   82
    Foreign Currency   83
    Currency Codes   84
    Value-Added Tax   84

Chapter 4   International Airfares   91

IATA Airfares   92
    Stopovers and Connections   92
    Normal Fares   94
    Excursion and Apex Fares   95
        Excursion/Apex Fare Basis Codes   96
    Infants' and Children's Fares   97
Interpreting IATA Airfare and Rule Displays   98
    Air Tariff Books   99
    Normal Fare Displays   99
    Excursion and Apex Fare Displays   102
    Automated Fare Displays   104

Chapter 5   International Ticketing   119

IATA Agent Responsibilities   120
The International Airline Ticket   121
    Name of Passenger   121
    Baggage Allowance   124
    Tax Computation and Currency Code   127
    Sales Indicator Code   129
    Fare Calculation Ladder   132
IATA Ticketing Procedures   132
    Normal-Fare Itineraries   132
    Excursion-Fare Itineraries   135
    Apex-Fare Itineraries   135

Chapter 6   The New Europe   149

The European Union   150
    Goals of the European Union   151
    Financial Concerns of the European Union   153
Travel and Tourism   154
    Travel Procedures   154

Travel Competition   154
Rail Travel   155
    European Rail Passes   156
        The Eurailpass   157
        The Europass   157
    The Channel Tunnel   160
    Le Shuttle   160
Major Destinations   162
  The Mediterranean   162
  The Riviera   162
    The French Riviera   164
    The Italian Riviera   164
    The Spanish Riviera   165
  Morocco   167
  Greece   167
  Turkey   168
  Israel   169
Off the Beaten Path   169
  The Orient Express   169
    London   172
    Paris   172
    Milan   173
    Venice   173
Historical Waterways   173
  The Rhine   173
  The Danube   176
Exploring Northern Europe   177

Chapter 7   The New Russia   185

The Commonwealth of Independent States   187
  Geography of the CIS   187
  Culture in the CIS   189
Travel and Tourism Russian Style   189
  Russian Air Travel   190
The Trans-Siberian Railroad   191
Major Destinations   191
  Moscow   191
  Yaroslaw   193
  Siberia   193
  Irkutsk   194

Lake Baikal　　194
　　　Ulan Ude　　195
　　　Khabarovsk　　195
　　　Vladivostok　　195
　　　China　　196
　　　Japan　　196
　　　Eastern Europe　　197
　　　Arctica　　198

Chapter 8　Asia and the Pacific　　207
The Eastern & Oriental Express　　210
　　Singapore　　211
　　Malaysia　　213
　　Ipoh and Butterworth　　214
　　Southern Thailand　　214
　　Bangkok　　215
　　Northern Thailand　　215
Vietnam　　216
　　The Reunification Express　　217
　　　　Ho Chi Minh City　　217
　　　　Nha Trang　　217
　　　　Da Nang　　219
　　　　Hue　　219
　　　　Hanoi　　220
Australia　　220
　　Indian Pacific　　221
　　The Ghan　　222
　　The Queenslander　　223
The South Pacific　　224
　　Tonga　　225
　　Fiji　　226
　　Easter Island　　226
　　Bora Bora　　227
　　American Samoa　　227
　　Tahiti　　227
　　Cook Islands　　227
　　New Zealand　　228

Chapter 9　Developing Nations　　233
Southern Africa　　236
　　The Blue Train　　238

    Cape Town 238
    Kimberley 240
    Johannesburg 240
  Zimbabwe 241
  Zambia 241
  Tanzania 241
The Nile River 242
  Egypt 244
  Sudan 245
  Ethiopia 246
The Zambezi River Valley 246
South America 248
  Quito 249
  Ambato 250
  Riobamba 250
  Cuenca 251
  Guayaquil 251
Argentina and Chile 251
  Patagonia 252
  Tierra del Fuego 252
  Ushuaia 252
  Punta Arenas 252
  Puerto Montt 254
Antarctica 254

Chapter 10 A Sustainable Future 261

Sustainable Tourism 262
  Embracing International Values 263
  Selling Sustainable Tourism 264
Ecotourism 264
  Defining Ecotourism 265
  Understanding Ecotourism 267
Adventure Travel 268
Maintaining Environmental Welfare 269
  The Amazon 270
  Protecting the Rain Forest 273
Preserving Social Structures 273
Protecting Animal Habitats 279

Appendices   287

Glossary   343

Index   351

Preface

OBJECTIVES OF THIS BOOK

International Travel and Tourism offers a refreshing approach to introducing the various and new aspects of traveling abroad through real-life, humorous, and relevant stories. It is a comprehensive source for discovering this fast-growing segment of the industry and exploring the growing need for specialized international travel professionals. This book presents a new perspective of international travel: that of the culturally aware ecotourist.

DESCRIPTION OF THIS BOOK

International Travel and Tourism contains several features that make it unique:

- Detailed coverage of international air-travel geography
- Extensive coverage of international airfares and ticketing procedures
- Reinforcement of each chapter through end-of-chapter activities
- Illustrations, objectives, and activities
- Introduction to what is new in Europe
- Critical analysis of ecotourism
- Broadening of global horizons to maximize cultural understanding

International Travel and Tourism continues where other international textbooks leave off. This book transitions naturally from domestic ticketing to advanced international fare construction. It stresses the importance of thoroughly knowing geography as it relates to efficient travel itinerary design. This book also encourages the reader to analyze the concept of ecotourism, and it emphasizes the importance of ethical travel. This book begins by discussing how to obtain passports and visas, then familiarizes the student with global time, travels through the New Europe and the New Russia, and ends with an in-depth exploration of "preservation-of-the-Earth" way of traveling.

Learning is reinforced with open-ended questions that encourage students to think critically and expand their horizons. After they read this book, international travel and tourism students will not be the same.

WHO SHOULD USE THIS BOOK

Travel professionals who are new to the field or are continuing their education will appreciate the daring and refreshing approach of this book. A smooth transition between classroom knowledge and on-the-job experience is stressed.

Acknowledgments

The author wishes to thank the travel and tourism students at the Community College of Denver for their utmost patience as I presented my rough draft of the manuscript.

Special thanks go to Michael McGuire of Denver who lent his support and read huge piles of manuscript during early developmental stages.

Very special thanks go to the author's parents residing in Denmark. Even during illness, her Father, Helge Sorensen, provided detailed updates on Europe. Her mother, Inge Sorensen, patiently served her favorite meals while the author worked on the final draft during her visits. My younger sister, Lise Sorensen, was kind enough to share her African experience and provide the chapter 9 photo. One of my goals with this text is to convince my older sister, Ulla Christensen, that the world is full of exciting and little explored places, begging to have her cast aside her fear of flying.

The rest of my heart goes to my close friends in the Rocky Mountain region. It would have been difficult to develop this text had they not been so understanding at seeing me so rarely.

All computer excerpts in this textbook are from United Airlines Apollo computer reservation system. United Airlines granted permission to reprint its fares and rules. This textbook also contains extracts of airfares from *Air Tariff Book 1—Worldwide*

Fares and rules from *Air Tariff Book 1—Worldwide Rules, Routings, and Mileages*. All airfares, rules, and exchange rates in this textbook are reprinted from air tariff books. The Airline Reporting Corporation (ARC) has granted permission to reprint all tickets appearing in this textbook.

REVIEWERS

Peter Wilmarth
Madison Area Technical College
Madison, WI

Donna Morn
Art Institute of Fort Lauderdale
Fort Lauderdale, FL

Diane Schafer
University of New Orleans
Metairie, LA

Scott Feinerman
West Los Angeles College
Los Angeles, CA

Russell Nauta
Northeastern Junior College
Sterling, CO

Ernest P. Boyer
Bethune-Cookman College
Daytona Beach, FL

About the Author

The author, Helle Sorensen, is an instructor in the Travel and Tourism Department of the Community College of Denver. Her work in the international field was sought by companies in Denmark, Great Britain, and the United States. Born and raised in Denmark, Sorensen resides in the majestic Rocky Mountains of Colorado. The serenity and beauty of living in the wilderness at 8,000 feet were her inspiration and motivation for writing this book. Sorensen's adventurous and far-reaching solo travels have exposed her to a wide variety of people from many different walks of life. She finds the incredible diversity of cultures and customs intriguing. One of Sorensen's travels led her to trek for days through the harsh Tibetan Himalayas to reach the peace and solitude of the highest monastery in the world at 16,500 feet. Mt. Everest loomed in the foreground.

Chapter 1

Introduction to International Travel and Tourism

Learning the Travel Profession
Historical Reasons for Travel
Growth of International Travel
    Emerging Nations
    Reasons for International Travel
The World Tourism Organization
Trends in Travel and Tourism
    Trends in Regional International Tourist Arrivals
    Trends in International Tourism Income
The World Travel & Tourism Council
Travel Employment
The World's Top Tourism Destinations
Health Issues when Traveling
    Jet Lag
    Altitude and Motion Sickness
    Food and Water
    Yellow Fever
    Cholera
    Typhoid Fever
    Hepatitis
    Tetanus
    Meningitis
    Malaria

2 International Travel and Tourism

OBJECTIVES

After completing Chapter 1, you should be able to:

- Understand the value of knowing geography
- Provide an overview of the international travel and tourism industry
- Explain why people travel
- Describe the influences on travel and tourism
- Discuss various health issues as they relate to travel

Many travelers find venturing through mysterious countries and experiencing different cultures intriguing. The allure of selling travel is finding out-of-the-way spots for clients. Travel professionals must carefully prepare to help their clients avoid unpleasant and unexpected events, because the unexpected almost always happens.

For example, imagine you are a travel professional who has sent a client backpacking in the unknown jungles and forests of Congo, Africa. Jet lagged and exhausted, your client is sitting by a campfire when she is surrounded suddenly by Bayaka pygmy people. Your client scrambles for her pocket guidebook, but it has no chapter on what to do in this situation. As a travel professional, you must help your clients prepare properly for events like these on their international journeys.

Learning the Travel Profession

Many travel professionals, especially those who have traveled, find selling travel rewarding. Travel experience is the best tool for educating travel professionals. In the travel business, nothing compares to firsthand knowledge and the ability to appreciate new places and events.

Becoming a knowledgeable travel professional begins with understanding geography. In fact, one of the biggest obstacles to selling travel efficiently is the lack of geographical knowledge. Professionals who sell travel with no cultural and geographical information can cause their clients to experience embarrassing moments. While it is impossible for travel professionals to know the geography of the entire world, it is possible for them to become highly familiarized with the geography and climate of a smaller region and to sell travel more efficiently as a result. For example, the travel professional who understands wind patterns knows that monsoon season is between December and March in Indonesia, instead of between May and October as in most other Southeast Asian nations. Similarly, the travel professional who knows ocean currents understands why the water in Los Angeles, California, is always cooler than that in Charleston, South Carolina, even though the two cities are at the same latitude.

Travel professionals who understand why people go abroad are more likely to satisfy their customers. Understanding the travel industry and its terminology fully helps the travel professional to determine the traveler's needs. The *Oxford Encyclopedic English Dictionary* defines a **traveler** as someone who makes a journey of some length. The World Tourism Organization (WTO) defines an **international visitor** as "... any person who travels to a country other than that in which he [or she] has his [or her] usual residence, the main purpose of whose visit is other than the exercise of an activity remunerated from within the country visited, and who is staying for a period of 1 year or less." An international visitor is classified as an **international tourist** if he or she is staying at least one night. Travelers have different expectations of accommodations, and it does not necessarily mean being accommodated in a hotel.

This text will broaden the knowledge base of the travel professional from these basic definitions to include the wide range of new travel products and destinations.

Historical Reasons for Travel

People have always traveled. In ancient times people needed travel. They traveled to hunt and to migrate with their food sources. For past civilizations travel was not pleasurable, particularly when it was needed to fight wars. Travel in ancient times was tedious, primitive, difficult, and often risky work.

Travel as we know it today evolved slowly. During the Greek Empirial and Roman Empirial times, travel expanded to include trading. During the Middle Ages (A.D. 500 to 1400), people organized large religious pilgrimages to cities like Jerusalem, Rome, and Mecca. During these pilgrimages, travelers began to require overnight accommodations and stayed at various monasteries en route. During the industrial revolution in the eighteenth century, people did not have vacation time to travel, even on weekends. They also had no additional income to fund their travel. The inception of railroads in 1802 revolutionized travel forever because trains made travel faster and more accessible. The automobile and the airplane, which followed in the late 1880s and 1903, respectively, made travel even more commonplace and attainable.

Growth of International Tourism

As reported by the *Countries of the World Yearbook,* at the beginning of World War II there were seventy recognized independent countries in the world. By January 1992, there were 184. During the last 40 to 50 years, nations have ceased to exist, and new nations have been created. For example, the Austrian-Hungarian Empire was divided into the countries of Austria and Hungary. Today, there are about 200 nations in the world. About 70 percent of these countries offer a rich multicultural travel experience.

EMERGING NATIONS

Many new international territories have emerged during the past 50 years, begging to be explored. Since World War II, the number of new sovereign nations has tripled. Most recently the former Soviet Union broke into fifteen independent nations. Many former European colonies also gained their independence. Great Britain suffered the greatest loss, releasing forty-two colonies throughout the world. Similarly, fourteen

French and five Portuguese colonies in Africa regained their freedom and independence.

REASONS FOR INTERNATIONAL TRAVEL

Today, many factors generate international travel. The two main factors are necessity and leisure. Like their ancestors, many people still travel out of necessity. Business travel, for example, is often crucial for prosperity. A large group of people travel for educational and health purposes. Some travelers take so-called "working vacations," such as trips to teach English in Indonesia or help build schools in Tanzania. For many athletes, traveling is a part of daily life. Traveling to visit family and friends can result both from necessary events, like weddings, and leisure pursuits, like relaxing and discovering the "roots" of a country. Religious pilgrimages are extremely popular leisure activities around Easter and Christmas.

Leisure travelers want to experience their destinations. Some may want to learn about other cultures. Participating in the Carnival in Rio de Janeiro, attending a bullfight in Spain, or watching a dance performance in Thailand widens the traveler's perspective. Natural environments of destinations also attract leisure travelers. People travel to warm climates to relax on white-sand beaches, enjoy good weather, and engage in water sports. Leisure travelers flock to cooler mountainous areas as well, where activities range from camping, hiking, and skiing to sightseeing. Sometimes a destination combines an attraction with wildlife, such as a safari park in Kenya.

The man-made attractions that attract many travelers are found mostly in or around the world's major cities. Religious structures, including Indonesian temples, Vietnamese pagodas, Japanese shrines, Tibetan monasteries, and German cathedrals, draw millions of tourists each year. Other famous structures include the Egyptian pyramids, the Forbidden City in Beijing, the Lost City of the Peruvian Incas, and London's Tower Bridge.

Whatever factor may be motivating the international traveler, the travel professional must examine the traveler's needs and interests carefully. With today's sometimes overwhelming and wide range of international travel products, the travel professional must be highly attentive to detail and genuinely interested in the international arena to become familiarized with and comfortable in the international market.

The World Tourism Organization

Once a year the **World Tourism Organization (WTO)**, the most widely used source of worldwide travel and tourism statistical information, publishes the latest statistics on domestic and international travel and tourism, as well as 10-year projections. For example, the WTO records tourism receipts and expenditures and indicates the most popular international destinations. Headquartered in Madrid, the WTO is a multinational organization that divides international travel and tourism into six regions: Africa, the Americas, East Asia/Pacific, Europe, the Middle East, and South Asia.

Trends in Travel and Tourism

The WTO statistics for worldwide international tourist arrivals in 1995 show a 3.9 percent increase over 1994 figures (Figure 1-1). The WTO defines **international arrivals** as "the number of arrivals of visitors and not the number of persons. The same person who makes several trips to a given country during a given period will be counted each time as a new arrival."

The WTO statistics also show that international tourist arrivals have grown steadily since 1985 (Figure 1-1). Although in-

International Tourist Arrivals Worldwide—1985–1995

	1985	1986	1987	1988	1989	1990	1991	1992	1993	1994	1995
Arrivals (millions)	330	341	367	402	431	459	466	504	518	546	567
Percent annual change	3.3	3.3	7.7	9.5	7.3	6.6	1.5	8.1	2.9	5.4	3.9

Source: World Tourism Organization (WTO). All figures have been rounded up.

FIGURE 1-1

ternational tourism declined drastically in 1991 due to the Persian Gulf War, it was still strong enough to increase 1.5 percent worldwide over 1990 statistics. In 1993, the industry again declined, this time due to economic recession throughout the industrialized nations.

TRENDS IN REGIONAL INTERNATIONAL TOURIST ARRIVALS

Even though the Americas and Europe remain the leaders in international tourism, accounting for almost 80 percent of tourist arrivals, the world's fastest growing tourism region in 1995 was the Middle East. That year this region boasted a 12.6 percent annual increase in international tourist arrivals (Figure 1–2). With its internal stability greatly improved, Egypt accounted for almost half the increase of tourist arrivals of the Middle East. The cultural riches of the entire Middle East contributed to the overall success of the region.

TRENDS IN THE MIDDLE EAST. Although the November 1995 assassination of Yitzhak Rabin, prime minister of Israel replaced the peace of a state with fear and uncertainty, 1995 was a record tourism year for Israel.[1] In 1995, Israel received more than 2.5 million visitors, the most in the 47-year history of the Jewish state. Visitors from the United States and Canada exceeded 550,000, an increase of more than 20 percent over 1994 figures.

TRENDS IN EAST ASIA AND THE PACIFIC REGION. The WTO statistics show East Asia and the Pacific region to have the second highest tourism growth of the six regions in 1995. This region received 84 million international arrivals in 1995, a 9.2 percent increase over 1994 numbers (Figure 1–2). East Asia and the Pacific region share 14 percent of the total world travel industry. The fastest growing destinations in East Asia/Pacific

---

[1]Waters, S. (1995–1996). *The travel industry yearbook: The big picture.* New York: Child and Waters.

International Tourist Arrivals by Region—1985–1995

	1985	1986	1987	1988	1989	1990	1991	1992	1993	1994	1995
World											
Arrivals (millions)	329.6	340.6	366.9	401.7	431.0	459.2	466.0	503.6	518.3	546.3	567.2
Percent annual change	3.3	3.3	7.7	9.5	7.3	6.6	1.5	8.1	2.9	5.4	3.9
Africa											
Arrivals (millions)	9.7	9.3	9.8	12.5	13.8	15.1	16.0	17.8	18.3	18.5	18.7
Percent annual change	10.2	-3.8	5.3	27.2	10.5	9.2	6.0	11.2	3.1	0.7	1.2
Americas											
Arrivals (millions)	66.4	71.6	76.6	83.2	87.1	93.6	97.0	103.6	104.0	107.2	111.9
Percent annual change	-1.8	7.7	7.0	8.7	4.6	7.5	3.6	6.8	0.4	3.0	4.4
East Asia/Pacific											
Arrivals (millions)	30.8	33.8	39.4	45.7	46.3	53.1	54.9	62.7	69.6	77.0	84.0
Percent annual change	10.9	9.7	16.4	16.2	1.3	14.6	3.4	14.2	11.0	10.6	9.2
Europe											
Arrivals (millions)	213.8	218.0	233.0	250.4	273.0	286.7	287.9	307.3	313.7	329.8	337.2
Percent annual change	3.6	2.0	6.9	7.5	9.0	5.0	0.4	6.7	2.1	5.1	2.3
Middle East											
Arrivals (millions)	6.2	5.1	5.4	7.0	7.7	7.6	7.0	8.6	9.0	9.9	11.1
Percent annual change	4.3	-17.8	5.8	28.2	10.1	-1.2	-7.7	23.6	3.9	9.9	12.6
South Asia											
Arrivals (millions)	2.5	2.7	2.7	2.9	3.1	3.2	3.3	3.6	3.6	3.9	4.2
Percent annual change	3.0	7.5	-0.9	6.4	6.0	4.1	3.2	10.0	-1.4	10.9	6.5

Source: World Tourism Organization (WTO).

FIGURE 1-2

in 1995 were Australia, New Zealand, and the South Pacific. Traditional destinations in the region, like Thailand and Indonesia, saw a healthy increase in visitor arrivals. Visitors are now flocking to the once-forbidden nations of Vietnam, Laos, and Cambodia and rediscovering a region full of natural beauty and historic sites. After 10 years of isolation, Laos opened for tourism in 1989.

TRENDS IN SOUTH ASIA. Although South Asia recorded the third highest tourism growth in 1995 at an annual increase of 6.5 percent (Figure 1–2), its figures translated into less than 1 percent of the total world travel industry, according to the WTO. In this region, India accounts for almost half the total international tourist arrivals, followed by Sri Lanka. Iran and Nepal share third place.

TRENDS IN THE AMERICAS. The Americas received 111.9 million international arrivals in 1995. While 4.4 percent is only slight growth for the region compared with 1994 totals (Figure 1–2), it translates into 20 percent of the total world travel industry. In 1995, the South American countries experienced a substantial growth in tourism, doubling the world average. The Caribbean nations enjoyed increased tourist arrivals, mostly because the popularity of cruises also grew. United States international tourist arrivals declined in 1995 from the previous year, mostly because the number of Canadian visitors to the United States dropped.

TRENDS IN EUROPE. While Europe received the greatest number of international tourist arrivals in 1995 at an impressive 337.2 million, or about 75 percent of the world total, it had only the fifth fastest annual tourism growth at 2.3 percent (Figure 1–2). In 1995, tourism in the nations of Eastern Europe, the Eastern Mediterranean, and the Baltic increased, while tourism in the countries of Western Europe decreased. Because many North Americans share their ancestry with the Europeans, Europe receives a large number of North American tourists. When

Germany reunified in 1989 and the Eastern European governments changed in 1990, the freedom to travel to these areas expanded greatly. In 1991, tourism in Europe declined drastically due to the Gulf War.

TRENDS IN AFRICA. Tourism is important to all African nations because they need tourism dollars. Unfortunately, international tourist arrivals to Africa in 1995 increased only 1.2 percent over 1994 levels (Figure 1–2). The nations of Southern Africa performed well, registering the highest growth of arrivals in the region, but Northern African nations, especially Morocco and Algeria, experienced a substantial drop in arrivals.

TRENDS IN INTERNATIONAL TOURISM INCOME

The WTO defines **international tourism receipts** as "the receipts of a country resulting from consumption expenditures, i.e., payment for goods and services, made by international visitors to use themselves or to give away." Tourism receipts are the income tourism makes. International tourism receipts have increased steadily since 1985 (Figure 1–3). In 1995, worldwide tourism receipts grew 7.5 percent over receipts from the previous year (Figure 1–3). From 1994 to 1995, all regions except the Americas attained international tourism growth. According to the WTO, the Middle East showed the largest gain in 1995 tourism receipts with an impressive 30.2 percent. Egypt contributed 95 percent to that figure.

Although the Americas recorded the lowest amount of international tourism receipts in 1995 according to the WTO, the Americas and Europe combined remain the world's top earners, accounting for 78 percent of all receipts. In fact, the United States is the world's top earner of tourism expenditures. In 1995, according to the WTO, the United States earned $58.4 billion in international receipts, a 60 percent contribution to the Americas' total and a 15 percent contribution to the world's total. The United States' income is unmatched internationally. It earns more than twice as much as Italy and France, which are competing for second place. European visitors spend more money during a vacation in the United States than do American

International Tourism Receipts by Region—1985–1995

	1985	1986	1987	1988	1989	1990	1991	1992	1993	1994	1995
World											
Receipts (in billions of US$)	117.6	142.1	174.2	201.5	218.4	264.7	271.8	308.6	314.0	346.7	372.6
Percent annual change	4.6	20.8	22.6	15.7	8.4	21.2	2.7	13.5	1.7	10.4	7.5
Africa											
Receipts (in billions of US$)	2.6	3.0	3.8	4.6	4.5	5.2	4.9	5.9	6.0	6.6	6.9
Percent annual change	2.8	14.2	27.8	20.9	−1.2	14.8	−6.2	21.2	1.7	9.1	5.6
Americas											
Receipts (in billions of US$)	33.6	38.0	42.5	50.9	59.7	69.5	76.8	84.8	90.7	95.1	95.2
Percent annual change	4.5	13.2	11.8	19.7	17.4	16.4	10.5	10.4	7.0	4.8	0.2
East Asia/Pacific											
Receipts (in billions of US$)	12.8	17.1	22.7	30.4	34.1	38.8	40.1	47.0	52.2	61.9	70.2
Percent annual change	7.7	33.7	32.2	34.1	12.3	13.7	3.4	17.2	10.9	18.7	13.4
Europe											
Receipts (in billions of US$)	62.4	78.3	98.1	108.7	112.6	144.0	143.3	162.6	157.5	174.8	189.8
Percent annual change	4.4	25.4	25.3	10.8	3.6	27.9	−0.5	13.5	−3.2	11.0	8.6
Middle East											
Receipts (in billions of US$)	4.8	4.0	5.3	5.1	5.4	5.1	4.3	5.4	4.8	5.1	6.7
Percent annual change	4.6	−16.1	31.6	−4.8	6.1	−4.3	−16.5	26.2	−11.0	6.3	30.2
South Asia											
Receipts (in billions of US$)	1.4	1.7	1.9	1.9	2.0	2.1	2.4	2.8	2.8	3.2	3.7
Percent annual change	−8.9	19.1	12.5	1.5	6.5	2.8	15.7	17.7	−1.6	13.1	16.8

Source: World Tourism Organization (WTO).

FIGURE 1–3

visitors during a European vacation because European currency has higher value.

The World Travel & Tourism Council

The **World Travel & Tourism Council (WTTC)** is a multinational organization with members from most sectors of the travel and tourism industry, including American Airlines, the American Automobile Association, Holiday Inn, British Airways, the Walt Disney Company, the American Express Company, and the Hertz Corporation. The WTTC's goal is to show governments how travel and tourism can benefit local and worldwide economies. The WTTC believes all barriers toward the growth and expansion of travel and tourism should be eliminated.

According to the WTTC, travel and tourism is the world's largest industry and a major contributor to global economic development. Travel and tourism generates more than $2.5 trillion in sales and is expected to more than triple that figure to $9.7 trillion by the year 2005.

Travel Employment

According to the WTTC, the travel and tourism industry is also the world's leading employer. The industry directly and indirectly employs more than 117 million people worldwide, or one in fifteen employees. This translates to 6.7 percent of all jobs worldwide. The industry has generated over 127 million jobs, and it is projected to grow 33 percent, or 157 million jobs, by the year 2005. This growth is unmatched by any other industry in the world.

In the United States the growth of travel and tourism employment is staggering. In 1995, tourism employees in the United States totaled 14.4 million, or 11.4 percent of the total workforce. That number is projected to climb to 16.8 million, or 11.5 percent of the total workforce, by the year 2005. In Africa, one in every ten workers is employed in the travel and tourism industry, compared to one in every twenty in Asia and the Pacific. These nations have higher employment rates than the nations of the European Union (predominantly western Europe). Although it is three times smaller than the United States, the European Union has about 325 million residents, compared to only 275 million in the United States. In 1995, tourism employees in the European Union totaled 19.4 million, or 13.2 percent of the total employees (Figure 1–4). That number is projected to reach 21.1 million, or 13.3 percent of the total employees, by the year 2005.

Growth of Travel Employment

The World Travel & Tourism Council (WTTC), a coalition of industry companies, has charted the growth of employment in the travel and tourism industry for the United States and the European Union during the last few years and projected figures for the years 1995 and 2005.

	United States		European Union	
Year	Tourism Employees (in millions)	Percent of Total Employees	Tourism Employees (in millions)	Percent of Total Employees
1987	12.5	11.2	18.9	13.1
1988	12.9	11.2	19.7	13.4
1989	13.1	11.2	20.3	13.6
1990	13.3	11.8	20.8	13.6
1991	13.0	11.1	20.7	13.6
1992	13.0	11.1	20.9	13.9
1995 (projected)	14.4	11.4	19.4	13.2
2005 (projected)	16.8	11.5	21.1	13.3

Source: *Travel Weekly*, February 26, 1996.

FIGURE 1–4

The World's Top Tourism Destinations

Figure 1–5 shows the top forty tourism nations in the world in 1995 by amount of international visitor arrivals and percent share of the world's total visitors. The top international destination was France, with an impressive 60.6 million tourist

The World's Top Forty Tourism Destinations

Rank 1985	Rank 1995	Country	International Tourist Arrivals* 1995	Percent Change 1995/94	Percent of Total 1995
1	1	France	60,584	−1.2	10.7
2	2	Spain	45,125	4.4	8.0
3	3	United States	43,493	−4.4	7.7
4	4	Italy	29,184	6.2	5.1
13	5	China	23,368	10.9	4.1
6	6	United Kingdom	22,700	7.9	4.0
11	7	Hungary	22,087	3.1	3.9
9	8	Mexico	19,870	16.1	3.5
23	9	Poland	19,225	2.3	3.4
5	10	Austria	17,173	−4.0	3.0
7	11	Canada	16,896	5.8	3.0
16 (1)	12	Czech Republic	16,600	−2.4	2.9
8	13	Germany	14,847	2.4	2.6
10	14	Switzerland	11,835	−3.0	2.1
14	15	Greece	11,095	3.6	2.0
19	16	Hong Kong	10,124	8.5	1.8
15	17	Portugal	9,513	4.2	1.7
22	18	Malaysia	7,936	10.3	1.4
28	19	Turkey	7,083	17.4	1.2
26	20	Thailand	6,900	11.9	1.2

FIGURE 1–5

arrivals, or a 10.7 percent share of the world's total. France well exceeded the United States' 4.5 million tourist arrivals. Paris, the cultural capital of Europe and fashion capital of the world, may have lured travelers. The culinary and wine experience by the river Seine with the grand Notre Dame Cathedral looming in the background is unmatched.

More than half the top 1995 tourism destinations were in Europe. Mexico ranked eighth with 19.9 million arrivals for a 3.5 percent share of the world's total traveling population. Mexico is a low-cost and year-round destination with exciting beaches and historic sites. While Africa is also a phenomenal destination, boasting white-sand beaches, exotic wildlife, tribal cultures, and antiquities like pyramids, it attracts only a small

Rank 1985	Rank 1995	Country	International Tourist Arrivals* 1995	Percent Change 1995/94	Percent of Total 1995
21	21	Netherlands	6,574	6.4	1.2
24	22	Singapore	6,422	2.5	1.1
17	23	Belgium	5,224	−1.6	0.9
18 (2)	24	Russian Federation	4,796	3.3	0.8
35	25	Macau	4,623	3.0	0.8
55	26	South Africa	4,488	22.3	0.8
25	27	Ireland	4,398	2.1	0.8
54	28	Indonesia	4,319	7.8	0.8
20	29	Bulgaria	4,125	1.7	0.7
32	30	Tunisia	4,120	6.8	0.7
38	31	Argentina	4,101	6.1	0.7
46	32	Australia	3,771	12.2	0.7
40	33	Korea Republic	3,753	4.8	0.7
36	34	Puerto Rico	3,297	8.4	0.6
33	35	Norway	2,880	1.8	0.5
41	36	Egypt	2,872	21.9	0.5
27	37	Romania	2,768	−1.0	0.5
29	38	Morocco	2,579	−25.6	0.5
—	39	Bahrain	2,483	9.4	0.4
39	40	Taiwan (Province of China)	2,332	9.6	0.4
		TOTAL 1-40	495,563	3.3	87.4
		WORLD TOTAL	567,213	3.9	100.0

*In thousands of arrivals; excludes same-day visitors.
(1) Former Czechoslovakia. (2) Former USSR.
Source: World Tourism Organization (WTO).

FIGURE 1–5 *(Continued)*

percentage of tourist arrivals because transportation costs are high. Developing nations in Africa, South America, and Asia do not appear on the list.

In the list of most popular international destinations for United States residents (Figure 1–6), the Caribbean soared to first place in 1995, a 19.2 percent increase over 1994 figures. American visitors also flocked to South Asia, which experienced a 14 percent annual increase in arrivals. Europe was near the bottom of the list in 1995, recording only a 1.9 percent increase over the previous year.

North America Outbound—Tourist Arrivals from North America

Destination	Total* 1995	Percent Change 95/94	Percent Change 94/93	Percent Change 93/92	Average Annual Growth Rate Percent 95/85	Market Share Percent of World Total 1985	Market Share Percent of World Total 1995
North America	54,750	−0.6	0.6	−5.2	3.0	54.5	60.5
Caribbean	8,392	19.2	2.8	9.8	4.3	7.3	9.3
South America	1,065	−8.7	16.1	4.0	4.9	0.9	1.2
Central America	1,129	7.4	6.5	8.1	12.1	0.5	1.2
Total America	65,336	1.6	1.2	−3.5	3.3	63.2	72.2
Europe	18,367	1.9	1.0	−0.9	−2.3	30.8	20.3
East Asia/Pacific	5,647	6.8	6.3	6.2	4.6	4.8	6.2
Africa	425	−4.1	6.2	6.9	0.6	0.5	0.5
South Asia	407	14.0	14.4	6.5	6.8	0.3	0.4
Middle East	334	8.8	4.4	−5.5	1.9	0.4	0.4
Total Long Haul	25,180	3.1	2.4	0.6	−0.9	36.8	27.8
World Total	90,516	2.0	1.5	−2.4	1.9	100.0	100.0

*In thousands.
Source: World Tourism Organization (WTO).

FIGURE 1–6

Over the last five years, many new travel destinations have surfaced in Asia and the Pacific. For example, since the United States lifted its trade embargo with Vietnam, this nation has blossomed into an exciting and exotic travel adventure. In fact, Asia/Pacific is the fastest growing tourism region in the world. International tourism in Europe and North America is predicted to lose some of its market share to the Asia/Pacific region by the turn of the century. It has also been predicted that growth in the Asia/Pacific region will double by the year 2000 and that by 2010, one in every five tourists will choose Asia/Pacific as a destination, thereby doubling the growth again. By 2010, Asia/Pacific may account for more than half the world's tourism trade.

Health Issues when Traveling

Being ill in a foreign country is typically not an enjoyable experience. Medical problems may result from exposure to extreme climates, diseases, and illnesses, but many travelers visit remote and exotic destinations with no problems. These travelers considered some of the following pieces of advice and exercised precautions.

JET LAG

Many international travelers suffer from a condition called **jet lag.** When travelers on long international flights cross several time zones quickly, their bodies' natural internal clocks, which control body temperature and eating patterns, become disturbed, resulting in jet lag. One of the most common effects of jet lag is a disturbance of daily sleeping patterns. For instance, assume a traveler takes a 26-hour flight that leaves Chicago at 3:20 P.M. and arrives in Nairobi, Kenya, at 8:00 A.M. 2 days later. When the traveler arrives, his internal body clock tells him it is time to sleep, but the external clock tells him it is time to rise and eat breakfast. The environmental factor of the sun rising affects the body's routine. Another external clock factor that may affect the body is adjusting to local eating patterns. For example, it is common in Mexico to eat dinner as late as 10 or 11 P.M. The easiest way to adjust to the time difference is to stay awake and retire early. Over time, the internal clock will adjust to the external one. Some travelers may need 5 or 6 days to readjust.

It is best for the traveler to follow the clock of the destination as soon as possible. For example, the traveler should set his watch to the time zone of his destination on his way to the airport. Matching eating and sleeping patterns with those of the destination by choosing late afternoon or early evening arrivals also helps the traveler acclimate more easily.

Some travelers acclimate to new surroundings more quickly than others. Individuals react differently to internal and external factors. External factors, like the stress of traveling, may induce jet lag in some travelers. Jet lag is difficult to avoid. One method to help minimize jet lag is to get plenty of rest before the trip and to arrive at the airport well ahead of scheduled departure.

Most travelers are really excited when they arrive at their destinations and wish to explore right away. Travelers should avoid rushing during the first few days of their trips and instead take the time to adapt to the time, climate, culture, and food of their new surroundings.

During the flight travelers should avoid consuming too much alcohol. Alcohol dehydrates the body at high altitudes because there is low humidity. As a result, most travelers feel more thirsty than normal and should drink plenty of water.

ALTITUDE AND MOTION SICKNESS

Traveling to mountain destinations can be tricky. Because high altitudes have low oxygen levels, it may be difficult for travelers to remain clearheaded. The air is also cool and dry. As a result, a traveler may become breathless, tired, lightheaded, dizzy, and dehydrated, while skiing, for example. The traveler can restore the moisture lost while breathing by drinking plenty of water. Once travelers have acclimated to a high altitude, they may experience severe headaches upon returning to sea level because the humidity level is much higher.

Motion sickness happens when the senses of balance and movement in the body are disturbed. Motions that cause the sickness are the movements of ships, cars, trains, and airplanes. Its symptoms are a cold sweat or queasiness. Some people may also experience headaches and drowsiness. If motion sickness is not treated, vomiting may occur. An empty stomach tends to worsen motion sickness.

To minimize a traveler's motion sickness on a cruise, try to book him or her in a cabin in the center of the ship where the motion of the ship is less apparent. Also recommend he or she eat lightly before and during the cruise.

FOOD AND WATER

The most common illness travelers experience in developing countries is **traveler's diarrhea,** which is caused by bacteria in food and water and may last from a day to a week. The diarrhea bacteria grow easily in developing countries because those countries have warm climates. Contaminated water is the source of many diarrheal illnesses. Therefore, travelers should avoid drinking and using the water in rural areas at all times, including when brushing the teeth. Travelers should also avoid food made with water, rinsed in water, and grown in water, including salads, uncooked vegetables and fruits, ice cubes, ice cream, raw oysters, raw meat, and milk products. The traveler's best precaution is to eat only well-cooked food and to drink bottled drinks or boiled water. The heat from cooking and boiling kills the bacteria.

Unpredicted events, such as flight cancellations, can lead a traveler to stay in a hotel with unhygienic standards. If the delay occurs in one of the African countries where delays can last several days, the traveler may run out of bottled water and risk contracting traveler's diarrhea. As a result, **immunizations** are much more important for land travelers than for cruise travelers who can enjoy controlled environments and food. Travelers to less developed countries in Africa, Asia, and Central and South America may require some immunizations. Immunizations are normally not required to travel to the Caribbean islands, Europe, Australia, New Zealand, and the developed countries of Asia (i.e., Japan and Singapore).

YELLOW FEVER

Yellow fever is caused by a virus that circulates in animals in certain tropical areas, particularly in the wet tropical areas of Africa. Its main symptom is high fever. Once travelers are immunized against this disease (one vaccination is used), their vaccination certificates are valid for 10 years after 10 days. Travel professionals should send their travel clients to their doctors for precautions and administration. Figure 1–7 illustrates the common areas of yellow fever.

CHOLERA

As Figure 1–8 shows, **cholera,** which is caused by contaminated food and drinking water, is common in less developed areas with low health standards. Its symptoms are diarrhea and sometimes vomiting. Travelers staying at popular tourist areas are at very low risk of contracting cholera, because person-to-person

20 International Travel and Tourism

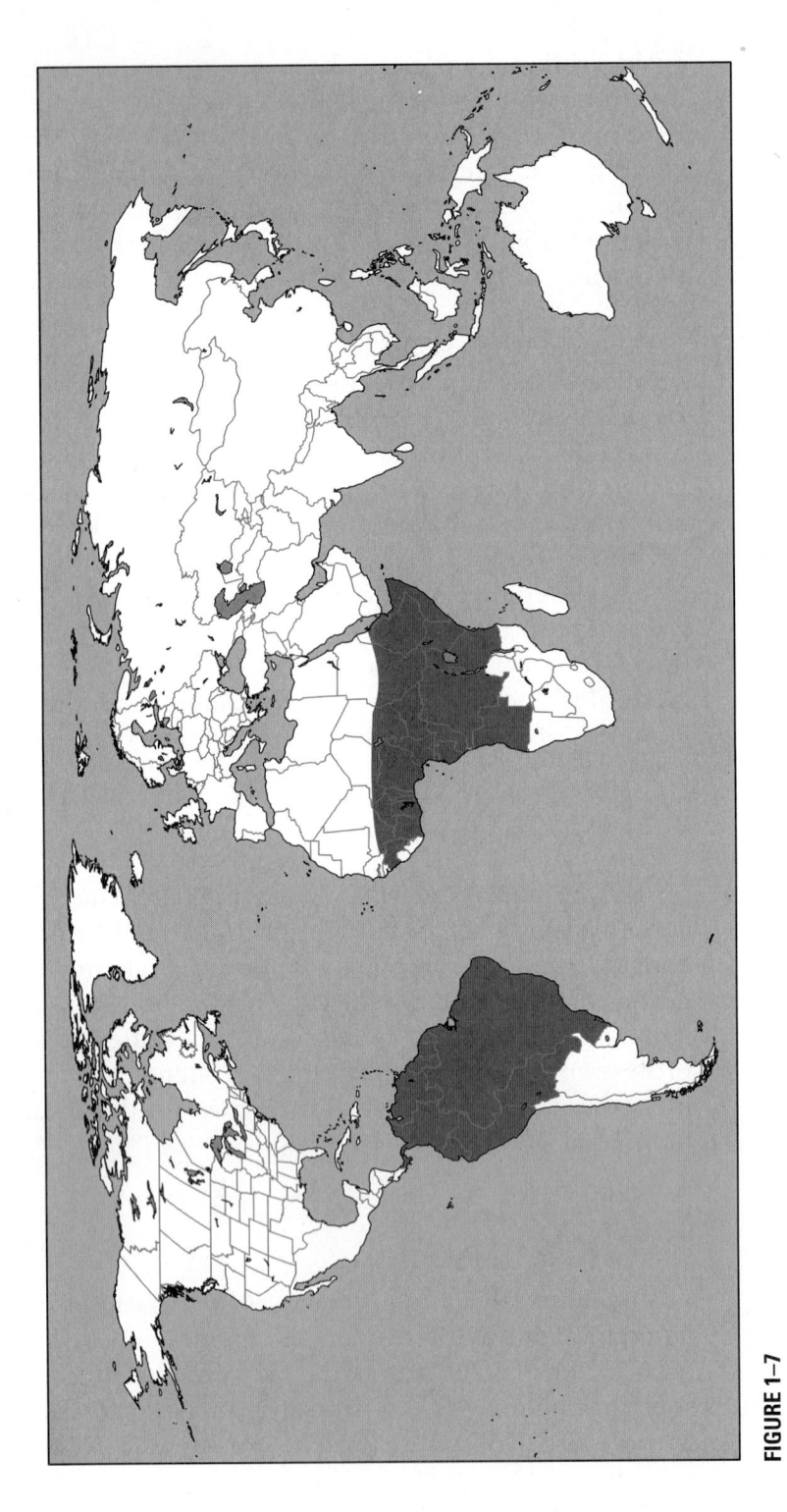

FIGURE 1-7
Yellow fever endemic areas

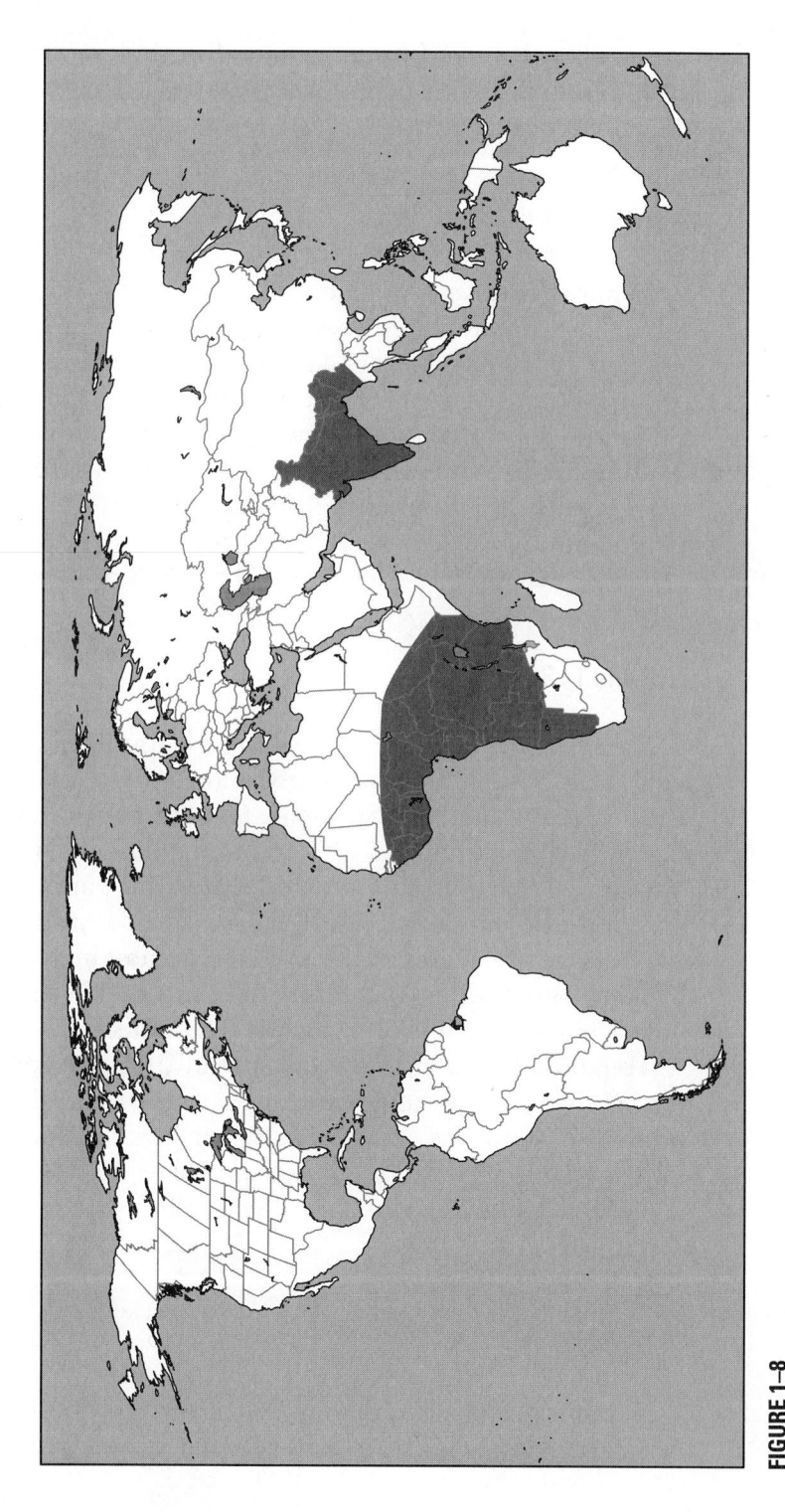

Chapter 1 Introduction to International Travel and Tourism *21*

FIGURE 1-8
Cholera endemic areas

transmission is rare. Immunizations for cholera are not to be given to infants under 6 months, because they may suffer severe side effects or reactions.

TYPHOID FEVER

Typhoid fever is a stomach infection that is caused by poor hygiene or contaminated food and water. Its symptoms are diarrhea and fever. Travelers who are living in rural areas away from usual tourist areas or eating out frequently are at higher risk for the disease than travelers staying at reputable hotels. Typhoid immunization, which is a capsule of live bacterial vaccine taken orally, is recommended for people traveling to less developed nations in Africa, Asia, and South America (see Figure 1–9). The vaccine provides up to 70 percent protection.

HEPATITIS

Two types of hepatitis are commonly found in the Amazon region of South America, Subsahara Africa, and Central/Southeast Asia (see Figure 1–10). **Hepatitis A** is a virus that is spread by contaminated food and water. Some of its early symptoms are fever, chills, fatigue, and aches and pains. These may be followed by appetite loss, darkened urine, and sometimes yellowing of the whites of the eyes. Treatment includes resting, drinking lots of water, and eating light meals. The gamma globulin vaccination will protect against Hepatitis A.

Hepatitis B is a virus that is spread through skin penetration. Tattoos, ear piercing, and injections should therefore be avoided in countries with poor hygiene and sanitation. While the symptoms and treatment are similar to those for Hepatitis A, gamma globulin is not as effective for protecting against Hepatitis B.

TETANUS

Tetanus, which is found in tropical and less developed countries (see Figure 1–11), is a germ that grows in an infected

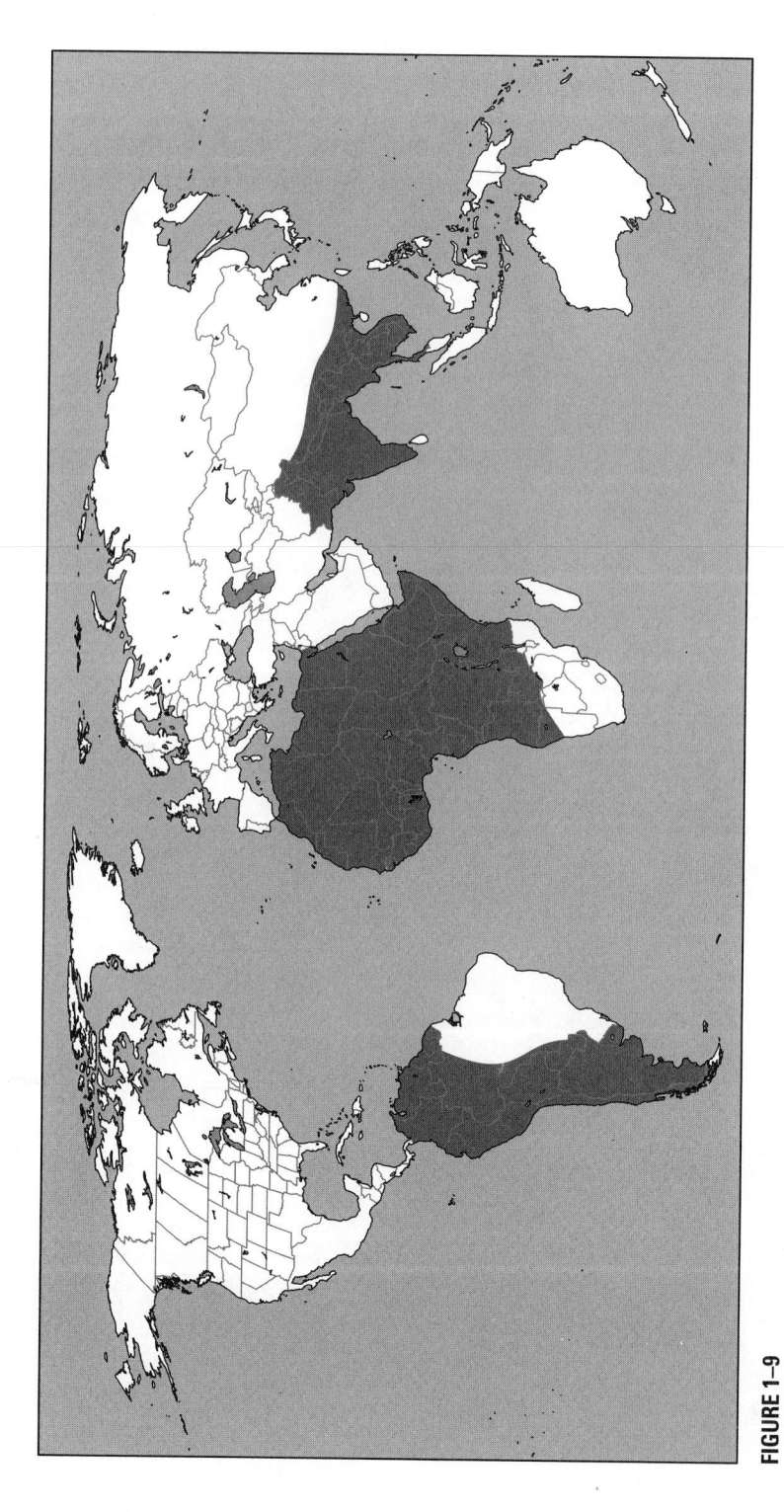

FIGURE 1-9
Typhoid fever endemic areas

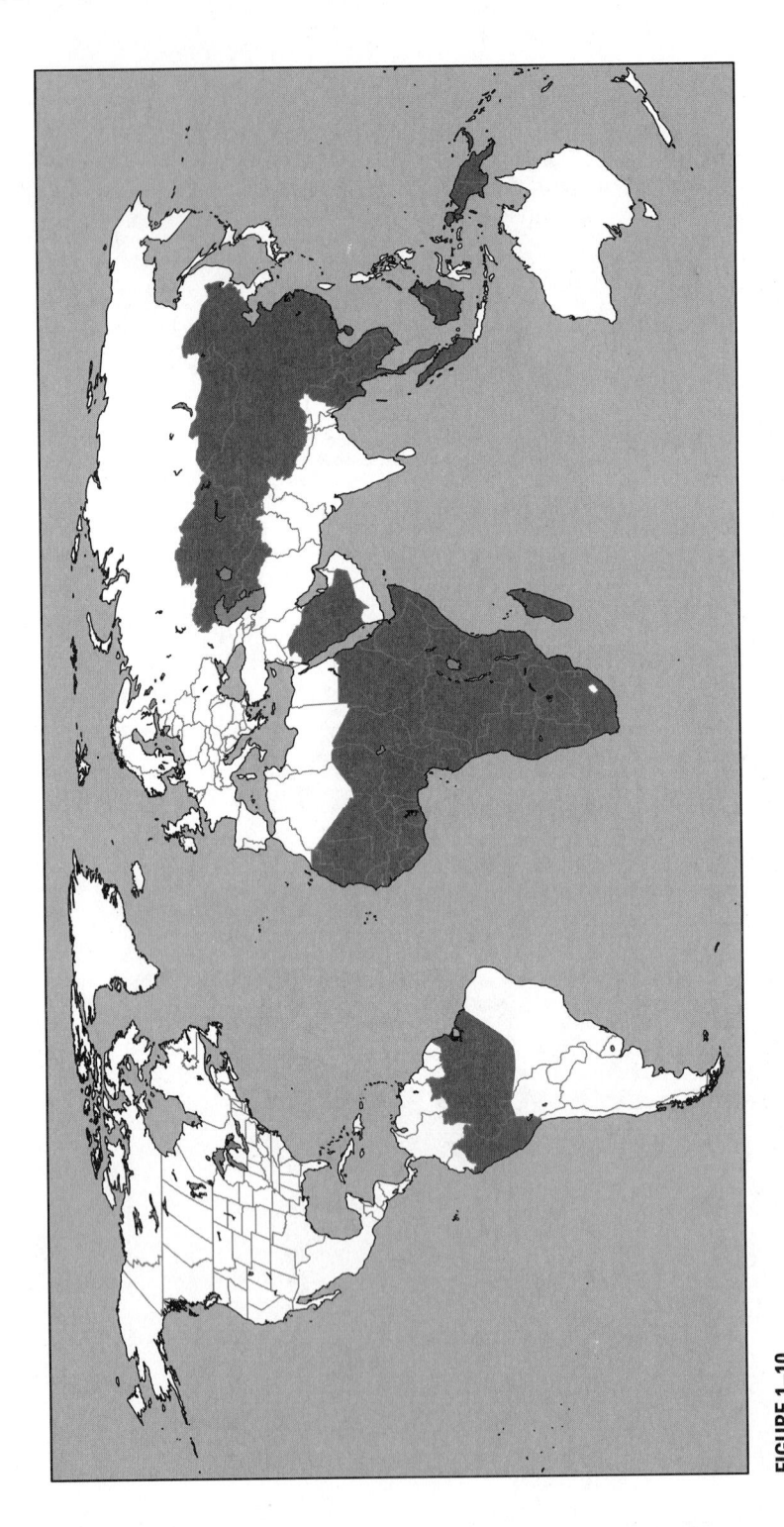

FIGURE 1-10
Hepatitis endemic areas

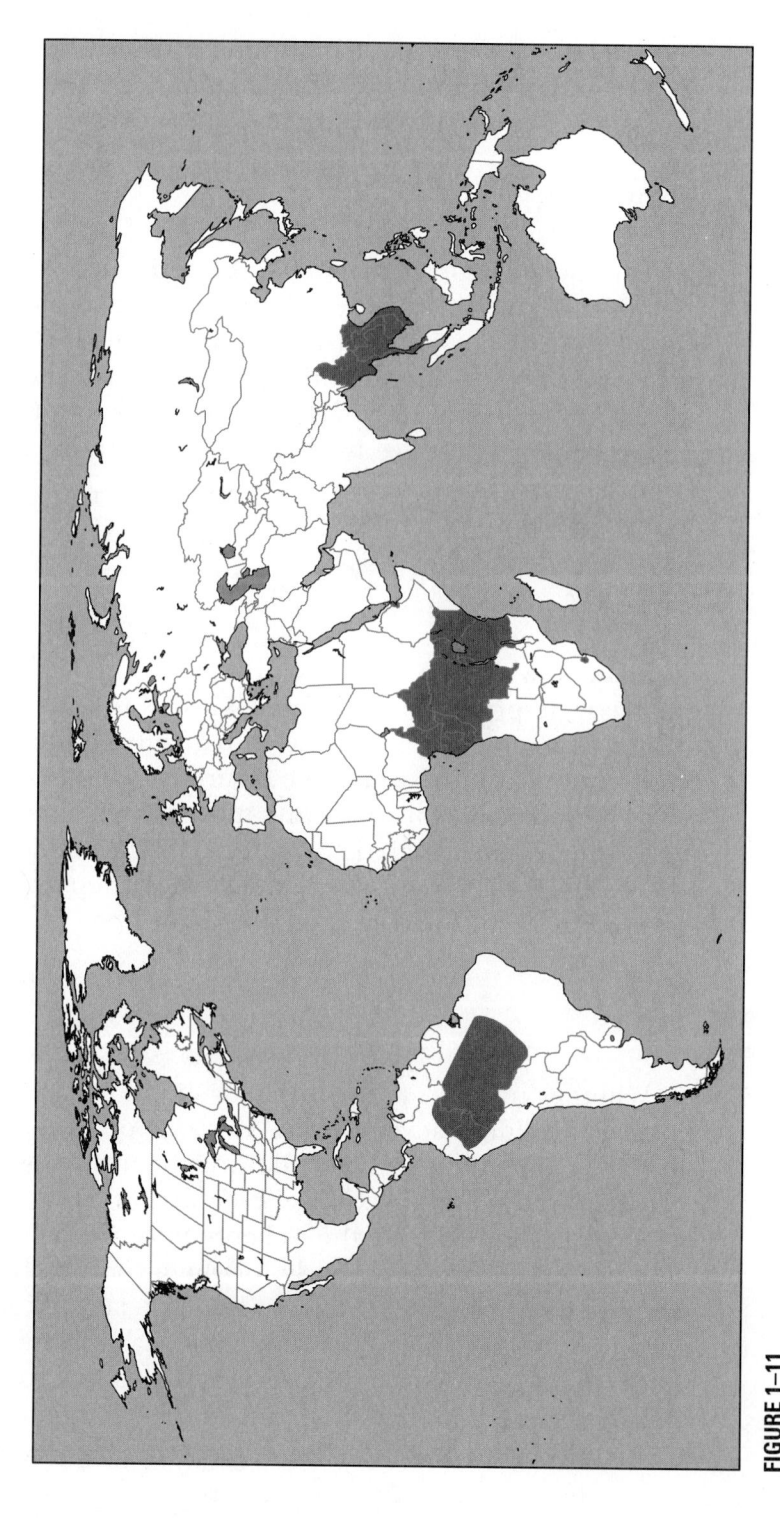

Chapter 1 Introduction to International Travel and Tourism 25

FIGURE 1–11
Tetanus endemic areas

wound. Its main symptom is stiffening of the jaw and neck, which results in painful seizures of all muscles in the body. Without immunization, this disease can lead to death.

MENINGITIS

The **meningococcal meningitis bacteria** circulates all over the world. Meningitis is serious because it affects the brain and can be fatal if not immunized. Its symptoms include severe headaches, neck stiffness, and light sensitivity. The dry areas bordering the southern Sahara region suffer frequent meningitis epidemics. As Figure 1–12 shows, Nepal, India, Kenya, and Tanzania experience occasional outbreaks. One injection is enough to obtain immunity.

MALARIA

Malaria, a disease caused by the bite of an infected mosquito, is widespread in Africa, but it is also common in the tropical and subtropical areas of the Indian subcontinent, parts of South America, and Turkey (see Figure 1–13). It is a flu-like illness with fever and shivers lasting more than 2 days. Currently there is no effective malaria vaccine, so malaria tablets must be taken with absolute regularity 1 week before departure, during the trip, and after the trip.

TRAVELING WISELY

Whether travelers are planning a shopping spree in Hong Kong or a wildlife adventure in Africa, good preparation ensures they will enjoy the trip. Following are travel tips to reduce inconveniences and maximize pleasure. Travel consultants must inform and educate their clients accordingly.

Travelers should leave early for the airport to begin their journeys free of stress. Travelers who leave late risk facing full parking lots and long check-in lines. Early arrival ensures check-in will be smooth and fast. Travelers also have a greater chance of getting preferred seating and having time to ensure the airline agent attaches the correct baggage tags. Finally,

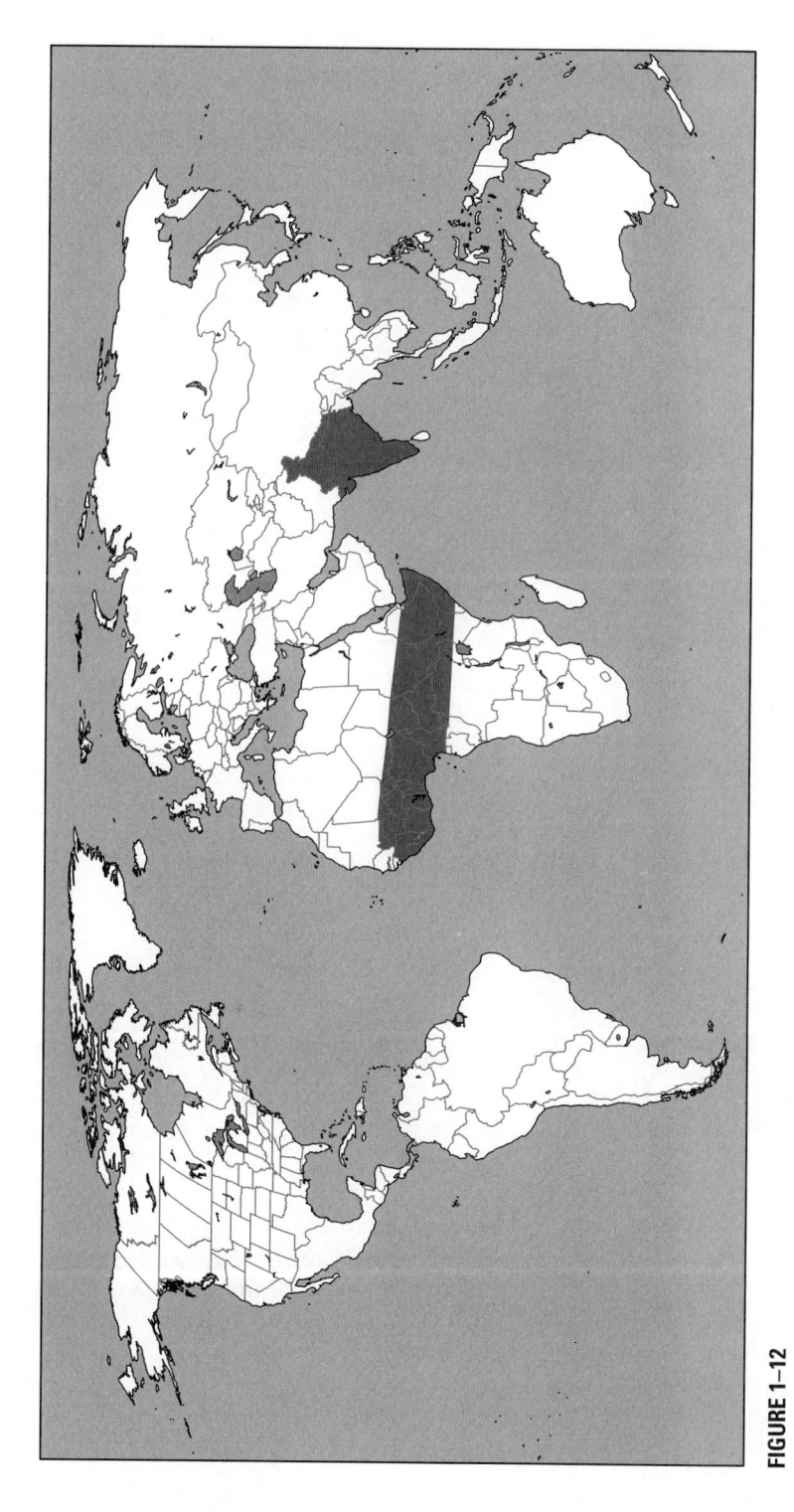

FIGURE 1-12
Meningitis endemic areas

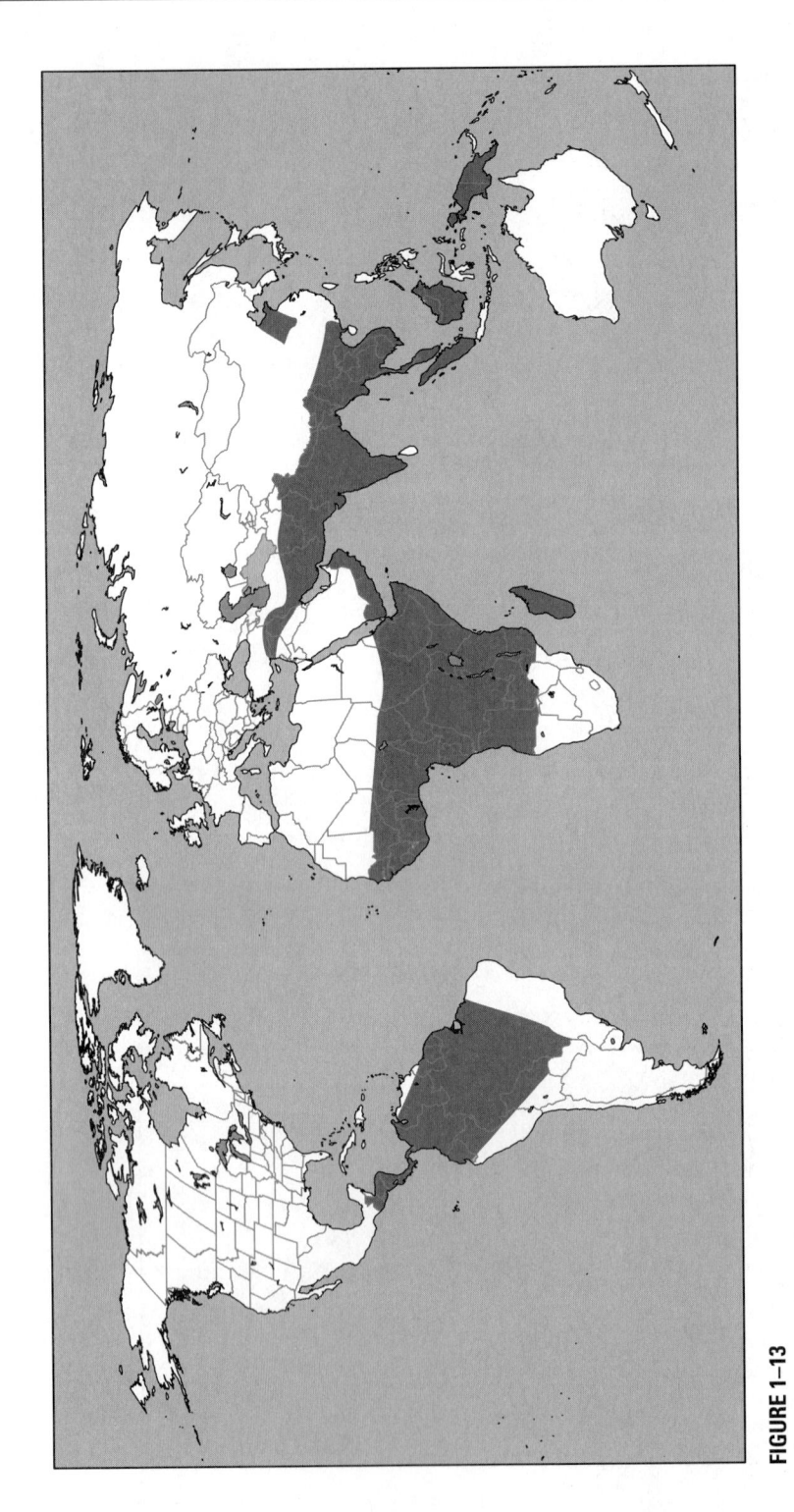

28 International Travel and Tourism

FIGURE 1-13
Malaria endemic areas

punctual travelers may board when their row numbers are called. Available seats are given to standby passengers.

It is best for travelers on short business trips that cross time zones frequently to keep their sleeping and eating patterns on home time. Some international business travelers spend a full day resting after arrival to adjust to local time.

A frequent mistake of international business travelers is failing to learn the culture in the country where they are conducting business. In Japan, for instance, business card presentation is important. The business card should be given and received with both hands, and the card of the Japanese business executive should be examined immediately. The business card must never be placed in a pocket, and it must never be written on.

SUMMARY

- The World Tourism Organization (WTO) is the most widely used source of worldwide travel and tourism statistical information.
- The United States is the world's top earner of tourism expenditures.
- Travel and tourism is the world's largest industry.
- The travel and tourism industry is the world's leading employer.
- One of the most common effects of jet lag is a disturbance of sleeping patterns.
- Travelers should avoid using the water in rural areas of developing countries at all times.

CHECK YOUR UNDERSTANDING 1–1

Construct a line graph that compares how the world's top forty tourism destinations in 1995 ranked in 1985.

CHECK YOUR UNDERSTANDING 1–2

Graph the top twenty North American tourism destinations in 1995 and 1994.

CHECK YOUR UNDERSTANDING 1–3

Write a report discussing why international tourism in Europe and North America is predicted to lose its market share to Asia and the Pacific. Analyze why Asia and the Pacific are among the fastest growing tourism regions in the world.

CHECK YOUR UNDERSTANDING 1–4

Directions: Answer true (T) or false (F) to each question.

1. ____ The stress of traveling may induce jet lag.
2. ____ Dehydration, shortness of breath, and dizziness are signs of motion sickness.
3. ____ Jet lag is basically a disturbance of the body's internal clock.
4. ____ The most common illness in developing countries is yellow fever.
5. ____ Immunizations are required to travel to Australia.
6. ____ Malaria is common in high-altitude destinations.
7. ____ Contaminated food is the source of many illnesses abroad.
8. ____ Immunizations are more important to a traveler on an escorted tour than to an independent traveler.
9. ____ Cholera is a stomach infection.
10. ____ Malaria is caused by the bite of an infected mosquito.

CHECK YOUR UNDERSTANDING 1–5

Directions: Use a Travel Planner or a similar publication to research the health requirements for the following nations.

1. Egypt

2. Peru

3. Nepal

4. Morocco

5. Thailand

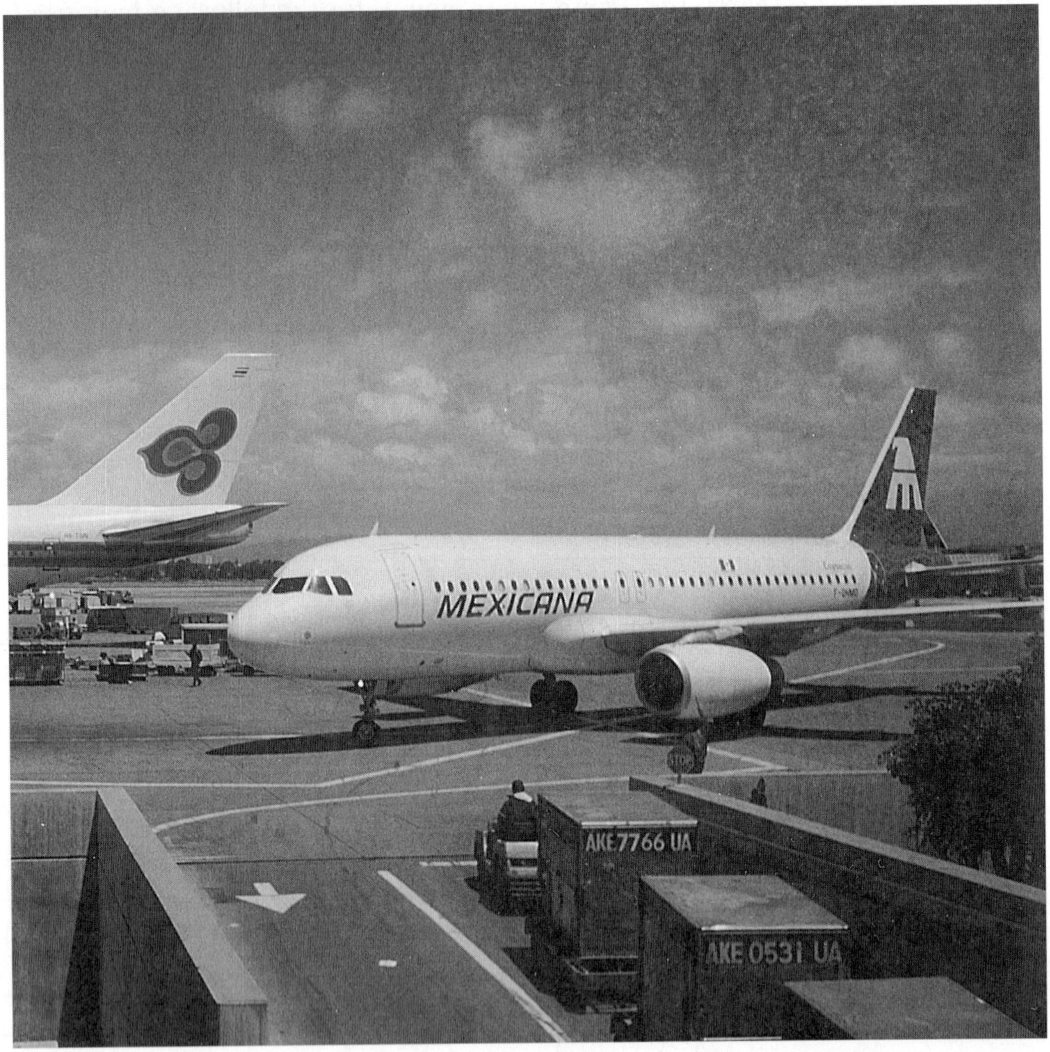
MEXICANA
AKE 7766 UA
AKE 0531 UA

Chapter 2

Air Travel Geography

Eight Freedoms of the Air
The International Air Transport Association
    The Roles of the IATA
        IATA Membership and Accreditation
The International Airlines Travel Agency Network
    Travel Agent Identification Cards
Interline Travel
IATA Geography
    IATA Areas
City, Airport, and Airline Codes
Air Routes
International Time
    The 24-Hour Clock
    Time Zones
    The International Date Line
    Elapsed Flying Time

OBJECTIVES

After completing Chapter 2, you should be able to:

- Discuss the Eight Freedoms of the Air
- Describe the International Air Transport Association (IATA) and its functions
- Define and discuss interline travel
- Recite and use city, airport, and airline codes
- Calculate international time

As Chapter 1 discussed, thoroughly knowing and understanding international travel geography is vital for success in the travel profession. Understanding air travel geography goes beyond knowing where London and Singapore are located. It provides a solid basis for visualizing the least expensive air routing. It also provides the background crucial to comprehending why a traveler on a 20-hour flight arrives in Australia 2 days after departure.

Eight Freedoms of the Air

Once travelers leave the the boundaries of their home countries, they must follow the governmental regulations of the country they are visiting. A **border** is a line that separates countries. Each country owns the land, ocean, and airspace within its borders. Therefore, an airline wishing to fly through the airspace of another country must secure permission from that country before doing so.

The traffic through international airspace is discussed and agreed upon through negotiations between national governments. When air traffic through United States airspace is negotiated, the United States Department of State, Department of Transportation, and Federal Aviation Administration (FAA) are involved. International air traffic agreements specify not only the frequency of flights, but also the number of air routes and the airports to be used. All governments must strictly follow these rules and agreements. If they did not, an aircraft with onboard medical problems would have to wait for permission to execute an emergency landing, for example. Fortunately, violations of airspace are rare.

The regulation governments must follow during air-traffic negotiations were established by the United Nations (UN) at a Chicago convention in 1944. Originally, five regulations or freedoms were established and called the "Five Freedoms of the Air." Since 1944, three more freedoms have been added. These **"Eight Freedoms of the Air"** follow:

1. The freedom to fly through the airspace of another country without landing.

    Itinerary: From Madrid, Spain to Frankfurt, Germany, via France

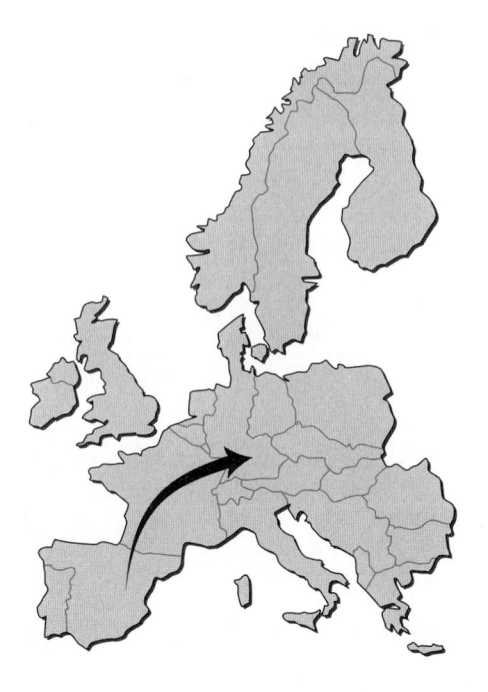

2. The freedom to land in another country for technical reasons only (i.e., to refuel or make repairs).

   Itinerary: From Cairo, Egypt to Nairobi, Kenya—to refuel—to Johannesburg, South Africa

3. The freedom to fly from one country to another country to drop off passengers and cargo.

   Itinerary: From Buenos Aires, Argentina to Rio de Janeiro, Brazil

4. The freedom to pick up passengers and cargo from one country and fly them back to the originating country.

   Itinerary: From Singapore, Singapore to Hong Kong.

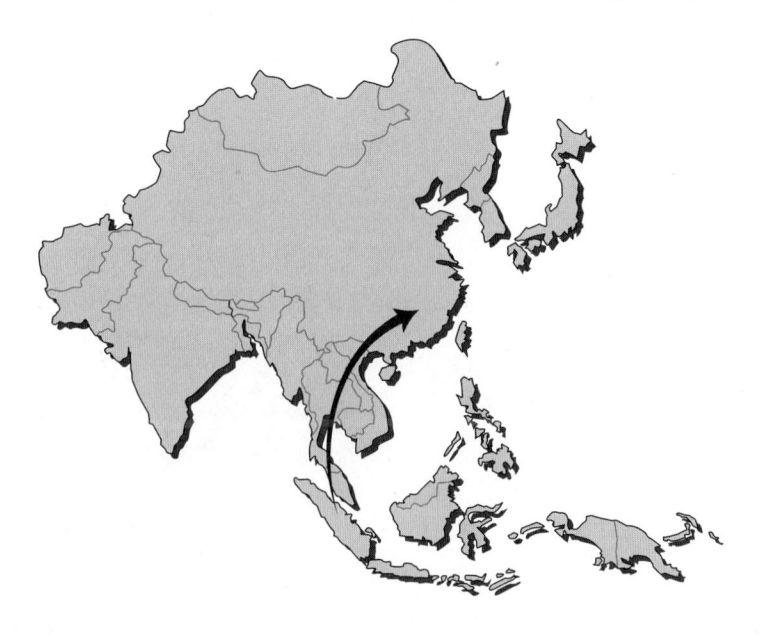

5. The freedom to fly from Country A to pick up passengers and cargo in Country B and drop them off in Country C.

   Itinerary: From Rome, Italy to Paris, France to London, Great Britain

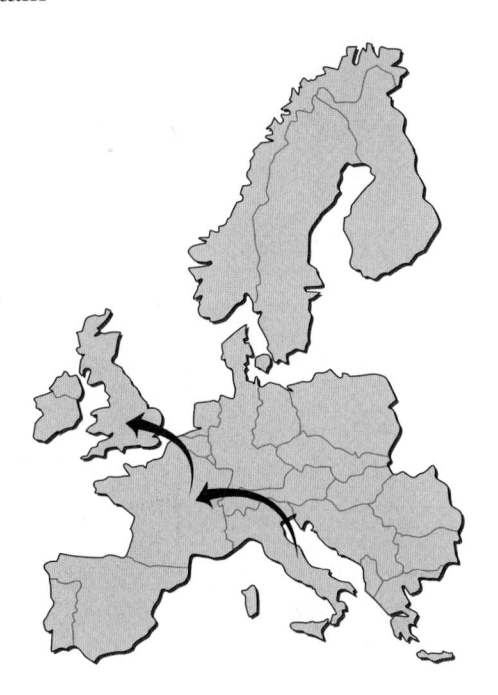

6. The freedom to fly between two countries other than the country of origin and to make a stopover in the country of origin.

   Itinerary: Hong Kong's national carrier, Cathay Pacific, flies from Tokyo, Japan to a stopover in Hong Kong, the country of origin, to Delhi, India

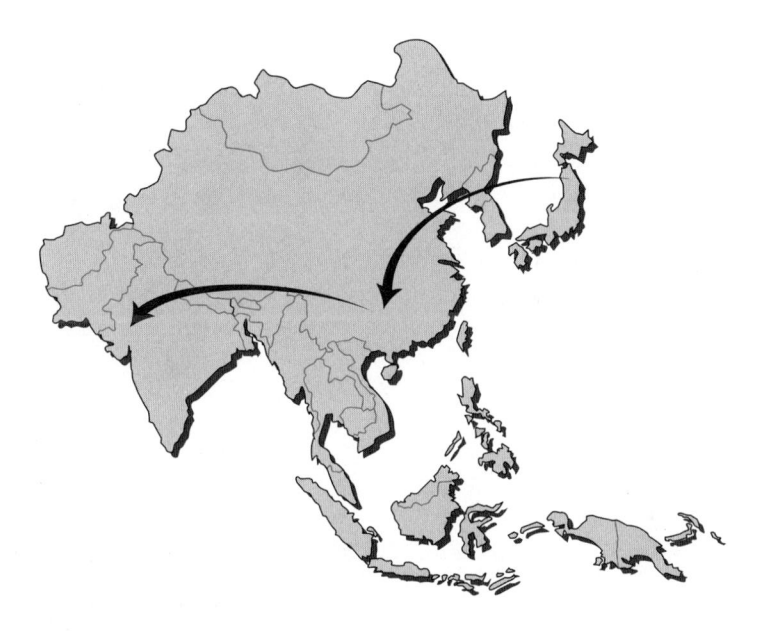

7. The freedom to fly between two countries other than the country of origin with no stopover in the country of origin.

   Itinerary: Air France flies from Vancouver, Canada to San Francisco, United States, without stopping in France, the country of origin

8. The freedom to fly solely within another country.

   Itinerary: Thai Airways flies from Perth, Australia to Sydney, Australia

Many countries have only one national carrier. National airlines carry the colors of their countries' flags on the tail sections of their planes or on their fuselages. Sometimes an airline will display an entire national flag or logo. These airlines are called **flag carriers** because they fly all over the world displaying their national colors. For example, Lufthansa is the national carrier of Germany, and Egyptair is the flag carrier of Egypt. In contrast, the United States does not have a flag carrier.

TRAVEL TIP

It is a lot of fun to arrive at a major international airport early and walk to the farthest gate to watch airplanes take off and land. At London's Heathrow Airport, the busiest airport in Europe, flights take off and land approximately every 2 minutes. You and your travel client can experience hundreds of flag carriers this way. Observe the colors of the flag carriers and guess their countries of origin.

The International Air Transport Association

The airline industry is a global business that needs a principal governing body to administer its worldwide operations. The **International Air Transport Association (IATA),** founded in 1945, is a private organization of scheduled international airlines that regulates international air traffic. Unscheduled airlines, such as charter airlines, are not members of IATA.

THE ROLES OF THE IATA

The IATA establishes safety standards; sets flight schedules; outlines reservation, passenger, and baggage check-in procedures; and investigates accidents. IATA also provides up to 10-year forecasts of passenger and cargo growth for many airports throughout the world and advises airport authorities how to minimize congestion and increase capacity.

IATA MEMBERSHIP AND ACCREDITATION

Most scheduled international carriers of the world are IATA members, including all major United States carriers. IATA-member airlines carry 98 percent of scheduled international air traffic. One advantage IATA members have is the ability to issue a ticket for another member airline. The IATA is the international equivalent to the United States **Airlines Reporting Corporation (ARC),** which is the organization that distributes payments of tickets between member carriers and thereby enables people to travel all over the world without hindrance. The IATA has simplified international ticket procedures similarly through a universal ticket format. An international ticket is issued the same way and in the same language regardless of where it is issued in the world. English is the universal language of the travel industry.

Travel agents and aviation workers across the world use universal aviation code to help minimize errors when spelling the names of passengers. For example, a travel professional making a reservation for Mrs. Lytton would use the universal alphabet that follows and spell her last name, "**L**ima, **Y**ankee, **T**ango, **T**ango, **O**slo, **N**ovember."

A Alfa
B Bravo
C Charlie
D Delta
E Echo
F Foxtrot
G Golf
H Hotel
I India
J Juliet
K Kilo
L Lima
M Mike
N November
O Oslo
P Papa
Q Quebec

R Romeo
S Sierra
T Tango
U Uniform
V Victor
W Whiskey
X X ray
Y Yankee
Z Zulu

Most travel agencies worldwide are IATA accredited and therefore are authorized to sell and issue international tickets. As IATA Resolution 800b states, an IATA-approved agent is responsible for adhering to IATA reservation and ticketing procedures. Every IATA-accredited travel agency has a seven-digit IATA code number.

The International Airlines Travel Agency Network

United States travel agencies may also be members of the **International Airlines Travel Agency Network (IATAN),** a group whose main focus is servicing United States travel agencies. IATAN is a subsidiary of IATA that links IATA airlines and United States travel agencies. Two of IATAN's functions are authorizing United States travel agencies to sell international tickets and setting higher professional standards within the industry.

TRAVEL AGENT IDENTIFICATION CARDS

The IATAN has introduced and now sells **travel agent identification (ID) cards.** These cards identify United States travel agents as professional travel industry employees. To apply for the card, an employee must work at least 20 hours per week in an IATAN travel agency selling travel, be at least 18 and earn an annual minimum of $4,080 in salary and commissions. The employee must submit the completed application form with a passport-size color photo, the signature of the agency's owner, and the fee.

Some suppliers grant trade benefits only to travel agents holding travel agent ID cards. A travel agent cannot obtain a travel agent ID card until the agency is an IATAN member. A travel agency's IATA membership does not mean the agency is also an IATAN member. Agencies must apply separately for IATAN membership.

Interline Travel

It is always to the passenger's advantage to fly on interlining carriers on international connecting flights. An **interline agreement** means two or more airlines have agreed to transport the other's passengers and to transfer the passengers' baggage at connecting points. Interline journeys benefit the travel professional as well because they can be issued on one ticket. This is possible because interline carriers agree to sell transportation over the routes of other interline carriers. Further, interline carriers agree to accept the tickets of other interline carriers. Interline carriers provide each other with the fares and rules necessary to complete a ticket sale.

Another advantage of interlining is passengers' bags are transferred to connecting airlines, provided the connections occur within 6 hours (12 hours if passengers arrive late at night and the first available, scheduled flight is the next morning). If the connection occurs in the same city but between two different airports, however, passengers are often required to transfer their own baggage. Live animals cannot be checked as interline baggage.

All bags that are bound for destinations in the fifteen member countries of the European Union (EU) or that are leaving EU countries are provided baggage claim tags that are edged in green. (The significance of the European Union is covered in detail in Chapter 6.) These tags mean the bags do not need customs control. These bags will be transferred automatically at a connecting EU point, mostly when interlining. As a travel professional, advise your clients to go through passport and immigration control. Ironically, passengers, not baggage are checked at customs.

IATA Geography

Thoroughly knowing international, as well as domestic, travel geography helps to increase the travel professional's efficiency in visualizing itineraries and flight patterns. For example, on a trip from Paris, France to Tokyo, Japan, is the shortest air route via the North Pole or via the United States? Which route is the least expensive? Which airlines service these routes? The travel professional finds these answers first by improving basic geography skills.

IATA AREAS

The IATA has divided the world into three areas for airfare purposes. The three areas, called Area 1, Area 2, and Area 3, are also called "Traffic Conferences" or "TC" and are labeled TC 1, TC 2, and TC 3, respectively. This text refers to the regions as areas. Each of the areas is listed and shown in Figure 2–1.

Area 1 consists of the Western Hemisphere and includes the following subareas:

- North America
- Central America (excluding Panama)
- South America (including Panama)
- The Caribbean
- Greenland
- Bermuda

Area 2 consists of Europe and Africa and includes the following subareas:

- Europe (including Morocco, Algeria, Tunisia, and Russia west of the Ural mountains)
- The Middle East (including Egypt and Sudan)
- Africa (excluding Egypt, Sudan, Morocco, Algeria, and Tunisia)

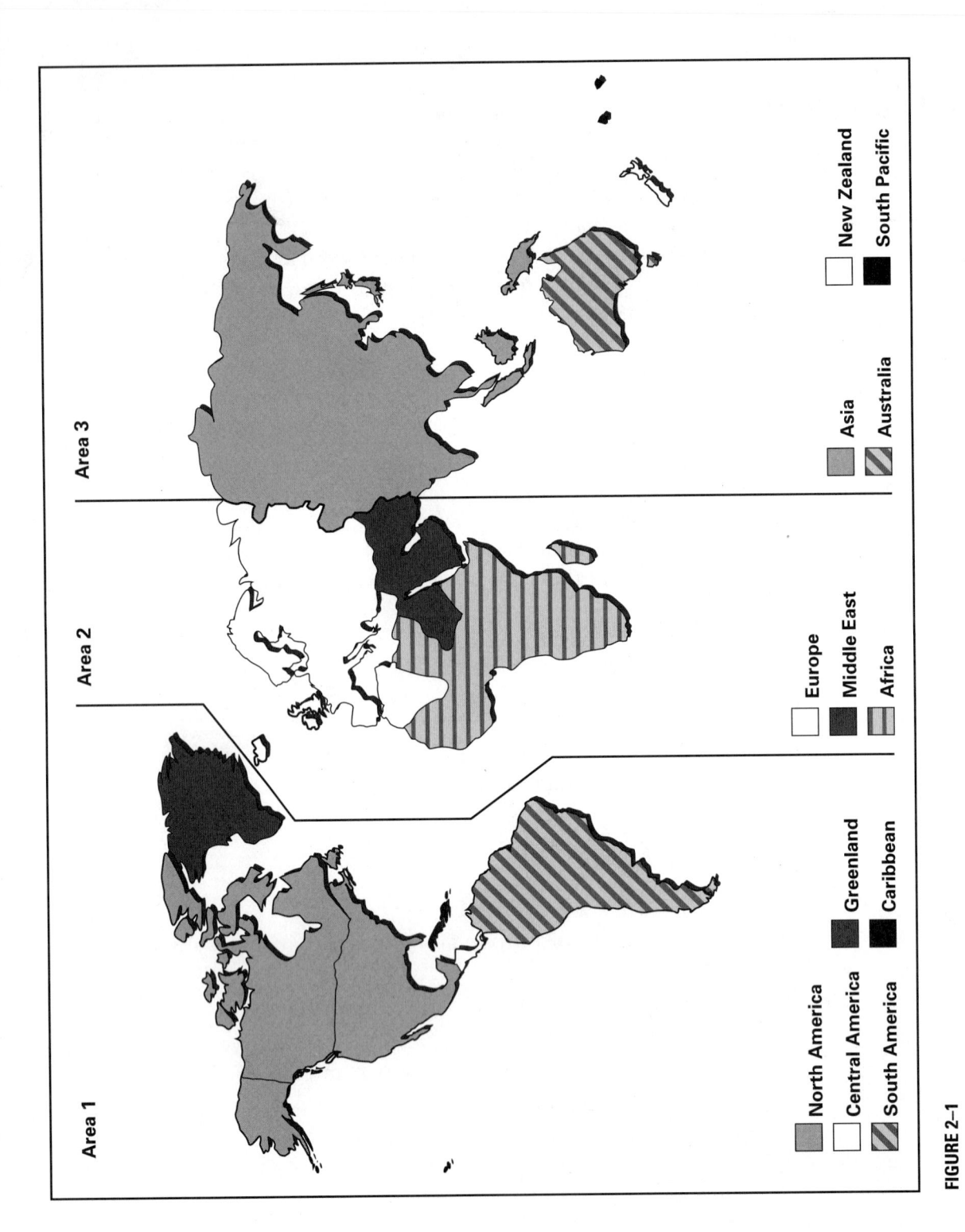

FIGURE 2–1
IATA areas. (*Courtesy of International Air Transport Association.*)

Area 3 consists of Australasia and includes the following subareas:

Asia (including Russia east of the Ural mountains)

Australia

New Zealand

The South Pacific

The travel professional should be aware of all three IATA areas and their respective subareas because fares and/or rules may apply to just one area. Area 2 differs most geographically. Note, for example, how Egypt is technically on the continent of Africa but appears on the Area 2 map in the Middle East subarea.

City, Airport, and Airline Codes

The IATA assigns codes to distinguish cities, airports, and airlines around the world (see Figure 2–2). A three-letter location code identifies a city or an airport. A two-letter code identifies an airline. These codes simplify communication and routing worldwide. Only one code is assigned to each city, airport, and airline. The IATA works closely with federal governments to ensure codes are not duplicated.

Most international city and airport codes are designated logically. Very few codes are unrecognizable. International location codes are often easier to recognize than domestic codes because they use the first three letters of the city's name. Following are some examples:

BUE	Buenos Aires, Argentina
CAI	Cairo, Egypt
DEL	Delhi, India
LON	London, Great Britain
PAR	Paris, France
RIO	Rio de Janeiro, Brazil
ROM	Rome, Italy
SIN	Singapore, Singapore
SYD	Sydney, Australia

Country	National Airline	Airline Code	Hub City	City Code	Airport Code
Argentina	Aerolineas Araentinas	AR	Buenos Aires	BUE	EZE
Australia	Qantas	QF	Sydney	SYD	
Austria	Austrian Airlines	OS	Vienna	VIE	
Belgium	Sabena	SN	Brussels	BRU	
Brazil	Varig	RG	Rio de Janeiro	RIO	GEG
Chile	Lan Chile	LA	Santiago	SCL	
China	Air China	CA	Beijing	BJS	PEK
Denmark	Scandinavian Airlines	SK	Copenhagen	CPH	
Egypt	Egyptain	MS	Cairo	CAI	
Fiji	Air Pacific	FJ	Nadi	NAN	
Finland	Finnair	AY	Helsinki	HEL	
France	Air France	AF	Paris	PAR	CDG	ORY
Germany	Lufthansa	LH	Frankfurt	FRA	
Great Britain	British Airways	BA	London	LON	LHR	LGW
Greece	Olympic Airways	OA	Athens	ATH	
Hong Kong	Cathay Pacific	CX	Hong Kong	HKG	
Hungary	Malev	MA	Budapest	BUD	
India	Air India	AI	Delhi	DEL	
Indonesia	Garuda	GA	Jakarta	JKT	CGK
Ireland	Aer Lingus	AE	Dublin	DUB	
Israel	El Al Israel	LY	Tel Aviv	TLV	
Italy	Alitalia	AZ	Rome	ROM	FCO
Japan	Japan Airlines	JL	Tokyo	TYO	NRT	HND
Kenya	Kenya Airways	KQ	Nairobi	NBO	
Korea	Korean Airlines	KE	Seoul	SEL	
Malaysia	Malaysian Airlines	MH	Kuala Lumpur	KUL	

FIGURE 2–2

Airline codes. Reprinted by special permission from the February 1966 issue of the OAG Desktop Guide— Worldwide Edition. *All rights reserved. Copyright 1966, Reed Travel Group.*

Some city and airport codes are formed using three letters from the city's name. These codes are also fairly easy to recognize. Following are some examples:

    BKK   **B**ang**k**o**k**, Thailand
    HKG   **H**ong **K**ong, Hong Kong
    HRE   **H**a**re**, Zimbabwe
    LGW   **L**ondon **G**at**w**ick Airport, Great Britain
    CCS   **C**ara**c**a**s**, Venezuela
    MUC   **M**unich, Germany

Country	National Airline	Airline Code	Hub City	City Code	Airport Code
Morocco	Royal Air Maroc	AT	Casablanca	CAS	
Nepal	Royal Air Nepal	RA	Kathmandu	KTM	
Netherlands	Royal Dutch Airlines	KL	Amsterdam	AMS	
New Zealand	Air New Zealand	NZ	Auckland	AKL	
Nigeria	Nigeria Airways	WT	Lagas	LOS	
Norway	Scandinavian Airways	SK	Oslo	OSL	FBU
Pakistan	Pakistan Airlines	PK	Karachi	KHI	
Papua New Guinea	Air Niugini	PX	Port Moresby	POM	
Peru	Aeroperu	PL	Lima	LIM	
Philippines	Philippine Air Lines	PR	Manila	MNL	
Portugal	Air Portugal	TP	Lisbon	LIS	
Russia	Aeroflot	SU	Moscow	MOW	
Saudi Arabia	Saudian Arabian Airlines	SV	Riyadh	RUH	
Singapore	Singapore Airlines	SQ	Singapore	SIN	
South Africa	South African Airlines	SA	Johannesburg	JNB	
Spain	Iberia	IB	Madrid	MAD	
Sweden	Scandinavian Airlines	SK	Stockholm	STO	ARN
Switzerland	Swissair	SR	Zurich	ZRH	
Tahiti	Air Tahiti	VT	Papeete	PPT	
Tanzania	Air Tanzania Corp.	TC	Dar es Salaam	DAR	
Thailand	Thai Airways	TG	Bangkok	BKK	
Turkey	Turkish Airlines	TK	Ankasa	ANK	
Uruguay			Montevideo	MVD	
Zambia	Zambia Airways	QZ	Lugaka	LUN	
Zimbabwe	Air Zimbabwe	UM	Harare	HRE	
Venezuela	Viasa	VA	Caracas	CCS	

FIGURE 2–2 *(Continued)*

NBO **N**ai**ro**bi, Kenya
TYO **T**o**ky**o, Japan
ZRH **Z**u**rich**, Switzerland

Each IATA area is illustrated with city and airport codes in Appendix A. For a compete list of worldwide city and airport codes, see Appendix B.

Unlike city and airport codes, airline codes can be difficult to recognize. Following are some examples:

AT Royal Air Maroc
AZ Alitalia

BA British Airways
JL Japan Air Lines
KE Korean Air Lines
KQ Kenya Airways
LA Lan Chile
MS Egypt Air
QF Qantas Airways
SQ Singapore Airlines

Most worldwide capital cities are hubs of international air traffic, and many international airlines are the national carriers of their home countries. National carriers almost always use their capital cities as their main operations areas for such things as maintenance work and connecting flights. Figure 2–2 helps you plan travel itineraries quickly and efficiently. A complete list of airline codes is shown in Appendix C.

Air Routes

Fares differ depending on air route. Therefore, travel professionals must understand the direction of travel to calculate air fares accurately and apply fare rules consistently. All directions of travel have two-letter global indicators that appear in fare and fare-rule displays. Following are the most commonly used global indicators and sample air itineraries. See Figure 2–3 for further information.

AF—via Africa
   Itinerary: From Miami to Nairobi to Delhi

AP—via the Atlantic and Pacific Oceans
   Itinerary: From Reykjavik to New York to Tokyo

AT—via the Atlantic Ocean
   Itinerary: From New York to Paris

EH—within the Eastern Hemisphere (Areas 2 and 3 only)
   Itinerary: From Paris to Bangkok

EM—via Europe and the Middle East
   Itinerary: From New York to Cairo to Delhi

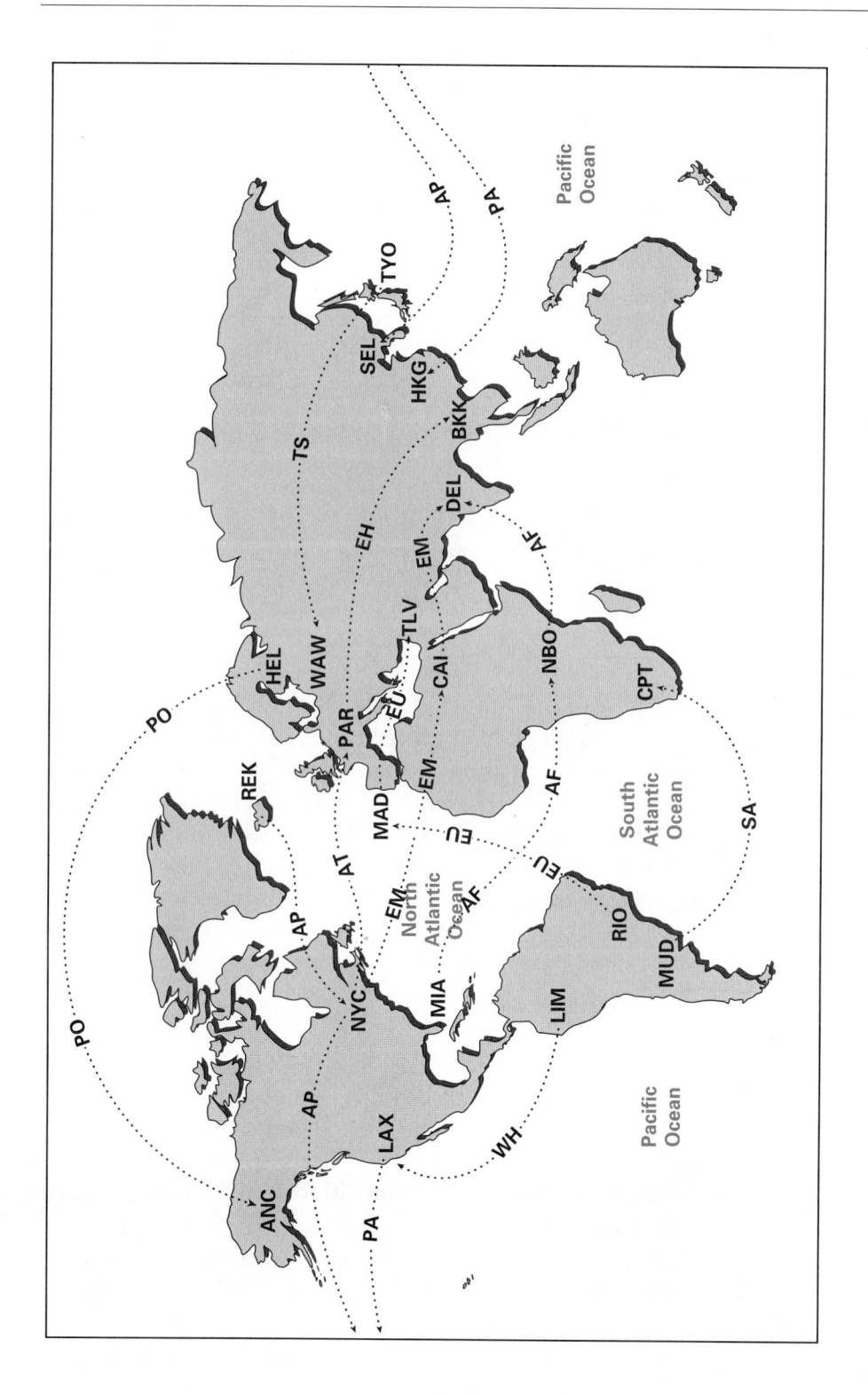

FIGURE 2-3
World air routes and global indicators. Reprinted by special permission from the February 1966 issue of the OAG Desktop Guide—Worldwide Edition. All rights reserved. Copyright 1966, Reed Travel Group.

EU—via Europe
    Itinerary: From Rio de Janeiro to Madrid to Tel Aviv

PA—via the North, Central, or South Pacific Ocean
    Itinerary: From Los Angeles to Hong Kong

PO—via the North Polar route
    Itinerary: From Helsinki to Anchorage

SA—via the South Atlantic Ocean only
    Itinerary: From Montevideo to Cape Town

TS—via the Trans Siberia route (nonstop flights only)
    Itinerary: From Tokyo to Warsaw

WH—within the Western Hemisphere (Area 1 only)
    Itinerary: From Lima to Los Angeles

International Time

A universal time standard is used in international travel to calculate travel times. This global time is based on the rotation of Earth about is axis and the "illusionary" east-to-west travel of the sun. Time is critical for the international travel professional to understand. Travel professionals use this knowledge to calculate time differences between foreign cities, the lengths of flights, and the best time to place international telephone calls.

THE 24-HOUR CLOCK

Civilians in the United States use the Latin terms *ante meridiem* (A.M.) and *post meridiem* (P.M.) to tell time. This system is called the "12-hour clock." The United States military and many foreign countries use the 24-hour clock system.

The 24-hour clock shows hours in four digits with no spaces or colons. The first two digits are hours; the last two are minutes. Because the first hour of each day begins 1 minute past midnight, that first minute is identified as *0001*. The noon hour (12 hours later) appears as *1200*. After noon, hours continue with *1300* (13 hours later, or 1:00 P.M.), *1400* (14 hours later, or 2:00 P.M.), and so on until midnight, identified as *2400*. The last hour in the day is usually *2400*; sometimes it is *0000*. As mentioned earlier, the first minute after midnight is *0001*, not *2401*. The hours before noon are similar in both clock systems. In the 24-hour clock system, all numbers higher than 1200 are afternoon or evening hours.

In the 24-hour clock system, all four digits are spoken and expressed in hundreds of hours. For example, *0100* is pronounced "oh one-hundred hours"; *0115* is pronounced "oh one-fifteen hundred hours."

The 24-hour clock system is more precise and less confusing than its 12-hour counterpart, because each clock hour has a different number in the former, and hence each hour is only counted once. Therefore, the travel professional who understands and uses the 24-hour clock makes fewer errors. International timetables, including flight schedules, are expressed using the 24-hour clock.

Following are easy ways to convert times between the two clock systems:

Example: Convert 2:00 P.M. to the 24-hour clock system.

$$\begin{array}{r} 2\!:\!00 \text{ P.M.} \\ +\,12\!:\!00 \text{ hours} \\ \hline 1400 \end{array}$$

In the example above, 12 hours are added to the 12-hour clock time because the 24-hour clock has 12 more hours than the 12-hour clock. To convert a 24-hour clock time to a 12-hour clock time, subtract 12 hours from the 24-hour time, because the 12-hour clock has 12 fewer hours than the 24-hour clock.

Example: Convert 2321 to the 12-hour clock system.

$$\begin{array}{r} 2321 \\ -\,12\!:\!00 \text{ hours} \\ \hline 11\!:\!21 \text{ P.M.} \end{array}$$

As explained earlier, all numbers higher than 12:00 noon are P.M. hours. Since the hours earlier than 12:00 noon are interchangeable between the two clock systems, it is only the clock hours higher than 1200 (or 12:00 noon) that can be used in the addition/subtraction method of 12 hours.

TIME ZONES

The time of day is not the same around the world. Because Earth rotates on its axis once every 24 hours, all countries cannot observe the same time. The relative east-to-west travel of the sun during these 24 hours causes times to differ around Earth. As a result, noon at one point on Earth is midnight at a point exactly halfway around the world. Travel professionals must know when to call parties at convenient local time. For example, if on Monday at 10:00 A.M. a travel professional in Los Angeles called her sister in London, her sister would be having dinner; her uncle in Sydney would be sleeping. A standard time zone system has been established throughout the world to simplify tasks like these.

At 0 degrees longitude is the meridian that runs north to south through Greenwich, a London suburb. **Greenwich Mean**

Time (GMT) is the mean solar time on this meridian. All time zones in the world are based on GMT (Figure 2–4). GMT became the legal time throughout Great Britain in 1884. Since 1928, GMT, which has been used for hundreds of years in navigation, has also been called **Universal Time.**

Earth is divided into twenty-four time zones, each separated by 15 degrees longitude and 1 hour. Therefore, there are twelve time zones east of GMT and twelve time zones west of GMT (Figure 2–4). While Earth spins, the sun traverses 15 degrees of longitude every hour. Because the sun rises in the east, countries in the time zones east of GMT start the day before countries west of GMT and are, therefore, ahead in time. These time zones are identified with a plus (+) character (Figure 2–4). For example, Paris, France is one time zone east of GMT, which means Paris is 1 hour ahead of GMT or GMT +1. When it is 2200 (10:00 P.M.) at GMT, it is 2300 (11:00 P.M.) in Paris. Bangkok is at GMT +7, which is seven time zones east or 7 hours ahead of GMT. When it is 2200 (10:00 P.M.) at GMT, it is 0500 (5:00 A.M.) in Bangkok the next day. Some countries have adjusted their time zones to ½ hour intervals instead of full-hour intervals. Iran's time zone is GMT +3½, Afghanistan's is GMT +4½, India's is GMT +5½, and Myanmar's zone is GMT +6½.

The countries in the time zones west of GMT are behind in time because the sun moves in a westerly direction. The countries in these time zones start the day later than those east of GMT. These time zones are identified with a minus (−) character. For example, New York City is five time zones west of GMT, which means New York is 5 hours behind GMT or GMT −5. When it is 2200 (10:00 P.M.) at GMT, it is 1700 (5:00 P.M.) in New York City. Honolulu is at GMT −10, which is ten time zones west of GMT or 10 hours behind GMT. When it is 2200 (10:00 P.M.) at GMT, it is 1200 (12:00 P.M.) in Honolulu.

CALCULATING TIME ZONE DIFFERENCES. Normal subtraction and addition do not apply when computing worldwide time differences across GMT. To make calculating time differences such as those between Sydney, Australia and Rio de Janeiro, Brazil, easier, refer to Figure 2–4. Sydney is at GMT +10, and Rio de Janeiro is at GMT −3. To travel *in time*

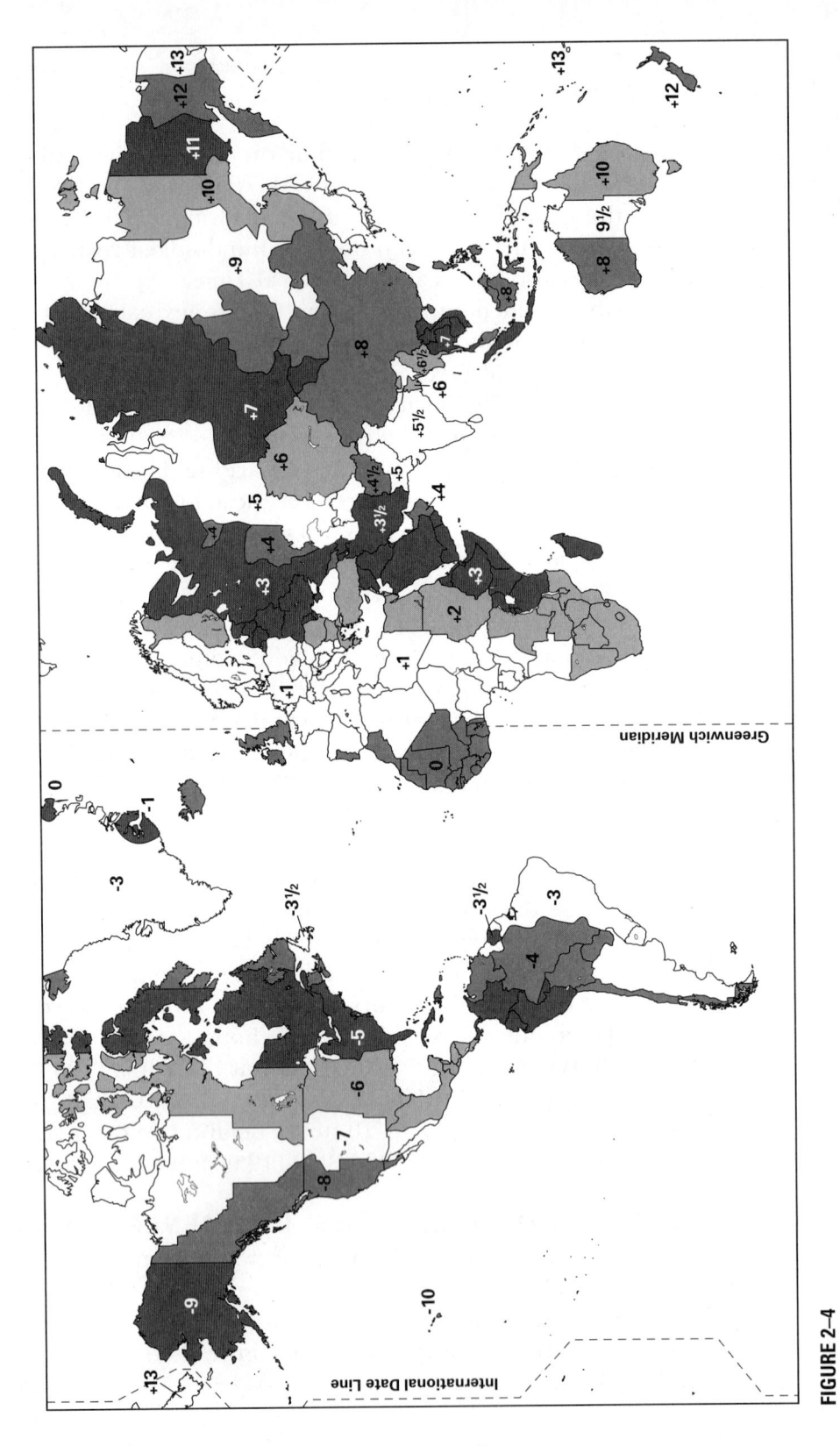

FIGURE 2–4
Map of world time zones. Reprinted by special permission from the February 1966 issue of the OAG Desktop Guide—Worldwide Edition. All rights reserved. Copyright 1966, Reed Travel Group.

from Sydney to Rio de Janeiro, a traveler must go via GMT. Calculating time differences throughout the world refers to traveling across time zones so that the arrival time at the destination becomes either earlier or later than the time at home. There are ten time zones from Sydney to GMT and three time zones from GMT to Rio de Janeiro. Because there are thirteen time zones between Sydney and Rio de Janeiro (10 + 3), there are 13 hours between the cities (13 time zones × 1 hour/time zone). Because Rio de Janeiro is west of GMT, it is 13 hours *behind* Sydney. A complete list of standard times throughout the world is found in Appendix D.

THE INTERNATIONAL DATE LINE

Separating GMT −12 and GMT +12 is the 180-degree longitude, which runs north to south through the Pacific Ocean. An imaginary line, called the **International Date Line,** partly follows this meridian and is exactly opposite the GMT. Since 1884, the International Date Line has been used to separate one day from another. The International Date Line deviates from the 180th meridian in some places to avoid separating communities.

CALCULATING TIME DIFFERENCES ACROSS THE DATE LINE.
When moving westbound across the International Date Line, the traveler loses a calendar day as the date changes to 1 day later. When moving eastbound across the International Date Line, the traveler gains a calendar day as the date changes to 1 day earlier. To calculate the time difference across the International Date Line, memorize and use the following easy calculation:

Westbound: Subtract 1 hour for each time zone crossed. Add 24 hours when crossing the International Date Line.
Eastbound: Add 1 hour for each time zone crossed. Subtract 24 hours when crossing the International Date Line.

Flying across the International Date Line is a unique experience in terms of time and days. A flight from Los Angeles to Sydney takes approximately 20 hours, yet technically 2 days elapse. The flight originates in Los Angeles, a point east of the International Date Line, at 8:05 P.M. and terminates in Sydney, a point west of the International Date Line, at 10:00 A.M. Because midnight has passed, the flight technically arrives the next day. However, because the International Date Line has been crossed westbound, another 24 hours must be added to the elapsed time, and hence the flight arrives 2 days later.

ELAPSED FLYING TIME

Many international travelers find crossing time zones outside the United States confusing. Not only do they want to know time differences but they are curious about lengths of flights. The total time spent flying from the point of origin to the point of destination is called the **elapsed flying time.**

When calculating elapsed flying time, it is important to remember to work with hours and minutes. Consider the following travel scenario:

Mr. and Mrs. Fickas are on a nonstop flight from Atlanta to Frankfurt. They depart Atlanta at 10:15 P.M. and arrive in Frankfurt at 11:15 A.M. the next day. Their elapsed flying time is calculated as follows:

Step 1. Convert the departure and arrival times to 24-hour clock time.

		10:15 P.M.	
Depart Atlanta	10:15 P.M.	+12:00 hour	= 2215
Arrive in Frankfurt	11:15 A.M.	2215	= 1115

Step 2. Convert the 24-hour clock departure and arrival times to GMT time. To compensate for the time differences, work with the same time zone. Use the International Standard Time Chart in Appendix D.

Depart Atlanta 2215 (GMT −5) = 0315

Add 5 hours to reach GMT time.

Arrive Frankfurt 1115 (GMT +1) = 1015

Subtract 1 hour to reach GMT time.

Step 3. Subtract the GMT departure time from the GMT arrival time. Remember to work with hours and minutes. Subtract minutes from minutes and hours from hours. The result is the elapsed flying time.

Arrival   1015
Departure − 0315
―――――――――
Elapsed time 0700

Calculating the elapsed flying time can be more complex, as the following scenario shows:

Mr. Nielsen departs New York City on a westbound flight at 11:30 A.M. on a business trip to Tokyo. He arrives at Tokyo's Narita Airport at 1:02 P.M. the next day.

Step 1. Convert all times to 24-hour clock time.

Depart New York City 11:30 A.M.
Arrive Tokyo   1:02 P.M.   1:02 P.M.
                                   +12:00 hours = 1130
                                     ―――――――――
                                      1302   = 1302

Step 2. Convert all 24-hour clock times to GMT time.

Depart New York City 1130 (GMT −5) = 1630
Add 5 hours to reach GMT time.
Arrive Tokyo 1302 (GMT +9)   = 0402
Subtract 9 hours to reach GMT time.

Step 3. Subtract the GMT departure time from the GMT arrival time.

Arrival   0402
Departure − 1630
―――――――――

To add and subtract time expressed in hours and minutes, separate the two. You must "borrow" time in full hour or minute increments. Therefore, to subtract 30 minutes in departure from 2 minutes in arrival, you must borrow 1 hour (60 minutes) from the 4 hours in the arrival and add it to the 2 minutes in arrival (0302 + 60 = 0362). You must also borrow 24 hours and add it to the remaining 3 hours in arrival (0362 + 2400 = 2762). (This calculation is based on

24 hours in one day and 60 minutes in 1 hour.) The revised subtraction looks as follows:

Arrival   2762
Departure   − 1630
Elapsed time 1132

In the final scenario, Helen and Andrew are traveling eastbound from Africa to Australia. They depart Johannesburg at 6:30 P.M. and arrive in Sydney at 7:25 P.M. the next day.

Step 1. Convert all times to 24-hour clock times.

Depart Johannesburg 6:30 P.M.   6:30 P.M.   = 1830
                                    +12:00 hours
                                     1830

Arrive Sydney   7:25 P.M.   07:25 P.M.   = 1925
                                    +12:00 hours
                                     1925

Step 2. Convert all 24-hour clock times to GMT time.

Depart Johannesburg 1830 (GMT +2) = 1630
Subtract 2 hours to reach GMT time.
Arrive Sydney 1925 (GMT +10)   = 0925
Subtract 10 hours to reach GMT time.

Step 3. Subtract the GMT departure time from the GMT arrival time.

Arrival   0925
Departure   − 1630

Revised subtraction:

0825 + 60 minutes = 0885
0885 + 24 hours   = 3285
Arrival   3285
Departure   − 1630
Elapsed time 1655

TRAVELING WISELY

Travel light. Dragging bags through airport terminals and watching them is not fun. It is stressful and tiring. Try to lay out on your bed everything you think you need, then cut it in half. In addition, buy inexpensive luggage. It does not draw as much attention as more expensive pieces do.

SUMMARY

- The IATA is an organization of international airlines that regulates international air traffic.
- IATAN is a subsidiary of IATA that services United States travel agencies.
- The Eight Freedoms of the Air are international air traffic agreements.
- A three-letter code identifies a city or an airport all over the world. A two-letter code identifies an airline all over the world.
- The IATA has divided the world into three areas (Area 1, Area 2, and Area 3) for airfare purposes.
- Travel directions have corresponding two-letter global indicator codes.
- To convert 12-hour clock time to 24-hour clock time, add 12 hours. To convert 24-hour clock time to 12-hour clock time, subtract 12 hours.
- Greenwich Mean Time (GMT) is always zero. Time zones around the world are based on GMT.
- The International Date Line follows the 180th meridian closely and separates one day from another.
- Elapsed flying time is the time spent flying from the point of origin to the point of destination.

CHECK YOUR UNDERSTANDING 2–1

Directions: For each city in the accompanying table, write the corresponding city code, country, IATA area, and IATA subarea in the spaces provided.

City	City Code	Country	IATA Area	Subarea
Zurich				
Manila				
Buenos Aires				
Stockholm				
Recife				
Istanbul				
Tokyo				
Winnipeg				
Karachi				
Dakar				
Singapore				
Quebec				
Tel Aviv				
Beijing				
Madrid				
Budapest				
Manaus				
Sydney				
Nairobi				
Caracas				
Kuala Lumpur				
St. Louis				
Dublin				
Cairo				
Papeete				
Rio de Janeiro				
Casablanca				
Paris				

CHECK YOUR UNDERSTANDING 2–2

Directions: Calculate the conversions in the accompanying table.

Convert to 24-Hour Clock Time		Convert to 12-Hour Clock Time	
11:15 P.M.		0315	
12:01 A.M.		1410	
8:10 A.M.		2100	
3:10 A.M.		0100	
9:31 P.M.		1745	
12:05 P.M.		0005	
1:37 P.M.		1631	
6:22 A.M.		2400	
4:50 P.M.		0510	
8:26 P.M.		0010	
11:58 A.M.		1210	
1:01 A.M.		2002	
10:47 P.M.		1055	
2:02 A.M.		0830	
12:00 A.M.		2313	

CHECK YOUR UNDERSTANDING 2–3

Directions: Calculate the elapsed flying times in the following scenarios.

1. A nonstop flight departs Johannesburg, South Africa at 5:25 P.M. and arrives in Nairobi, Kenya at 10:15 P.M.

   Elapsed flying time: _____

2. A direct flight departs Singapore, Singapore at 7:30 A.M. and arrives in San Francisco, USA at 9:25 A.M. the same day.

   Elapsed flying time: _____

3. A nonstop flight departs Nadi, Fiji Island at 2:35 A.M. and arrives in Los Angeles, USA at 8:15 P.M. the previous day.

   Elapsed flying time: _____

4. A connecting flight departs Chicago, USA at 4:50 P.M. and arrives in Budapest, Hungary at 5:55 P.M. the next day.

   Elapsed flying time: _____

5. A nonstop flight departs London, Great Britain at 8:00 P.M. and arrives in Cape Town, South Africa at 11:45 A.M. the next day.

   Elapsed flying time: _____

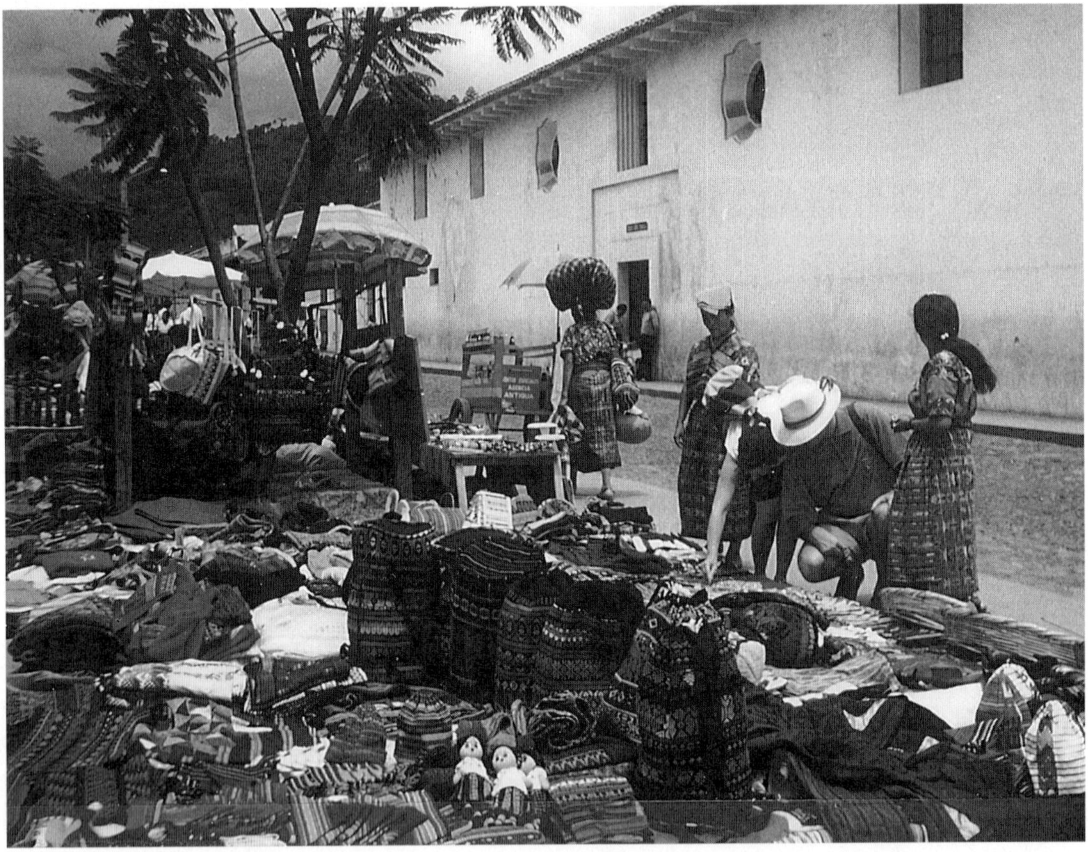

Chapter 3

Travel Requirements

Travel Documents
    The Passport
    The Visa
    The Tourist Card
    Proof of Citizenship
Customs and Immigration
    Customs Inspection
    Immigration Procedures
    Customs Procedures
    Duty-Free Shopping
    Restricted Items
Money Matters
    Foreign Currency
    Currency Codes
    Value-Added Tax

OBJECTIVES

After completing Chapter 3, you should be able to:

- Identify the documents needed for international travel
- Understand international customs and immigration procedures
- Demonstrate a functional understanding of document requirements for international travel
- Identify five prohibited items while traveling abroad

It is important for the travel professional to plan an international itinerary so the traveler will experience little inconvenience. To do so, the travel professional must follow the many rules and regulations that control travel between countries. These rules and regulations vary widely depending upon the country, the traveler's status, the purpose of the traveler's visit, and the length of stay.

Travel Documents

Preparing an international itinerary is time-consuming, and it requires special attention to details like passports, visas, tourist cards, and proof of citizenship.

THE PASSPORT

A **passport** is a government-issued document that identifies the bearer as a citizen of the country that issued it or the country where the bearer was officially naturalized. Governments use these documents to allow passport holders to travel between foreign countries. Passport holders also use these documents to request protection while visiting foreign lands. Therefore, it is important for travelers to watch their passports closely. Passports request their holders to be permitted across borders safely and soundly.

Everyone, including infants, must obtain passports to travel to countries requiring them. An adult passport is valid for 10 years; a child's passport (under 18 years) is valid for 5 years. All passports are valid from the date of issue.

To obtain a United States passport, travelers must complete an application. A United States passport application form is shown in Figure 3–1. Applicants must submit the following items with their applications to prove their citizenship:

- Proof of United States citizenship. This can be verified by an original birth certificate, an expired United States passport, or a Certificate of Naturalization.
- Proof of identity. A valid, permanent driver's license suffices as proof because it shows the bearer's signature and photograph. If applicants cannot provide proof of their identities, they must bring with them identifying witnesses who are United States citizens. An expired United States passport, a Certificate of Naturalization, or a military identification card also suffice as proof of identity.
- Two recent and identical photographs (2" × 2"), taken within the last 6 months.
- Passport fees. In 1996 passport application fees were $65.00 for an adult and $40.00 for a child.
- If married, a copy of the marriage certificate. If applicants are divorced, they must produce copies of their divorce papers.

A traveler requesting a passport for the first time must appear in person at a major post office, a passport agency, or any federal or state court building with the completed application and supporting documents. The passport agent then verifies that the application is complete. The applicant signs the form in front of the agent.

It takes approximately 4 to 8 weeks to process a passport application. This passport is then mailed to the applicant's residence. In an emergency, a passport can be issued within 3 days, but there is an additional fee. The applicant must provide all necessary documents or airline tickets and appear at a passport agency office personally. A traveler who has a passport can renew it by mail using a renewal application. The traveler must produce the same documents as first-time applicants and pay a renewal fee.

In the United States, the most commonly issued passport is the **regular passport.** This passport is for people traveling on business or vacation. Other types of passports are the **diplomatic**

FIGURE 3–1

United States passport application

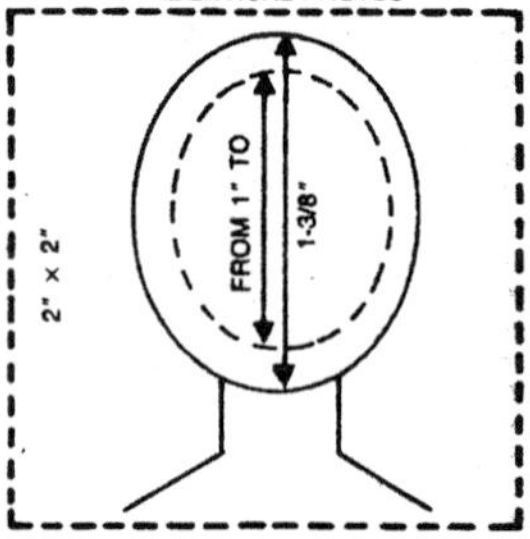

passport, for diplomats traveling on government assignment, and the **official passport,** for all other government workers.

THE VISA

A **visa** is an endorsement on one of the blank pages of the passport, which allows the traveler to enter another country. Visas are issued by the governments of countries being visited. A visa confirms that a passport has been accepted and a traveler is authorized to enter a country. The visa outlines the conditions of entry, such as length of stay and reason for entry. Some visas allow multiple entries for indefinite periods; others allow just one entry for a short time.

Most foreign countries have **embassies** and **consulates** to protect their citizens and the interests of their citizens. A United States citizen may wish to travel to Nepal, for example. That citizen would have to apply to the Nepalese embassy in New York City for a tourist visa. A tourist visa application for visiting Nepal is shown in Figure 3–2. Before leaving the United States, the citizen must submit the visa application to the Nepalese embassy personally or through a visa service agency, because the traveler, not the travel agent, is responsible for obtaining visas.

Because all visas are stamped on passports, the passport, which is valid for at least 6 months after the scheduled departure date, must be submitted with the completed visa application, passport-size photographs, and a fee. The cost of visas varies according to the number of days left before departure. Visa processing rules, times, and fees also vary. For example, a traveler visiting the Russian Federation must supply the names of the cities on the itinerary, travel dates, and hotel confirmation numbers.

A person traveling on business is sometimes required to obtain a **business visa,** which involves submitting the visa application with a letter on company letterhead that states the company is financially responsible for the trip. A person traveling abroad to study needs a **student visa.** Normally, although only full-time students are granted this type of visa, and they are not allowed to work, apprenticeships are permitted in some fields of study.

ROYAL NEPALESE CONSULATE GENERAL
820 SECOND AVENUE, SUITE 202
NEW YORK, N.Y. 10017

Please check one of the following:

___ Single entry visa, 15 days and under - $15.00
___ Single entry visa, 30 days and under - $25.00
___ Double entry visa, 30 days and under - $40.00
___ Multiple entry visa, 60 days and under- $60.00

VISA APPLICATION FORM
(one copy along with one photograph required)

PLEASE ATTACH

PHOTOGRAPH

HERE

1. Name: _____
   (last)   (middle)   (first)

2. Nationality: _____

3. Address: _____
   (street block)   (city)
   _____ Telephone No. _____
   (state)   (zip code)

4. (a) Date of Birth: _____ (b) Place of Birth _____

5. Particulars of Passport: (Diplomatic/Special/Regular)
   (a) Passport No. _____
   (b) Date of Issue _____ (c) Date of Expiry _____

6. Expected date of arrival in Nepal _____

7. Date of Departure from U.S. _____

8. Duration of stay in Nepal _____

9. Purpose of visit to Nepal _____

10. Date and purpose of previous visit to Nepal _____

11. Name, Date of birth and Passport no. of every member of the family if accompanied:

NAME	DATE OF BIRTH	PASSPORT NO.
_____	_____	_____
_____	_____	_____
_____	_____	_____
_____	_____	_____

_____   _____
Date   (Signature of Applicant)

For Official use only (Do not detach)

(a) No. and Category of Visa _____
Date _____
Remarks _____

_____
(Signature of Officer)

(PLEASE SEE THE REVERSE SIDE FOR INSTRUCTIONS)

FIGURE 3–2

Nepal visa application

While United States citizens are **tourist visa exempt** in many countries, which means they do not need visas to visit those countries, situations change constantly. Western European countries do not currently require United States citizens to obtain tourist visas for stays up to 3 months. A few nations in Asia, such as Thailand, Indonesia, Japan, Hong Kong, and Fiji, do not require visas from United States citizens for stays between 14 and 30 days.

Countries that are open only to tour groups on organized itineraries include Tibet, where approximately 1,000 visas are granted per year, and the Commonwealth of Independent States, where travelers must submit letters confirming their entry and exit dates, their itineraries, and their means of transportation. Sometimes travelers can obtain visas at the airport upon arriving. In Nepal, for example, a 7-day **transit visa** is available at the airport.

Because the visa application merely requests permission for a person to enter a foreign country, it is not unusual that a request is denied. A government can refuse a visa for anyone it does not wish to admit. Many countries do not explain why they deny requests. Therefore, submitting passport and visa applications several months before the intended departure date is recommended. If problems or delays occur, the departure date can be adjusted accordingly. The risk of experiencing a problem with obtaining a visa can be minimized by completing the paperwork as fully, accurately, and honestly as possible.

A traveler who holds a valid passport and visa is not guaranteed entry to a foreign country. Immigration inspectors in any city in the world can refuse to allow a traveller to enter and rarely do they inform them of their decisions. For example, inspectors can "turn away" citizens who try to bring prohibited items into the country. If a traveler attempts to bring in weapons or drugs, he or she will be detained. When travelers enter a country without the proper papers and documentation, they may be detained or deported. Sometimes they are even arrested. Therefore, the travel professional should never assume that the traveler is a United States citizen. While many foreign nationals in the United States have obtained permanent residency (they have obtained **green cards,** which are documents that verify the holders have permanent resident status) and are fluent in English, they are still citizens of their home countries. Travelers should always ask which passport is used for traveling, because passport and visa requirements depend on the traveler's nationality.

The following advisory information from the United States Department of State is of great value to the travel professional. It should be used to educate the traveler as to crucial information relevant to the destination.

State Department Advisory

Entry Requirements: For information on entry requirements for both France and Monaco, travelers may contact the Embassy of France at 4101 Reservoir Road, NW, Washington, DC 20007, tel: (202) 944-6000, or the nearest French Consulate General in Boston, Chicago, Detroit, Honolulu, Houston, Los Angeles, Miami, New Orleans, New York, San Francisco, or San Juan. Travelers to Monaco may also contact the nearest Honorary Consulate of Monaco in Boston, Chicago, Dallas, Los Angeles, New Orleans, New York, Palm Beach (Florida), Philadelphia, San Francisco, San Juan, or Washington, DC.

Medical Facilities: Medical care is widely available. United States medical insurance is not always valid outside the United States, however. In some cases, travelers have found supplemental medical insurance with specific overseas coverage to be useful. Further information on health matters can be obtained from the Centers for Disease Control and Prevention's International Travelers Hotline at (404) 332-4559.

Crime Information: France and Monaco both have relatively low rates of violent crime, but crimes involving larceny are becoming more common. Pickpocketing, theft of unattended baggage, and theft from rental cars or vehicles with out-of-town or foreign license plates occur daily. Criminals often operate around popular tourist attractions like museums, monuments, restaurants, hotels, and beaches and on trains and subways. Americans in France and Monaco should be particularly alert to pickpockets on trains and subways, as well as in train and subway stations. Travelers are advised to carry only whatever cash and personal checks are absolutely necessary and to leave extra cash, credit cards, personal documents, and passport copies at home or in the hotel safe.

The loss or theft of a United States passport overseas should be reported immediately to the local police and to the nearest United States embassy or consulate. United States citizens can refer to the Department of State's pamphlet "A Safe Trip Abroad," which provides useful information on guarding valuables and protecting personal security while traveling abroad. The pamphlet is available from the Superintendent of Documents, United States Government Printing Office, Washington, DC 20402.

Drug Penalties: United States citizens are subject to the laws of the country in which they are traveling. In France, the penalties for possessing, using, and dealing in illegal drugs are very strict. Convicted offenders can expect significant jail sentences and heavy customs fines; failure to pay can result in upward of an additional 2 years imprisonment.

Dual Nationality: United States citizens who have also acquired French citizenship may be subject to compulsory military service and other aspects of French law while in France. Those who might be affected can inquire at a French Embassy or consulate regarding their status. In some instances, dual nationality may hamper United States government efforts to provide protection abroad.

Other Information: Certain Air France flights between France and various Middle Eastern points (usually Damascus or Amman) make en-route stops in Beirut. However, United States passports are not valid for travel to, in, or through Lebanon unless special validation has been obtained from the Department of State.

Terrorist Activities: Civil disorder is rare in France. However, in the past, terrorist groups have committed violent acts in France, including a few closely targeted political assassinations. Recent bombings in Paris, which also appear to be the work of terrorists, have killed or injured French citizens and foreign visitors. There is no indication that these acts have been directed at American citizens, American businesses, or American interests. These bombings have increased the police presence at travel centers like airports, metros, and train stations.

The Basque Separatist Party (ETA) and the National Front for the Liberation of Corsica (FLNC) continue to operate in southern France and have occasionally bombed local government institutions, travel agencies, and so on. ETA and FLNC attacks usually occur late at night, an apparent attempt to minimize casualties. Recently, terrorist groups have committed other terrorist acts, including a few closely targeted political killings and kidnappings, but no Ameri-cans have been affected.

Registration and Embassy Location: United States citizens may register at the Consular Section in the United States Embassy or at one of the three consulates, where they may obtain updated information on travel and security in France. There is no United States embassy or consulate in Monaco. For assistance and registration in Monaco, United States citizens can contact the United States consulate general in Marseille or the United States Consular agent in Nice.

The United States Embassy in Paris is located at: 2 Avenue Gabriel, tel: (33) 1-42-96-12-02, fax (33) 1-42-66-97-83. The Consular Section is located one block away, across the Place de la Concorde, at 2 Rue St. Florentin, fax (33) 1-42-86-82-91.

The United States Consulate in Bordeaux is located at: 22 Cours du Marechal Foch, tel: (33) 56-52-65-95, fax (33) 56-51-60-42.

The United States Consulate in Marseille is located at: 12 Boulevard Paul Peytral, tel: (33) 91-54-92-00, fax (33) 91-55-09-47.

The United States Consulate in Strasbourg is located at: 15 Avenue d'Alsace, tel: (33) 88-35-31-04, fax (33) 88-24-06-95.

There is a Consular Agent in Nice, at 31 Rue du Marechal Joffre, tel: (33) 16-93-88-89-55, fax (33) 16-93-87-07-38.

THE TOURIST CARD

Since World War II, international tourism has had many sociocultural and economic benefits. Many nations, especially those in North America and western Europe, have eased their passport and/or visa restrictions since then. In addition, nations agreed to admit travelers without passports and visas.

In some nations, like Mexico, the **tourist card,** which is a piece of paper used to identify travelers and regulate who enters and leaves, has replaced the passport/visa. United States nationals who are vacationing in Mexico or visiting for health, sports, scientific, or artistic reasons can enter the country with a tourist card instead of a passport or visa. The tourist card is valid for 6 months and is easy to obtain. To do so, travelers must bring proof of United States citizenship to the Mexican Embassy, a travel agency, or the air carrier who flew them to Mexico. Travelers must present proof of citizenship and the tourist card upon arriving in Mexico. Clients can also be issued tourist cards at the Mexican border. Divorced parents must show certified letters or custody papers to bring children into Mexico.

PROOF OF CITIZENSHIP

United States citizens staying fewer than 6 months can sometimes enter countries without valid passports. These countries include Canada, the Bahamas, Bermuda, the Cayman Islands, Jamaica, Puerto Rico, the United States Virgin Islands, and Mexico. However, other evidence of United States citizenship and identity is required. Documents that prove United States citizenship include a(n):

- Original birth certificate
- Expired passport
- Certificate of naturalization
- Certificate of citizenship
- Valid driver's license
- Government identification card

A valid passport is always the best proof of citizenship, and it secures the holder's reentry into the United States. Therefore, a traveler who has one should use it. Most foreign nationals need passports and possibly visas to enter Mexico. Therefore, the travel professional should always check the traveler's nationality.

Customs and Immigration

Customs and immigration services are present in over 300 international ports of entry throughout the United States and protect over 90,000 miles of borders. Each port of entry regulates the flow of people and goods leaving and entering the country. New York City is the busiest port of entry. All international travelers must go through a customs and immigration control check at each international port of entry. For example, on a flight from Seattle to Hong Kong via Tokyo, a traveler must go through customs and immigration in Japan and Hong Kong.

CUSTOMS INSPECTION

Immediately when travelers arrive in a foreign country, immigration authorities thoroughly check each traveler and his or her travel documents. These **immigration officers** decide if arriving travelers may enter their country. After this inspection, travelers are directed to a customs control area where **customs officers** search personal baggage for prohibited items. Some countries also require departing passengers to go through customs. Thailand officials, for example, thoroughly search departing travelers for drugs. (Thailand carries out the death penalty for the possession of drugs. No one, including presidents, prime ministers, embassies, or monarchies, may interfere in such a situation, because the local law of that country has been broken.) Israel also has strict departing controls. In this country, officials open and search every suitcase. In addition, they direct each passenger into a small, enclosed room where the passenger is questioned and sometimes asked to undress so a body search can be conducted.

IMMIGRATION PROCEDURES

Since 1891, all travelers arriving in and departing the United States, including United States citizens, have been checked by **Immigration and Naturalization Services (INS)**. The main job of INS is to control who enters and leaves America. Although the visa states the purpose of the traveler's visit, the immigration officer sometimes asks questions about the visa. As a travel professional, you should advise your client to answer all questions patiently, because the officer's job is to verify information and identify "unwanted aliens" and others involved in criminal activity, such as people traveling on stolen passports.

TRAVEL TIP

One unfortunate, but patient, traveler named Rita experienced the complexities of immigration laws at London's Heathrow Airport. As Rita can attest, a visa does not guarantee a traveler will be admitted to a foreign country.

Since the December 1988 Pan Am disaster in Lockerbie, Scotland, travelers have been recommended to arrive at Heathrow at least 6 hours before their scheduled international departures because security has become extremely tight. Five months after the disaster, Rita was to fly on a complimentary round-trip, business-class ticket from London to Tokyo on a United States carrier. She was waiting in the very important person (VIP) check-in line, wearing a comfortable jogging outfit and carrying a backpack and a sleeping bag. She was not allowed to check her baggage, however. At the check-in counter, three security men interrogated Rita and left with her passport, airline ticket, and credit cards. When the men returned her personal identification an hour later, they thoroughly searched her backpack and showed a particular interest in her Walkman®. Rita then realized she was suspected of something. She thought she may have fit the description of an unwanted alien or a terrorist.

Almost 3 hours after her ordeal began, Rita was allowed to check her luggage. She now had less than 3 hours to go through passport control before her departure. By the time officials searched her carry-on luggage, Rita had just enough time to arrive at the gate just as the flight crew was closing the airplane's doors.

The future immigration procedure will be remarkable. INS has developed INSPASS, a new immigration system for airline passengers arriving in the United States. **INSPASS** permits member citizens of the United States, Canada, Bermuda, and the Visa Waiver Pilot Program to avoid waiting in line for immigration checks.

Each INSPASS member is issued a wallet-size membership card. At the INSPASS machine, the member inserts the card and places a hand on a glass plate. The machine reads the hand's geometry and compares it with the information on file. New York's John F. Kennedy Airport, Newark International Airport, and Toronto's Pearson International are using INSPASS machines on a trial basis. Applications for INSPASS cards can be obtained at any one of these airports.

CUSTOMS PROCEDURES

To regulate the items entering a nation and help prevent smuggling, customs officers inspect the baggage of most incoming travelers. Customs officers also assess and collect taxes, or **customs duties,** on imported items and, therefore, must identify all items acquired abroad. Incoming travelers must declare all items they purchased and received as gifts abroad and pay taxes to the government of the country where the items were acquired. An estimated $12 billion is collected each year in customs duties.[1]

All travelers to the United States must complete a **Customs Declaration Form** before arriving (Figure 3–3). If the travelers are arriving via cruise ship or airplane, the crew provides the form. The form must state the retail value of all items acquired abroad.

---

[1] *The World Book Encyclopedia,* vol. 4. Chicago: World Book, Inc., 1991.

FIGURE 3–3

United States Customs Declaration Form

DUTY-FREE SHOPPING

Duty-free shopping is tempting, because **duty-free** means an item is not subject to sales tax in the country of purchase. However, travelers must comply with the American duty-free limit upon entering the United States. Upon entering any country, you must comply with the duty-free limit. It is, therefore, wise to keep all receipts. For example, if a traveler purchased a bottle of Christian Dior perfume in London's Heathrow duty-free airport store, she would not pay British sales tax. If her total purchases exceeded a predetermined maximum allowance, however, she would pay United States tax upon entering the United States. The maximum allowance is determined by the government. A traveler can learn the maximum allowance from a travel professional or the customs declarations posted at airports.

A United States resident returning from a stay abroad of less than 48 hours may bring back $25 worth of items. United States residents returning from stays abroad of at least 48 hours may bring back up to $400 worth of duty-free items. Nonresidents may bring back up to $100 worth of items. Such items may include cameras, chinaware, games, jewelry, tobacco (100 cigars or 200 cigarettes), alcohol (1 liter if the traveler is over 18), musical instruments, paper products, perfume, records, tape recorders, toys, and wood carvings. The tax exemption for United States residents is $600 if the traveler is returning from a select list of twenty-four Caribbean nations, including Jamaica and the Bahamas. If he or she is returning from American Samoa, Guam, or the United States Virgin Islands, the tax exemption is $1,200, including cigarettes. The traveler may also transport up to $10,000 in foreign or United States currency, money orders, or travelers checks into or out of the United States without filing a report with United States Customs.

RESTRICTED ITEMS

Most countries strictly prohibit certain items. These items include illegal drugs, weapons and ammunition, pornographic materials, hazardous articles (i.e., fireworks), and switchblade knives. Customs officers use specially trained dogs to find drugs in baggage. A dog can search 500 pieces of luggage in about 30 minutes and thoroughly and accurately search a car in about 2 minutes. Most countries also prohibit most fruits, vegetables, plants, animals, and meats, because these items have a high risk of carrying infectious diseases to humans, livestock, or crops.

Some countries allow certain items only with **import permits.** For example, weapons and ammunition for hunting purposes must be registered before they leave the United States to prove they were not purchased abroad. In contrast, drugs accompanied by written doctor's prescriptions do not require import permits, but medications should be kept in pharmacy bottles. Items made from endangered animals are illegal, and import permits cannot be obtained for them. Such products include alligator skin, whalebone, tortoise shell, crocodile skin, African ivory, and fur. All prohibited items may be seized on the spot and destroyed. Moreover, the traveler can be fined or even arrested.

A traveler must be careful about collecting souvenirs abroad, particularly archaeological and historical items such as stones from the Acropolis ruins outside Athens. Such items are nationally protected treasures, and violators can be arrested. Export restrictions may also apply to religious products. For example, Thailand prohibits the export of images of Buddha. The customs officers, who are appointed all over the world to detect international smuggling, frequently detect art and archaeological items and drugs and narcotics in travelers' baggage and have the authority to make arrests.

Money Matters

Even in this shrinking world with an increasing open global market economy, the United States dollar is not universally accepted as currency. Most nations have their own individually named currency with corresponding denominations. For example, the notes of the Japanese Yen are in denominations of ¥10,000, 5000, 1000, and 500 with coins of ¥100, 50, 10, 5, and 1.

FOREIGN CURRENCY

When traveling abroad, United States dollars cannot always be used as currency. Instead, local currency must be used. For example, before your client leaves on a trip to Italy, advise him or her to go to a bank to exchange his or her American dollars for Italian currency, the Italian lire.

The **banker's selling rate (BSR)** is the rate at which a bank sells foreign currency. In America, the United States dollar is multiplied by the BSR to calculate the equivalent amount of foreign currency. If a traveler is exchanging 500 United States dollars and the exchange rate is 1514.90, the traveler will receive 757,450 Italian lire (500 × 1514.90). Current exchange rates can be obtained from computer reservation systems, banks, or newspapers.

Buying foreign currency at BSR may not be most economical, because a limited number of nationwide banks in the United States and other countries carry foreign currency. Some travel agencies, like Thomas Cook and American Express, sell foreign currency at rates that compete aggressively with banks. American dollars can be exchanged for foreign currency, travelers checks in United States dollars, or travelers checks in foreign currency.

Traveling with **traveler's checks** in United States dollars is the easiest and safest alternative. Many foreign banks cash traveler's checks. If the checks are stolen or lost, they can be replaced. With the high value of the United States dollar on the international market, many foreign countries accept United States traveler's checks for restaurant meals, hotel accommodations, and shopping items.

It is a good idea for travelers to exchange a few dollars for foreign banknotes before leaving the United States. It can be frustrating to have to pay a bank's exchange rates and fees at an international airport just to buy bus fare or a cup of coffee. Before travelers return to the United States, they should spend all their foreign currency. When foreign currency is exchanged for United States dollars, value is almost always lost.

Many countries, primarily those with weak and unstable local currencies, use the United States dollar. The American dollar must not be confused with the dollars of other countries.

Canada, Australia, and Singapore, for example, have dollar values and exchange rates that differ from those in the United States.

Some countries have unusual currency exchange procedures. For example, China's currency, Renminbi, is only available to travelers as **Foreign Exchange Certificates (FEC)**. Travelers cannot remove Renminbi from China. The FECs, which come in the same denominations as Renminbi, can be exchanged for travelers checks in Hong Kong or China.

CURRENCY CODES

Each country in the world has a three-letter currency code that consists of a two-letter country code followed by the first letter of the name of the currency. For example, the currency code for the United States is *USD* (US = United States, D = dollar). The **International Organization for Standardization (ISO),** founded in 1946, standardizes international commercial and industrial regulations and has established the country codes. Figure 3–4 provides a few examples of the ISO country and IATA currency codes.

VALUE-ADDED TAX

Europe's **value-added tax (VAT)** is equivalent to a national sales tax. The VAT ranges from 6.5 percent in Switzerland to 25 percent in Denmark. Under the refundable tax program called **Europe Tax-Free Shopping (ETS),** travelers shopping in Europe's participating tax-free shops, which display "Tax-Free for Tourists" signs, can receive a refund of the VAT. However, the VAT refund is only available for items to be taken out of the country. Additionally, to qualify for the VAT refund, the shopper must be a non-European resident who is shopping in a European nation. Most European nations participate in the ETS program.

When a shopper qualifies for the refund, the salesperson completes a tax-free shopping check with the shopper's passport information. Travelers must present their passport infor-

Country	ISO Country Code	IATA Currency Code
Australia	AU	AUD
Belgium	BE	BEF
China	CN	CNY
Egypt	EG	EGP
France	FR	FRF
Greece	GR	GRD
Hong Kong	HK	HKD
Italy	IT	ITL
Japan	JP	JPY
Kenya	KE	KES
Luxembourg	LU	LUF
Morocco	MA	MAD
Nepal	NP	NPR
Portugal	PT	PTE
Saudi Arabia	SA	SAR
Thailand	TH	THB
United States	US	USD
Zimbabwe	ZW	ZWD

FIGURE 3-4

ISO country and IATA currency codes

mation to sales representatives to prove their non-European status and thereby qualify for the VAT refund. A customs officer stamps the shopping check when the traveler leaves Europe. The traveler can obtain the refund at the airport.

Often the traveler must show the items claimed on the VAT refund form at customs. Upon passing customs at the airport, travelers must go to the tax refund service desk called "Tax-Free Shopping" for a cash, check, or credit card refund. Airports that do not have such service desks mail refund checks to the travelers' home addresses several weeks later.

Before travelers can claim tax refunds, most European countries require a minimum amount of purchase. The minimum spending amount is expressed in local currency and varies according to nation. Therefore, the equivalent amount in United States dollars also varies depending on the exchange rate.

TRAVELING WISELY

Many countries, including the United States, refuse to allow passengers arriving on one-way tickets to enter. Therefore, travelers must have confirmed onward or return airline tickets when entering foreign countries. In addition, travelers should always travel with copies of their passports, visas, credit cards, and other important documents, and they should keep them separate from the original documents in case the originals are lost or stolen. Finally, travelers should leave handbags at home and use belt pouches for carrying valuables.

SUMMARY

- A passport is a document that identifies the bearer as a citizen of the country. This country is normally the one in which the traveler was born.
- A visa is an endorsement on one of the blank pages in the traveler's passport that permits the traveler to enter another country.
- Immigration inspectors decide if travelers may enter their countries.
- Most countries prohibit certain items, including drugs, weapons, knives, and products made from endangered animals.
- United States residents returning from stays abroad of at least 48 hours may bring back $400 worth of items without paying duties.

CHECK YOUR UNDERSTANDING 3–1

Directions: Fill in the following blanks:

1. A _____ is a document that identifies the bearer as a citizen of the country in which the traveler was born.

2. A visa outlines the conditions of entry to a foreign country, such as _____ and _____.

3. The holder of a passport is approved by _____ to travel between foreign countries.

4. A tourist card is good for travel to _____.

5. An adult passport is valid for _____ years.

6. The passport application form must be submitted with the following four documents: _____, _____, _____, and _____.

7. A _____ is an endorsement on one of the blank pages of the traveler's passport.

8. Proof of citizenship is good for travel to _____, _____, and _____.

9. A valid passport and visa do not guarantee _____.

10. The United States is tourist visa exempt with many countries, including _____, _____, _____, _____, _____, and _____.

CHECK YOUR UNDERSTANDING 3–2

Directions: Fill in the following blanks:

1. _____ decide if arriving travelers may enter their country.

2. United States residents returning from stays abroad of at least 48 hours may bring back $_____ worth of items without paying duties.

3. Most countries prohibit certain items, including _____, _____, _____, _____, and _____.

4. At customs, most travelers are checked for _____.

5. When travelers return to the United States, customs officers search their personal baggage for _____.

6. All travelers arriving in the United States must complete a _____.

7. A United States resident returning from a stay abroad of less than 48 hours may bring back $_____ worth of items without paying duties.

8. Europe's value-added tax (VAT) program is equivalent to _____.

9. INSPASS is _____.

10. The term *duty-free* means _____.

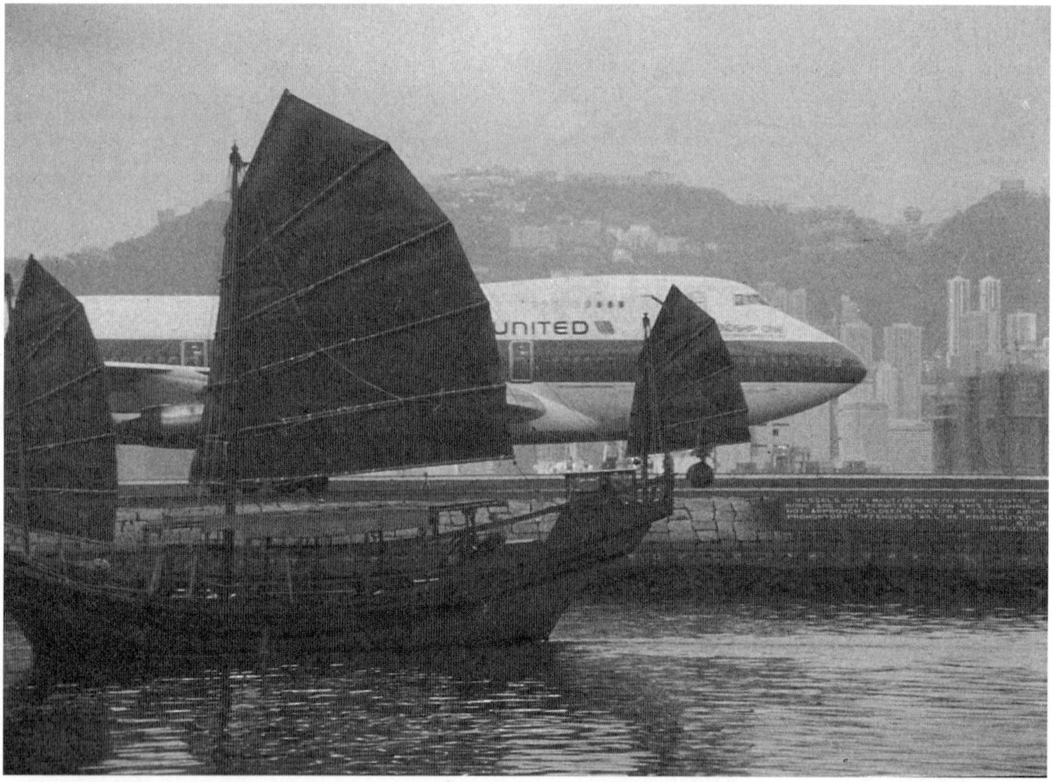
UNITED

Chapter 4

International Airfares

IATA Airfares
    Stopovers and Connections
    Normal Fares
    Excursion and Apex Fares
    Infants' and Children's Fares
Interpreting IATA Airfare and Rule Displays
    Air Tariff Books
    Normal Fare Displays
    Excursion and Apex Fare Displays
    Automated Fare Displays

OBJECTIVES

After completing Chapter 4, you should be able to:

- Define *stopover* and *connection*
- Interpret international airfares
- Interpret international rules for airfares

The travel professional may wonder why it is important to learn to read manual airfare displays when computer reservation systems provide airfares automatically. First, thoroughly understanding airfare structures enables travelers to convert their knowledge to any computer reservation system easily, thereby increasing their computer literacy. Second, travelers cannot rely on computers to automatically search for the lowest airfare. Most computer reservation systems contain only airfare information for major international carriers on major international routes. A computer may not access airfare on a smaller carrier flying to a smaller city.

IATA Airfares

Because all United States airlines are privately owned and financed, they determine their domestic airfare structures. Most international carriers are owned and controlled by their governments who authorize airfares and routes. These IATA-established airfares and rules are predetermined and negotiated by those governments. Thus, the fierce airfare wars and competition continually being waged in the United States rarely occur internationally.

STOPOVERS AND CONNECTIONS

When calculating international airfares and compiling an itinerary, it is important to understand how a connection and a stopover differ. Figure 4–1 illustrates the differences. A **connection**, also called a transfer, is any point between the point of origin and the point of destination that does not interrupt the traveler's journey and lasts for fewer than 6 hours. A fare is not charged for a connection. A **stopover** occurs when a traveler voluntarily interrupts the journey for more than 6 hours at any point between the point of origin and the point of destination.

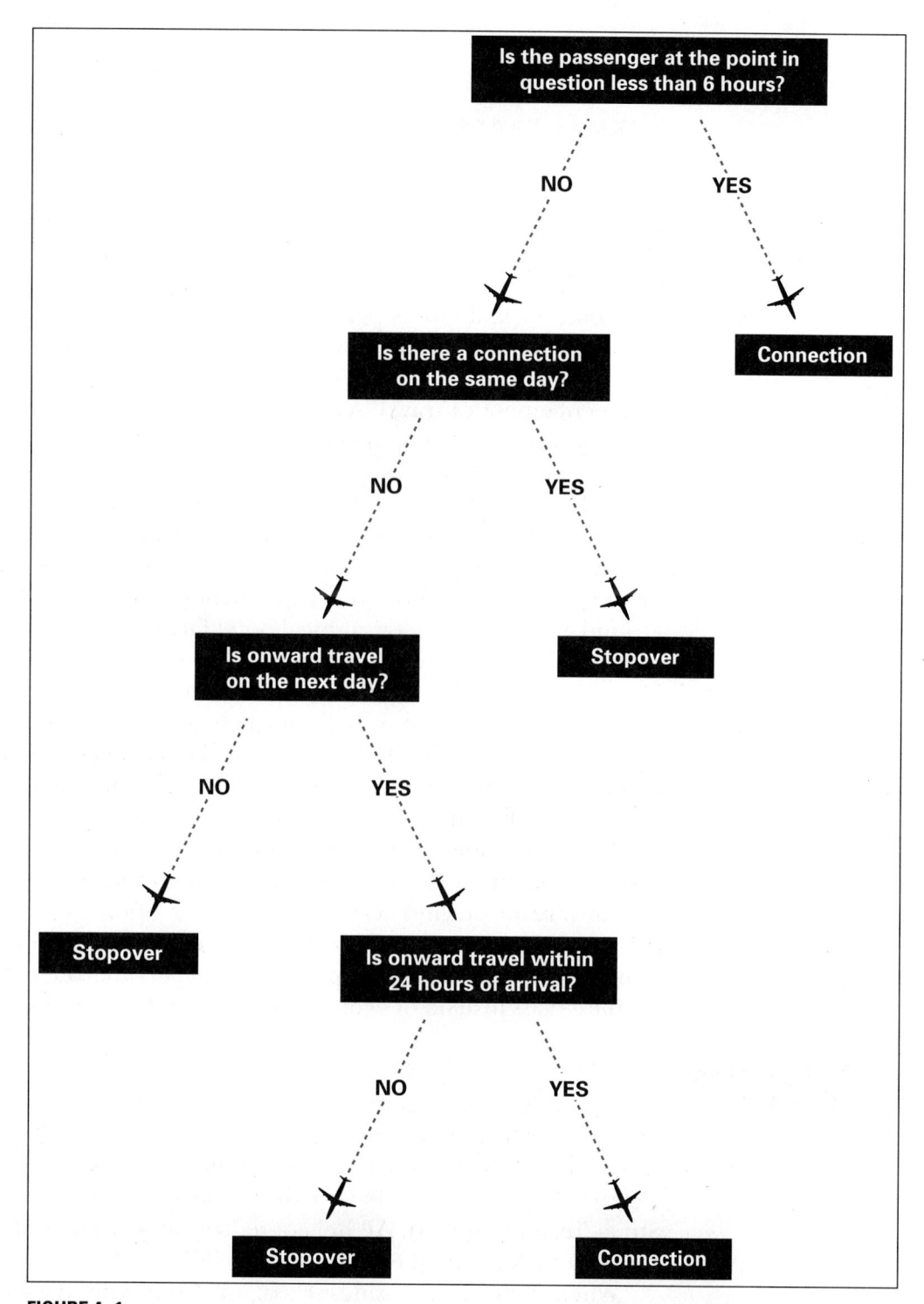

FIGURE 4–1

Stopovers versus connections. Adapted from IATA Ticketing Handbook, *26th ed. (June 1994).*

NORMAL FARES

A **normal fare** is an unrestricted and totally flexible airfare. A normal-fare ticket can be purchased at the last minute without a minimum stay requirement, and the purchaser can travel on any day throughout the year. Any change, exchange, or refund of a normal fare is permitted without penalty. Unlimited stopovers are also often allowed. Discounts, however, are rarely available. Normal airfares are valid for 1 year from the date of commencement of travel. A normal fare can be purchased for one-way or round-trip journeys.

A normal airfare allows stopovers at any point unless the airfare rule prohibits such a stop. The airfare and its corresponding rule is determined by the individual airline. The cost of a stopover, if any, depends on the fare rule and/or the type of journey. On round-trip and circle-trip journeys, the point of turnaround, which is the geographical point farthest from the point of origin, is not counted as a stopover. A journey from Boston to Miami is round-trip if both the outbound and inbound flight segments are complete mirror images, such as flying the same airline in both directions with the same class of service. A circle-trip journey is of a round-trip nature, but differs in that the outbound and inbound portions are not mirror images.

There are four main categories of normal airfares (see Figure 4–2). Each has a corresponding two-letter fare basis code. The airfare in business class category C is often the same as the airfare in economy class category Y. The advantage of common rated fares is that travel professionals can offer their clients business-class instead of economy-class accommodations.

TRAVEL TIP

When first-class, business-class, or Concorde passengers originate or terminate their journeys at New York City's John F. Kennedy Airport (JFK), free helicopter travel is available to Newark Airport (EWR), LaGuardia Airport (LGA), or the 34th Street Terminal (TSS). All helicopter services are operated by the New York Helicopter Corporation (HD).

When first-class, business-class, or Concorde passengers originate or terminate their journeys at Los Angeles International Airport (LAX), free helicopter travel is available to Burbank (BUR), Long Beach (LGB), Commerce Business Plaza

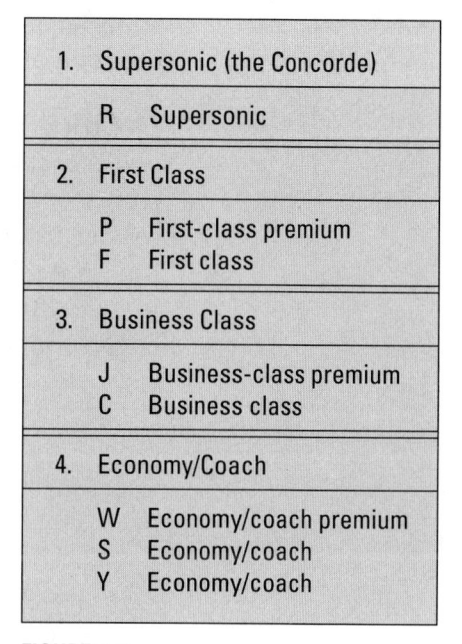

1.	Supersonic (the Concorde)	
R	Supersonic	
2.	First Class	
P	First-class premium	
F	First class	
3.	Business Class	
J	Business-class premium	
C	Business class	
4.	Economy/Coach	
W	Economy/coach premium	
S	Economy/coach	
Y	Economy/coach	

FIGURE 4-2

Normal airfares and their codes

(JBP), or the City of Industry (JID). All helicopter services are operated by LA Helicopter.

EXCURSION AND APEX FARES

Excursion fares and **apex fares** are discounted economy fares. An excursion fare has some restrictions, which may include minimum stay and/or travel limitation to specific seasons. Excursion fares can only be purchased for round-trip journeys, and they must be purchased 7 to 14 days in advance. A few stopovers are sometimes allowed, but changes, exchanges, and refunds are penalized. An excursion fare is valid from 4 months to 1 year from the date of commencement of travel.

An apex fare is really an advance-purchase excursion fare because it must be purchased at least 21 days before departure. Apex is the least expensive international airfare, but it is also the most restricted. A specific airline must be flown or a specific city must be used as a connection, or both. Therefore, stopovers are not permitted. An apex fare can only be purchased for round-trip journeys, and they are valid for 3 to 6 months from the date of commencement of travel.

EXCURSION/APEX FARE BASIS CODES. The fare basis codes in the excursion/apex fare category contain multiple letters. The first letter of the fare basis, also known as the class of service, identifies the type of fare. First letters include, but are not limited to, *B, H, L, M, N, Q, T,* and *V.* The remaining letters identify the conditions of travel. Each condition of travel and its corresponding letter(s) appear in Figure 4–3.

SEASONAL CODES	
H	Highest fare season
Q	Christmas-fare season
O	Middle (shoulder) fare season
L	Lowest fare season
PARTS-OF-THE-WEEK-CODES	
W	Weekend-fare level (for weekend travel only)
X	Weekday-fare level (for weekday travel only)
FARE- AND PASSENGER-TYPE CODES	
AB	Advance-purchase fare (lowest fare season)
AD	Agent fare
AN	Nonrefundable advance-purchase fare
AP	Advance-purchase fare
BT	Bulk inclusive tour
CD	Senior citizen
CH	Child
DG	Government officials
DP	Diplomats and dependents
EE	Excursion
GV	Group inclusive tour
IN	Infant
IT	Inclusive tour
NR	Nonrefundable fare
RW	Round-the-world
SD	Student
UU	Standby fare
VU	Visit-USA fare
ZZ	Youth fare

FIGURE 4–3

Travel conditions and their codes

Following are two examples that combine basis codes in a fare basis. The general rule is the longer the fare basis, the more restricted the fare.

Example 1: An apex fare from London, Great Britain to North Bay, Canada, with a senior-citizen discount.

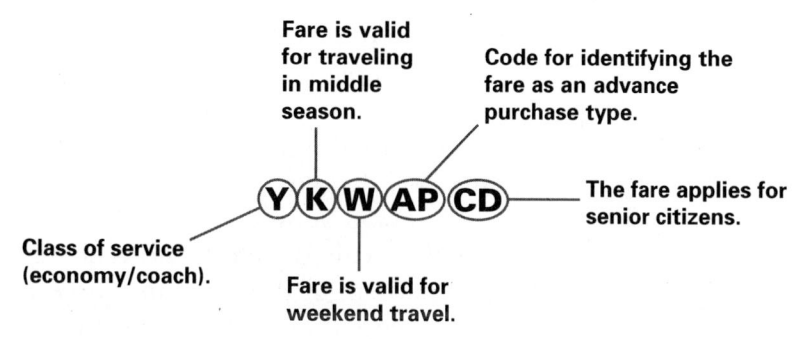

```
        Fare is valid
        for traveling    Code for identifying the
        in middle        fare as an advance
        season.          purchase type.
                │                │
            (Y)(K)(W)(AP)(CD) ──── The fare applies for
             │       │              senior citizens.
Class of service     │
(economy/coach).     Fare is valid for
                     weekend travel.
```

Combining basis codes in a fare basis, more restricted

Example 2: A group fare from Conakry, Guinea to New York City, USA.

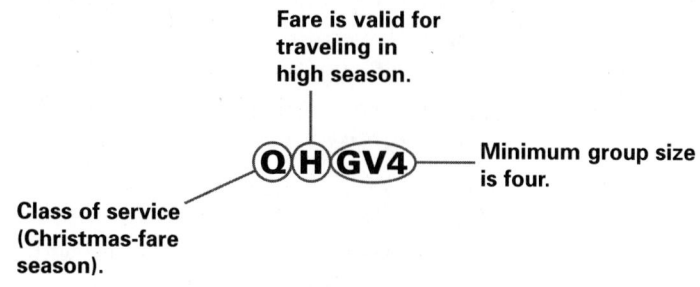

```
              Fare is valid for
              traveling in
              high season.
                    │
              (Q)(H)(GV4) ──── Minimum group size
               │                 is four.
Class of service
(Christmas-fare
season).
```

Combining basis codes in a fare basis, less restricted

INFANTS' AND CHILDREN'S FARES

Discounted airfares for infants and children are calculated as percentages of adult airfares. A person under 2 years old on the date of commencement of travel is called an **infant.** The airfare for an infant is 10 percent of the accompanying adult's fare, provided the infant does not occupy a seat (the adult holds the infant). For example, on a round-trip journey from Bangkok, Thailand to Manila, Philippines, an adult passenger using an excursion airfare pays $1,652. The fare for the infant, who does not occupy a seat, is 10 percent of the adult's fare, or $165.20 (1,652 × 0.10). If an adult has two infants, the second infant must occupy a seat and, therefore, must be charged child's airfare, which is usually 50 percent of the accompanying adult's airfare. When travel is wholly within Area 3 of the world (see Chapter 1), 67 percent of the accompanying adult airfare must be charged. Occasionally infants fly free on Trans-Pacific journeys provided they do not occupy seats. If an infant occupies a seat, child's airfare must be charged. No discounts apply for unaccompanied infants. When an infant flies alone, adult airfare must be charged.

A person between 2 and 11 years old on the date travel commences is called a **child** and is charged a child's airfare, which is 50 percent of the accompanying adult's airfare. On all journeys, except those within Area 1 of the world (see Chapter 1), a child between 2 and 7 years must be accompanied by an adult. A child between 8 and 11 years need not be accompanied. No discounts apply for unaccompanied children, however. When a child travels unaccompanied, an adult airfare must be charged. The airfare for a child traveling in Area 1 with an adult is 67 percent of the adult airfare. If travel is wholly within Area 3 on any carrier, 67 percent is also usually charged. For example, on a journey from Atlanta to Paris an adult passenger on an apex fare pays $947.00. If the adult's child occupies a seat on the same flight, the child's fare is 67 percent of the adult's, or $634.49 (947 × 0.67). Refer to the carrier for any exceptions.

A person who is 12 years or older on the date travel commences is called an **adult.**

Interpreting IATA Airfare and Rule Displays

As was mentioned earlier, international airfare information can be obtained from a computer reservation system or from a manual display. While a computer reservation system is the fastest means of obtaining airfare information, most computer reservation systems only contain airfare information for major international carriers on major international routes. Not all travelers want to visit London and Singapore. Travelers who want to go home for Christmas to Innamincka, Australia, should consult an air tariff book.

AIR TARIFF BOOKS

An **air tariff book** contains comprehensive airfare information. Several kinds of air tariff books, as well as airfare rule books, are available. Because airfares and their corresponding rules change frequently, these books are published several times a year. Air Canada, British Airways, Japan Airlines, Qantas, Swissair, and Trans World Airlines produce and publish these books jointly.

Travel professionals must use the air tariff books to determine which international airfare and corresponding rule are effective the date travel commences. The traveler's point of origin is important when reading an airfare display. The **point of origin** is the city in which the journey originates. The point of origin appears at the top of each fare column. When researching an airfare, first locate the point of origin, then locate the point of destination down the columns. To see how to read a fare display examine Figure 4–4.

NORMAL FARE DISPLAYS

All normal fares, such as supersonic (R), first class (F), business class (J or C), and economy/coach (Y or S), are listed at the beginning of a fare display. In the fare display in Figure 4–5, two economy/coach fares (Y), two business fares (J/C), two first-class fares (F), and one excursion fare (YE30) are offered from Jakarta to Kuala Lumpur. Note that one-way airfares appear in normal type, and round-trip fares appear in bold. The Eastern Hemisphere air route must be used for all four normal fares such as Jakarta to Singapore to Kuala Lumpur. The right-hand column explains the air route allowed for each fare level. This is also referred to as the route reference (RTE REF), appearing in the column heading.

As was mentioned earlier in this chapter, a normal fare is completely flexible in terms of routing choice, air carrier, and stopover points. However, normal airfares are also the most

All fare types are valid for traveling on any carrier. When a two-letter carrier code appears, it means the fare is valid for travel on that particular carrier only.

All the types of fares from Jakarta to Kuala Lumpur are listed here. Three normal fares Y, J/C, and F, and one excursion fare (YE 30), are available.

Point of origin.

Point of destination.

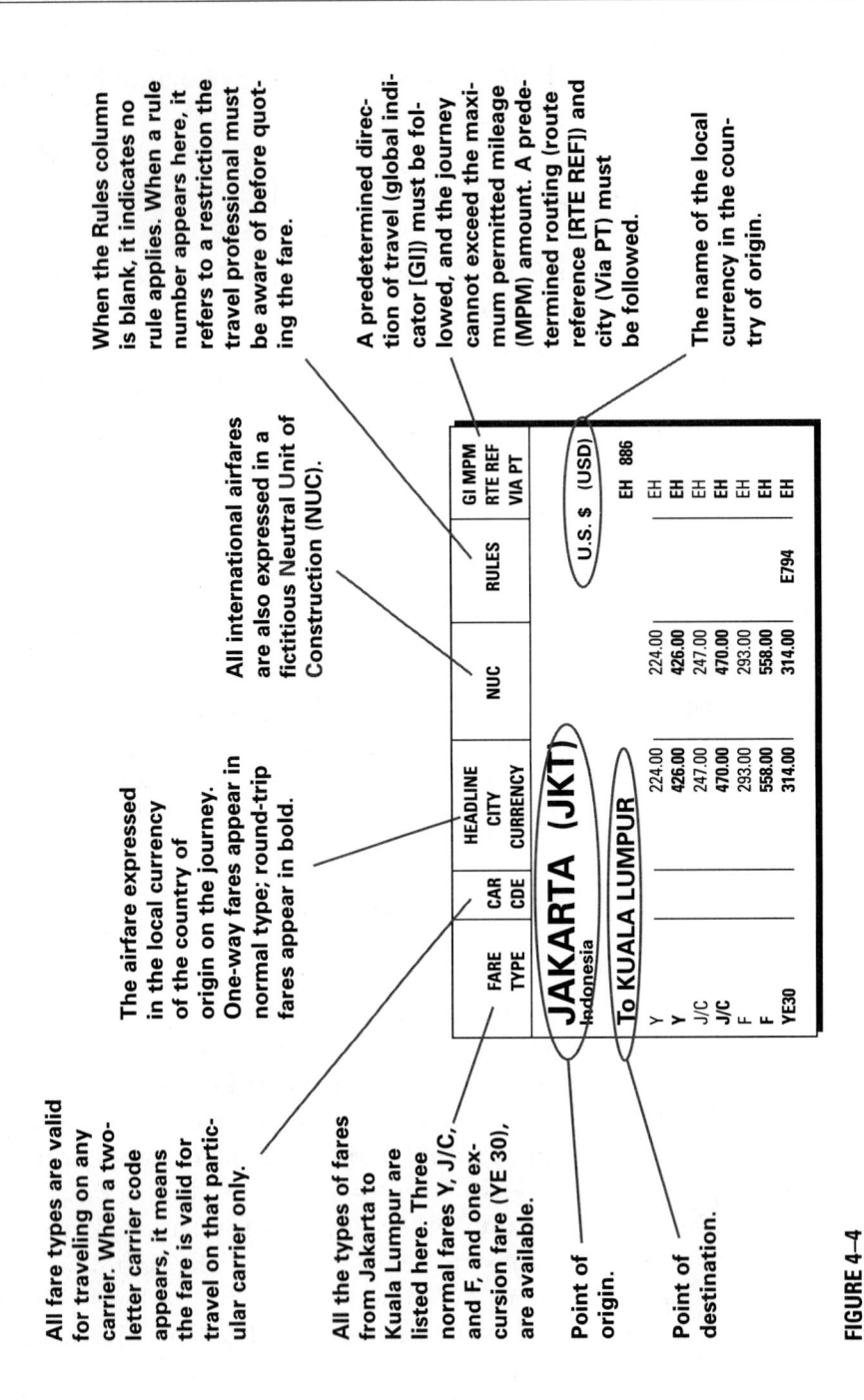

When the Rules column is blank, it indicates no rule applies. When a rule number appears here, it refers to a restriction the travel professional must be aware of before quoting the fare.

A predetermined direction of travel (global indicator [GI]) must be followed, and the journey cannot exceed the maximum permitted mileage (MPM) amount. A predetermined routing (route reference [RTE REF]) and city (Via PT) must be followed.

The name of the local currency in the country of origin.

The airfare expressed in the local currency of the country of origin on the journey. One-way fares appear in normal type; round-trip fares appear in bold.

All international airfares are also expressed in a fictitious Neutral Unit of Construction (NUC).

FARE TYPE	CAR CDE	HEADLINE CITY CURRENCY	NUC	RULES	GI MPM RTE REF VIA PT
JAKARTA (JKT) Indonesia					
To KUALA LUMPUR				U.S. $ (USD)	EH 886
Y		224.00	224.00		EH
Y		**426.00**	**426.00**		EH
J/C		247.00	247.00		EH
J/C		**470.00**	**470.00**		EH
F		293.00	293.00		EH
F		**558.00**	**558.00**		EH
YE30		**314.00**	**314.00**	E794	EH

FIGURE 4–4
Fare display. Source: Air Tariff Worldwide Fares Book 1, June 1993. (Courtesy of Air Tariff Development, Trans World Airlines.)

Chapter 4　International Airfares　101

One-way first-class fare in the local currency is USD 293.00.

Round-trip first-class fare in the local currency is USD 558.00.

FARE TYPE	CAR CDE	HEADLINE CITY CURRENCY	NUC	RULES	GI MPM RTE REF VIA PT.
JAKARTA (JKT) Indonesia				U.S. $	(USD) EH 886
To KUALA LUMPUR					
Y		224.00	224.00		EH
Y		426.00	426.00		EH
J/C		247.00	247.00		EH
J/C		470.00	470.00		EH
F		293.00	293.00		EH
F		558.00	558.00		EH
YE30		314.00	314.00	E794	EH

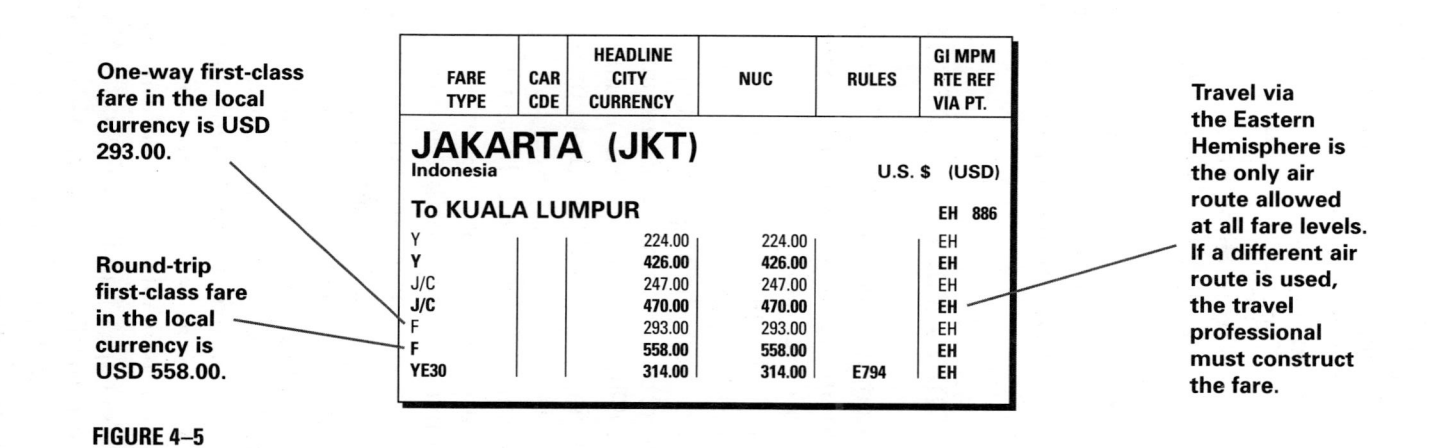

Travel via the Eastern Hemisphere is the only air route allowed at all fare levels. If a different air route is used, the travel professional must construct the fare.

FIGURE 4–5

Fare display. Source: Air Tariff Worldwide Fares Book 1, June 1993. (Courtesy of Air Tariff Development, Trans World Airlines.)

expensive. Sometimes a passenger can enjoy most of the privileges of a normal fare but fly at a discounted rate. Sometimes travel professionals will discover discounted normal fares for their clients. In Figure 4–6, note the discounted Y2 fare British Airways offers from Hong Kong, Hong Kong to Glasgow, Scotland. The one-way Y2 fare is HKD 8280, and Rule E025 applies. See the bottom of Figure 4–6 to examine Rule E025 and determine the difference between a normal fare and a discounted normal fare. As the figure shows, Rule E025 restricts the number of stopovers, routing, and choice of carrier.

EXCURSION AND APEX FARE DISPLAYS

A discounted economy/coach or excursion fare is listed toward the bottom of a fare display. Note that in Figure 4–7, one low-season excursion fare and one high-season excursion fare from Cairo, Egypt to Auckland, New Zealand are offered. Rule E687 must be applied toward the excursion fares from Cairo to Auckland. Note the stopover rule in Figure 4–8. One stopover is allowed both on the outbound and inbound portions of the journey. Therefore, it does not matter whether the journey is routed via Singapore, Bangkok, or Nairobi as long as it is not routed via Europe. The lowest fare level for traveling to Auckland is available between February 1 and August 31 because the seasons are reversed in the Southern Hemisphere.

Some excursion fares are not very restricted, as Figure 4–9 shows. Two stopovers are permitted outbound and inbound. Suggest your clients take advantage of them. They have 3 months to complete their journeys. Be daring with your clients. Offer them all options even though they may not ask for them.

The least expensive and most restricted airfare is an apex fare. These fares are purchased as point-to-point journeys, because no stopovers are allowed on apex fares. As a travel professional, it may take you a few minutes to quote your traveler the correct apex fare from Boston, USA to Zurich, Switzerland, if you use the fares in Figure 4–10. With eight different apex fares offered between these cities, there are more restrictions to look for. The date travel commences must always be the primary focus, because travel dates determine the seasonal fare level.

Chapter 4 International Airfares 103

FARE TYPE	CAR CDE	HEADLINE CITY CURRENCY	NUC	RULES	GI MPM RTE REF VIA PT.

HONG KONG (HKG)
Hong Kong   Hong Kong $ (HKD)

To GLASCOW   EH 9094

y		12650	1632.01	E653	EH
y		25300	3264.03	E653	EH
Y2	BA	8280	1068.24	E025	EH *Z02
YLIPO	BA	5170	666.40	E047	EH
YKIPO	BA	5720	737.36	E047	EH
YHIPO	BA	6430	828.95	E047	EH
J/C		14030	1810.05	E653	EH
J/C		26860	3465.29	E653	EH
J	BA	25100	3238.23	E091	EH
J2	BA	11950	1541.71	E001	EH *Z02
J2	BA	22900	2954.41	E001	EH *Z02
F		22670	2950.50	E653	EH
F		43690	5636.54	E653	EH
F	BA	22450	2896.32	E091	EH
F	BA	42890	5533.33	E091	EH
YLPX	BA	9910	1278.62	E077	EH
YKPX	BA	11080	1426.96	E077	EH
YHPX	BA	12500	1612.76	E077	EH
YLAPBO	BA	4910	632.86	E019	EH *Z02
YLAPB		4340	559.32	E019	EH *Z02
YLAP	BA	5360	690.91	E014	EH *Z02
YKAPB	BA	5330	687.04	E019	EH *Z02
YKAP	BA	5990	772.19	E014	EH *Z02
YHAPBO	BA	6060	781.22	E019	EH *Z02
YHAP	BA	6780	874.11	E014	EH *Z02

E025   ECONOMY FARES: Ⓐ
        HONG KONG ➤ UK

1. Application Y OW/RT Point to Point via BA only.

5. Children and Infants Fares:
   A. Children: 67%
   B. Infants: 10%

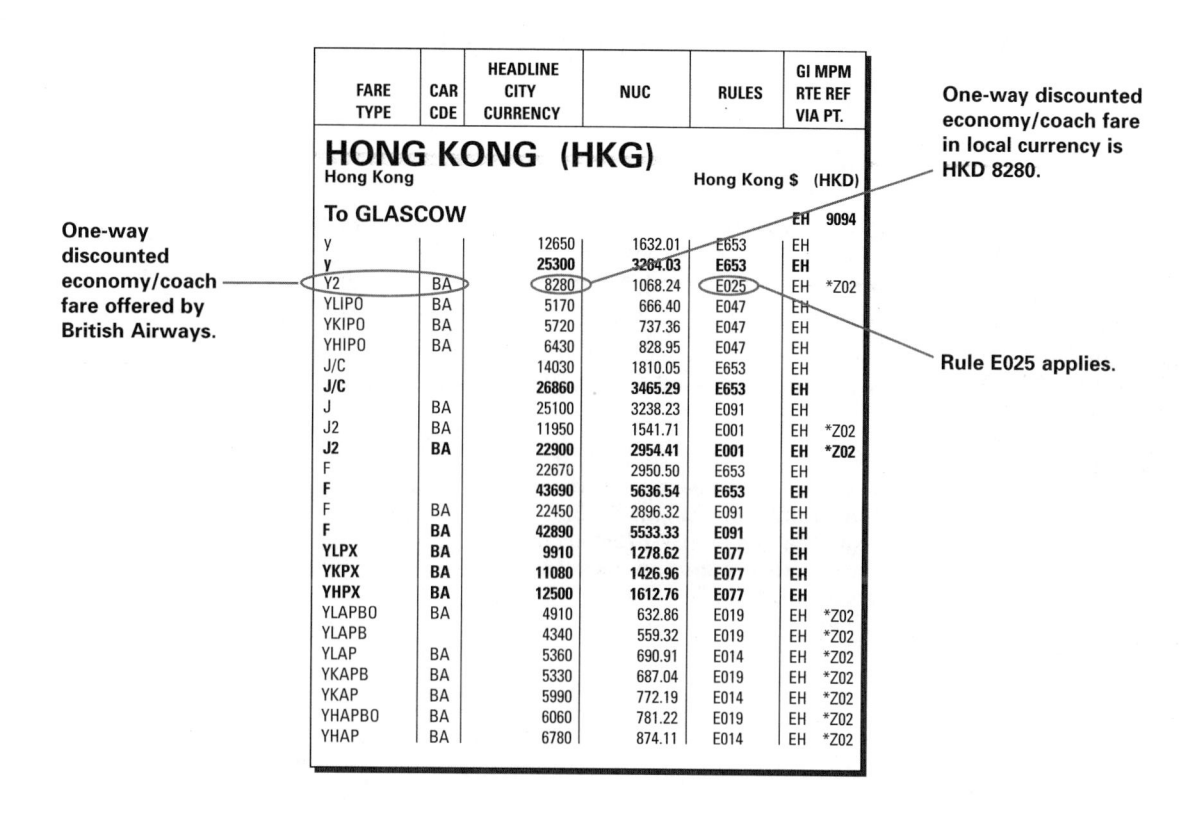

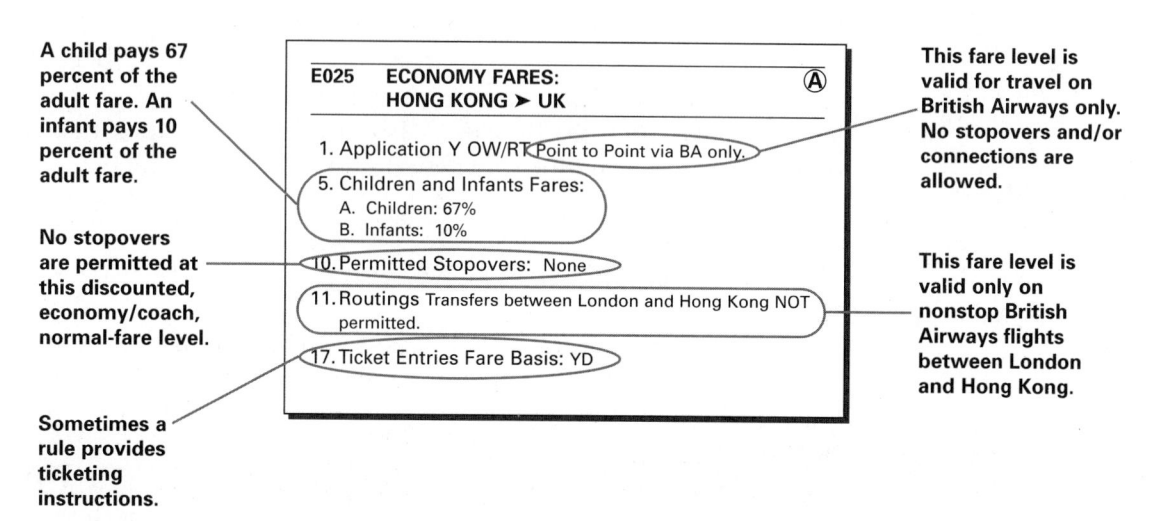

10. Permitted Stopovers: None

11. Routings Transfers between London and Hong Kong NOT permitted.

17. Ticket Entries Fare Basis: YD

FIGURE 4–6

Fare display and Rule E025. Source: Air Tariff Worldwide Fares Book 1, *June 1993. (Courtesy of Air Tariff Development, Trans World Airlines.)*

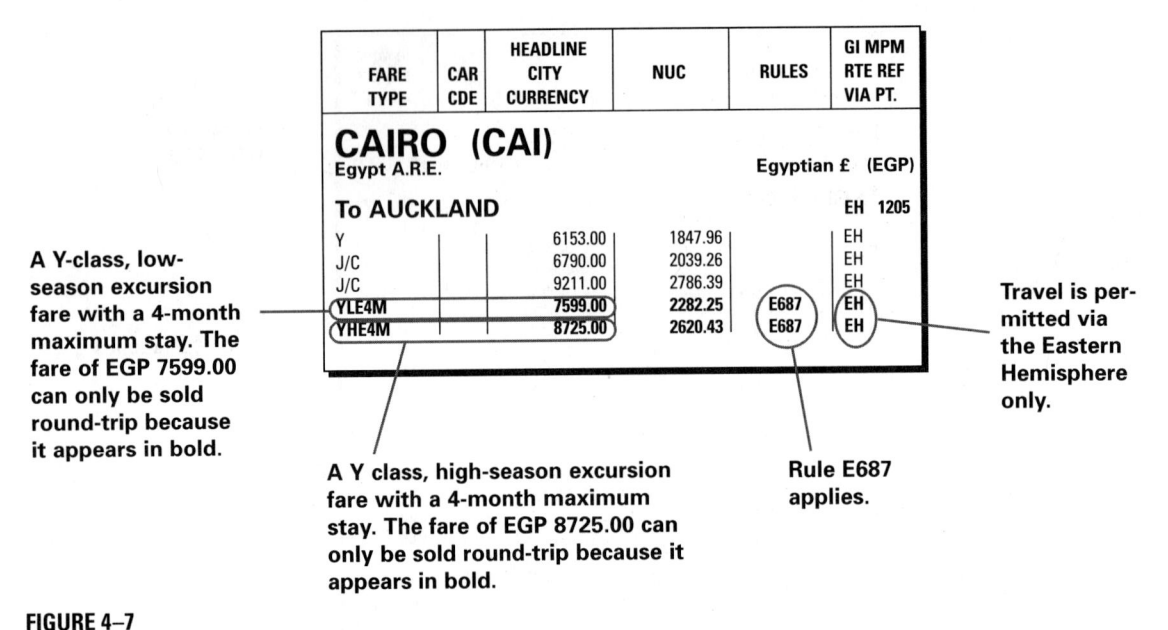

	FARE TYPE	CAR CDE	HEADLINE CITY CURRENCY	NUC	RULES	GI MPM RTE REF VIA PT.

CAIRO (CAI)
Egypt A.R.E.   Egyptian £ (EGP)

To AUCKLAND   EH 1205

Y			6153.00	1847.96		EH
J/C			6790.00	2039.26		EH
J/C			9211.00	2786.39		EH
YLE4M			7599.00	2282.25	E687	EH
YHE4M			8725.00	2620.43	E687	EH

A Y-class, low-season excursion fare with a 4-month maximum stay. The fare of EGP 7599.00 can only be sold round-trip because it appears in bold.

A Y class, high-season excursion fare with a 4-month maximum stay. The fare of EGP 8725.00 can only be sold round-trip because it appears in bold.

Rule E687 applies.

Travel is permitted via the Eastern Hemisphere only.

FIGURE 4–7

Rule E687. Source: Air Tariff Worldwide Fares Book 1, *June 1993. (Courtesy of Air Tariff Development, Trans World Airlines.)*

For example, travel professionals with clients traveling home for Christmas and leaving on December 19, should use the Q fare level according to Rule N3615 in Figure 4–11. If December 19 outbound travel originates on a Wednesday, the MQXAP fare level of USD 905 must be used. Also, note that this apex ticket must be booked, paid for, and issued 21 days before travel begins.

AUTOMATED FARE DISPLAYS

Reading automated fare displays is similar to reading manual displays. Figure 4–12 shows a computer display of normal fares from Cairo, Egypt to Nairobi, Kenya, for travel on June 10, 1996 on Egyptair.

Automated fares are listed from lowest to highest, which means the most economical normal fare, economy/coach (Y), appears at the beginning of the display. In the fare display in Figure 4–12, one economy/coach fare (Y), one business fare

E687	**EXCURSION FARES:**		Ⓐ
	MIDDLE EAST ➤ SOUTH WEST PACIFIC		

1. Application Y RT / CT / OJ.
   BETWEEN Middle East (except Israel)
   AND Australia / New Zealand.
   NOTE: These fares do not apply retroactively.

2. Periods of Application
   A. From Australia:

1 Jan - 31 Jan	Low Shoulder	YJE4M
1 Feb - 29 Feb	Basic	YLE4M
1 Mar - 31 Mar	Low Shoulder	YJE4M
1 Apr - 30 Apr	High Shoulder	YKE4M
1 May - 31 Aug	Peak	YHE4M
1 Sep - 30 Sep	High Shoulder	YKE4M
1 Oct - 30 Nov	Basic	YLE4M
1 Dec - 10 Dec	High Shoulder	YKE4M
11 Dec - 23 Dec	Peak	YHE4M
24 Dec - 31 Dec	High Shoulder	YKE4M

   B. To Australia/New Zealand:

1 Jan - 31 Jan	Peak	YHE4M
1 Feb - 31 Aug	Basic	YLE4M
1 Sep - 31 Dec	Peak	YHE4M

   C. From New Zealand:

1 Jan - 29 Feb	Basic	YLE4M
1 Mar - 31 Mar	Off Peak	YJE4M
1 Apr - 30 Apr	Shoulder	YKE4M
1 May - 31 Jul	Peak	YHE4M
1 Aug - 31 Aug	Shoulder	YKE4M
1 Sep - 30 Sep	Off Peak	YJE4M
1 Oct - 30 Nov	Basic	YLE4M
1 Dec - 31 Dec	Peak	YHE4M

5. Children and Infants Fares
   A. Children: 67%
   B. Infants: 10%

6. Minimum Stay 10 days

8. Maximum Stay 4 months

10. Permitted Stopovers One in each direction

11. Routings
    A. Not permitted via Europe.
    B. From Australia/New Zealand: For travel via a ticketed point, any higher return promotional fare from point of origin to this point (excluding side-trips), must be charged.
    C. In Australia, travel must be via the fare construction points.
    D. From Middle East: Any higher intermiate fare in South Asian Sub-continent may be ignored, provided passengers and baggage are through booked and checked.
    E. Permitted Transfers:
       1. Two in each direction.
       2. From/ to New Zealand: One additional in each direction at Auckland between an International and Domestic service.
       Note: Each stopover taken counts as a permitted transfer.

17. Ticket Entries Fare Basis: YLE4M/ YJE4M/ YKE4M/ YHE4M.

18. Voluntary Rerouting Permitted.

23. Passenger Expenses Permitted in the Middle East and the South Asian Sub-continent, (except via BA/QF).

25. Agents Discounts Permitted.

The lowest fare level for traveling to Auckland is between February 1 and August 31. Note that the low-season travel dates for leaving Auckland are different.

One stopover at any point in each direction of travel is allowed at no additional cost.

The flight from Cairo to Auckland is not permitted as a connection or a stopover in Europe.

FIGURE 4-8

Stopover rule. (Courtesy of Air Tariff Development, Trans World Airlines.)

FARE TYPE	CAR CDE	HEADLINE CITY CURRENCY	NUC	RULES	GI MPM RTE REF VIA PT.

BUENOS AIRES (BUE)
Argentina   U.S. $ (USD)

To CALCUTTA   AT 13720
                                                                  AT 13720

Y		2752.00	2752.00	S500	AT
J/C		3165.00	3165.00	S500	AT
F		4119.00	4119.00	S500	AT
Y2		2792.00	2792.00	P8502	PA
C1		3211.00	3211.00	P8501	PA
F1		5207.00	5207.00	P8500	PA
YGV10		3211.00	3211.00	P8504	PA
YE		3238.00	3238.00	S520	AT

Round-trip Y class excursion fare of USD 3238.00. (circles YE and 3238.00)

Travel is permitted via the Atlantic Ocean only.

Rule S520 applies.

**S 520   S.ATL. EXCURSION FARES: S.ATL. AREA ▶ Ⓐ
         S.E. ASIA/SOUTH ASIAN SUBCONTINENT**

1. Application Y RT/CT/SOJ.
   NOTE: These fares do not apply retroactively.

5. Children and Infants Fares:
   A. Children: 75% except from Pakistan: 67%
   B. Infants: 10%

6. Minimum Stay: 13 days.

8. Maximum Stay: 3 months.

10. Permitted Stopovers
    A. Free: Two in each direction.
    B. Additional: Unlimited at CNY 360 / HKD 600 / INR 1400/ LKR 3000 / MMK 510 / MYR 250/ NPR 2210 / PKR 1650/ SGD 150/ THB 2000/ USD 75 each.

12. Permitted combinations Fares within Area 1, South East Asia and South Asian Subcontinent.
13. Advertising and Sales Within Area 3 limited to South East Asia and South Asian Subcontinent.

17. Ticket Entries Fare Basis: YE3M

Two stopovers at any point in each direction of travel are allowed at no additional cost.

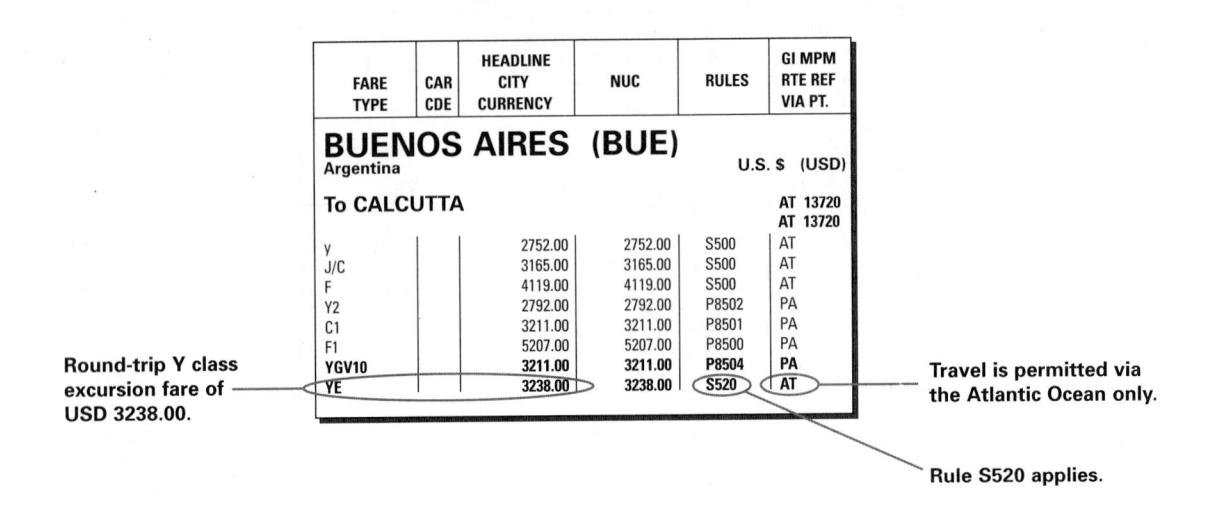

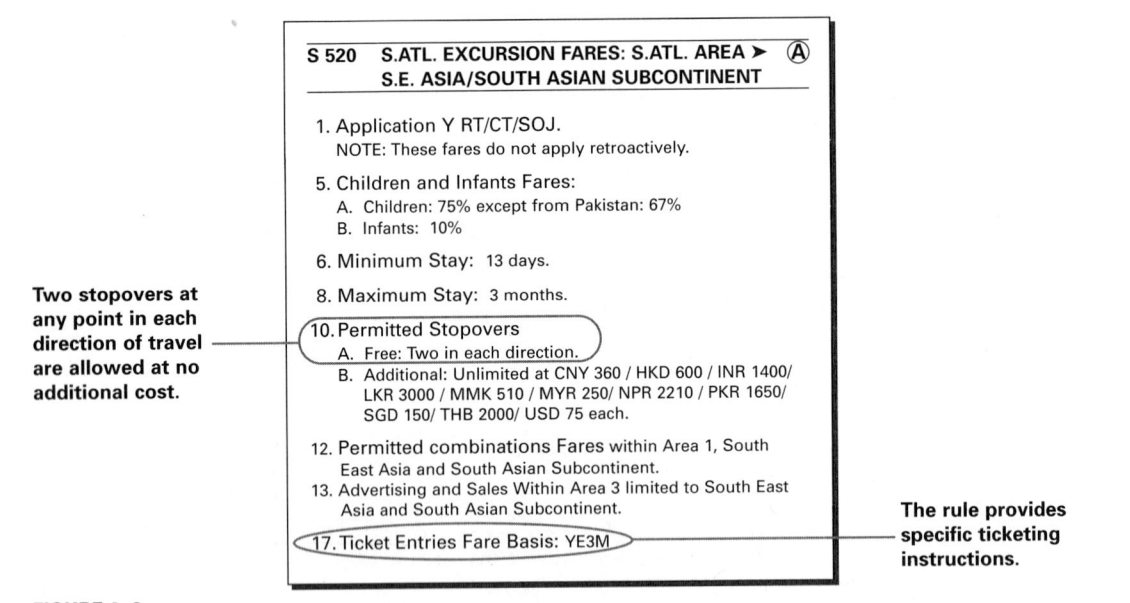

The rule provides specific ticketing instructions.

FIGURE 4-9

Lightly restricted airfares. (Courtesy of Air Tariff Development, Trans World Airlines.)

FARE TYPE	CAR CDE	HEADLINE CITY CURRENCY	NUC	RULES	GI MPM RTE REF VIA PT.

BOSTON (BOS)
Mas., U.S.A — U.S. $ (USD)

To ZURICH — AT 4482

Fare Type	Car	Headline	NUC	Rules	GI
J	BA	1426.00	1426.00	N0110	AT
F	BA	2539.00	2539.00	N0110	AT
S1	BA	1065.00	1065.00	N0110	AT
MQXAP	BA	905.00	905.00	N3615	AT
MQWAP	BA	965.00	965.00	N3615	AT
MLXAP	BA	791.00	791.00	N3615	AT
MLWAP	BA	851.00	851.00	N3615	AT
MOXAP	BA	960.00	960.00	N3615	AT
MOWAP	BA	1060.00	1060.00	N3615	AT
MHXAP	BA	1146.00	1146.00	N3615	AT
MHWAP	BA	1206.00	1206.00	N3615	AT
MLXE	BA	1066.00	1066.00	N1245	AT
MLWE	BA	1146.00	1146.00	N1245	AT
MQXE	BA	1262.00	1262.00	N1245	AT
MQWE	BA	1322.00	1322.00	N1245	AT
MHXE	BA	1347.00	1347.00	N1245	AT
MHWE	BA	1407.00	1407.00	N1245	AT

Eight round-trip M-class apex fares are offered in Q, L, O, or H seasons for traveling on weekdays or weekends. All apex fares are valid for travel on British Airways only. Rule N3615 applies, and travel is permitted via the Atlantic Ocean only.

FIGURE 4–10

Apex fares. (Courtesy of Air Tariff Development, Trans World Airlines.)

(C), and one first-class fare (F) are offered for travel on any carrier (YY) via the Eastern Hemisphere (EH) only. It is important to note that these are one-way fares that must be doubled for round-trip journeys. Round-trip fares are followed by the letter *R*. All three normal fares are valid for travel all year, and no advance-purchase or minimum/maximum stay requirements apply.

The corresponding fare rule is accessed by line number. As Figure 4–13 illustrates, the rule for the fare on Line 3 has been accessed. There are no restrictions for the first-class normal fare.

Note from Figure 4–14 that the high-season excursion fare from Cairo to Auckland is slightly higher than the manual-fare display in Figure 4–7. This is because the automated display requests a specific airline. Also note that the rules, such as minimum and maximum stay requirements, global direction of travel, and seasons, remain the same.

108 International Travel and Tourism

**N 3615 NORTH ATLANTIC APEX FARES:
USA ➤ AUSTRIA/SWITZERLAND**   Ⓐ

1. Application Y RT / CT / SO. via BA
2. Periods of Application

25 Dec - 21 Mar	Basic	MLXAP/MLWAP
22 Mar - 31 Mar	Shoulder	MOXAP/MOWAP
1 Jun - 30 Sep	Peak	MHXAP/MHWAP
1 Oct - 31 Oct	Shoulder	MOXAP/MOWAP
1 Nov- 13 Dec	Basic	MLXAP/MLWAP
14 Dec - 24 Dec	Holiday	MQXAP/MQWAP

6. Minimum Stay 7 days
8. Maximum Stay 3 months
10. Permitted Stopovers None (except to Austria: One free at LON)
11. Routings Permitted Transfers: One at the North American gateway, one in Europe and one in the UK in each direction (except where otherwise noted in the published routings).
14. Reservations
    A. Deadline: 21 days.
    B. Changes: Reservations/Routings:
        1. Up to Payment Deadline: No restrictions.
        2. After Payment Deadline: Including After Departure:
            a. Not permitted for the outbound journey.
            b. Permitted for the return journey at a charge of USD 100 for each transaction. The applicable fare for revised itinerary must be re-calculated from the point of origin.
15. Payment Deadline: 21 days.
16. Ticketing Deadline: 21 days.
17. Ticket Entries
    A. Fare Basis: As shown in Paragraph 2, followed by the maximum stay, e.g. MLXAP3M.
    B. Endorsements: NON REF / APEX which must be carried forward to all re-issued / upgraded tickets.
    C. IMPORTANT NOTICE: Required.
    D. Confirmed reservations for the entire journey must be shown.
18. Voluntary Rerouting Not permitted except as provided for in Subparagraph 14.B.
20. Cancellations and Refunds
    A. Before departure - Up to the Payment Deadline
        Cancellation: Full refund.
    B. Before departure - After the Payment Deadline
        Cancellation/ No Show forfeit: USD 75.
    C. After departure: The refund, if any, will be the difference between the fare paid and the fare for the journey completed less USD 75.
    D. In the case of certified death/illness of passenger/member of immediate family: Full refund.
    E. At any time:
        1. An APEX fare ticket may be upgraded to a higher fare type without forfeit, or change for reservations/routing changes.
        2. If the higher fare ticket re-issue is subsequently cancelled, the original forfeit or charge for reservations/ routing changed will apply.

Annotations:
- The fares in this rule are for travel on British Airways only.
- No stopovers are allowed at any direction of travel.
- If connecting flights are chosen, three connecting points are allowed in each direction of travel. One is in the United States, one is in Europe, and one is in Great Britain.
- The reservation must be made 21 days before travel. The ticket must also be paid for and issued 21 days before travel.
- Make sure all ticketing instructions are carried forward on the ticket.

FIGURE 4–11

Rule N3615. (Courtesy of Air Tariff Development, Trans World Airlines.)

Chapter 4 International Airfares *109*

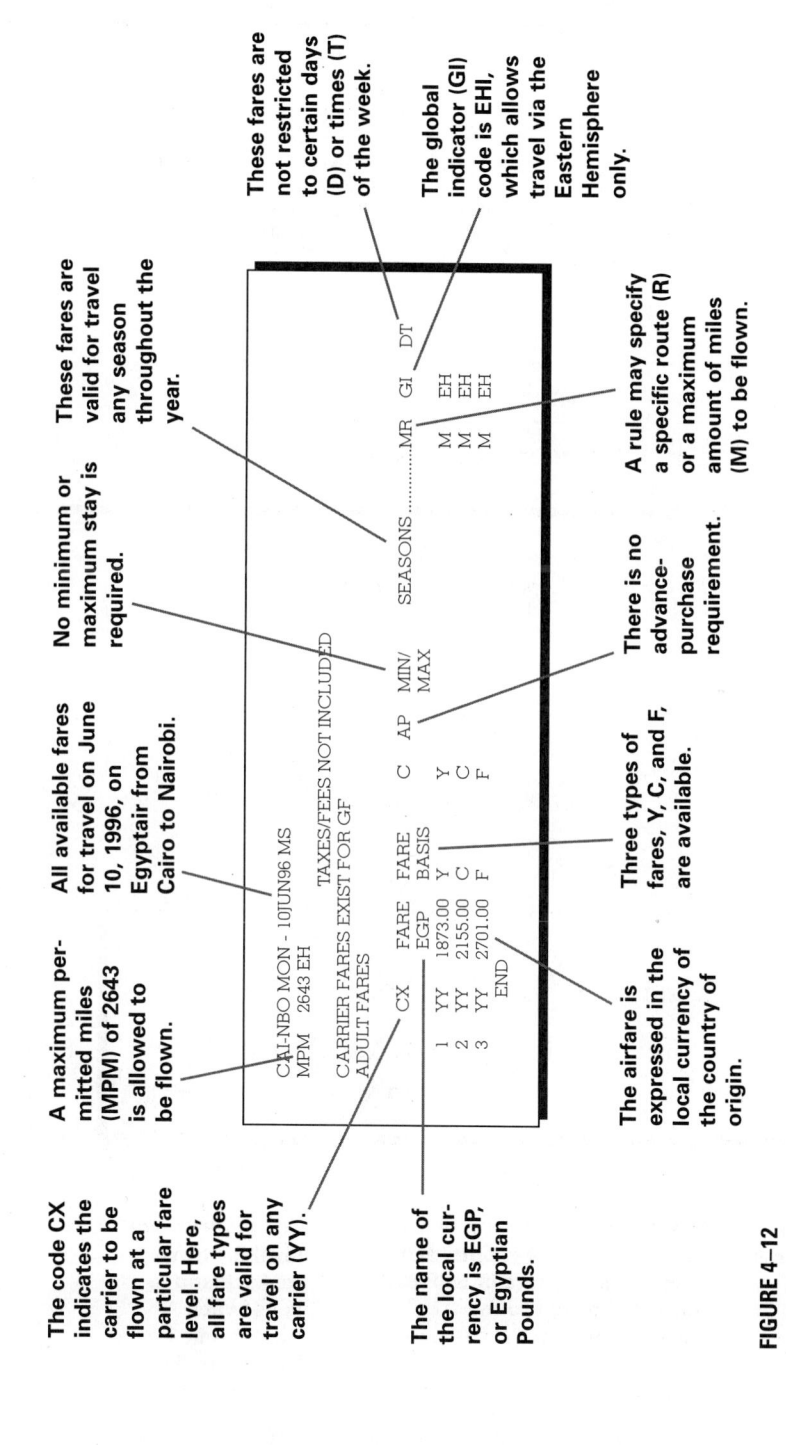

The code CX indicates the carrier to be flown at a particular fare level. Here, all fare types are valid for travel on any carrier (YY).

A maximum permitted miles (MPM) of 2643 is allowed to be flown.

All available fares for travel on June 10, 1996, on Egyptair from Cairo to Nairobi.

No minimum or maximum stay is required.

These fares are valid for travel any season throughout the year.

These fares are not restricted to certain days (D) or times (T) of the week.

The global indicator (GI) code is EH, which allows travel via the Eastern Hemisphere only.

```
CAI-NBO MON - 10JUN96 MS
MPM  2643 EH       TAXES/FEES NOT INCLUDED
CARRIER FARES EXIST FOR GF
ADULT FARES
   CX  FARE    FARE   C  AP  MIN/  SEASONS......MR  GI  DT
       EGP     BASIS             MAX
 1 YY  1873.00 Y      Y                         M   EH
 2 YY  2155.00 C      C                         M   EH
 3 YY  2701.00 F      F                         M   EH
       END
```

The name of the local currency is EGP, or Egyptian Pounds.

The airfare is expressed in the local currency of the country of origin.

Three types of fares, Y, C, and F, are available.

There is no advance-purchase requirement.

A rule may specify a specific route (R) or a maximum amount of miles (M) to be flown.

FIGURE 4-12
Automated fares. (Courtesy of Apollo Travel Services.)

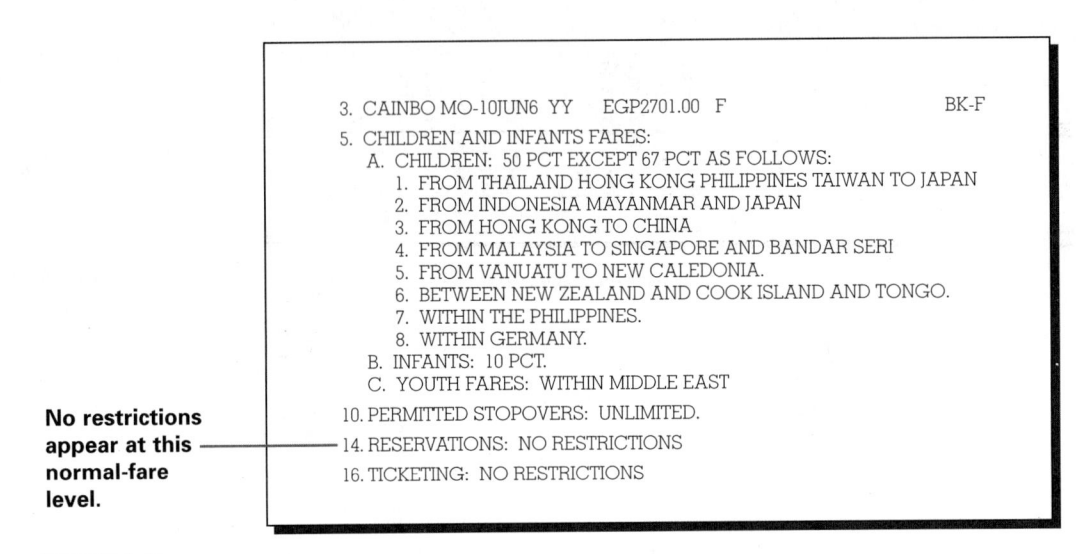

```
            3. CAINBO MO-10JUN6  YY    EGP2701.00  F                    BK-F
            5. CHILDREN AND INFANTS FARES:
               A. CHILDREN: 50 PCT EXCEPT 67 PCT AS FOLLOWS:
                  1. FROM THAILAND HONG KONG PHILIPPINES TAIWAN TO JAPAN
                  2. FROM INDONESIA MAYANMAR AND JAPAN
                  3. FROM HONG KONG TO CHINA
                  4. FROM MALAYSIA TO SINGAPORE AND BANDAR SERI
                  5. FROM VANUATU TO NEW CALEDONIA.
                  6. BETWEEN NEW ZEALAND AND COOK ISLAND AND TONGO.
                  7. WITHIN THE PHILIPPINES.
                  8. WITHIN GERMANY.
               B. INFANTS: 10 PCT.
               C. YOUTH FARES:  WITHIN MIDDLE EAST
           10. PERMITTED STOPOVERS:  UNLIMITED.
           14. RESERVATIONS:  NO RESTRICTIONS
           16. TICKETING:  NO RESTRICTIONS
```

No restrictions appear at this normal-fare level.

FIGURE 4–13

Nonrestricted airfare. (Courtesy of Apollo Travel Services.)

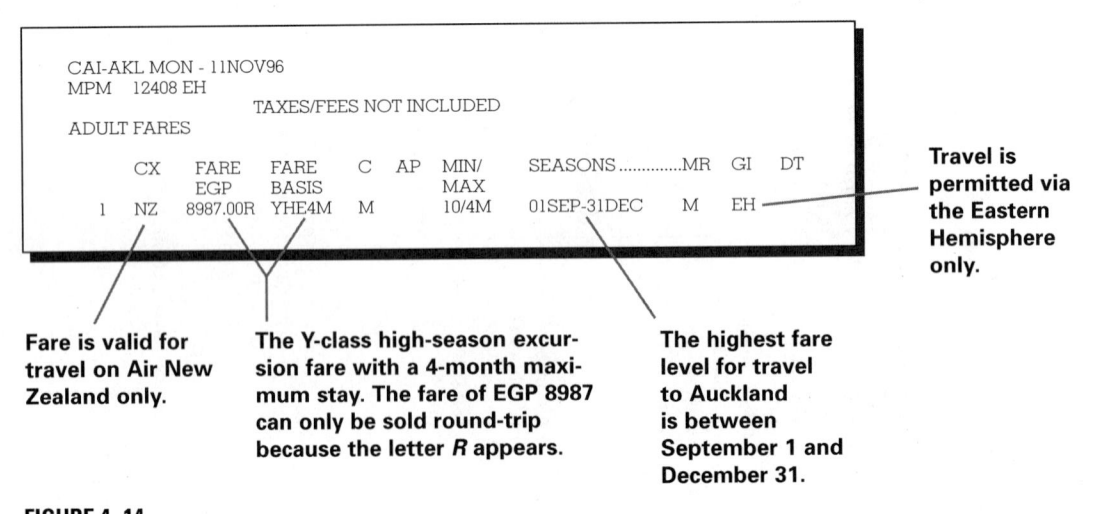

```
   CAI-AKL MON - 11NOV96
   MPM   12408 EH
                       TAXES/FEES NOT INCLUDED
   ADULT FARES

        CX    FARE    FARE    C  AP  MIN/    SEASONS.......MR  GI   DT
              EGP     BASIS           MAX
     1  NZ   8987.00R YHE4M   M      10/4M   01SEP-31DEC    M   EH
```

Fare is valid for travel on Air New Zealand only.

The Y-class high-season excursion fare with a 4-month maximum stay. The fare of EGP 8987 can only be sold round-trip because the letter *R* appears.

The highest fare level for travel to Auckland is between September 1 and December 31.

Travel is permitted via the Eastern Hemisphere only.

FIGURE 4–14

High-season excursion fare. (Courtesy of Apollo Travel Services.)

The corresponding fare rule in Figure 4–15 states the same stopover rule as expressed in the manual fare rule: One stopover is allowed at any point both on the outbound and inbound portions of the journey.

Because the least expensive and most restricted airfare is an apex fare, the letter *R* appears in the MR column in Figure 4–16, indicating a certain route must be followed. The fare level is valid for travel between October 1 and October 31.

The corresponding apex rule in Figure 4–17 states that this apex ticket must be booked, paid for, and issued 7 days before travel begins.

One stopover at any point in each direction of travel is allowed at no additional cost.

The flight from Cairo to Auckland is not permitted a connection or a stopover in Europe.

```
1. CAIAKL MO-11NOV6 NZ   EGP8987.00R  YHE4M   STAY 10/4M    BK-M
2. PERIODS OF APPLICATION:
   SEASONALITY:
        BETWEEN NEW ZEALAND AND MIDDLE EAST FOR HIGH SEASON FARES
        ORIGINATING NEW ZEALAND -
        PERMITTED 01JAN THROUGH 31JAN OR 01DEC THROUGH 31DEC.
        ORIGINATING MIDDLE EAST -
        PERMITTED 01JAN THROUGH 31JAN OR 01SEP THROUGH 31DEC.
5. CHILDREN AND INFANTS FARES:
   UNLESS OTHERWISE SPECIFIED
        AN ACCOMPANIED CHILD 2-11 YEARS OF AGE WILL BE CHARGED 67
        PERCENT OF THE ADULT FARE WHEN ACCOMPANIED ON ALL FLIGHTS
        AND IN THE SAME COMPARTMENT BY AN ADULT AT LEAST 12 YEARS
        OF AGE.
        THE TICKETING CODE FOR THE DISCOUNTED FARE IS THE BASE FARE
        CODE PLUS CH.
        OR - AN INFANT UNDER 2 YEARS OF AGE AND OCCUPYING A SEAT
        WILL BE CHARGED 67 PERCENT OF THE ADULT FARE WHEN
        ACCOMPANIED ON ALL FLIGHTS AND IN THE SAME
10. PERMITTED STOPOVERS:
    UNLESS OTHERWISE SPECIFIED
        NOTE - GENERAL RULE DOES NOT APPLY
    2 FREE STOPOVERS PERMITTED - 1 IN EACH DIRECTION.
        NOTE -EACH STOPOVER UTILIZES ONE OF THE PERMITTED TRANSFERS.
11. ROUTING:
    FLIGHT APPLICATION:
    UNLESS OTHERWISE SPECIFIED
        NOT VALID VIA EUROPE.
        NOTE -VIA LY/QF ONLY TRAVEL FROM AUSTRALIA TO
        ISRAEL IS PERMITTED VIA FRANKFURT/LONDON/
        ROME IGNORING ANY MILEAGE SURCHARGE.
    TRANSFERS:
    UNLESS OTHERWISE SPECIFIED
```

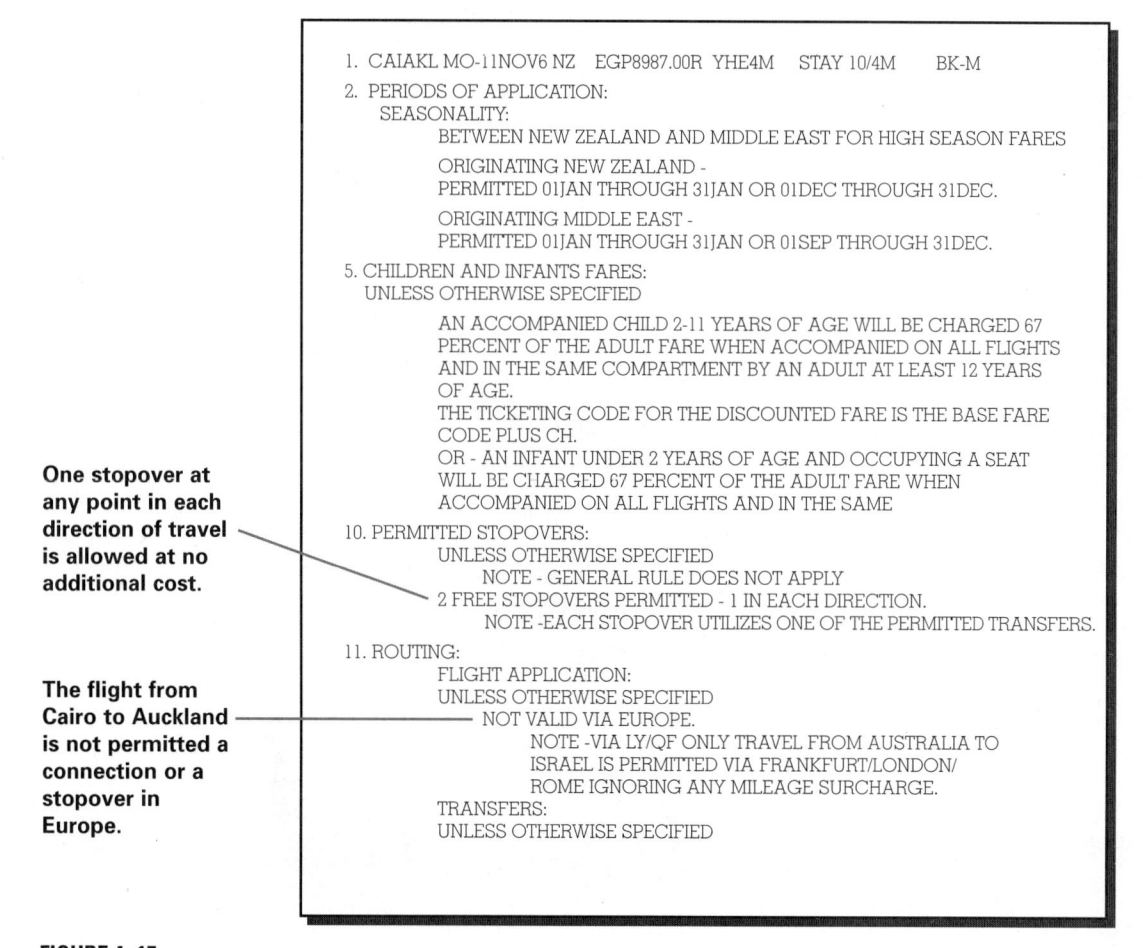

FIGURE 4–15

Stopover rule revisited. (Courtesy of Apollo Travel Services.)

```
CHI-LON TUE - 15OCT96  BA
MPM  4740 AT          TAXES/FEES NOT INCLUDED
ADULT FARES

     CX   FARE     FARE    C   AP   MIN/    SEASONS........MR  GI  DT
          USD      BASIS                MAX
 1   BA   726.00R  LKXAN   L   21^   07/1M   01OCT-31OCT    R   AT  D
 2   BA   776.00R  LKWAN   L   21^   07/1M   01OCT-31OCT    R   AT  D
 3   BA   826.00R  KKXAN   K   14^   07/2M   01OCT-31OCT    R   AT  D
 4   BA   876.00R  KKWAN   K   14^   07/2M   01OCT-31OCT    R   AT  D
 5   BA   926.00R  BKXAP   B   7^    SU/6M   01OCT-31OCT    R   AT  D
 6   BA   976.00R  BKWAP   B   7^    SU/6M   01OCT-31OCT    R   AT  D
 7   BA   788.00   S2      S                                M   AT
 8   BA   1498.00  S       S                                M   AT
 9   BA   2234.00  J       J                                M   AT
10   BA   3839.00  F       F                                M   AT
     END
```

(Lines 5 and 6 circled with annotation:) Two round-trip B-class apex fares are offered in K season for travel on weekdays or weekends. Both apex fares are valid for travel on British Airways only via the Atlantic Ocean and along a particular route. The ticket must be purchased 7 days before travel. The minimum stay of "SU" means the first day of return travel cannot begin until the first Sunday. Maximum stay of 6 months (6M) means the ticket is valid for 6 months.

FIGURE 4–16

Restricted route. (Courtesy of Apollo Travel Services.)

Chapter 4 International Airfares **113**

```
     5 CHILON TU-15OCT6 BA    USD926.00R BKXAP    STAY SU/6M    BK-B
  5. CHILDREN AND INFANTS FARES:
     BETWEEN THE UNITED STATES AND UNITED KINGDOM
       AN ACCOMPANIED CHILD 2-11 YEARS OF AGE WILL BE CHARGED 75
       PERCENT OF THE ADULT FARE WHEN ACCOMPANIED ON ALL FLIGHTS
       AND IN THE SAME COMPARTMENT BY AN ADULT AT LEAST 12 YEARS
       OF AGE.
       THE TICKETING CODE FOR THE DISCOUNTED FARE IS THE BASE FARE
       CODE PLUS CH.
       OR - AN INFANT UNDER 2 YEARS OF AGE AND OCCUPYING A SEAT
            WILL BE CHARGED 75 PERCENT OF THE ADULT FARE WHEN
            ACCOMPANIED ON ALL FLIGHTS AND IN THE SAME
            COMPARTMENT BY AN ADULT AT LEAST 12 YEARS OF AGE.
       OR - THE FIRST INFANT UNDER 2 YEARS OF AGE AND NOT
            OCCUPYING A SEAT WILL BE CHARGED 10 PERCENT OF THE
            ADULT FARE WHEN ACCOMPANIED ON ALL FLIGHTS AND IN
            THE SAME COMPARTMENT BY AN ADULT AT LEAST 12 YEARS
            OF AGE.
       OR - AN UNACCOMPANIED CHILD 5-11 YEARS OF AGE WILL BE
            CHARGED 75 PERCENT OF THE ADULT FARE.
 10. PERMITTED STOPOVERS:
     NONE BETWEEN THE UNITED STATES AND UNITED KINGDOM
 11. ROUTING:
       TRANSFERS:
         BETWEEN THE UNITED STATES AND UNITED KINGDOM
         4 TRANSFERS PERMITTED - 2 IN EACH DIRECTION.
 14. RESERVATIONS/TICKETING:
       ADVANCE RES/TICKETING:
         BETWEEN THE UNITED STATES AND UNITED KINGDOM
           ORIGINATING THE UNITED STATES -
             RESERVATIONS FOR ALL SECTORS ARE REQUIRED AT LEAST 7
             DAYS BEFORE DEPARTURE.
             TICKETING MUST BE COMPLETED WITHIN 72 HOURS AFTER
             RESERVATIONS ARE MADE OR AT LEAST 7 DAYS BEFORE
             DEPARTURE WHICHEVER IS EARLIER.
           ORIGINATING THE UNITED KINGDOM -
             RESERVATIONS FOR ALL SECTORS ARE REQUIRED AT LEAST 7
             DAYS BEFORE DEPARTURE.
             TICKETING MUST BE COMPLETED WITHIN 48 HOURS AFTER
             RESERVATIONS ARE MADE OR AT LEAST 7 DAYS BEFORE
             DEPARTURE WHICHEVER IS EARLIER.
       SALES RESTRICTIONS:
         NONE BETWEEN THE UNITED STATES AND UNITED KINGDOM
 17. TICKET ENTRIES:
     BETWEEN THE UNITED STATES AND UNITED KINGDOM
       THE ORIGINAL AND THE REISSUED TICKET MUST BE ANNOTATED -
       SUB TO PENALTIES/APEX - IN THE FORM OF PAYMENT BOX.
         NOTE -
```

Annotations:
- No stopovers are allowed at any direction of travel.
- If connecting flights are chosen, two connecting points are allowed in each direction of travel.
- The reservation must be made 7 days before travel. The ticket must also be paid for and issued 7 days before travel.
- Make sure all ticketing instructions are carried forward on the ticket.

FIGURE 4–17

Apex rule. (Courtesy of Apollo Travel Services.)

TRAVELING WISELY

Have you ever considered traveling with a small tape recorder? It helps to capture the local language, music, and culture for longlasting enjoyment. Remember to bring extra batteries, and write your thoughts and feelings in a diary. You will enjoy reading the diary many years later, particularly during retirement.

SUMMARY

- A connection is an involuntary interruption of a journey for less than 6 hours. A fare is not charged.
- A stopover is a voluntary interruption of a journey for more than 6 hours. A fare is charged.
- A normal fare is unrestricted and allows an unlimited amount of stopovers.
- Apex and excursion fares are discounted economy fares with no or a limited number of stopovers.
- A person who is under 2 years old is called an infant.
- A person who is between 2 and 11 years old is called a child.

CHECK YOUR UNDERSTANDING 4–1

Directions: Decipher the following airfare basis codes:

1. P   _____
2. YOX   _____
3. YE141YR   _____
4. R   _____
5. YEXC4M   _____
6. BGV10   _____

7. QHAPOW _____

8. VLXZZ _____

9. BDG _____

10. KOWAB4 _____

CHECK YOUR UNDERSTANDING 4-2

Directions: Study the following airfare and rule displays and fill in the following blanks:

FARE TYPE	CAR CDE	HEADLINE CITY CURRENCY	NUC	RULES	GI MPM RTE REF VIA PT.
NEW YORK (NYC) N.Y., U.S.A.				U.S. $ (USD)	
To SHANGHAI					
F	CA	2172.00	2172.00	P0100	PA
YAB	CA	1641.00	1641.00	P0139	PA
YAB0	CA	830.00	830.00	P0139	PA
YAPB	CA	1641.00	1641.00	P0139	PA r70
YAPB0	CA	830.00	830.00	P0139	PA r70
YLAP	CA	1646.00	1646.00	P0129	PA r70
YHAP	CA	1704.00	1704.00	P0129	PA r70
YLGV	CA	1627.00	1627.00	P0225	PA
YHGV	CA	1674.00	1674.00	P0225	PA r70
Y	CO	2751.00	2751.00	N9999	AT
J	CO	3164.00	3164.00	N9999	AT
P	CO	4790.00	4790.00	N9999	AT
MLAPB	JL	1774.00	1774.00	P0461	PA r157
MLAPB0	JL	890.00	890.00	P0461	PA r157
MHAPB	JL	1898.00	1898.00	P0461	PA r157
MHAPB0	JL	953.00	953.00	P0461	PA r157
YD	JL	1336.00	1336.00	P0102	PA r158
C	JL	1711.00	1711.00	P0100	PA r158
C2	JL	1470.00	1470.00	P0100	PA r158
F	JL	2600.00	2600.00	P0100	PA r158
MLAP	JL	1894.00	1894.00	P0261	PA r158
MLAPJL	JL	1871.00	1871.00	P0261	PA r157
MHAP	JL	1963.00	1963.00	P0261	PA r158
MHAPJL	JL	1894.00	1894.00	P0261	PA r157
Y	TW	2595.00	2595.00	N0310	AT
C	TW	2854.00	2854.00	N0305	AT
F	TW	4519.00	4519.00	N0301	AT

N 0301 NORTH ATLANTIC FIRST CLASS FARES: Ⓐ
USA ⇔ AREA 2/AREA 3

1. **Application**
   A. OW/RT/CT/OJ via AC/AI/CO/PA (except at FP fares)/TW.
   B. OW/RT/CT via KL.
   C. OW/RT via PA at FP fares.
   FROM Chicago.
   TO Krakow/Warsaw.

5. **Childrens and Infants Fares**
   A. **Children:**
      1. **Via AI/PA from/to Area 3:** 67% (except from Japan, 50%).
      2. **Via KL:** To Area 3 and from/to Jordan: 67%.
      3. **Via TW:** From/to Area 3 (except Bangladesh): 67%.
      4. **All other journeys:** 50%.
   B. **Infants:** 10% (via KL, from/to New York).

10. **Permitted Stopovers**
    A. **Via CO at POX 4 fares:** One at New York in each direction.
    B. **Via KL at F1 Fares:**
       1. **Eastbound:** None.
       2. **Westbound:** One in each direction. The applicable higher intermediate point must be charged.
    C. **All other Journeys:** Unlimited.

14. **Reservations**
    A. **Via CO at POX 4 fares:** Deadline: 24 hours.
    B. **All other journeys:** No special requirements.

15. **Payment**
    A. **Via CO at POX 4 fares:** Deadline: 24 hours.
    B. **All other journeys:** No special requirements.

1. The point of origin is _____ .

2. The point of destination is _____ .

3. The city code for the origin city is_____.

4. Continental Airlines offers fares via the_____ air route only.

5. Low-season group airfare in local currency on Air China is_____.

6. The rule for Japan Airlines high-season apex fare is _____.

7. The fare basis code for traveling first class on Continental Airlines is_____.

8. Rule N0301 belongs to the_____ fare basis, traveling on _____ Airlines.

9. The one-way first class child's fare traveling on Trans World Airlines is_____.

10. A passenger is allowed_____ stopovers when traveling westbound on Japan Airlines.

11. The reservation must be completed_____ before departure on Continental Airlines.

12. The ticket must be paid for_____ before departure on Air China.

CHECK YOUR UNDERSTANDING 4-3

Directions: Study the following airfare and rule displays and fill in the following blanks:

```
HKG-GLA  WED-07FEB96  YY
MPM    9098  EH
                  TAXES/FEES NOT INCLUDED
ADULT FARES
       CX       FARE     FARE      C   AP   MIN/      SEASONS......  MR GI DT
                HKD      BASIS                MAX
   1   CX       17680R   Y2        W                                 MR EH
   2   CX        9160    Y2        W                                 MR EH
       END
```

```
    1 HKGGLA WE-07FEB6 CX        HKD17680R Y2                    BK-W
 1. APPLICATION:
    RULE: V307
    CX SPECIAL /POINT TO POINT/ ECONOMY FARES
    BETWEEN HONG KONG AND UNITED KINGDOM
    BETWEEN HONG KONG
    AND      UNITED KINGDOM
    ECONOMY...OW/RT...OOJ /EX UK/...TOJ /EX HR/...TRVL
    SEAMAN DISCOUNT DO NOT APPLY TO THIS FARE.
 5. CHILDREN AND INFANTS FARES:
    CHILDREN - 67 PCT OF APPLICABLE ADULT FARE.
10. STOPOVERS:
    NOT PERMITTED
11. ROUTING:
    VIA CX DIRECT SERVICES BETWEEN HK AND LON/MAN. WHEN THE
    FARE IS COMBINED WITH UK ADD ONS OR UK DOMESTIC FARES
    TRAVEL WITHIN UK PERMITTED ON ANY BRITISH CARRIER.
    TRANSFERS
    NOT PERMITTED  EXCEPT VIA LONDON WHEN THE
    FARE IS COMBINED WITH UK ADD ONS.
```

1. Fares are shown for traveling from_____ to_____.

2. The type of fare offered is _____
   _____

3. The route for this fare level is
   _____

4. The fare applies for travel on_____ Airways.

5. The fare can be used between points in Area_____
   and Area_____.

6. Travel is permitted in the_____ Hemisphere only.

7. The following stopover rule applies:
   _____

8. The following reservation rule applies:
   _____

9. The adult one-way fare is_____.

10. The cost for a child traveling round-trip is_____.

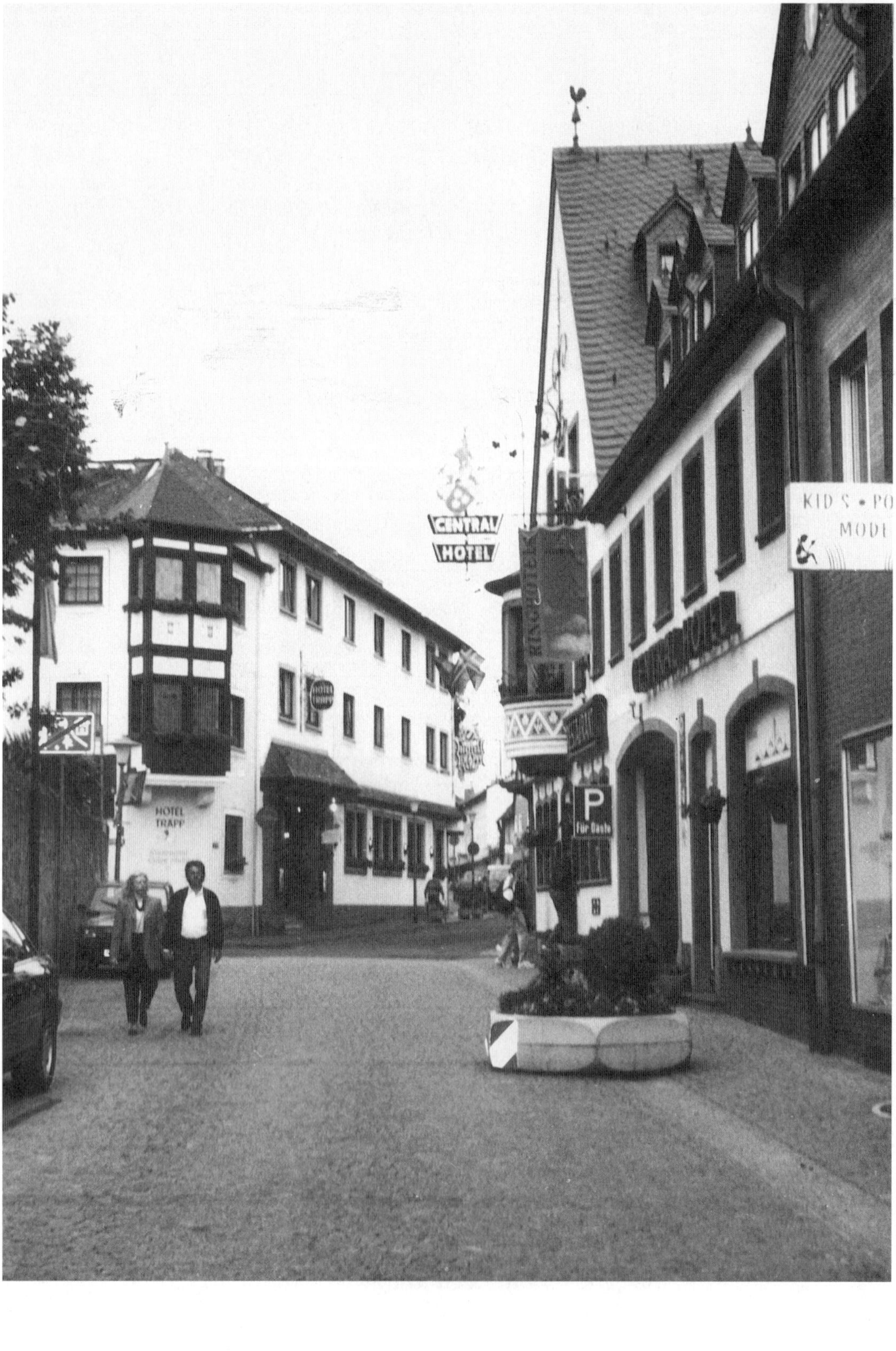
CENTRAL
HOTEL
HOTEL
TRAPP
P
Für Gäste

Chapter 5

International Ticketing

IATA Agent Responsibilities
The International Airline Ticket
    Name of Passenger
    Baggage Allowance
    Tax Computation and Currency Code
    Sales Indicator Code
    Fare Calculation Ladder
IATA Ticketing Procedures
    Normal-Fare Itineraries
    Excursion-Fare Itineraries
    Apex-Fare Itineraries

OBJECTIVES

After completing Chapter 5 you should be able to:

- Describe IATA ticketing procedures
- Explain how to issue adult excursion, apex, and normal-fare tickets
- Discuss how to issue children's and infants' excursion, apex, and normal-fare tickets

IATA Agent Responsibilities

The *IATA Ticketing Handbook* provides detailed instructions on how to issue and reissue interline passenger airline tickets. These instructions are based on the **IATA Passenger Services Conference Resolutions** related to tickets and ticketing procedures. According to IATA Resolution 800b, IATA-approved agents are responsible for adhering to ticketing procedures as stated in the following.

"The agent undertakes that all traffic documents, as well as all reservations or reservations alterations entered in connection with such transactions, shall be made according to the carrier's tariffs, regulations, or other applicable, published instructions.

The consequences of violating the ticketing procedures (IATA Resolution 830a) may be loss of IATA accreditation. Violations include, but are not limited to, the following:

- Entering incomplete or incorrect reservation entries on a ticket, thereby allowing travel at less than the applicable fare
- Changing the point of origin
- Changing or omitting the name of the passenger
- Changing the form of payment
- Using a reservations alteration sticker to alter a flight date without observing a consequential requirement [When IATA states a 'consequential requirement,' they mean that you cannot make any changes to the dates on a ticket using an alteration sticker without checking the fare rule for possible consequences. For example, the fare rule may limit the time frame (the dates) within which a change may be allowed. A fare rule may even prohibit a change of travel dates completely.]

- Issuing a ticket for more than one passenger
- Making different entries on flight and audit coupons of the same ticket"[1]

This chapter strictly adheres to IATA format, style, and procedures.

The International Airline Ticket

International ticket issuance differs from domestic ticket issuance in the following areas:

1. Name of passenger
2. Baggage allowance
3. Tax computation
4. Currency code
5. Sales indicator code
6. Fare calculation ladder

To clarify these differences, the fares from Figure 4–4 have been used to issue a business-class fare, round-trip ticket from Jakarta, Indonesia to Kuala Lumpur, Malaysia (see Figure 5–1).

NAME OF PASSENGER

On an international ticket, it is imperative that the passenger's name appear exactly as it does on the passenger's passport. As the ticket in Figure 5–2 shows, the passenger's surname, followed by an oblique, and the passenger's first name and title are entered in the "Name of Passenger" box. If the passenger's surname is hyphenated or separated by a space, the hyphen or space is omitted.

Sometimes it is necessary to add a passenger identification code after the passenger's name. The passenger in Figure 5–2

---

[1] *IATA Ticketing Handbook,* 26th ed. (1994), p. VIII.

122   International Travel and Tourism

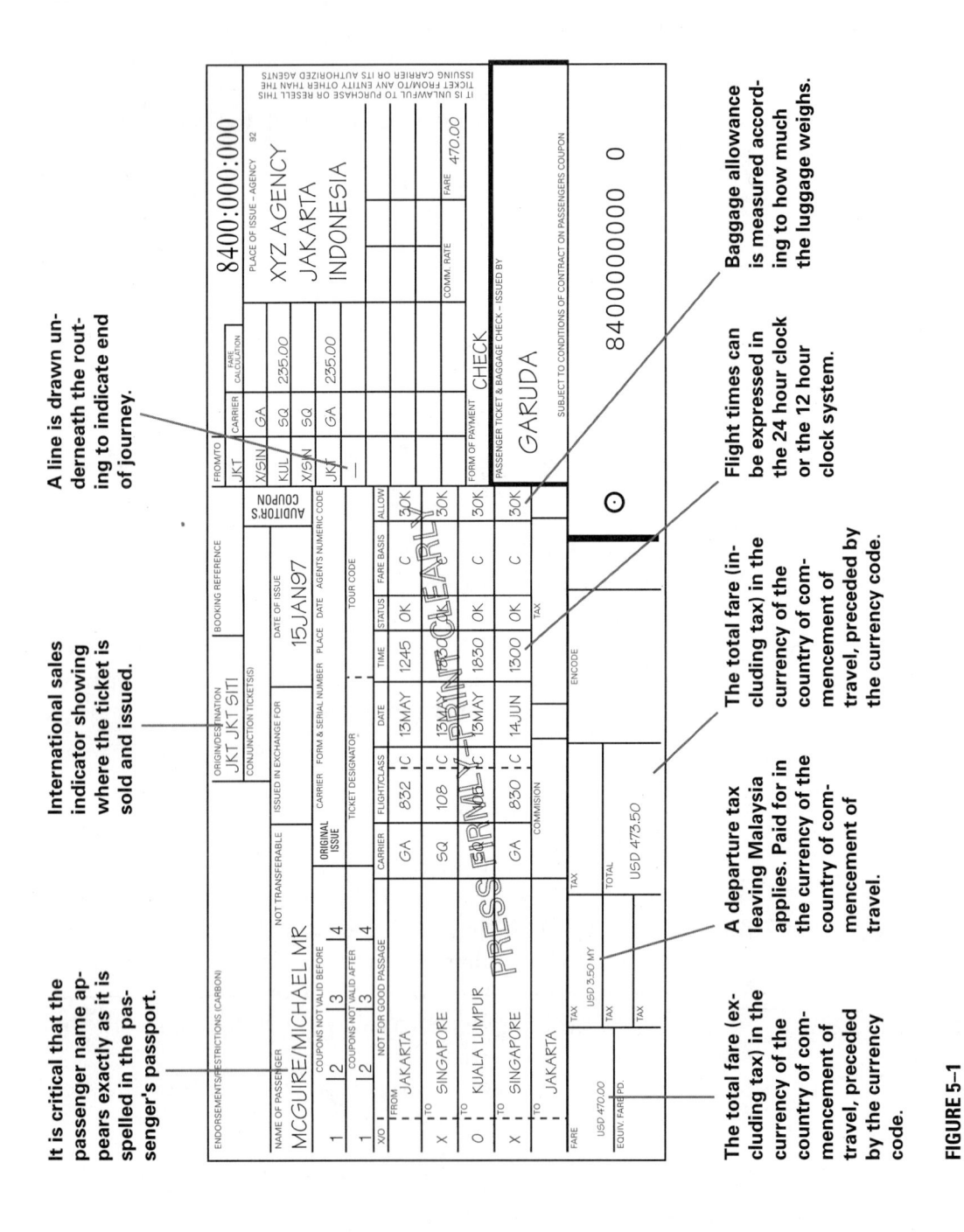

FIGURE 5–1

International ticket. Source: Industry Agents' Handbook, *October 1994. (Courtesy of Airlines Reporting Corporation.)*

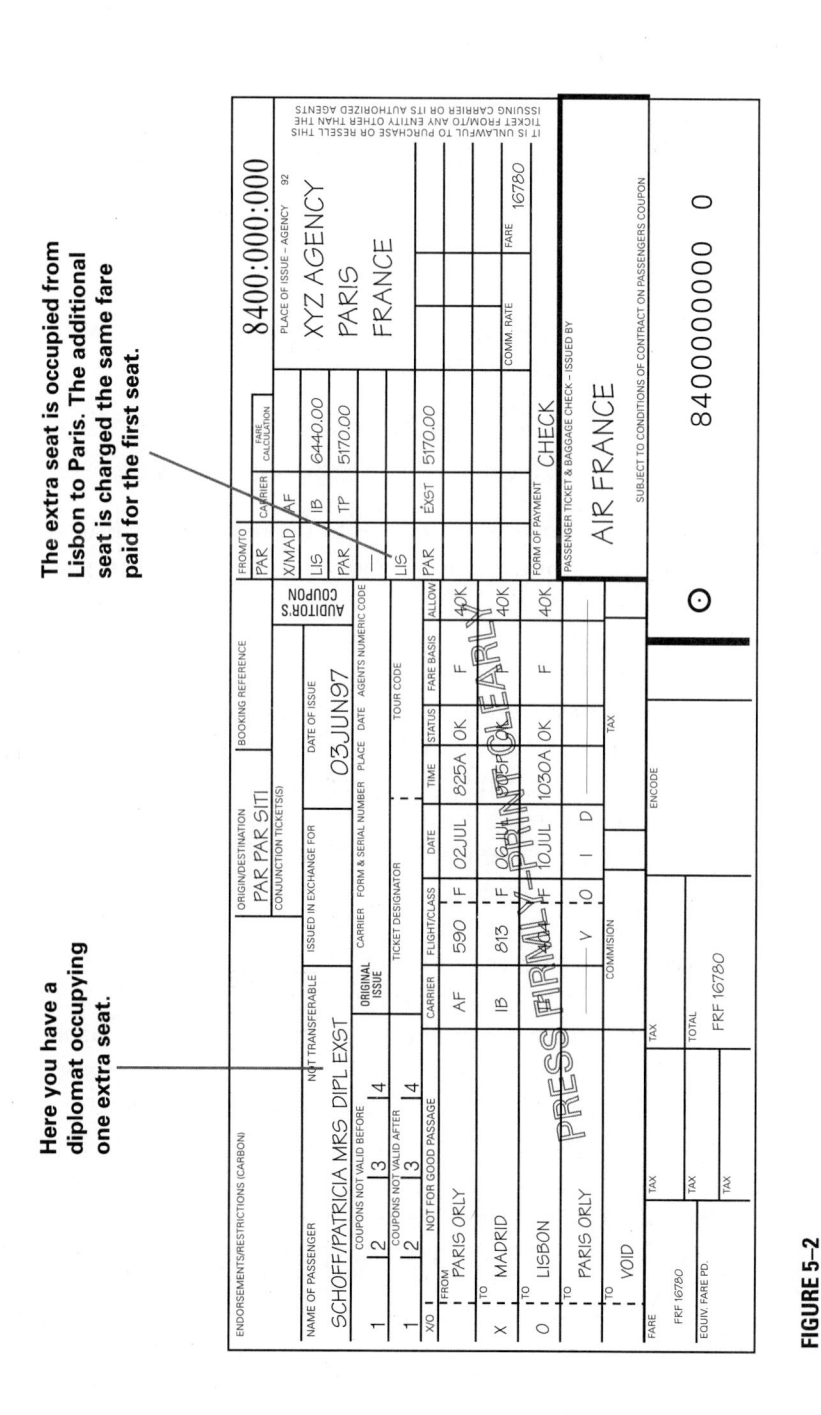

Chapter 5 International Ticketing 123

FIGURE 5-2

Diplomat's international ticket. Source: Industry Agents' Handbook, October 1994. (Courtesy of Airlines Reporting Corporation.)

is a diplomat, and the diplomat code, DIPL, follows her name on the ticket. Some other common examples are as follows:

INF	Infant's discount fare
CBBG	Cabin baggage, when a passenger seat is used for baggage
CHD	Child's discount fare, followed by the child's age
UM	Unaccompanied minor, followed by the minor's age (i.e., UM08)
03NOV96	Date of birth required for youth fare
EXST	Extra seat
DIPL	Diplomat
DEPU	Deportee unaccompanied
DEPA	Deportee accompanied by an escort

Airfare allows a passenger to occupy one airline seat. Sometimes a passenger must occupy two seats, as the passenger requires in Figure 5–2. The fare for the additional seat cannot be lower than that for the first seat. Normally, no extra baggage is allowed.

When passengers request extra seats from Cathay Pacific, All Nippon Airways, Northwest, Trans World Airlines, and United Airlines, they are charged two fares for the portion of the journey during which they occupy two seats. Each passenger is allowed twice the baggage for that part of the journey.

When passengers who desire additional seats travel on American Airlines, Continental Airlines, or Delta Airlines, they are charged 150 percent of the normal adult fare for the portion of the journey during which they occupy two seats. Each passenger is allowed twice the baggage for that portion of the journey.

When passengers fly Japan Air System or Japan Airlines, they are charged 200 percent of the normal adult fare for the portion of the journey during which they occupy two seats. Each passenger is allowed twice the baggage for that portion of the journey.

BAGGAGE ALLOWANCE

Passengers in all service classes—first, business, economy, and discounted economy—are allowed two free pieces of checked baggage for travel within the United States and

Canada, to/from the United States and Canada, and to/from South America via the Pacific Ocean. Free baggage is not limited to suitcases and backpacks. Golf bags, skis, sleeping bags, musical instruments, surf boards, bicycles, and hunting rifles are also considered pieces of free baggage. Each piece of baggage must not exceed 70 pounds, however.

When travel does not include the United States and/or Canada and to/from South America across the Pacific, the free checked-baggage allowance is measured according to how much the luggage weighs. International airlines and flights use the metric system. The baggage allowance in first class is 40 kilos (88 pounds). In business class, the baggage allowance is 30 kilos (66 pounds). In all economy classes, the baggage allowance is 20 kilos (44 pounds). It can be expensive to check baggage exceeding the free baggage allowance. Normally the charge is 1 percent per kilo of the normal adult one-way, first-class fare. For example, on a round-trip flight from Chicago to London on a $926.00 apex fare (see Figure 5–9), the charge for bringing 10 kilos of excess baggage one way is calculated from the first class one way fare of $3839.00. The cost for checking 1 extra kilo is 1 percent of $3,839 (3,839 × 0.01 = 38.39). Therefore, the cost for 10 extra kilos is 10 percent of 3,839 which is $383.90 (3,839 × 0.10 = 383.90). Many exceptions to the baggage rules exist, however. It is always a good idea to check with carriers for more detailed information on what is or is not acceptable.

The amount of free baggage is entered in the "Allow" box on the ticket (Figure 5–3) with one of the following codes:

40K 40 kilos (88 pounds)
30K 30 kilos (66 pounds)
20K 20 kilos (44 pounds)
PC   pieces
NO   No free baggage allowed
NIL No free baggage allowed
NS   No free baggage allowed (infant not occupying a seat)

A passenger who is paying for first and/or business class but is traveling economy is allowed the first- and/or business-class free-baggage allowance. A child paying at least 50 percent of the adult fare is allowed the same free baggage allowance as an

126　International Travel and Tourism

The code "INF" after the passenger name indicates the infant is flying discounted.

The infant travels free when not occupying a seat.

Free fare passengers always pay any applicable taxes.

Infant not occupying a seat. The code "NS" indicates no seat.

An infant not occupying a seat is not allowed free baggage allowance.

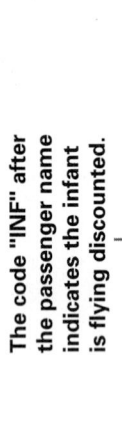

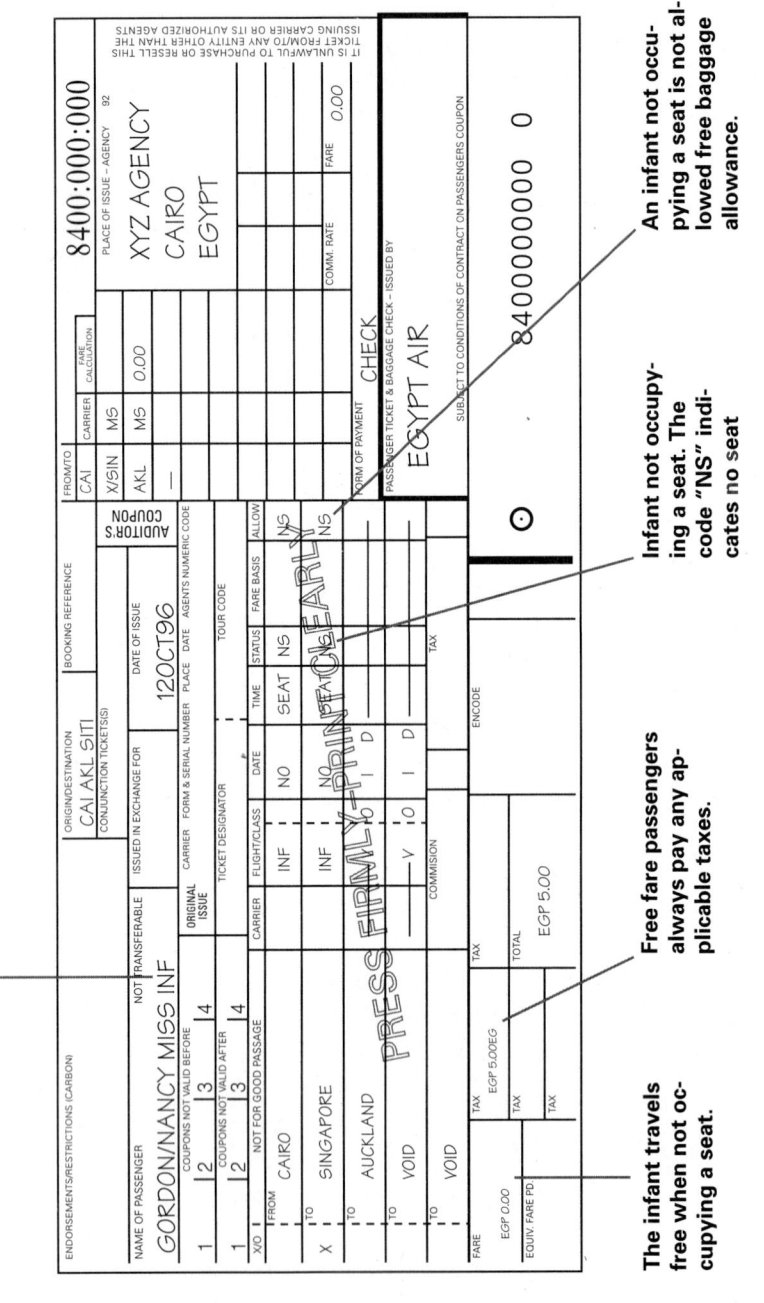

FIGURE 5–3

Free baggage code. Source: Industry Agents' Handbook, October 1994. (Courtesy of Airlines Reporting Corporation.)

adult. An infant paying 10 percent of the adult fare is allowed one free piece of checked baggage. An infant not occupying a seat is not allowed any free baggage.

TAX COMPUTATION AND CURRENCY CODE

On international journeys, the 10 percent federal tax charged domestic travelers does not apply. International taxes are fixed, but they vary from country to country. International taxes must be added to airfares because all international fares are listed without tax.

All taxes must be paid when the ticket is purchased, and the taxes must be entered in the "Tax" boxes of the ticket in the currency of the country in which the journey originates, followed by its two-letter tax codes (Figure 5–4). It is not mandatory to show the three-letter currency code. Some international taxes and their codes follow:

- XA   United States Agriculture, Animal and Plant Health Inspection service fee
- XC   Guatemala passenger service charge
- XD   Mexico departure tax
- XE   Algeria International Airport tax
- XF   United States passenger facility charge
- XG   Canadian goods and service tax
- XK   Egypt ticket-issuance fee
- XL   Egypt stamp tax
- XO   Mexico International Airport tax
- XP   Prepaid Ticket Advice (PTA) service charge
- XQ   Quebec, Canada, sales tax
- XR   Argentina Airport tax
- XT   Combined United States taxes
- XV   Mexico domestic airport departure tax
- XW   Warsaw, Poland, Airport tax
- XY   United States INS Fee
- YA   Sweden security charge
- YC   United States Customs user fee, $6.50
- YP   Portugal passenger service charge
- YV   Venezuela international departure tax

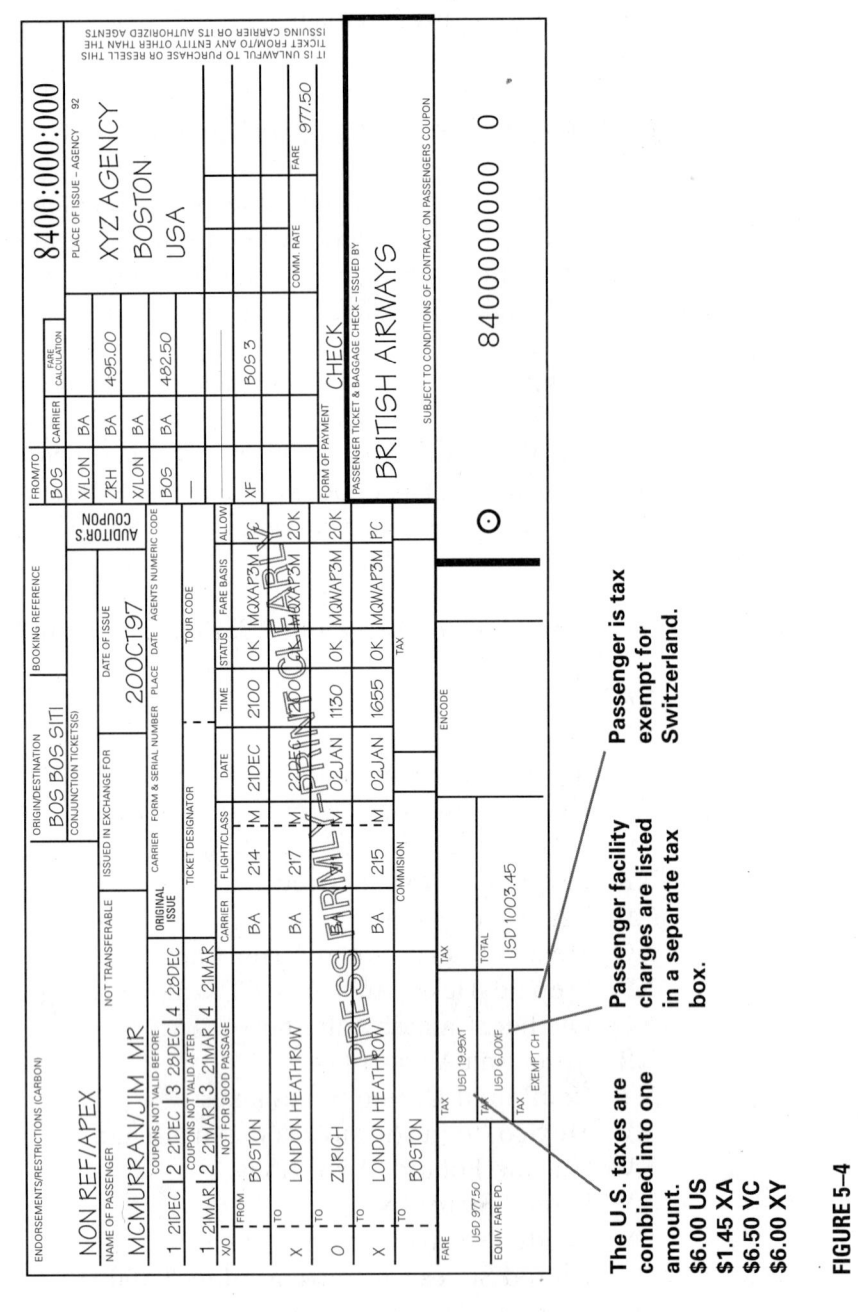

The U.S. taxes are combined into one amount.
$6.00 US
$1.45 XA
$6.50 YC
$6.00 XY

Passenger facility charges are listed in a separate tax box.

Passenger is tax exempt for Switzerland.

FIGURE 5–4

Tax-exempt passenger. Source: Industry Agents' Handbook, October 1994. (*Courtesy of Airlines Reporting Corporation.*)

Taxes for each country must be shown separately on the ticket. Some countries, including the United States, charge airport departure taxes. The United States departure tax is charged every time a passenger leaves the United States. The United States departure tax must be collected when the ticket is sold, but many other countries collect the departure tax when passengers check in to leave. The code for an international departure tax is always the two-letter country code.

If multiple taxes apply to a country, those taxes can be combined into one amount. When this is done, the code XT replaces the two-letter country code on the ticket. If a passenger is tax exempt, the word *Exempt* appears in one of the "Tax" boxes. See Figure 5–4 for an example.

SALES INDICATOR CODE

International airfares are constructed based on where tickets are sold and issued. Most tickets are sold and issued in the country where travel commences. When travel originates in Scandinavia, all Scandinavian countries (Denmark, Norway, and Sweden) are considered one country, except when the ticket is a SOTO. Similarly, when travel originates in Canada or the United States, Canada and the United States are considered one country.

A four-letter international sales indicator code appears in the "Origin/Destination" box of the ticket (Figure 5–1) to indicate which fare construction method was used. Figure 5–3 shows a ticket that was purchased and issued in Egypt. The fare construction methods follow:

SITI: Ticket is Sold Inside and Ticketed Inside the country where international travel commences

Example: Ticket is purchased and issued in South Africa

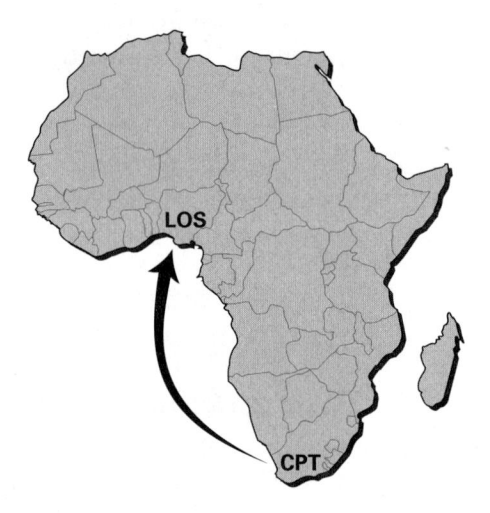

SOTI: Ticket is Sold Outside but Ticketed Inside the country where international travel commences

Example: Ticket is purchased inside New Zealand but issued in Australia

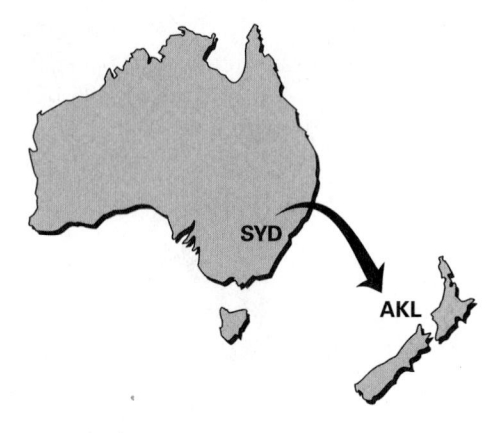

SOTO: Ticket is Sold Outside and Ticketed Otside the country where international travel commences

Example: Ticket is purchased and issued in France

SITO: Ticket is Sold Inside but Ticketed Outside the country where international travel commences

Example: Ticket is sold in Peru but issued in Brazil

FARE CALCULATION LADDER

The fares entered in the **fare calculation ladder,** which is a detailed breakdown of how the airfare was constructed, must be in the local currency of the country where travel commences. The fare calculation ladder should always be completed in the event reroutings, refunds, or changes occur. The IATA rules for completing the fare calculation ladder follow:

- City codes (*not* airport codes) are entered in the "From/To" column.
- Airline codes are entered in "Carr." column. When no specific airline is used to calculate the fare, the code "YY" is entered instead.
- Half the round-trip fare is entered by the point of turnaround, and the second half of the round trip fare is entered by the final destination.
- Surcharges like the passenger facility charge and the charge for stopovers are entered separately at the end of the itinerary.
- A line is drawn below the itinerary in the "From/To" column to separate the routing and the additional surcharges.
- The "X/" is entered by each connecting point in the "From/To" column.

Figure 5–5 illustrates how IATA rules are used to complete the fare calculation ladder.

IATA Ticketing Procedures

The local currency fare can be quoted when a through fare is used from the point of origin to the point of destination. These local currency fares are called **point-to-point fares.** All apex and excursion fares are point-to-point fares and can therefore be quoted in local currency.

NORMAL-FARE ITINERARIES

Study again the fare display in Figure 4–5 (see page 101) from Jakarta to Kuala Lumpur. Figure 5–6 shows the journey is routed via points in the Eastern Hemisphere. A child

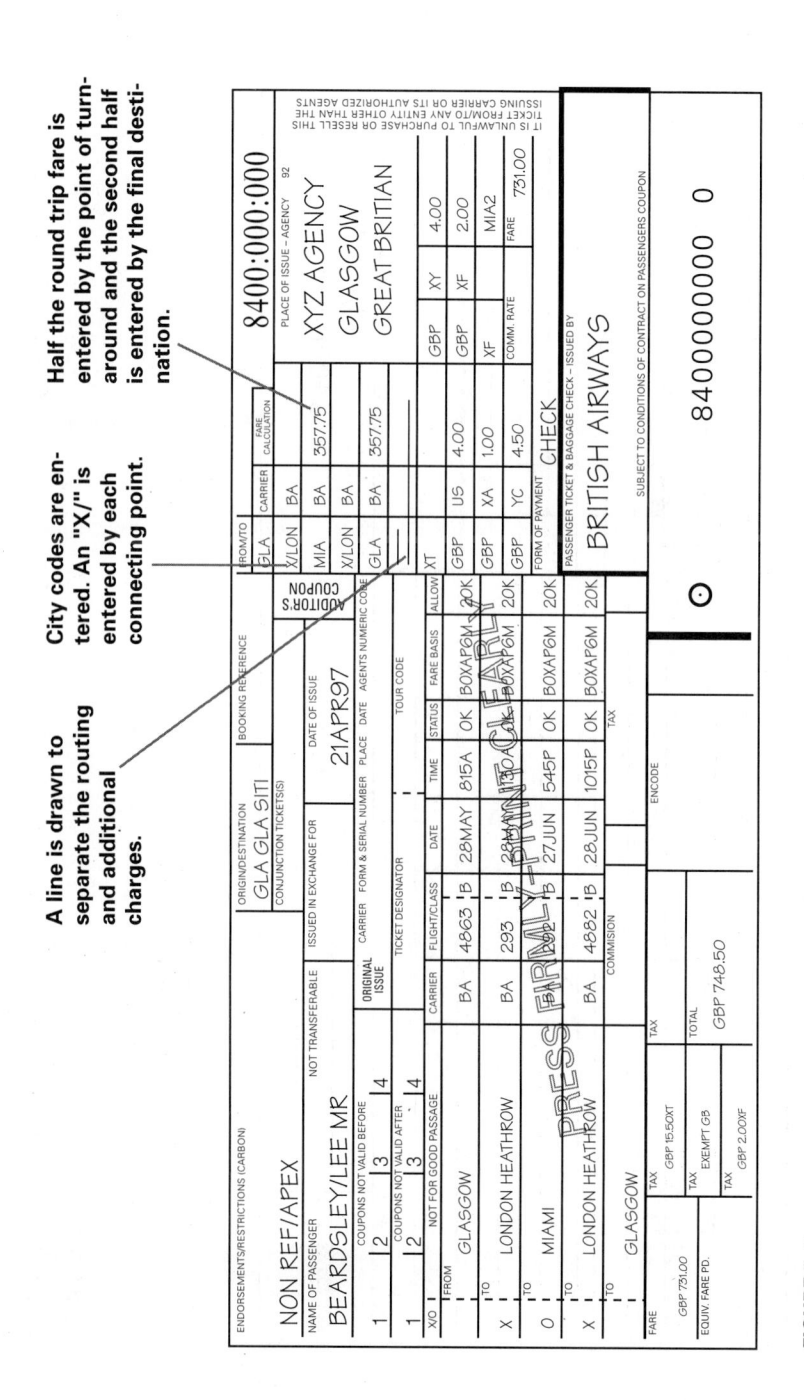

Chapter 5 International Ticketing *133*

FIGURE 5-5
Completing the fare calculation ladder. Source: Industry Agents' Handbook, October 1994. (Courtesy of Airlines Reporting Corporation.)

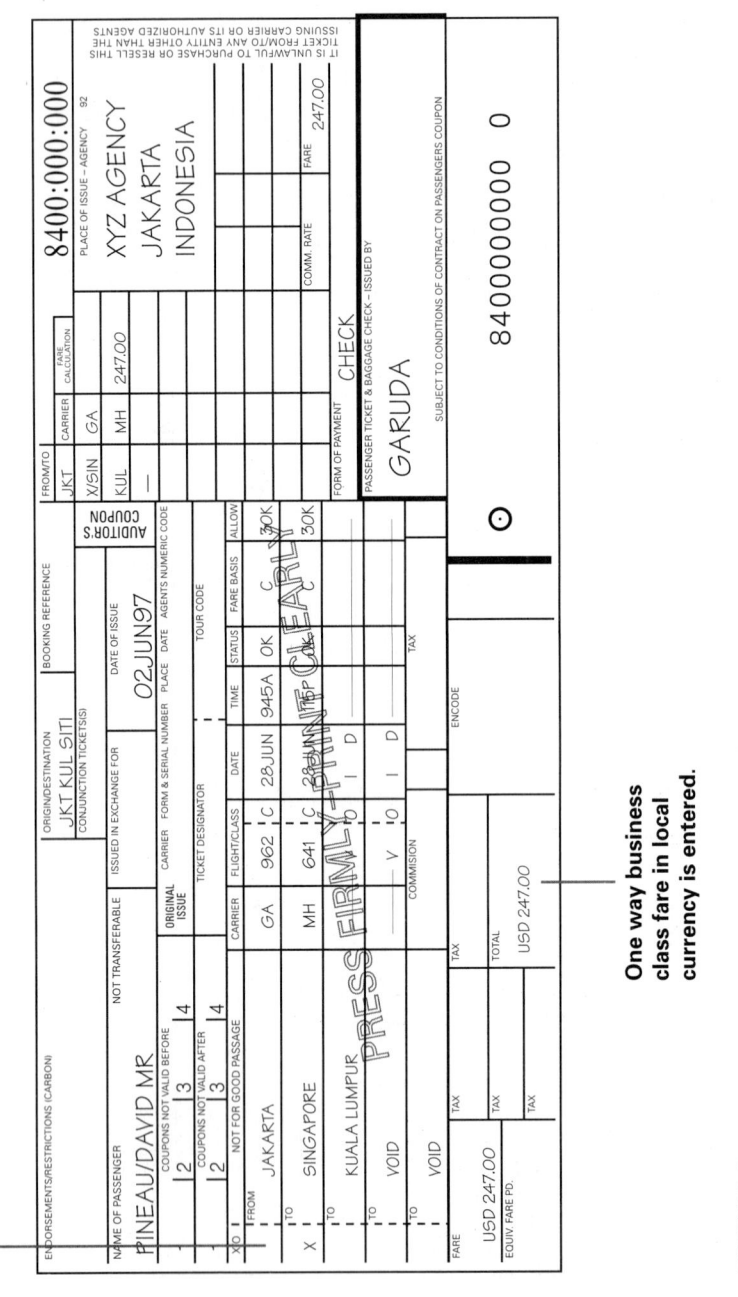

FIGURE 5-6

Travel via the Eastern Hemisphere. Source: Industry Agents' Handbook, October 1994. (Courtesy of Airlines Reporting Corporation.)

accompanied by an adult often receives a discount on international fares. Rule category 5 in the lower half of Figure 4–6 on page 103 explains that a child receives a 33 percent discount of the adult Y2 fare level.

EXCURSION-FARE ITINERARIES

An excursion fare is the most flexible discounted economy/coach fare ticket. One or two stopovers are often permitted for free. Figure 5–7 illustrates a free stopover in Singapore and how it is entered in the fare calculation ladder. The fares from Cairo, Egypt to Auckland, New Zealand in Figure 4–7 and its corresponding Rule E687 in Figure 4–8 are used as guides.

On many international journeys, an infant who occupies a seat receives a 90 percent discount. When the adult excursion fare of EGP 8987 (Figure 4–14) is compared with the infant's fare level in the corresponding rule (Figure 4–15), the infant flies at a 33 percent discount. Figure 5–8 illustrates this concept.

APEX-FARE ITINERARIES

The most restricted and least expensive international fare is the advance-purchase excursion fare or apex fare. As the apex fare level in Figure 4–16 and its corresponding rule in Figure 4–17 (see pages 112–113) show, no stopovers are allowed in either direction of travel. This fare level is only valid for travel on British Airways. See Figure 5–9 for an adult apex ticket.

A child normally does not receive a discount on an apex fare. In Figure 4–17 note that the child pays 75 percent of the adult apex fare level of USD 926 in Figure 4–16. See Figure 5–10 for clarification.

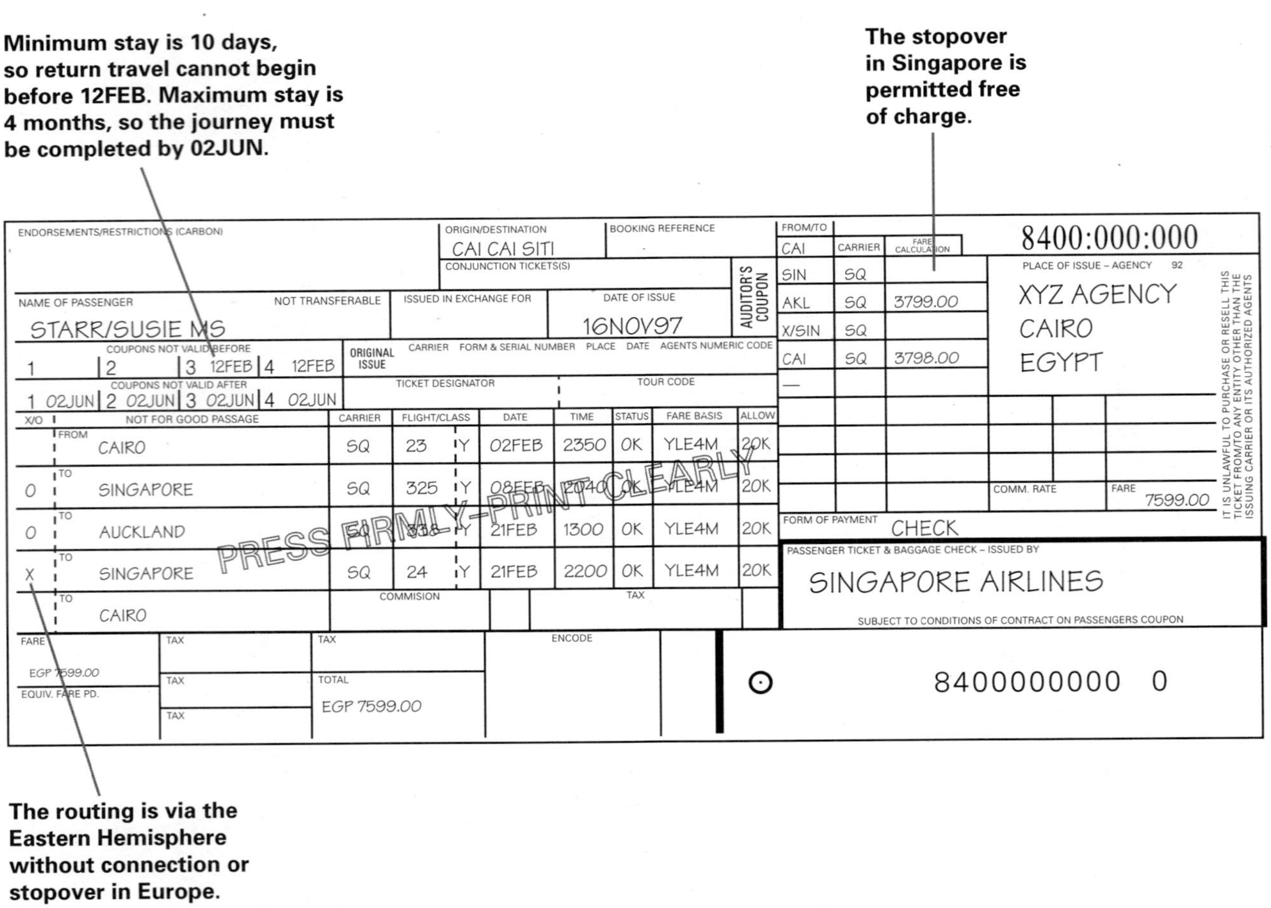

136　International Travel and Tourism

FIGURE 5-7

Free stopover. Source: Industry Agents' Handbook, October 1994. (Courtesy of Airlines Reporting Corporation.)

Chapter 5 International Ticketing 137

The passenger identification code "INF" followed by the age, identifies the traveler as a discounted infant.

ENDORSEMENTS/RESTRICTIONS (CARBON)				ORIGIN/DESTINATION CAI CAI SITI CONJUNCTION TICKET(S)		BOOKING REFERENCE			
NAME OF PASSENGER CHAPIN/DEBORAH INF 1YR		NOT TRANSFERABLE		ISSUED IN EXCHANGE FOR					PLACE OF ISSUE – AGENCY 92
	COUPONS NOT VALID BEFORE					DATE OF ISSUE 16NOV97			XYZ AGENCY
1	2	3 12FEB	4 12FEB	ORIGINAL ISSUE	CARRIER FORM & SERIAL NUMBER PLACE DATE AGENTS NUMERIC CODE				CAIRO
	COUPONS NOT VALID AFTER					TOUR CODE			EGYPT
1 02JUN	2 02JUN	3 02JUN	4 02JUN						8400:000:000
X/O	NOT FOR GOOD PASSAGE	CARRIER	FLIGHT/CLASS	DATE	TIME	STATUS	FARE BASIS	ALLOW	
	FROM CAIRO	SQ	23 Y	02FEB	2350	OK	YLE4M	10K	FROM/TO CARRIER FARE CALCULATION
O	TO SINGAPORE	SQ	325 Y			OK	YLE4M	10K	CAI SIN SQ 379.95
O	TO AUCKLAND	SQ	Y	21FEB	1300	OK	YLE4M	10K	SIN AKL SQ 379.95
X	TO SINGAPORE	SQ	24 Y	21FEB	2200	OK	YLE4M	10K	X/SIN
	TO CAIRO								CAI
FARE		TAX		TAX		TAX			COMM. RATE FARE 759.90
EGP 759.90									FORM OF PAYMENT CHECK
EQUIV. FARE PD.		TAX		TOTAL EGP 759.90		COMMISSION		ENCODE	PASSENGER TICKET & BAGGAGE CHECK - ISSUED BY **SINGAPORE AIRLINES**
									SUBJECT TO CONDITIONS OF CONTRACT ON PASSENGERS COUPON
									8400000000 0

PRESS FIRMLY - PRINT CLEARLY

IT IS UNLAWFUL TO PURCHASE OR RESELL THIS TICKET FROM/TO ANY ENTITY OTHER THAN THE ISSUING CARRIER OR ITS AUTHORIZED AGENTS

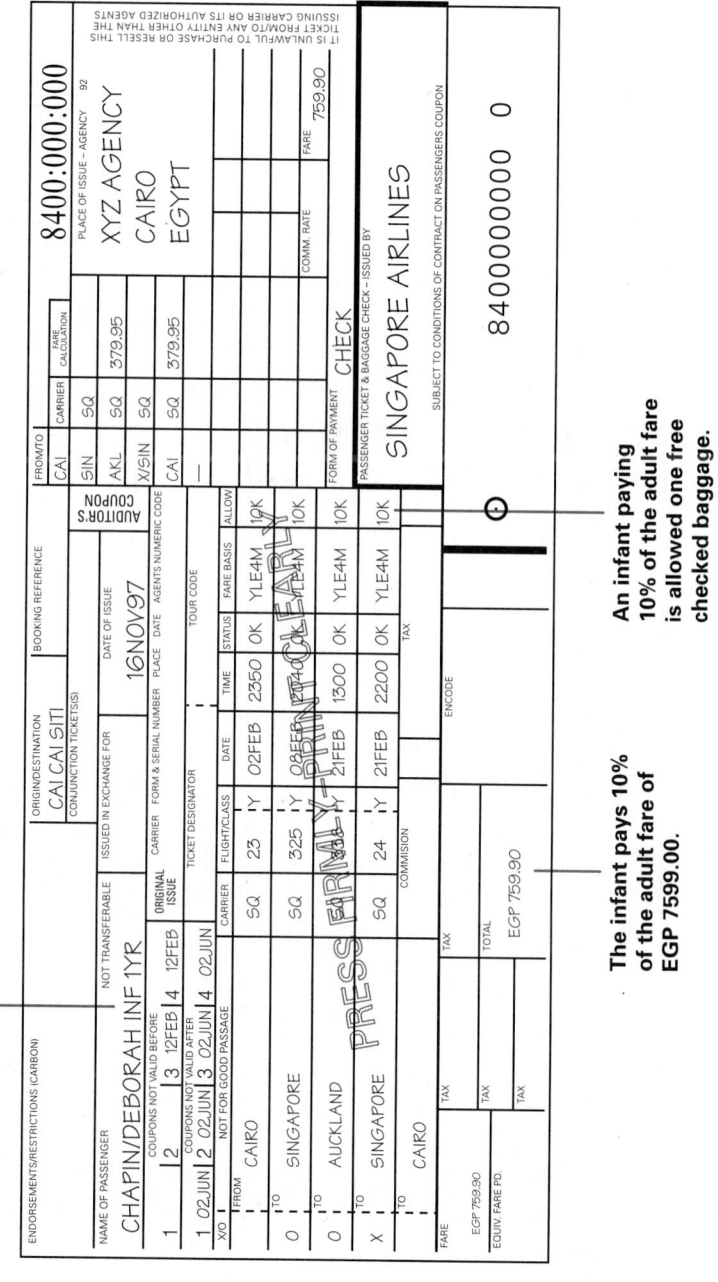

AUDITOR'S COUPON

The infant pays 10% of the adult fare of EGP 7599.00.

An infant paying 10% of the adult fare is allowed one free checked baggage.

FIGURE 5–8

Infant's discounted fare. Source: Industry Agents' Handbook, October 1994. (Courtesy of Airlines Reporting Corporation.)

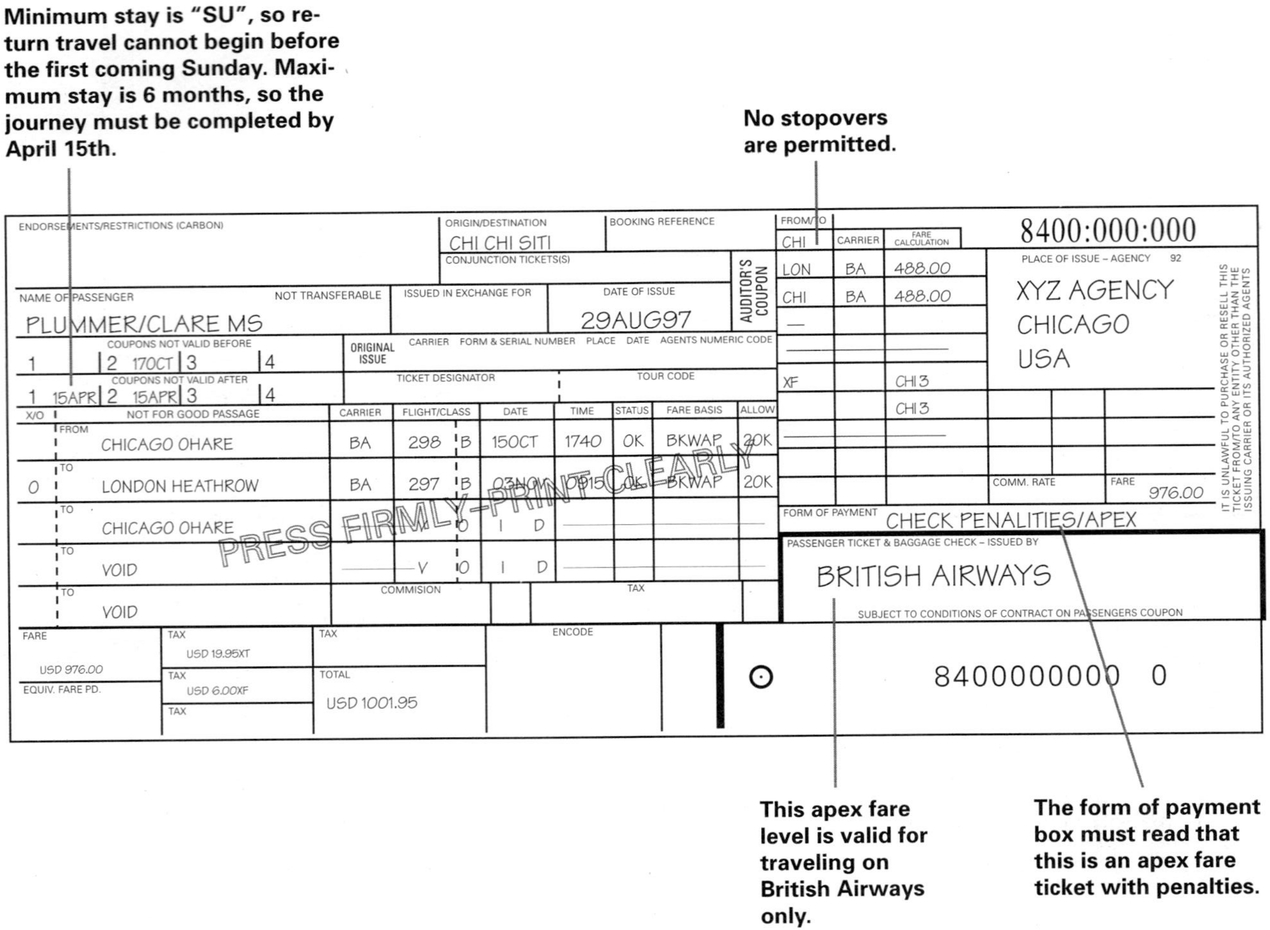

138　International Travel and Tourism

FIGURE 5-9

Airline-specific airfare. Source: Industry Agents' Handbook, October 1994. (Courtesy of Airlines Reporting Corporation.)

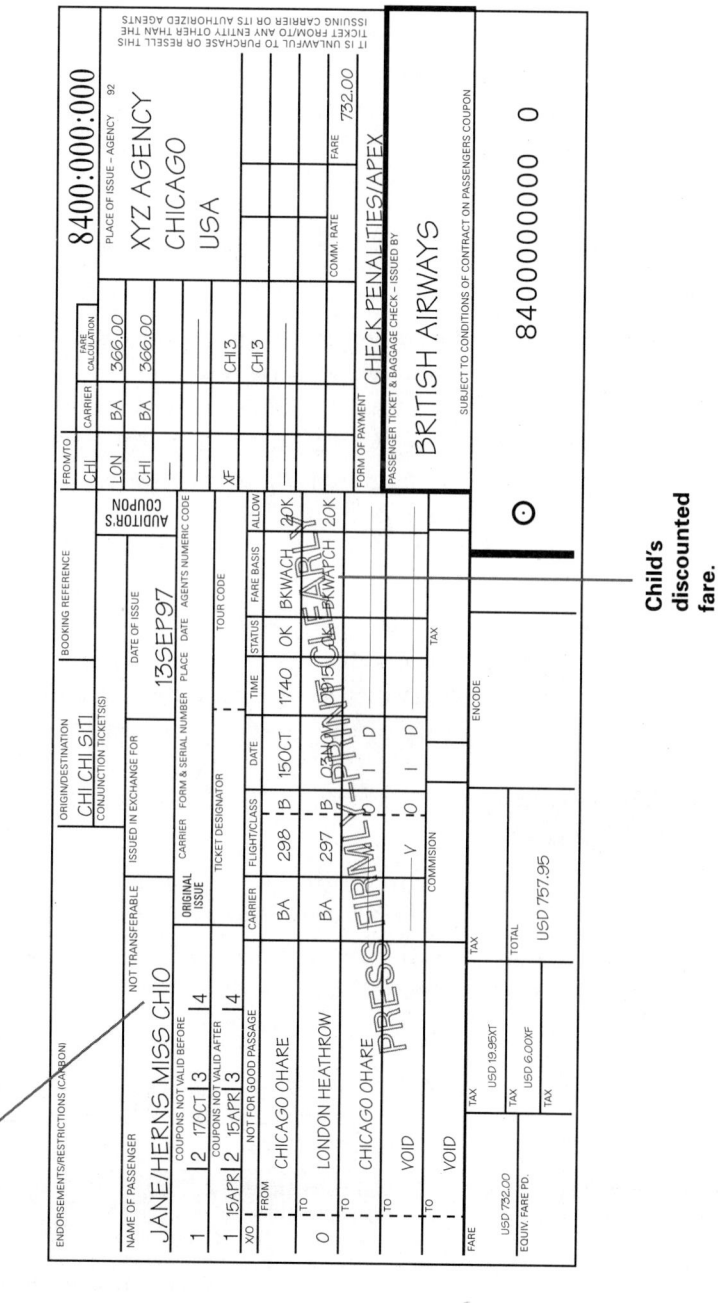

FIGURE 5-10

Child's discounted adult apex fare. Source: Industry Agents' Handbook, October 1994. (Courtesy of Airlines Reporting Corporation.)

TRAVELING WISELY

Never expect a trip to go as planned. Be flexible and open-minded. View unexpected events as challenging and enjoyable surprises and experiences. Above all, travel at a relaxed and pleasant pace. Do not rush trying to see five capital cities in a week. Peace and serenity are important to absorbing experiences and impressions.

SUMMARY

- The passenger's name must appear on the ticket exactly as it appears on the passenger's passport.
- When travel does not include the United States and/or Canada or to/from South America via the Pacific, the amount of free checked baggage is measured according to how much the baggage weighs.
- International ticket taxes are fixed amounts that vary from country to country.
- International air fares are constructed based on where the ticket is sold and issued.
- The fares entered in the fare calculation ladder must be in the local currency of the country where travel commences.

CHECK YOUR UNDERSTANDING 5–1

Use an official airline guide or a computer reservation system to find the best flight schedule in the following example. Study the fare and rule display provided to calculate the excursion fare and issue the ticket. Create the name of the passenger, the dates of travel, and the date of issue.

FARE TYPE	CAR CDE	HEADLINE CITY CURRENCY	NUC	RULES	GI MPM RTE REF VIA PT
PENANG (PEN) Malaysia		Ringgit (MYR)			
To TOKYO					EH 4158
Y		1848	706.67		EH
J/C		2033	779.61		EH
F		2628	1007.78		EH
YE30		3041	1166.16	E792	EH
YGV15		2278	873.56	F982	EH

E 792   EXCURSION FARES: BRUNEI/INDONESIA/ MALAYSIA/SINGAPORE ♦ JAPAN   Ⓐ

1. **Application** Y RT/CT.
5. **Children and Infants Fares** Not permitted.
6. **Minimum Stay** 5 days.
8. **Maximum Stay** One month.
9. **Extension of Ticket Validity** Not permitted.
10. **Permitted Stopovers** Unlimited.
12. **Permitted Combinations** Not on a half RT basis.
17. **Ticket Entries Fare Basis:** YE1M.
18. **Voluntary Rerouting** Permitted.
24. **Tour Conductors Discounts** Permitted.
25. **Agents Discounts** Permitted.

Chapter 5 International Ticketing *141*

From/To	Carrier	Flight/Cl	Date	Departure	Arrival

CHECK YOUR UNDERSTANDING 5-2

Use an official airline guide or a computer reservation system to find the best flight schedule in the following example. Study the fare and rule display provided to calculate the best youth round trip fare and issue the ticket. Create the name of the passenger, the dates of travel, and the date of issue.

FARE TYPE	CAR CDE	HEADLINE CITY CURRENCY	NUC	RULES	GI MPM RTE REF VIA PT
NAIROBI (NBO) Kenya					U.S. $ (USD)
To VANCOUVER					AT 10722
Y		1422.00	1421.71	G308	AT
J/C		1589.00	1588.71	G308	AT
F		2332.00	2332.45	G308	AT
YLAP		1463.00	1463.31	G560	AT
YHAP		1632.00	1632.31	G560	AT
YE3M		2041.00	2041.31	G409	AT
YZ		1958.00	1958.31	G362	AT

G 362 NORTH ATLANTIC YOUTH FARES: CANADA ↔ AFRICA

1. **Application** Y RT/CT/SOJ.
   NOTES:
   1. To Ethiopia: only available to Addis Ababa.
   2. These fares do not apply retroactively.

5. **Children and Infants Fares** Not applicable.

11. **Routings Permitted Transfers:** Two in each direction.

12. **Permitted Combinations** Domestic fares.

13. **Advertising and Sales** Permitted worldwide (except Nigeria)

14. **Reservations** Must not be confirmed or entered on the ticket more than 5 days before the respective dates of each Transatlantic departure. However, if the youth passenger is accompanied by a passenger paying a full adult fare, normal reservation/procedures apply.

17. **Ticket Entries**
    A. Fare Basis: Y.
    B. Ticket Designator: ZZ.
    C. Name of Passenger: Date of birth immediately following name.

18. **Voluntary Rerouting** Permitted.

21. **Eligibility**
    A. From 12th to before 24th birthday:
    B. Journeys ex Africa: Fares are also available to full-time students before their 27th birthday. Certified proof of attendance at a recognised Educational Establishment is required.

22. **Documentation** For Travel originating in Africa: A copy of the passenger's Identity Card/passport particulars must be attached to the ticket.

From/To	Carrier	Flight/CI	Date	Departure	Arrival

CHECK YOUR UNDERSTANDING 5–3

Use an official airline guide or a computer reservation system to find the best flight schedule in the following example. Study the fare and rule display provided to calculate the fare for a 1-year-old infant accompanied by an adult and issue the ticket. Create the name of the passenger, the dates of travel, and the date of issue.

```
LAX-SYD MON-12AUG96 YY
                TAXES/FEES NOT INCLUDED
ADULT FARES                                         *SHORT $D*
      CX    FARE    FARE     C  AP  MIN/   SEASONS......  MR GI DT
              USD   BASIS            MAX
   1  AA  1098.00R  QLXAP    Q   7  07/3M  01APR -31AUG    R  PA D
      END
*
  1 LAXSYD MO-12AUG6 AA     USD1098.00R QLXAP    STAY 07/3M    BK-Q
2. PERIODS OF APPLICATION:
   DAY/TIME:
     BETWEEN SYD AND THE UNITED STATES FOR QLXAP TYPE FARES

     TO SYD -
       PERMITTED 1100AM TO 300PM MON/TUE/WED FROM THE GATEWAY.

     FROM SYD -
       PERMITTED 400PM TO 800PM MON/TUE/WED FROM THE GATEWAY.

   SEASONALITY:
     BETWEEN THE UNITED STATES AND AUSTRALIA FOR BASIC SEASON
       PERMITTED 400PM TO 800PM MON/TUE/WED FROM THE GATEWAY.

   SEASONALITY:
     BETWEEN THE UNITED STATES AND AUSTRALIA FOR BASIC SEASON
     FARES

     ORIGINATING THE UNITED STATES -
       PERMITTED 01APR THROUGH 31AUG ON THE OUTBOUND
       TRANSPACIFIC SECTOR.

     ORIGINATING AUSTRALIA -
       PERMITTED 01FEB THROUGH 31MAR OR 16OCT THROUGH 30NOV ON
       THE OUTBOUND TRANSPACIFIC SECTOR.
```

```
5. CHILDREN AND INFANTS FARES:
   BETWEEN THE UNITED STATES AND AUSTRALIA

     IF TRAVEL IS VIA TRANSPACIFIC SECTORS
       AN ACCOMPANIED CHILD 2-11 YEARS OF AGE WILL BE CHARGED
       67 PERCENT OF THE ADULT FARE WHEN ACCOMPANIED ON ALL
       FLIGHTS AND IN THE SAME COMPARTMENT BY AN ADULT AT LEAST
       12 YEARS OF AGE.
       THE TICKETING CODE FOR THE DISCOUNTED FARE IS THE BASE
       FARE CODE PLUS CH
       OR - AN INFANT UNDER 2 YEARS OF AGE AND OCCUPYING A SEAT
            WILL BE CHARGED 67 PERCENT OF THE ADULT FARE WHEN
            ACCOMPANIED ON ALL FLIGHTS AND IN THE SAME
            COMPARTMENT BY AN ADULT AT LEAST 12 YEARS OF AGE
       OR - THE FIRST INFANT UNDER 2 YEARS OF AGE AND NOT
            OCCUPYING A SEAT WILL BE CHARGED 10 PERCENT OF THE
            ADULT FARE WHEN ACCOMPANIED ON ALL FLIGHTS AND IN
            THE SAME COMPARTMENT BY AN ADULT AT LEAST 12 YEARS
            OF AGE
       OR - AN UNACCOMPANIED CHILD 5-11 YEARS OF AGE WILL BE
            CHARGED 100 PERCENT OF THE ADULT FARE.
            NOTE -
            UNACCOMPANIED CHILDREN 5 6 AND 7 YEARS OF AGE WILL
            ONLY BE TRANSPORTED OVER THE LINES OF AA NON-STOP
            OR THROUGH PLANE SERVICE.

10. PERMITTED STOPOVERS:
    BETWEEN THE UNITED STATES AND AUSTRALIA FOR QLXAP TYPE FARES
    NOTE - GENERAL RULE DOES NOT APPLY

      ORIGINATING AUSTRALIA -
       6 STOPOVERS PERMITTED
          LIMITED TO 1 FREE AND 5 AT AUD 110.00 EACH.
          CHILD/INFANT DISCOUNTS APPLY.

      ORIGINATING THE UNITED STATES -
       UNLIMITED STOPOVERS PERMITTED
          LIMITED TO 1 FREE AND UNLIMITED AT USD 125.00 EACH.
          CHILD/INFANT DISCOUNTS APPLY.

      NOTE - THE CITY PAIRS BELOW ARE CONSIDERED THE SAME POINT -
          BWI-WAS FLL-MIA OAK-SFO OAK-SJC SFO-SJC
          LAX-ONT LAX-BUR LAX-LGB LAX-SNA ONT-BUR
          ONT-LGB ONT-SNA BUR-LGB BUR-SNA LGB-SNA
          NYC-EWR
```

```
11. ROUTING:
    FLIGHT APPLICATION:
    BETWEEN THE UNITED STATES AND S.W. PACIFIC

      FARES ONLY APPLY ON ANY AA FLIGHT.
          NOTE -
          EXCEPT THAT INTERLINE TRANSPORTATION IS
          PERMITTED WHERE SPECIFIED ON THE ROUTING.
    TRANSFERS:
    BETWEEN THE UNITED STATES AND S.W. PACIFIC

      4 TRANSFERS PERMITTED - 2 IN EACH DIRECTION
         ONLINE EXCLUDING THE PUBLISHING CARRIER/INTERLINE.
      AND - UNLIMITED TRANSFERS PERMITTED
         ONLINE ON THE PUBLISHING CARRIER.

14. RESERVATIONS/TICKETING:
    ADVANCE RES/TICKETING:
    BETWEEN THE UNITED STATES AND S.W. PACIFIC FOR QLXAP TYPE
    FARES

      ORIGINATING S.W. PACIFIC -
      RESERVATIONS AND TICKETING ARE REQUIRED AT LEAST 7 DAYS
      BEFORE DEPARTURE.
      NO STANDBYS PERMITTED.
          NOTE -
          WAITLIST SEGMENTS MAY NOT BE RETAINED BEYOND THE
          RESERVATION DEADLINE.

      ORIGINATING THE UNITED STATES -
      RESERVATIONS AND TICKETING ARE REQUIRED AT LEAST 14 DAYS
      BEFORE DEPARTURE.
      NO STANDBYS PERMITTED.
          NOTE -
          WAITLIST SEGMENTS MAY NOT BE RETAINED BEYOND THE
          RESERVATION DEADLINE.
    SALES RESTRICTIONS:
    BETWEEN THE UNITED STATES AND S.W. PACIFIC
```

```
17. TICKET ENTRIES:
    BETWEEN THE UNITED STATES AND S.W. PACIFIC

    THE ORIGINAL TICKET MUST BE ANNOTATED - VLD ON AA ONLY -
    IN THE ENDORSEMENT BOX
    OR - THE REISSUED TICKET MUST BE ANNOTATED - APEX/NONREF
       USD - IN THE ENDORSEMENT BOX.
        NOTE -
         //APPLICABLE NON-REFUNDABLE AMOUNT//
```

From/To	Carrier	Flight/Cl	Date	Departure	Arrival

(Courtesy of Venice Simplon Orient Express, Ltd.)

Chapter 6

The New Europe

The European Union
    Goals of the European Union
    Financial Concerns of the European Union
Travel and Tourism
    Travel Procedures
    Travel Competition
    Rail Travel
Major Destinations
    The Mediterranean
    The Riviera
    Morocco
    Greece
    Turkey
    Israel
Off the Beaten Path
    The Orient Express
Historical Waterways
    The Rhine
    The Danube
Exploring Northern Europe

OBJECTIVES

After completing Chapter 6, you should be able to:

- Describe and evaluate the development of the European Union
- Discuss the impact of the European Union
- Identify and describe the various European rail passes
- Identify and describe the variety of destinations and itineraries in Europe

The yearning for a unified Europe rose from the ruins of World War II. Unification efforts started in 1952 when a European Coal and Steel Community organized to rebuild Europe's shattered industry and devastated economy. In 1957, six Western European countries, Belgium, France, Germany, Italy, the Netherlands, and Luxembourg, signed the Treaty of Rome and thus established the **European Economic Community (EEC).** The EEC is a political organization that is based on the idea of free trade within Western Europe. After its inception, the EEC expanded, and six other nations, Denmark (1973), Great Britain (1973), Ireland (1973), Greece (1981), Portugal (1986), and Spain (1986), also joined.

Since World War II, Europe has experienced its longest period of peace. There may be a direct correlation with the Treaty of Rome, which, in addition to free trade, also calls for peace and prosperity for its member nations. Funded by the EEC, Greece, for example, has benefited from improved infrastructure, a healthier environment, and a higher quality of goods.

The European Union

Many European nations share a strong cultural heritage, which may explain why the twelve EEC nations quickly learned that working together meant increasing their collective ability to compete with the North American and Japanese economies. In December 1991, EEC leaders met in Maastricht, Netherlands and agreed to European sovereignty by signing the Treaty on European Union. The **Maastricht Treaty,** as it is called, proposed for its members common security, common foreign policy, common defense policy, common immigration policy, and a monetary union. Hence, on January 1, 1993, the twelve EEC-member nations formed a united Europe called the **European Union (EU).** Austria, Finland, and Sweden joined the EU on November 13, 1994 (see Figure 6–1). Norway declined EU membership on November 30, 1994.

Brussels is at the center of the fifteen EU nations and therefore is considered the "capital" of the new Europe. The Berlin Wall crumbled in October 1989, signifying the end of Eastern European Communism. Since the fall of Russian Communism, Western and Eastern Europe have merged into one Europe. Several years ago, Switzerland, the Czech Republic, Cyprus, Hungary, Malta, Poland, Slovakia, and Turkey filed applications for EU membership.

The move toward Western European unity began long before 1993. The Channel Tunnel, completed in 1995, for example, was built to connect Great Britain with continental Europe. A similarly large project was begun in 1994 in Scandinavia. A bridge/tunnel will connect Denmark with Sweden by the year 2000.

GOALS OF THE EUROPEAN UNION

The EU's main goal is to break down political and economic barriers and create one inner market where labor, business, goods, and monetary funds move freely between nations. Since the EU formed in 1993, goods and monetary funds have flowed freely between member nations. Another EU goal is to establish one common European language, which has been the dream of many Europeans for centuries.

One of the primary goals of the Maastricht Treaty is to gradually create an **Economic and Monetary Union (EMU).** The main objective of the EMU is to create one European currency that is one of the world's most stable and strong. This currency, which will be called the **European Currency Unit (ECU),** will be a mixture of European currencies. It will replace the national currencies of the fifteen EU members. The EMU and the ECU are goals set for the year 2000.

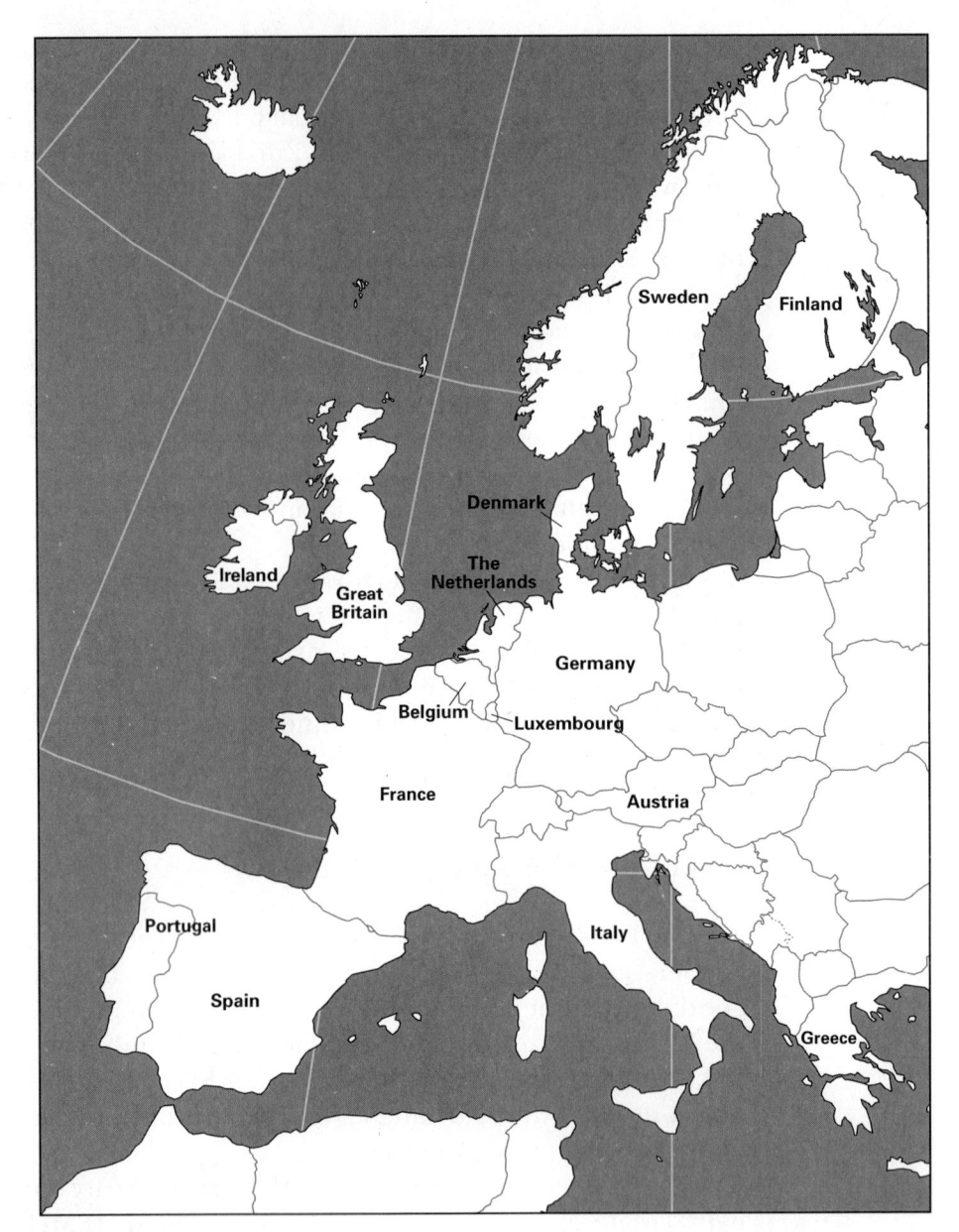

FIGURE 6–1

European Union members

FINANCIAL CONCERNS OF THE EUROPEAN UNION

Transitioning to the EMU will profoundly impact hundreds of millions of European lives in all aspects. Europeans will face unfamiliar payment methods, such as **banknotes,** checks, credit cards, and money orders. The ECU will also have different denominations than the current national currencies, and national exchange rates will disappear. Bonds, investment funds, taxes, insurance policies, government debts, and investors must all switch to the ECU. Marketing materials, like cruise brochures in the travel industry, will have to be altered. Because many promotional pieces are printed 12 months in advance, they may have to show dual pricing.

The EU member nations are still discussing the denomination of the ECU and how the banknotes and coins will look. At printing time, the majority favored ECU 2 as the highest valued coin. The denomination of banknotes would be ECU 5, 10, 20, 50, 100, and 500. Two kinds of banknotes were being considered. Either the banknotes will look the same throughout the EMU, or they will carry nation-specific features or logos.

The EMU could prove advantageous to exchange rates. Companies will be able to do business across borders without the expense and hassle of exchange rates. Foreign exchange transaction fees will vanish between EU member nations, benefiting all citizens. Imagine a traveler on a trip to four EU member nations under the current system. He leaves Germany with 500 marks. At the border of France, he changes the 500 marks for French currency. At an exchange rate of 3.312, he receives 1,656 francs. When he enters Italy, he exchanges the 1,656 francs for Italian lira. With an exchange rate of 278.14, he receive 460,600 lire. While driving through Austria, he exchanges the 460,600 lire for Austrian schillings. At an exchange rate of 0.0071, he receives 3,271 schillings. When the traveler returns to Germany, he exchanges the schillings for German marks. At an exchange rate of 0.124, he receives 405 marks, 95 marks fewer than he started with and he purchased nothing. With one uniform ECU exchange rate, citizens will not experience such a loss.

The experienced traveler to Europe will notice many changes. One change is that, since 1993, international borders within EU member nations have effectively disappeared. Another change is that travelers and goods are only cleared at the first port of entry. Once travelers are inside the EU, they can circulate freely.

Travel and Tourism

The EU has made traveling in Europe much easier. Traveling within the EU is now treated almost as a domestic market.

TRAVEL PROCEDURES

All baggage that is bound for a destination within the EU or that is leaving the EU is given baggage claim tags edged in green. These tags mean the baggage does not require a customs control check. Thus, the baggage will be transferred automatically at a connecting EU city.

There are no country-to-country customs and immigration procedures when traveling within the EU. Travelers go through passport and immigration control only once at the first EU-member-nation port of entry. Travelers also go through customs control only once when departing the EU.

Seven EU nations, Belgium, France, Germany, Luxembourg, the Netherlands, Portugal, and Spain, have combined to form a visa-free zone, which means travelers from 120 countries, including the United States, must go through immigration only once when entering one of these countries. These seven nations also have one standard visa, which means there is only one visa/immigration control check.

TRAVEL COMPETITION

For the first time in European history, airfares are beginning to become more competitive. For example, Lufthansa started a fare war December 29, 1992, and cut its fares nearly in half for certain destinations within the EU. Since January 1993, government control of airfares for routes within the EU has relaxed slightly. For the most part, carriers can set any intra-European fares they like.

Fares can go low, but not too low, and some routes may become more competitive, but not too competitive. The New Europe is competitive but very cautious because the European nations remember the results of United States deregulation. Some of the effects of deregulation that make Europeans wary include an unstable and erratic airfare structure and airlines going into bankruptcy. Many airlines are looking to expand and/or merge. As a result, many small countries, like Ireland, are now wondering if there is room on the market for their national carriers. Other EU countries are negotiating airline agreements jointly. Joint airline agreements mean governments give up control. Scandinavian Airlines System (SAS) has combined its network with that of Lufthansa, Germany, and together the two may become one of the largest airlines in the world. Lufthansa has already joined with United Airlines (UA), Thai Airways (TG), and Varig (RG), but the Scandinavian merger might be challenged because Scandinavian Airlines is partly owned by Norway, a non-EU member. Frankfurt (FRA) and Munich (MUC) are now serving as hubs for trans-Atlantic and intra-European flights. Copenhagen (CPH) is the hub for flights to Asia, to/from Scandinavia and to/from the Baltic countries.

The reorganization in Europe is gradual. The EU is attempting to establish that no single country can monopolize EU air routes beginning April 1997. Until then, carriers can exercise the seventh Freedom of the Air, the freedom to fly between two countries other than the country of origin without making a stopover in the country of origin. This freedom among EU airlines may toughen competition. The EU air carriers seem to be moving from government control and ownership to privatization and open markets.

A true "open-skies" policy in EU is a sensitive issue. Open skies mean some sense of nationality will be lost, because EU airlines will be treated as citizens of Europe rather than citizens of their home countries.

RAIL TRAVEL

Traveling by rail in Europe can be quite eventful. Train travel is a journey through diverse histories and a multitude of cultures. Trains allow the independent traveler a flexible and relaxed vacation. Among Europeans, rail travel is a way of life, whether it is commuting to school or work, or visiting friends or family. Often, the train is the first choice of transportation for Europeans taking vacations. To join Europeans in celebrating this practical way of traveling, a rail traveler must bring an adventurous spirit and the highest patience.

First, a rail ticket does not guarantee a seat on a train unless the passenger has made advance seating arrangements. The trains are often very crowded, particularly on the most traveled routes. In fact, trains can be so crowded that standing room only space is available, even on overnight trains. Occasionally, however, trains prove more efficient than airplanes. The rail passenger will not experience airport hassles like delays because trains are extremely punctual. On some routes, for example, between Rome and Florence and between Munich and Salzburg, trains travel faster than airplanes. Many European train stations are conveniently located in the centers of towns, near business districts, or near tourist attractions. The airports in London, Paris, Rome, Amsterdam, Brussels, Frankfurt, Geneva, Vienna, and Zurich are directly linked to rail networks.

Deciphering the timetable at a European train station may take some effort. Many train stations display their departure times on yellow posters and their arrival times on white posters. All times are listed in the 24-hour clock system. Next to each time is the number of the train and the platform number. Boarding the right train as well as finding the correct car on the train is important. Many trains split en route. A traveler may discover the car he thought was headed for Paris is headed instead for Rome.

EUROPEAN RAIL PASSES. The best way to explore Europe is to purchase a rail pass. A **rail pass** is the most flexible and economical way of traveling. The European rail network has over 10,000 miles of tracks. Tucked-away regions can be reached with a slower scenic train; the highlights of Europe can be reached via a high-speed train.

There are eleven different rail passes. All types of rail passes permit unlimited travel within participating countries for the number of days purchased. *Unlimited* means the traveler chooses on which days and how many days to travel. A rail travel day is from midnight to midnight. Deciding which pass is best involves determining which countries are to be visited and for how long. The two most frequently used passes are the Eurailpass and the Europass.

The Eurailpass: The **Eurailpass** is the most popular rail pass. As Figure 6–2 shows, Eurailpass offers unlimited rail travel within seventeen countries. It is important for travelers to ensure their journeys do not take them through **nonparticipating countries.** Travelers who pass through nonparticipating countries are assessed extra fees. People under age 26 can travel on a special youth pass. Children aged 4 to 11 on the first day of travel pay half the adult fare. Children up to 3 years old travel free.

Eurailpass comes with bonuses such as free bus, ferry, and steamer transportation. This includes some Rhine and Danube river journeys and trips on Swiss Lake steamers. Ferries connecting Sweden with Finland, Ireland with France, Greece with Italy, Germany with Denmark, and Denmark with Sweden are included in the cost of the pass.

The Europass: The **Europass** offers unlimited rail travel within five of the seventeen Eurailpass countries: France, Germany, Italy, Spain, and Switzerland. The Europass offers three options: (1) three countries in 5 to 7 days, (2) four countries in 3 to 10 days, or (3) five countries in 11 to 15 days. Young people under age 26 can travel on a special youth pass. Children aged 4 to 11 years on the first day of travel pay half the adult fare. Children up to three years old travel free. All Europasses are valid for 2 months. The Europass comes with the same travel bonuses as the Eurailpass.

Note from Figure 6–2 that Great Britain does not participate in the Eurailpass or Europass programs. A separate ticket or **BritRail Pass** must be purchased if a person is traveling by rail to, from, or within Great Britain. The ferry link between France and Great Britain costs extra as well.

If a person wants unlimited and extensive travel within one country or a smaller area, a great variety of other rail passes, such as the BritFrance Railpass, the European East Pass, and Spain's Flexipass, abound.

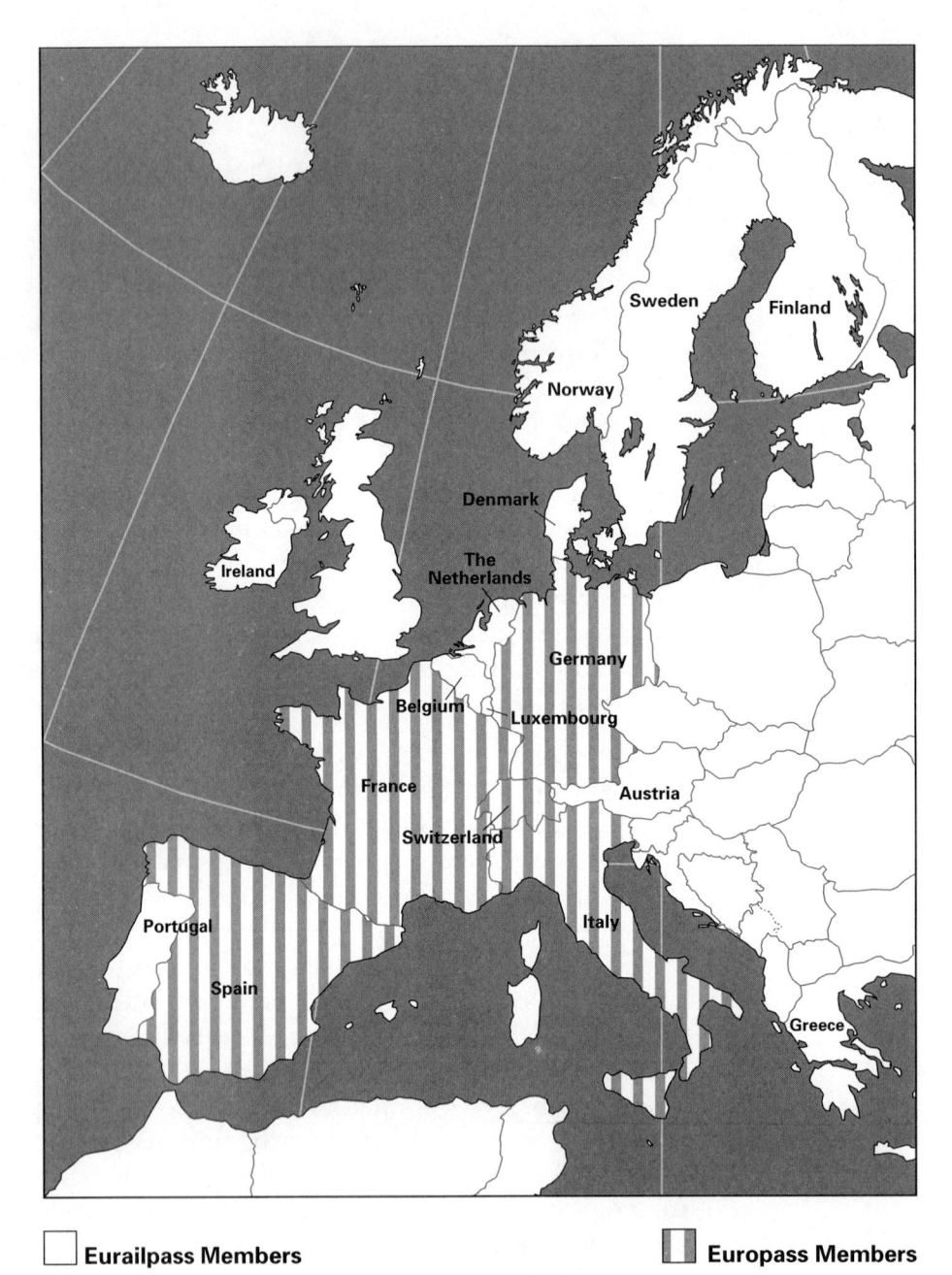

Eurailpass Members

Europass Members

FIGURE 6–2

Eurailpass and Europass members

Welcome aboard! Thanks for stopping by our World Wide Web Site, Europe by Eurail! We've put together a variety of resources to help make planning and taking your trip much more convenient and enjoyable. While you're here, take a look at who we are and see what's new!

Europe by Eurail and Britain by BritRail

Not sure what to expect when you get to Europe or how to travel with a rail pass? Look no further than the Ferguson guidebooks, *Europe by Eurail* and *Britain by BritRail.* These popular guidebooks feature the Base-City/Day-Excursion method of seeing Europe at your own pace.

Cafe Elysees Now Serving

Looking for advice on traveling Europe or want to share your rail-travel experiences? Stop by our on-line conference, Cafe Elysees, where topics range from choosing the right pass to first-hand advice from the authors of *Europe by Eurail* and *Britain by BritRail.*

Planning Your Eurail Trip

You need to start planning your trip, but where do you begin? We have a number of articles to get you started . . . from budgeting and getting there to money and packing tips. Even search for point-to-point tickets or download a free copy of *EuroData,* a European trip planning program.

European and British Rail Passes

A variety of rail passes are available . . . from the 17-country Eurailpass to the design your own Europass valid for travel in the five most visited countries of Europe. Those traveling to Britain will find a BritRail Pass or country pass fits their needs.

Traveling Europe by Eurail

"Travel Europe by train" has long been the slogan of the European railways. Take a look at what to expect when using your pass and other important tidbits to help you get more out of your rail pass and your trip.

Eurostar Service via the Channel Tunnel

Travel in high-speed comfort on the Eurostar train linking London with Paris or Brussels in just 3 hours. Order a Eurailpass, Europass, or BritRail Pass and take advantage of discounted Eurostar tickets.

THE CHANNEL TUNNEL. The **Channel Tunnel,** sometimes called the Eurotunnel or the "Chunnel," is a 31-mile long rail tunnel under the English Channel connecting France with Great Britain. It is the second longest rail tunnel in the world. Only the tunnel under the Strait of Tsugaru in Japan is longer.

The Channel Tunnel rail service, the Eurostar, competes directly with the airlines. Flight time from London to Paris and from London to Brussels is 55 minutes. Additional time is needed to travel to and from each airport and to and from downtown in each city.

The **Eurostar** is a high-speed passenger train service operating between London, Paris, and Brussels (see Figure 6–3). The Eurostar travels between London's downtown Waterloo station and Paris' downtown Gar du Nord in just 3 hours on each of its fifteen daily round-trip departures. It takes the Eurostar 3½ hours to travel from London's Waterloo station to Brussels' downtown Midi on each of its six daily departures. Reservations are required for all depatures. The Channel crossing takes 20 minutes. The Eurostar travels 186 miles per hour through France. While in the tunnel and Great Britain, the Eurostar travels at 100 miles per hour.

The Eurostar is jointly owned and operated by the French National Railroads (50 percent), BritRail (35 percent), and Belgium National Railroads (15 percent). Travelers from North America holding French Rail passes can receive a 33 percent discount. A child under 12 travels at a 50 percent discount, and a child under 4 travels free. The Eurostar Channel crossing is not included in any of the rail passes.

LE SHUTTLE. Le Shuttle is a ½-hour train service between Calais, France and Folkeston, Great Britain, that transports vehicles and their passengers through the Channel Tunnel (see Figure 6–3). Without purchasing a ticket in advance, a traveler can transport a bicycle, car, van, truck, motorcoach, or motorcycle on Le Shuttle in Folkeston or Calais. During the crossing, the traveler stays with the vehicle. No foot passengers are allowed. Each Le Shuttle train can carry 180 vehicles and departs every 20 minutes.

Hertz® offers a Le Swap program to Le Shuttle customers, which allows a Hertz rental-car customer to swap cars in Calais

FIGURE 6–3

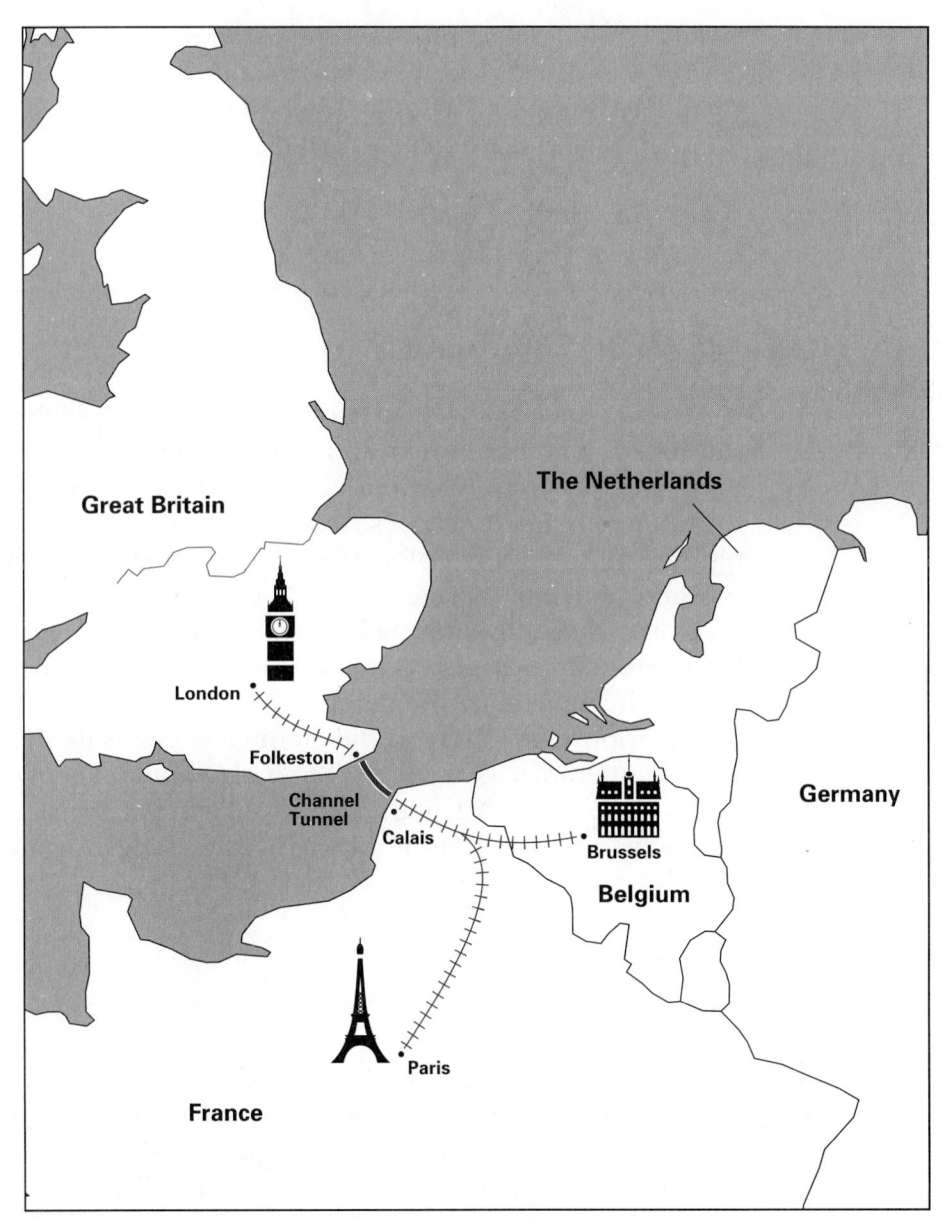

The Channel Tunnel

or Folkeston. For example, a traveler can rent a left-hand-drive Hertz car in Paris, drive to Calais, take Le Shuttle through the Channel Tunnel to Folkeston, trade the left-hand-drive vehicle for a right-hand-drive vehicle, and drive to London.

Major Destinations

THE MEDITERRANEAN

The Mediterranean area, which is blessed with 300 days of sunshine a year, has lured travelers from all over the world for thousands of years. Nowhere else exist such beguiling waterfronts and intimate beaches, mixed with one of the greatest histories in antiquity. Colorful landscapes bathed in blinding sunshine and tiny villages perched on mountain tops blend with Grecian philosophy, Italian art, Spanish architecture, and fashionable French resorts. Many find the sparkling beauty of the Mediterranean mesmerizing.

An important feature of the Mediterranean is its consistent water temperature. The narrow Strait of Gibraltar keeps out the colder water of the Atlantic Ocean (see Figure 6–4). As a result, the water near the bottom of the Mediterranean Sea is only slightly cooler than that on the surface.

THE RIVIERA

The Riviera, which stretches from Toulon, France to La Spezia, northwestern Italy (see Figure 6–4), is one of Europe's most visited bathing places. Its mild climate, fine beaches, and outstanding scenic beauty lure millions of visitors each year. Small fishing ports and colorful towns are scattered all along the Riviera.

In France and Italy, the Alps extend brilliantly all the way to the shoreline, creating thousands of small coves, ranging from good sand beaches to rocky inlets. The Alps act as a natural barrier, keeping the mild climate in the south from mixing with the cold climate of the north.

Chapter 6 The New Europe **163**

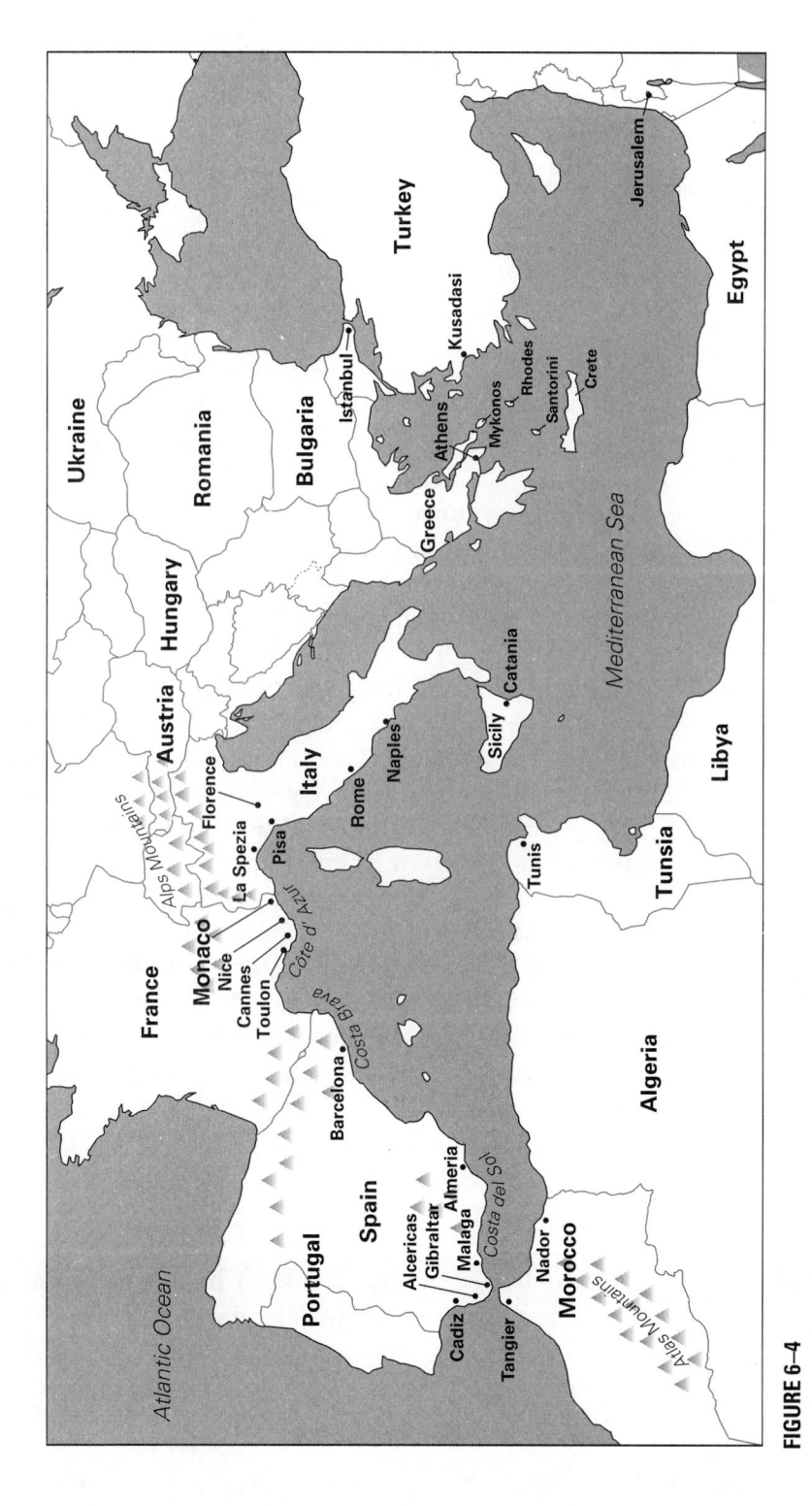

FIGURE 6–4
The Mediterranean

THE FRENCH RIVIERA. Lined with tropical gardens, the fashionable French Riviera, or Cote d'Azur, extends from Cannes to Monaco. The dazzling and sophisticated cities of Cote d'Azur are built into the coast's steep hillsides. With its azure blue waters, mountains, lakes, rivers, and gorges, the Cote d'Azur is often described as one of the most beautiful resort areas in the world. Excellent museums and historic structures add to the immense popularity of this exceptional international playground.

With its famous seaside Promenade des Anglais filled with elegant boutiques, sidewalk cafes, and bistros, Nice is the queen of the French Riviera. This broad, tree-lined avenue overlooks beautiful beaches. Although its beaches are rocky, the natural beauty of the surroundings have made Nice one of the most popular tourist resorts in Europe. Every month, Nice boasts a maximum daytime temperature of over 70 degrees.

From the Royal Palace perched atop a cliff, the elegant and tiny sovereign principality of Monaco boasts a magnificent view of its picturesque port and beaches. The Royal Palace of the Prince, which dates back to the sixteenth century, has a nineteenth-century cathedral. Changing of the guards occur daily at the Palace at 11:55 A.M. The Prince's Palace Square offers museums, restaurants, and boutiques. Monaco is chiefly famous for the casino in Monte Carlo.

THE ITALIAN RIVIERA. Italy's rocky coastline has only a few natural habors. La Spezia is the most beautiful. Many of the beaches along the 200-mile Italian Riviera are beautifully located at the bottom of cliffs or steep green hills. Among the most attractive Italian resorts are Portofino and San Remo.

The Romanesque cathedral of Pisa, built between 1063 and 1092, with its freestanding Leaning Tower (completed about 1350), is the landmark of Pisa. Presently the circular tower is about 181 feet high and leans about 17 feet from perpendicular. Over the last 100 years, the tower has tilted 1 foot. It has be estimated the tower could crash in about 50 years.

From Pisa there is easy and quick access to Florence, which houses the world's finest collection of fifteenth-century Renaissance art and the architecture of Leonardo da Vinci and Michelangelo. Much of Italian art is associated with this beautiful city, which is situated in a natural bowl between hills. Pitti Palace contains many splendid museums. The River Arno runs through Florence, adding to the city's allure. The most famous bridge across the river is the Ponte Vecchio. The dome of the Cathedral of Santa Maria dominates the city's skyline.

In the ancient Colosseum stadium at the "Theatre of Death" in Rome, it is easy to imagine being thrown to the lions. The Arch of Constantine can be seen at the Colosseum, which dates back to A.D. 80. The Trevi Fountain, completed in 1762, and the Spanish Steps are lively areas and among the most popular evening gathering places for young people who want to eat, talk, sing, and play music.

The heart of Catholicism, Vatican City, is located in the center of Rome. The sight best known to visitors is the architectural wonder of St. Peter's Basilica, famed for its Michelangelo-designed dome. The superb St. Peter's Square was created between 1656 and 1667 by Giovanni Bernini. In the center of the Square is an Egyptian obelisk, and to one side is the Pope's residence, the Vatican Palace. Here the most famous feature is the Sistine Chapel, famed for its Michelangelo-painted ceiling.

The castle-dotted hills above Naples offer a sweeping view of the city. Naples is the gateway to the ruins of Pompeii, once covered by the lava of the still-active volcano, Mt. Vesuvius, in A.D. 79. Travelers can drive within a few hundred yards of the summit. Energetic visitors climb to the rim, where a bedazzling view of the steam-filled crater and a startling view over the Bay of Naples await them.

Founded in the eighth century B.C., Catania sits near the foot of Europe's largest active volcano, Mt. Etna, on the island of Sicily. Damaged extensively by earthquakes and lava, the city has been almost entirely rebuilt in eighteenth-century style. Its fine beaches attract many tourists.

THE SPANISH RIVIERA. The Gold Coast of Spain, or Costa del Sol, extends over 100 miles along the southern coast from Algericas east to Almeria. Costa del Sol is one of the most popular tourist areas in southern Europe and one of the world's most visited because of its mild winters and fine beaches.

The most popular resort in Costa del Sol is Malaga. Backed by hills, Malaga is in the center of Costa del Sol and has an 85-mile-long beach. The River Guadalmedina separates the old part of town from the modern. In the hills above the city is a sixteenth-century cathedral, which is connected to a ninth-century Moorish citadel by a double wall. Medieval towns and spectacular caves make Malaga a very popular vacation spot. Another famous resort town in Spain is Nerja, which is perched high above the sea with fabulous views of the Mediterranean. Nerja has earned its nickname "Balcony of Europe."

The 40-mile stretch of Costa Brava northeast of Barcelona is the second most popular and intensely developed resort area in Spain. Costa Brava attracts mostly tourists seeking the sea, sun, and fun, because cultural experiences are few.

Barcelona has been the cultural and artistic center of Spain since the Middle Ages. Spain's oldest city has a museum with art treasures like Picasso's early sketches. The old-city section also houses the fourteenth-century Cathedral of Santa Aulalia and a remarkable unfinished church of the Sacred Family. A cable-car ride up Montjuich to a seventeenth-century castle reveals gorgeous views of the city and sea. The site of the ancient city walls, the Ramblas, is now a popular area.

Other popular Costa Brava resorts include Tossa de Mar, which tries to retain a small-town flavor. Cadaques is an enchanting fishing village nestled on the coast. Ampurias boasts impressive Greco-Roman remains.

Gibraltar is an eighteenth-century British colony town that overlooks the Strait of Gibraltar. Gibraltar is situated on a rocky and mountainous point that juts southward into the Mediterranean Sea. A spectacular activity in this town is a cable-car ride to the top of the Rock of Gibraltar. The Rock is a natural fortress that contains miles of tunnels and many caves. The Mediterranean Steps Walk from O'Hara's Battery, the highest point in Gibraltar, snakes down the cliff and ends at the western side of the Rock. Another popular tourist activity is to walk around the almost-complete city walls built by the Moors.

A drive north from Algericas to Cadiz offers spectacular views of the Strait of Gibraltar, Morocco, and the Atlas Mountains. Cadiz is one of the oldest towns in Spain, dating back to around 1000 B.C. Ferries run from Algericas to Tangier in Morocco.

MOROCCO

Tangier is an interesting gateway to Morocco. The twelve nations that have occupied Tangier over the centuries have clearly left their marks, not only in the three-language street signs but in the colorful and active market, Grand Socco.

Morocco is mainly mountainous. The Atlas Mountains run through the country. The beaches along the country's Mediterranean Shore between Tangier and Nador lie sheltered in creeks and bays.

GREECE

Nineteen percent of Greece, and evidence of ancient Greek civilization, is scattered throughout the many Greek Isles. Ancient civilization is also quite evident in Athens on the mainland. This ancient city is built around the flat-topped hill of the Acropolis, where four ancient structures still stand. The most famous structure is the fabled 2,400-year-old Parthenon. Built completely of white marble in approximately 450 B.C., the Parthenon still dominates the Athenian skyline and offers a splendid view of Athens below. The old town, Plaka, provides an interesting atmosphere of *tavernas,* or Greek eating houses, shops, and narrow winding streets. Although Greece is no longer a monarchy, the Efzones, or guards, still protect the Royal Palace. The guards' uniforms resemble the Greek national costume with their white tunics and raised-toe slippers decorated with bobbles.

The Greek island of Crete was home to Europe's earliest civilizations and is rich with historical remains. Venetian castles, Byzantine churches, and Minoan palaces lie scattered alongside modern beach resorts. Crete has an interesting walled city called Heraklion. Within these walls is King Minos' palace at Knossos. Nearby, a marketplace blends with the castles. Crete is also rich in scenic beauty because the island is mostly mountainous. The highest point on the island is Mt. Ida at 8,058 feet.

Brilliant white houses with flat roofs lining narrow, winding alleys characterize the island of Mykonos. Quaint, small boutiques and many windmills are scattered throughout the island. On Santorini, a neighboring island, spectacular volcanic cliffs have created black-sand beaches. A donkey ride up the zigzag path to the tiny cliff-top village of Thera reveals a splendid view.

Rhodes is one of the most popular islands in the Mediterranean. With its well-developed beach resorts, Rhodes offers a diverse nightlife, top-class hotels, and excellent shopping. Sports enthusiasts are attracted to the island's varied sports activities, such as fishing and golf. Rhodes is also an island of impressive ruins, including the Temple of Apollo. Many Greek legends came from this island.

TURKEY

A side excursion from Greece to Kusadasi, Turkey displays the Temple of Artemis, one of the original seven wonders of the world. Kusadasi is also an attractive beach resort. Within easy reach of Kusadasi to the northeast is Ephesus. The Roman ruins of Ephesus are magnificant, with their thermal baths and amphitheathers. Ephesus is the city most completely excavated. Recent excavations have revealed temple ruins from around 560 B.C.

Farther up the Turkish coast lies the former Constantinople, the capital of the Roman and Byzantine Empires for 700 years and the capital of the Ottoman Empire for over 450 years. No longer the acting capital, Constantinople has been renamed Istanbul. Its impressive mosques, palaces, and museums display exotic architecture from its many occupiers. Straddling the continents of Asia and Europe, Istanbul is a colorful city with an overwhelming blend of cultures and an exhilarating atmosphere. Among Istanbul's attractions is the Blue Mosque, the only mosque in the world with eight praying towers. In addition, the Topkapi palace of the Ottoman sultans magnificently overlooks the sea.

ISRAEL

For many tourists, Israel is the Holy Land. Religious tours are abundant. In Jerusalem, the fascinating Old City is surrounded by an impressive town wall built in approximately 1542. The Old City can only be entered through one of its eight gates, the most famous of which is the Damascus Gate. Inside the Old City is the Wailing Wall and via Dolorosa—Christ walked to the crucifixion. Religious tours to Mount Zion and Bethlehem are available.

Off the Beaten Path

A wide range of ferries, steamers, ships, and trains travel the European waterways and countrysides. There are plenty of opportunities to discover the delights and splendors of Europe from the luxury trains in the south to the hidden fjords in the "Land of the Midnight Sun," the portion of the Scandinavian countries located north of the Arctic Circle.

THE ORIENT EXPRESS

Unity in Europe began in 1883 when the Orient Express rail service began transporting both mail and passengers. It was the fastest and most luxurious route between Europe and the East. It ensured an exotic journey for those who could afford it. In fact, the train was so elegant it was quickly nicknamed the "King of Trains and the Train of Kings." The wealth and power of Orient Express passengers symbolized an unreachable way of life for most people. Huge crowds would gather to glimpse the sleek cars and their elite travelers.

The Orient Express also became a popular mode of transportation for secret agents, who nicknamed the Orient Express the "Spies' Train." The train was a convenient and easy way to access many different nations. It provided rapid escape across borders as well. The train was, therefore, a magnet for burglars, jewelry thieves, and international smugglers. The Orient Express is legendary as the milieu of murder and mystery. During its heyday between the world wars, no other means of public transportation carried as many travelers involved in massive plots.

During World War II, the cars of the Orient Express scattered all over Europe. Many disappeared due to bombings or sabotage, and many were used as military barracks and headquarters. After the war only a few cars could be located and refurbished as beautiful reminders of a great era. The Orient Express started service again between London and Venice in the early 1980s.

Today, The Orient Express has once again become the prime example of grace, elegance, and luxury. In fact, the train's popularity is astounding. Its passenger list is impressive. Many noble passengers such as royal families, rajahs, barons, dukes, and duchesses have enjoyed pampered rides. Stars of the theater and cinema, circus performers, and entire ballet companies have made the Orient Express their first choice of transportation. Even classical violinists and pianists use the train to travel between concerts. The real attraction of the Orient Express is the train itself. Its French and Italian staff pamper every passenger, and everything is done in style. Passengers often enter the spirit of this magical era by dressing in 1930s style.

As Figure 6–5 shows, the original route of the Orient Express took 56 ½ hours. It departed every Monday from Paris for Stuttgart, Munich, Vienna, Budapest, and Bucharest to a ferry ride through the Black Sea to Istanbul. When tracks through Bulgaria were completed in 1889, the journey between Paris and Istanbul could be made without the ferry.

Completion of the 12-mile long Simplon Tunnel through the Swiss Alps in 1906 shortened the route of the Orient Express. The Simplon Tunnel begins in the Rhone Valley and climbs to 6,592 feet before descending to the Lake District in northern Italy. When the tunnel opened, the Simplon Orient Express began running from London or Paris to Milan, Venice, and Zagreb via the tunnel, and then it continued to Belgrade, Sofia, and Istanbul. Today, the route terminates in Venice.

The Simplon Orient Express offers many traveling options. Travel can begin and end at any of the main stopping points en route.

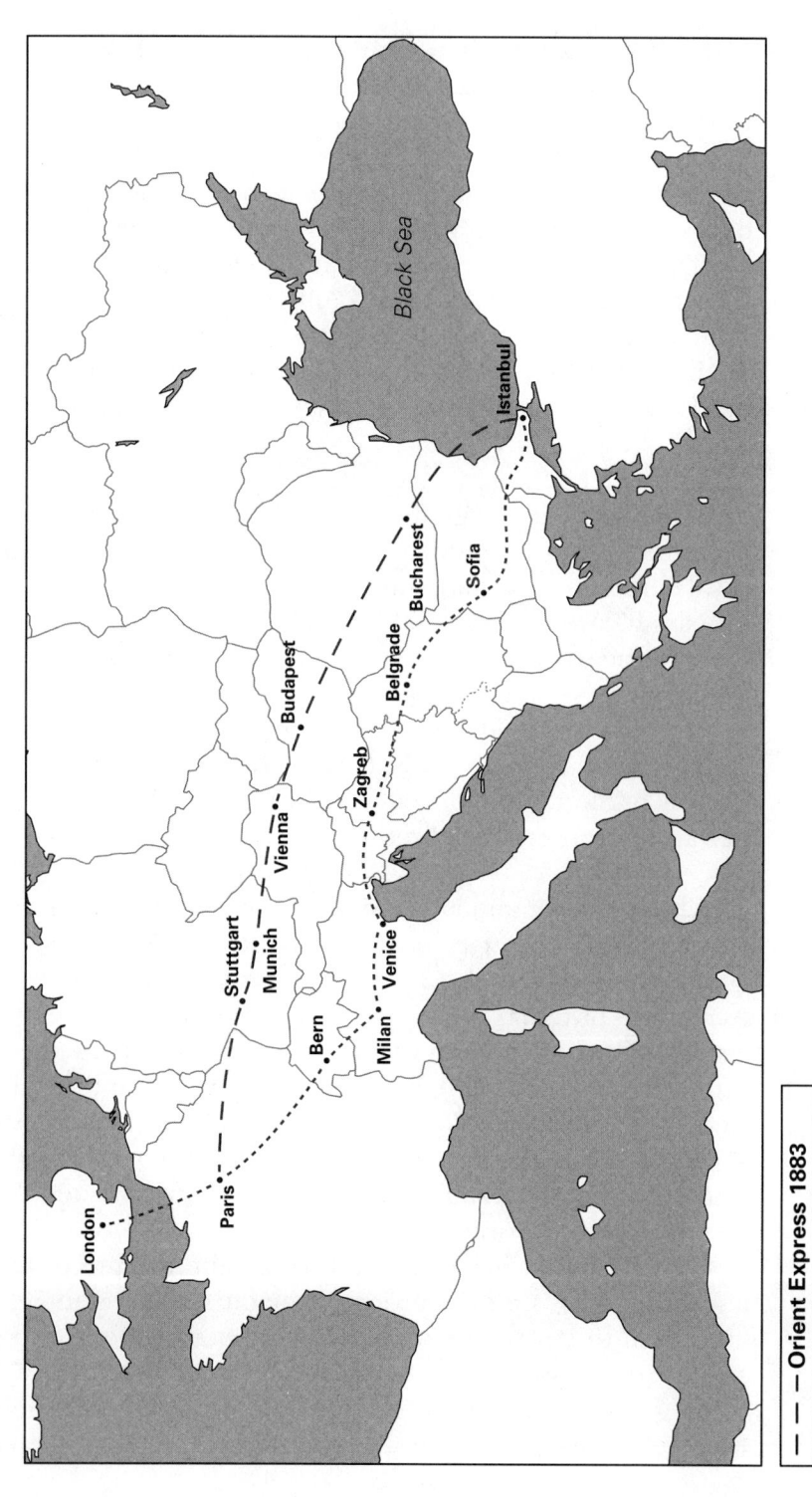

FIGURE 6–5
The Simplon Orient Express

LONDON. London's wealth of attractions is staggering. A traveler could easily spend 1 week in the city before boarding the Orient Express. Because London is on the Thames River, a cruise to Great Britain's largest castle, Windsor Castle, is a popular first-day activity. The castle has been the chief residence of the royal family since the twelfth century.

The Tower of London, built in the eleventh century, houses the crown jewels of the royal family. Nearby is Tower Bridge, built in the nineteenth century, one of the most famous bridges in the world. Big Ben is one of London's most famous landmarks. It is the clock of the Houses of Parliament. Big Ben began striking on July 1, 1859.

Henry III began constructing London's Westminster Abbey in 1245. Nearly all kings and queens of Great Britain have been crowned in Westminster Abbey. The Abbey is also where many royal family members are buried. Built from 1703 to 1705, Buckingham Palace is also a residence of the royal family, but it is not open to the public. Changing of the guards occurs at the Palace at 11:30 A.M.

If a traveler is seeking entertainment, lunch in a pub by Piccadilly Circus or Trafalgar Square is always fun. Both places are centers of attention, particularly during New Year's Eve festivities and post-soccer celebrations.

PARIS. Many famous Parisian tourist attractions are within short walking distances of the Seine River. The oldest bridge across the Seine is the Pont Neuf, which was built in 1578. Across the bridge is the Louvre. Once the royal palace of Francis I in about 1550, the Louvre is now one of the greatest museums in the world. The landmark of Paris is the Eiffel Tower, which was built in 1889. The Cathedral of Notre Dame is on a small island in the Seine. Built between 1200 and 1245, the Cathedral is a remarkable piece of architecture. Statues of many sizes elegantly decorate its portals.

Paris' Avenue des Champs Elysees, the avenue of fashion and sumptuous shops, is probably the most famous and elegant avenue in the world. People go to the Avenue to see and to be seen. Prospective models occasionally promenade the avenue, hoping to be "discovered." At one end of the 1¼-mile long avenue sits the Arc de Triomphe. Napoleon I began its construction in 1806, and turned it into the largest arch of its kind in the world.

MILAN. Before the Orient Express reaches Venice, travelers should make a stop in Milan. Construction of Milan's Gothic Cathedral began in 1386. It is now the second-largest church in the world. This cathedral boasts 3,159 statues and 135 pinnacles, the highest of which dominates the city skyline from a height of 354 feet.

VENICE. Venice, with its 160 canals, 400 bridges, singing gondoliers, and plentitude of art, attracts tourists. Venice is built on an island in a lagoon. There are over 100 hundred islands in the lagoon, and Venice sits on the largest, Rialto. The charm of Venice is that motor traffic is not allowed. The Grand Canal is 2 miles long and serves as the lagoon's main waterway. The famous Rialto Bridge, built between 1588 and 1592, crosses the Grand Canal in a single arch of 90 feet. The House of Gold, built between 1421 and 1440, is the most famous of the buildings on the Grand Canal.

Historical Waterways

Major European rivers have always been important waterways for both international trade and warfare.

THE RHINE

Even today the Rhine, which flows from southeast Switzerland in the Alps to the North Sea in the Netherlands, serves as a significant shipping route from the industrial cities of the Ruhr district to the North Sea. At the border with Liechtenstein, the Rhine forms Lake Constance, then drops in a 70-foot waterfall at Schaffhausen. The river continues north, creating a natural boundary between France and Germany, then flows to the Netherlands before draining into the North Sea (see Figure 6–6).

The 820-mile-long Rhine was developed by the Romans, who named it Rhenus. During the Middle Ages the Rhine was a shipping highway that separated the Romans from the Germans.

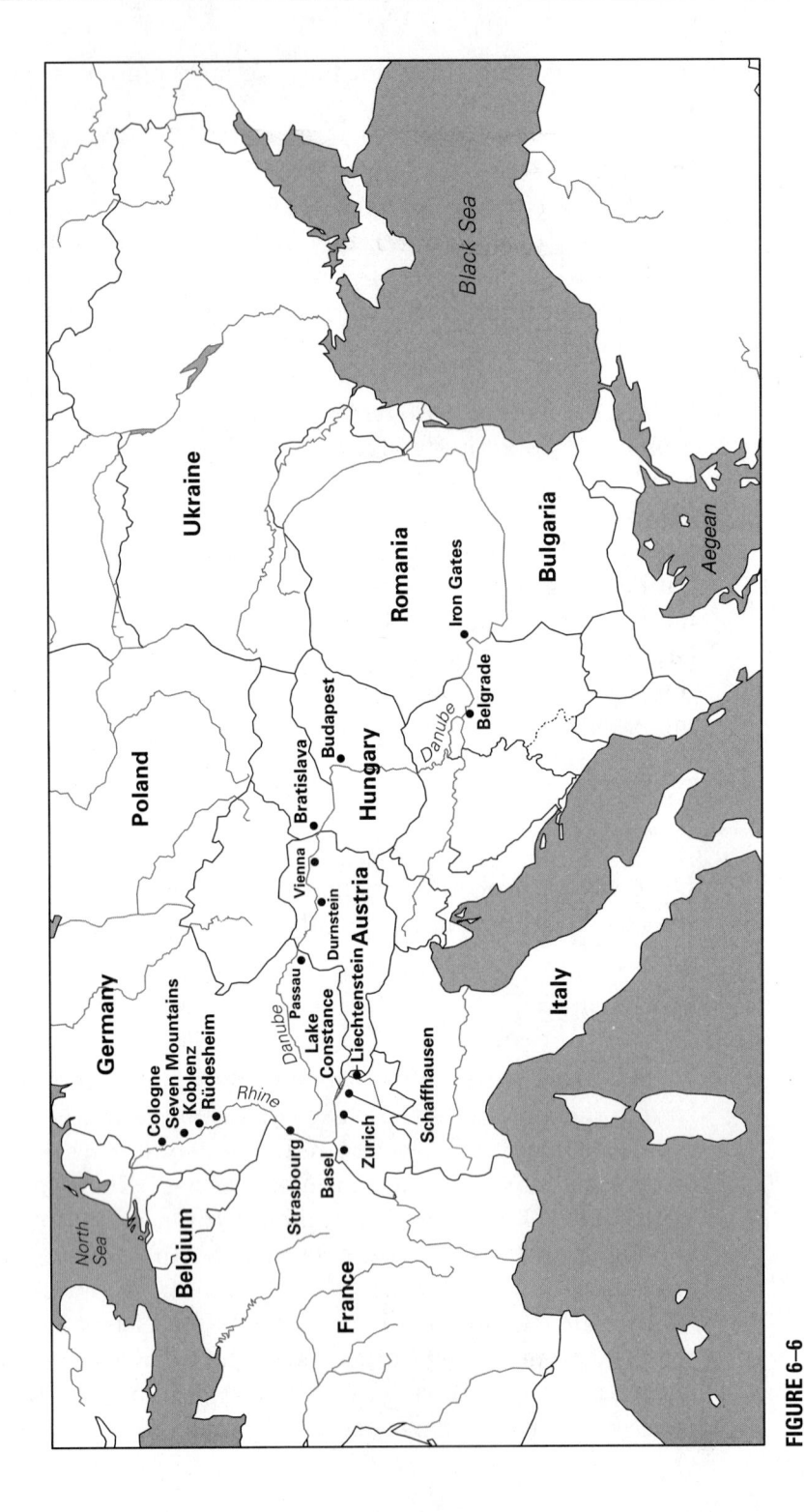

FIGURE 6–6
Historical waterways

Many cities along the Rhine were founded by the Romans. In addition to its practical uses, the Rhine is a major river for sight-seeing, and millions of tourists are attracted to its castle-covered banks.

The most popular portion of the Rhine is from the Alps foothill city of Basel, Switzerland to the 2,000-year-old culturally and artistically rich city of Cologne, Germany. This portion of the river boasts the spectacular scenery of the Swiss and Bavarian Alps and a glorious history, complete with gothic cathedrals and romantic castles. The German section of the Rhine is ancient, dotted with hundreds of primeval castles with moats, towers, and spires intact. These Middle-Age castles were built by powerful rulers as defensive structures, not romantic homes. A ruler increased his power and influence when he owned a castle in the Rhine valley because he could fully control the river traffic through his territory. During this time, there were thirty toll barriers between Mainz and Cologne. Therefore there are a large number of castles between Cologne and Mainz. Today, the 35-mile stretch between Koblenz and Rudesheim boasts more castles than any other river valley in the world. Some castles are in ruins, but many have been restored as museums with unique furniture, housewares, and art collections.

Many visitors begin a Rhine cruise southbound from Cologne. Cologne's landmark is the largest cathedral in Europe, the breathtaking and soaring Gothic Cathedral of St. Peter and St. Mary (from between the thirteenth and nineteenth centuries). In 1998, the city celebrated the "Gothic Year of Cologne" to mark the 750 year anniversary of the cathedral's foundation, laid in 1248. As river cruise travelers sail upstream and southbound on the Rhine, both river banks become increasingly steep. The banks rise to seven mountain peaks called the Siebengebirge, which are volcanic in origin. The "Seven Mountains," located halfway between Koblenz and Cologne, rise dramatically, and picturesque villages are scattered on their hillsides.

The Rhine becomes most romantic and spectacular in the gorge between Koblenz and Rudesheim. Here the river cuts through mountains in a narrow gorge and becomes less than 200 yards wide at times. There are no bridges on this section of the Rhine, which adds to its pristine flavor.

Koblenz is strategically situated where the Rhine and the Moselle rivers meet. Just past Koblenz on the Rhine, the thirteenth-century Stolzenfels castle appears perched high on a hill. The only fully preserved knight's castle on the Rhine, the Marksburg, appears soon after as the cruise progresses. Between vine-covered slopes on a bend in the Rhine is Boppard Castle, the "Pearl of the Rhine." Soon the castle Pfalz appears on a rock in the middle of the river. By the time the river cruisers reach Rudesheim, it is evident Germany's Rhineland is a large, old, and outdoor cultural museum.

THE DANUBE

River cruisers interested in adding music to their itineraries may continue to the Danube region (see Figure 6–6). Since 1937, the Rhine has been linked to the Danube River via the Main River and Ludwigs Canal. This part of Europe is particularly attractive because it is where the great Habsburg Empire, which flourished from the sixteenth to nineteenth centuries, clearly left its mark.

The Danube is the second longest river in Europe after the Volga River. The 1,800-mile-long river flows through seven countries. It originates in the Black Forest in southwestern Germany, continues through Austria, the Slovak Republic, Hungary, Yugoslavia, Bulgaria, and Romania, and empties into the Black Sea. Before barriers in Europe were broken, the Danube served as a dividing line between the West and the East. The Danube is navigable to Regensburg, Germany, 200 to 250 days of the year.

One of the most beautiful sections of the Danube is between Passau, Germany and Budapest, Hungary, because idyllic Roman, medieval, and renaissance ruins are scattered along the banks of the river. In Passau, which is where the Danube, Inn, and Ilz rivers meet, the most famous attraction is the Baroque Cathedral containing the world's largest church organ.

Continuing along the Danube, Durnstein, which is in the heart of Austria's Wachau Valley, is covered with terraced vineyards, castles, and little riverside towns on steep slopes. The ruined castle of Durnstein held Richard the Lionheart prisoner there in 1192. Vienna, Austria, which appears next along the Danube, was the center of the Habsburg Empire from 278 to 1918. The grand composers Beethoven, Haydn, Mozart,

Schubert, and Strauss lived in this city. With its zigzag roof pattern, the cathedral of St. Stephen (1137 to 1578) dominates Vienna's skyline.

Bratislava has grand views of the Danube and the bridge leading to Austria. After the Danube passes Bratislava, the new capital of the Slovak Republic, it flows through the middle of Budapest, Hungary. Budapest used to be two separate towns, Buda and Pest. Buda, the older and more historic section with cobblestone streets and medieval structures, is about two hills west of the Danube. The Buda section is dominated by a "castle hill" where a stone fort was built in the thirteenth century. From the hill is a sweeping view of the city and mountains. East of the Danube is the more modern Pest. Buda and Pest merged in 1873 to become the Hungarian capital Budapest. Budapest is the most "Western" city of the former Eastern European nations. It is a fun city, rivaling London and Paris with its fine theatrical performances, ballets, and operas.

After the Danube forms the border with Hungary, it winds through an impressive gorge in the Carpathian Mountains on the Yugoslavian-Romanian border. This 60-mile section of the Danube, called the "Iron Gates," is the most spectacular part of the river. The gorge is only 560 feet wide and 2 miles long, with several tumultuous rapids.

Exploring Northern Europe

Visiting Northern Europe, also known as Scandinavia, is like traveling back in time. This land where the Vikings once roamed is very quiet. It is easy to imagine a Viking attack breaking the stillness of a quaint fishing village. It is a place where natural wonders are abundant. The tranquility and beauty of majestic mountains, calm fjords, and dramatic glaciers is hard to match. Many North European ports are set against dramatic mountain backdrops.

In the far north of Scandinavia is the "Land of the Midnight Sun," so called because the sun never sets above the Arctic Circle for about 2 months in the summer. The sun sinks low on the horizon at midnight, but it never really gets dark. The "Midnight Sun" is spectacular, appearing as a red ball, even on a cloudy night. A few minutes past midnight the sun starts to rise again.

The Arctic Circle is an imaginary line that follows the latitude 66 degrees north, which is 1,650 miles from the North Pole (see Figure 6–7). Climatic patterns are determined by the magnitude of heat and light received from the sun. During the winter months the tilt of the Earth blocks the sun's rays north of the Arctic Circle, and the sun never rises as a result.

In Lapland, Scandinavia's remote area above the Arctic Circle, the hardy Sami people, or Lapps, may gather in front of their tents. Many dress up for tourists. Lapland encompasses extreme northern Norway, Sweden, Finland, and the Russian Kola Peninsula. The Lapp population is fairly small, comprising only about 1 percent of the total population. Most Lapps live north of the 62nd parallel.

The reindeer-based Lapp culture originated in Russia and migrated west through Finland, settling mostly in Sweden and Norway. The Lapp people brought their Samic language and nomadic lifestyle of herding reindeer with them. They do not use clocks much. The Lapps consider reindeer as important as people. In years past, they lived for the reindeer and during the winter stayed with the reindeer constantly. Lapps wear colorful, traditional Sami attire and live in reindeer-skin tents. Today, only about 15 percent of Lapps live seasonally nomadic lives. The rest have settled in small towns. Modern Lapps are extraordinary; most still speak the Lapp language. Today, Lapps follow the reindeer only 1 to 2 weeks each year.

Seafaring is essential to Scandinavian heritage. The Norwegian Viking, Leif Ericsson, son of Eric the Red, landed in North America in a small oar boat hundreds of years before Columbus. Travelers who want to experience the traditional Scandinavian way of travel should try "cruising." The Coastal Voyage, or Hurtigruten (the fast route), sails into the very deep, blue fjords of Norway. Many of the fjords are only 330 feet wide with vertical cliffs that rise over 3,300 feet on both sides. Hurtigruten is a big part of daily life along the Norwegian coast. For the past 100 years, Hurtigruten, or Highway 1, has carried locals, mail, cargo, and goods. Picturesque and remote coastal towns and fishing villages dot the hillsides from Bergen in the south to Kirkenes in the north.

The city of Bergen, founded in 1070, is where Hurtigruten departs daily at 10:00 P.M. (see Figure 6–7). The ship sails

FIGURE 6–7
Scandinavia

into Norway's longest and deepest fjord, Sognefjord, which runs over a hundred miles into the interior. Europe's largest glacier is nearby. Geirangerfjord is Norway's most spectacular fjord with its overhanging cliffs and Seven Sisters and Bridal Veil waterfalls.

Trondheim would make an interesting stopover on a Scandinavian trip. This ancient capital of Norway is located on a fjord surrounded by hills. All Norwegian kings are still crowned and buried in the Cathedral of Trondheim, founded in 1075.

Just north of the Arctic Circle is Norway's second largest glacier, the Svartisen (Black Ice). Svartisen is surrounded by mountains and forks into many glacial branches that lead to valleys and fjords. Hammerfest, the northernmost European town, is the gateway for venturing into the rugged Arctic tundra. On the island of Mageroya is the world's northernmost fishing village of Honningsvag. From here an overland excursion through lunar landscapes ends at the North Cape, the northernmost point in Europe. Kirkenes is Hurtigruten's last stop. Kirkenes is located at the Varangerfjord and borders Russia. The vast Finnmark tundra, where the Lapplanders and their reindeer roam, lies beyond.

The traveler can pass the 80th parallel to visit the remote and strange Spitsbergen Islands. The Norwegian Spitsbergen Islands are only 625 miles from the North Pole. The famous Norwegian Roald Amundsen originated his explorations of the North Pole in Spitsbergen in 1925. This true Arctic wilderness is home to seals, walruses, polar bears, reindeer, and arctic fox. The massive icebergs, gigantic glaciers, and steep-sided mountains of these untouched Arctic islands are spellbinding.

TRAVELING WISELY

A visitor to a foreign country should always read as much literature as possible about the country, including culture and customs, before departing. If the visitor is planning to rent a car, it is also a good idea to note which countries drive on the left side of the road.

SUMMARY

- The European Union (EU) is an organization of fifteen Western European member nations whose main goal is to break down political and economic barriers and work toward one European market where labor, business, goods, and monetary funds move freely from country to country.
- The Maastricht Treaty has proposed one common European currency of the future to be called the European Currency Unit (ECU).
- Many internal borders between EU member nations have effectively disappeared.
- Seven EU nations have together implemented a passport-and-visa-free zone.
- The best way to explore Europe is to purchase one of the many available rail passes.
- The Eurostar travels the Channel Tunnel, also called the Eurotunnel, carrying passengers between London, Paris, and Brussels.
- The Simplon Orient Express is a luxurious rail service between London and Venice.
- The Rhine is the most romantic and legendary river in Europe.
- The Danube is the second longest river in Europe.
- The far northern region of Europe is called the "Land of the Midnight Sun."

CHECK YOUR UNDERSTANDING 6-1

Discuss the developments in Europe, including the following:

- The advantages and disadvantages of the European Union (EU)
- How the New Europe benefits visitors
- The impacts of a borderless Europe
- The prospect of one common European language
- The prospects of a European Currency Unit (ECU)

CHECK YOUR UNDERSTANDING 6–2

Directions: Fill in the following blanks:

1. What type of visitor to Europe would travel on the Orient Express and why?

2. Name the most important selling feature of the Orient Express.

3. Describe how the Orient Express competes with the European rail passes.

4. Explain how a Rhine river cruise compares with the Coastal Voyage.

5. What type of visitor to Europe would travel on the Coastal Voyage and why?

CHECK YOUR UNDERSTANDING 6-3

Directions: Fill in the following blanks:

1. Define *rail pass*.

2. Distinguish between the Eurailpass and the Europass.

3. Describe the Channel Tunnel rail service.

4. Describe the Le Shuttle program.

5. Identify the advantages and disadvantages of traveling by rail in Europe.

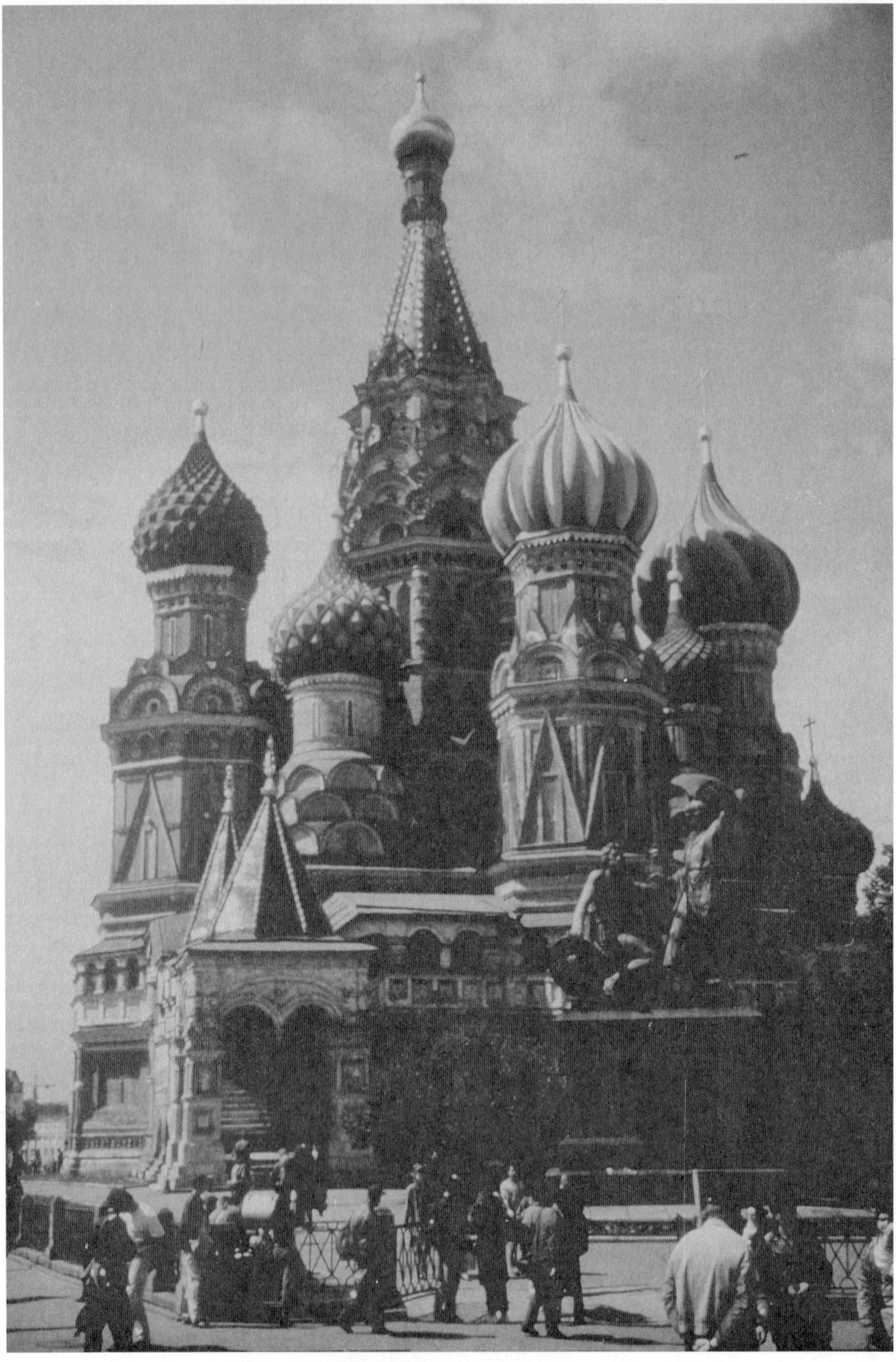

Chapter 7

The New Russia

The Commonwealth of Independent States
    Geography of the CIS
    Culture in the CIS
Travel and Tourism Russian Style
    Russian Air Travel
The Trans-Siberian Railroad
Major Destinations
    Moscow
    Yaroslaw
    Siberia
    Irkutsk
    Lake Baikal
    Ulan Ude
    Khabarovsk
    Vladivostok
    China
    Japan
    Eastern Europe
    Arctica

OBJECTIVES

After completing Chapter 7, you should be able to:

- Describe and evaluate the development of the Commonwealth of Independent States (CIS)
- Discuss the impact of the CIS
- Identify and describe the variety of destinations and itineraries throughout the CIS

The turmoiled history of Russia and its devastating economic failure and political decay of 1917 were followed by social turmoil that grew dramatically and overwhelmingly through the early 1990s when the Soviet Republics began to challenge and resist the Communist-centralized government. The dissolution of the domineering Communist Party was inevitable. In December 1991, the Soviet Union, and thus the 70-year-long era of Communism organized by Lenin, ceased to exist. The first open elections in Russia followed the dissolution, and the people began transitioning to a market economy and democratic government in 1992.

Reorganizing to a market economy in Russia has been painfully slow. While foreign investors may be interested in the Russian free market, many goods are slow to become available. Russia experiences scarcities of food, consumer products, electricity, and fuel. As a result, most products are imported, and their prices are outrageous. The transition to a market economy and national socialism has brought the Russian people other extreme difficulties. It will take the Russian people many more years to convert from a government monopoly to privatization. Under Communism the government owned all farmland. The Russian people had little or no incentive to work hard and produce because the government took most of their earnings. This land has now been given back to farmers, but they do not know what to do with it because they have not been trained to be competitive and produce. They require extensive training and education.

A complete transformation to democracy has yet to be witnessed in the former Soviet Union. Because the Communist Party still boasts many members, the future of Russia is difficult to predict. Time will show if these changes will be fruitful or devastating for the lives of the Russian people. In any form, the New Russia offers immense historical and cultural treasures and an amount of architectural beauty that is surprising to most visitors.

The Commonwealth of Independent States

Now that Communism has dissolved, the former republics of the Soviet Union have reappeared as the fifteen independent nations, shown in Figure 7–1. On September 23, 1989, Azerbaijan was the first Russian Republic to declare its sovereignty. Lithuania was the first to declare its independence on March 11, 1990. The remaining thirteen Russian Republics quickly followed. Georgia was the last to declare its independence in October 1993. Eleven of these republics were established by treaty of the **Commonwealth of Independent States (CIS)** on December 8, 1991. The four remaining, Estonia, Georgia, Latvia, and Lithuania, decided not to join the CIS.

GEOGRAPHY OF THE CIS

The CIS, which is headquartered in Minsk, Belarus, does not replace the Soviet Union as a country with a centralized government. The CIS is instead a loose union that is located within the borders of the former Soviet Union. With a coastline of more than 36,000 miles, the CIS borders twelve nations: Afghanistan, China, Finland, Hungary, Iran, Mongolia, North Korea, Norway, Poland, Romania, the Slovak Republic, and Turkey. The CIS stretches 5,595 miles from the European region west of the Ural Mountains to the Asian region, also called Siberia, east of the Ural Mountains, and 2,485 miles from the arctic Siberian tundra in the north to the low-lying subtropics in the south. Covering eleven time zones and more than 100 ethnic groups that total 150 million people, one former Soviet Republic, the Russian Federation, remains the largest country in the world, stretching 5,250 miles from east to west (see Figure 7–1). This country is more than twice as large as the United States. Geographically, the CIS is isolated. About 90 percent of the CIS nations are closer to the North Pole than to the Equator. One fourth of the landmass is north of the Arctic Circle. Despite its vast boundaries and central location in Eurasia, the CIS has surprisingly few connections with bordering nations. The easiest mode of transportation is by plane or train.

United States citizens must have visas to travel to all the newly independent Russian states except Estonia. Most of the

FIGURE 7–1

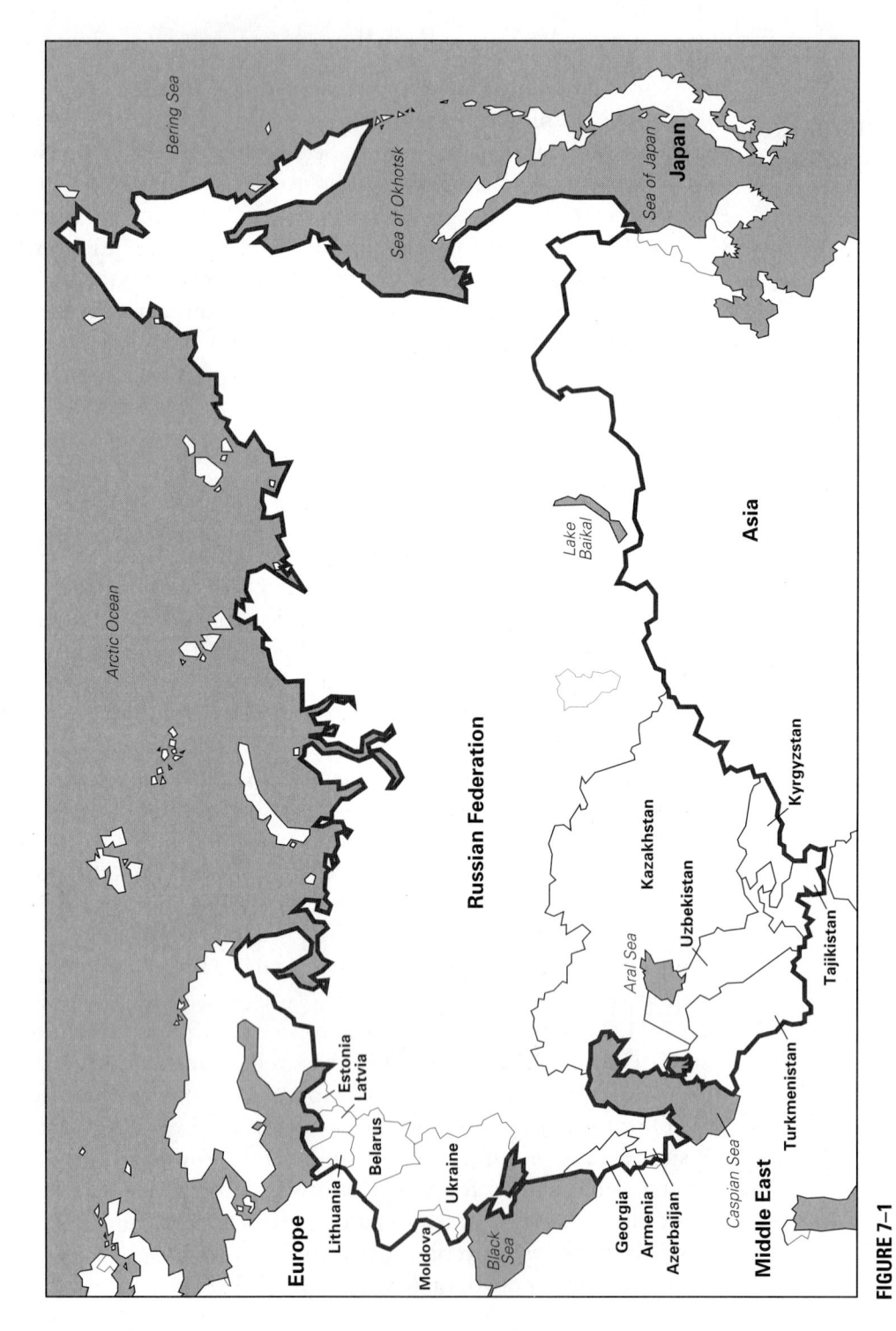

The New Russia

independent states have changed their names as a means of regaining their original cultures and identities. In the Russian Federation, for example, St. Petersburg was renamed Petrograd during World War I. In 1924, Petrograd was changed to Leningrad to honor Communist leader Nikolai Lenin's death. The city was renamed St. Petersburg in 1991. It is difficult to keep current with the name changes. Many occur as original cultures and heritages revive.

CULTURE IN THE CIS

Russia's cultural patterns have changed with its political and economic systems over the last century. Russian culture has characteristically been chaotic. During the Soviet Communist regime, all religions and churches were prohibited, including the Russian Orthodox Church, which was suppressed for decades. Many religious structures were destroyed. Today, Russian citizens once again attend monasteries, cathedrals, churches, and mosques. These buildings have been reopened or restored or are being rebuilt. Church bells are again allowed to ring, and religion in Russian is recapturing social importance.

Russians have revived nationalism in a struggle to regain their ancient heritage and disassociate themselves from their Soviet past. Folk songs and musical performances with traditional costumes are becoming commonplace. Under Soviet rule, the Russian language was written in the Cyrillic alphabet. Today, Latin has been reintroduced to replace Russian.

Travel and Tourism Russian Style

The former Soviet Union was not a major destination for tourists with luxury and entertainment in mind. All travel itineraries were predetermined, fully packaged, and escorted at all times. A fully packaged itinerary is a tour where all tour components, such as accommodations, meals, and sight-seeing options, are prearranged and included in the cost of the tour. Free time or optional tours were not allowed because independent travel in the Soviet Union was not allowed. Until 1989, the government-controlled travel agency Intourist had a monopoly on travel arrangements in the Soviet Union, including hotel choices, sightseeing, and transportation. Intourist, which was headquartered in Moscow and founded in 1929, had offices in most capital cities throughout the world. Although most tourists still travel with Intourist, they are no longer required to obtain their tickets and itineraries from the agency. A startling number of new, private travel organizations, such as Intourservice and Sputnik, have emerged. A traveler can now bypass Intourist and book directly with hotels and tour companies.

Independent travel in the New Russia is less difficult. Because all internal and external travel restrictions have now been relaxed, today's traveler is free to explore and experience the nations of the CIS. However, Russia's drastic economic, political, and social changes have made visiting less exciting than it was just a few years ago. Western-style luxuries and services, especially in Moscow and St. Petersburg, are more widespread. For example, more privately owned restaurants have opened in Moscow and St. Petersburg. Moscow now has over 100 casinos, and high-quality, privately owned hotels are under construction in the city. In addition, infrastructure in Russia's bigger cities has improved greatly.

In 1995, foreign visitors to the fifteen new Russian nations increased. Few other travel destinations offered such scenic variety and cultural diversity. Each CIS nation is unique because it has a different history and background. Russia was once ruled by powerful Czars and inhabited by Tartars, Eskimos, and Cossacks. The Russian Federation is an interesting, multicultural nation. With its many nationalities and ethnic groups, this giant presents a myriad differences.

RUSSIAN AIR TRAVEL

Air travel within the former Soviet Union was chaotic. The former Soviet Union's national airline, **Aeroflot** (SU), was totally unreliable, despite being the world's largest. The airplanes had a poor safety record, the service was substandard, and pilots were usually overworked. Flights would be delayed by days, the customs procedures were tedious, and the staff were often rude. Further, the airport facilities were designed to completely control passengers. Each passenger was screened, one at a time, compared to the random spot-checks at United States airports. No one could escort passengers to the gate to say farewell.

Aeroflot is now divided into 320 smaller airlines, 286 of which are in the Russian Federation. Many independent Russian nations have created their own national carriers.

The Trans-Siberian Railroad

The **Trans-Siberian Railroad** is one of the best ways to see Russia. Its construction began in 1891. It was meant as a main trading route between Europe and the Far East. Upon its completion in 1916, the Trans-Siberian Railroad became the world's longest rail line and created opportunities for trade and industry to develop in remote Siberia.

Before the Trans-Siberian Railroad was completed, it could take up to 1 year to travel the 5,800 miles from Vladivostok via reindeer-drawn sleigh across the Siberian tundra to Lake Baikal, a ferry across Baikal, and horse and carriage to Moscow (see Figure 7–2). Today, the Trans-Siberian train runs entirely in the Russian Federation. It departs daily during the summer months and four times weekly during the winter. The journey from Moscow to Vladivostok now takes 8 days. The trip crosses eight times zones in 1 week, which means travelers must adjust their clocks approximately once daily. The 5,750-mile-long Trans-Siberian Railroad is a remarkable journey. The railroad has greatly helped to unify the Russian people and their cultures.

Major Destinations

MOSCOW

Moscow was built on the banks of the Moscow River 800 years ago. The heart of Moscow is Red Square, around which are found many of Moscow's famous attractions. One famous

FIGURE 7-2

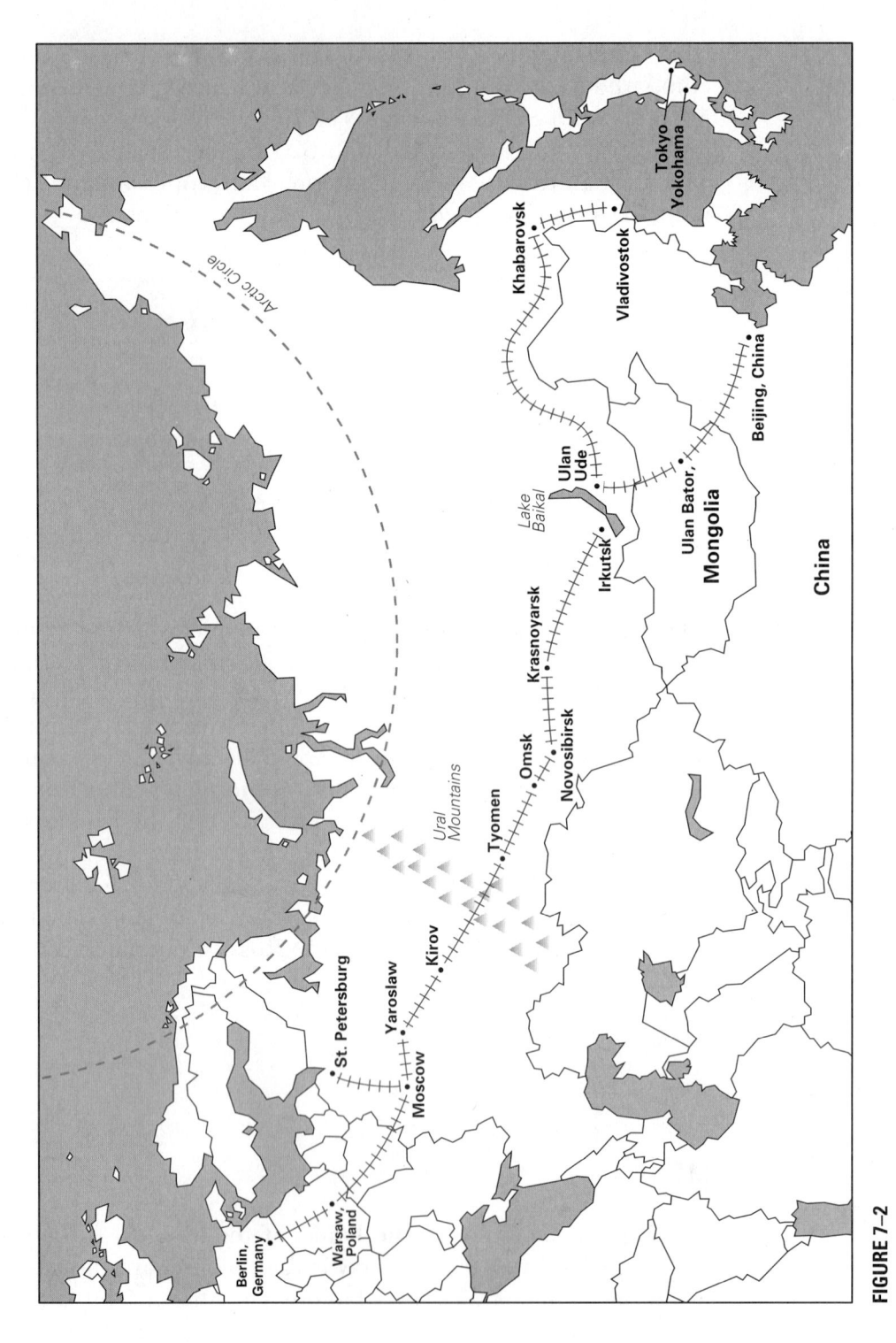

The Trans-Siberian Railroad

sight is the Kremlin, which is surrounded by the red fortress wall that inspired the name "Red Square." The Kremlin houses the offices of the Soviet government. On the Kremlin grounds are the Fourteenth-century Grand Kremlin Palace and the Uspensky Cathedral, which was built between 1475 and 1479. Moscow also holds Lenin's mausoleum, which is on the outer Kremlin wall in Red Square.

At one end of Red Square is St. Basil's Cathedral, which was built between 1555 and 1560. The Cathedral is one of Moscow's best-known structures. It symbolizes the famous and traditional Russian architectural style. Another Moscow attraction is the Bolshoi Theatre, home of the world-famous Russian ballet and opera.

YAROSLAW

Prince Yaroslaw the Wise of Kiev founded the city of Yaroslaw in 1010. Yaroslaw stretches for many miles along the Volga River and retains many noteworthy monuments to its colorful past, including the thirteenth-century Spasky Monastery.

SIBERIA

Siberia extends from the Ural Mountains to the Pacific Coast, covering an area of over 4 million square miles or about 76 percent of the Russian Federation. Siberia is covered mostly by taiga forest. The taiga is like an ocean of conifer trees, blending with the tundra in the far north. The tundra is a marshy arctic area that is devoid of trees. Only hardy vegetation and low bushes grow there. The Siberian taiga is broken by three major rivers (Ob, Yenisei, and Lena), thousands of lakes, and 53,000 smaller rivers. Most of the Russian Federation's population is found along the route of the Trans-Siberian Railroad.

Novosibirsk, meaning "new Siberia," is the first taste of Russian Siberia (see Figure 7–2). This "capital" of Siberia is on the River Ob. Novosibirsk was founded in honor of Czar Nicholas II in 1896, while the Trans-Siberian Railroad was being constructed across the River Ob. The Famous Opera and Ballet Theatre, the

Bolshoi Theatre of Siberia, is located in Novosibirsk. Krasnoyarsk, a city east of Novosibirsk along the Trans-Siberian Railroad, was founded by Cossacks in 1626. From Krasnoyarsk, the Trans-Siberian Railroad crosses eighty-two bridges. One is almost 1 mile long and is built of thick granite to resist the immense pressure icebergs in the river exert.

IRKUTSK

Irkutsk, a beautiful, colorful, and romantic city, is located on the Angara River along the rail line. Irkutsk is one of the few Russian cities without Communist concrete architecture. It is clean and beautiful, full of eighteenth-century wood houses, Baroque churches, wide avenues, and greenery. Its tree-lined streets and charming traditional wooden and stone houses have contributed to its nickname, "Paris of Siberia." Historically, Irkutsk is a 300-year-old Cossack fort city. The Cossacks defeated the Buryats, the aboriginal Mongols, so they could use Irkutsk as a military base. Today, Irkutsk has an interesting blend of Buryats, Chinese, Mongolians, and Russians. Irkutsk has grown steadily as the gateway to spectacular Lake Baikal and Mongolia.

LAKE BAIKAL

From Irkutsk, the Trans-Siberian Railway travels the rocky southern shore of Lake Baikal, the deepest lake in the world. Lake Baikal formed between 20 and 30 million years ago, making it the oldest lake in the world as well. This body of water is remarkably clean. At a depth of 5,315 feet, the bottom of the lake can be seen. Lake Baikal is surrounded by the Yablonovy Mountains. Slightly larger than Belgium, the 395-mile-long lake houses an astonishing variety of 2,500 plants and animals, many of which can only be found in Baikal. One of the most impressive species is the gray Nerpe seal, the only freshwater seal on earth. Even though over 300 rivers feed Lake Baikal, its only outlet is the Angara River near Irkutsk.

ULAN UDE

On the eastern side of Lake Baikal is Ulan Ude (see Figure 7–2). This interesting frontier town was founded in the 1660s as a winter refuge for the Cossacks. Therefore, most of its inhabitants are Mongolian Bhuddists, and many of its structures are Bhuddist temples and pagodas. A southbound route winds through a landscape dotted with the traditional and colorful tents of the Mongolian nomadic tribes toward Ulan Bator in Mongolia. In 1238, Genghis Khan traveled through Ulan Ude on his way to Moscow.

KHABAROVSK

Khabarovsk, a city located on the eastern end of the Trans-Siberian Railroad, was founded in 1858 and named after the Russian explorer Yerofey Khabarov. Stretching 28 miles along scenic hills on the banks of the Amur River, Khabarovsk is the scientific, industrial, and cultural center of the Russian Far East. The Khabarovsk Museum holds interesting artifacts from the many cultures of the Amur people. Just outside Khabarovsk is the vast expanse of the taiga where Siberian tigers still roam.

VLADIVOSTOK

The last stop on the Trans-Siberian route is the major Pacific seaport of Vladivostok where Czar Nicholas II laid the first stone of the railroad in 1891. Cable cars traverse the city's hilly streets, and the bay, Golden Horn, boasts spectacular beaches. Vladivostok is nicknamed "Rule of the East" because of its political and military importance.

The vast expanse of the Siberian frontier combine with the dramatic history of nomadic Mongol occupiers and Czarist growth to captivate visitors. The Irkutsk, Ulan Ude, and Ulan Bator area has broad appeal. From nature trips to the natural wonders of the Baikal region, sleigh rides in the taiga, and the ancient homeland of Ghengis Khan, this region has great potential in the travel industry.

CHINA

From Ulan Bator in Mongolia, the tracks of the Trans-Siberian Railway continue south to the great city of Beijing in China (see Figure 7–2). Beijing, the capital of China, consists of three walled, rectangular cities. In the heart of Beijing is the most visited rectangular region, the Forbidden City. The Forbidden City was the residence of the Ming and Qing emperors. The Imperial Palace, which is found inside the Forbidden City, is decorated with many glorious bronze statues. It was built between 1406 and 1420, and it was home to twenty-four emperors. With 9,999 chambers and over 1 million glorious art objects from the dynasty eras, the Imperial Palace is the largest royal complex in the world. Other places of interests in China include Tiananmen Square, the largest public square in the world, and the Summer Palace, the resort of the Qing dynasty emperors.

North of Beijing is one of the greatest structures and wonders in the world, the Great Wall of China. The Wall was constructed to protect against invaders 2,600 years ago in circa 210 B.C., but it was not completed until the Ming Dynasty, which lasted from 1368 to 1644. The Wall stretches from west to east for more than 3,750 miles, from the Jiayuguan Pass to the Yellow Sea. Most tourists visit its best preserved section at Badaling where the wall is 8 meters high and 6 meters wide. The wall is also famous for being the only man-made structure that is visible from the Moon.

JAPAN

From Vladivostok, the farthest point east on the Trans-Siberian Railroad (see Figure 7–2), a ferry crosses the Sea of Japan to Yokohama, the gateway to Japan for sea vessels coming from all over the world. Located 18 miles southwest of Tokyo, Yokohama is connected to Tokyo via fast rail service. Tokyo is one of the most highly populated cities in the world and among the most fascinating. Western values coexist peacefully with 2,000-year-old traditions in the city. Kimonos and *sashimi* (raw fish) stalls blend with blue jeans and McDonald's. Many visitors choose to attend a centuries-old Kabuki or Noh theater performance or a class in Japanese flower arranging.

The Imperial Palace is located in the oldest part of Tokyo. The Palace is surrounded by an enormous wall that rises around a picturesque moat. At 1,093 feet tall, another landmark, the steel-structured Tokyo Tower, is one of the world's highest. The Ginza is Tokyo's liveliest street at night, displaying a vast array of luxury shops, theaters, and entertainment.

No trip to Japan is complete without a ride on the Shinkansen (Bullet Train). The most popular route is from Tokyo to Kyoto via Mt. Fuji. The Fuji Five-Lake District is one of the most sought-after side trips from Tokyo. Snow-capped Mt. Fuji is the main attraction, and it stands like a symbol of Japan. The five lakes at the base of Mt. Fuji form a scenic resort that offers year-round recreational activities. To truly experience Japanese life, travelers must spend at least one night at a *ryokan* in Kyoto. A *ryokan* is a traditional Japanese-style inn. Overnight guests stay on soft futon mattresses on *tatamis* (straw mat floors). Guests must remove their shoes, change into slippers, and wear kimonos.

EASTERN EUROPE

Westbound from Moscow, the tracks of the Trans-Siberian Railway continue to Berlin, Germany, via Warsaw, Poland (see Figure 7–2). During World War II, 87 percent of Warsaw was destroyed. Today, much of the city has been rebuilt in its original form. The Royal Castle, for example, was beautifully reconstructed. The reconstructed Wilanow Palace has a rare collection of paintings and furniture. North of Warsaw is Gdansk, which will celebrate its 1,000 year anniversary in 1997. This city offers cobbled streets and historical architecture from the Gothic and Renaissance sixteenth century.

Berlin is a newly united city. Even though most of the concrete panels of the Berlin Wall fell in November 1989, portions remain as eerie reminders of a painful past. Since the Berlin

Wall collapsed, streets have connected the two parts of the city east and west.

Alexanderplatz in the former East Berlin was one of the main centers of 1920s Berlin. Unter den Linden is an avenue lined with diplomatic buildings. At the western end of the avenue sits the Brandenburg Gate, once abruptly cut off by the Berlin Wall. The Gate was completed in 1791 and stands 66 feet high and 204 feet wide. For nearly 30 years the Brandenburg Gate symbolized a divided Berlin. Today the gate is accessible from both East and West Berlin for the first time since 1961.

West down Unter den Linden through the Brandenburg Gate is Kurfurstendamm, the heart of West Berlin. Lined with cafes, *Kneipen* (pubs), restaurants, and 24-hour shops, Kurfurstendamm is the place to be.

The most popular branch rail line is between Moscow and St. Petersburg. Established in 1703 by Czar Peter the Great, St. Petersburg was the capital of Czarist Russia for 200 years until World War I. Hundreds of canals, bridges, and rivers made the city famous as the "Venice of the North." With its many elegant buildings, St. Petersburg is a truly classic and historic city. The Winter Palace, built between 1754 and 1762, is a true architectural wonder. The Hermitage (1840–1852) is attached to the Winter Palace and houses one of the world's most outstanding art collections of the Czars. The Summer Palace of Peter the Great was erected between 1710 and 1712. The Kazan Cathedral (1801–1811) houses a museum. The gold-domed St. Isaac's Cathedral, built between 1817 and 1858, is one of the largest domed structures in the world.

ARCTICA

The North Pole, or Arctica, lies in the center of the 4-million-square-mile Arctic Ocean. Arctica is a frozen ocean, more than half of which has ice all the time. Much of the ice is a drifting and tangled pile called pack ice that freezes and spreads during the 6 winter months of no direct sunlight. The ice melts and shrinks during the 6 summer months of long hours of sunlight.

Arctica experiences only one day and one night each calendar year. Travelers to this mystic area at 90 degrees north latitude decide themselves to which time zone to set their clocks, because all longitude lines meet at the North Pole. Therefore time does not matter. What is critical is the ice condition. The constantly moving and massive ice floes and thick pack ice riddled with cracks and ridges make it difficult and dangerous for ships to reach the destination safely. Many ships have become trapped and sometimes crushed in the ice. The only ship to make it to this latitude thus far was a vessel powered by nuclear engines and manned by a Russian crew. It takes the nuclear-powered vessel 15 days to travel round-trip (1,460 miles) from Murmansk in Russia to the North Pole (see Figure 7–3). Because the entire cruise takes place north of the Arctic Circle, the sun shines for 24 hours a day every day during the cruise.

Since 1991, this nuclear-engine vessel has been chartered by an American cruise company. The vessel tries to reach Arctica only during the summer months when the ice floes are only an average of 10 feet thick. During the winter months, some of the ice floes measure up to 160 feet thick. Many ice floes can be as large as several square miles in area and remain that way for 1 or 2 years before breaking and scattering into smaller ice floes. Since the North Pole is an ocean with no land under the ice, the Arctic region is flat, devoid of mountains, glaciers, and icebergs.

The race for the North Pole began in the 1840s after Britain's 130-person expedition team vanished while exploring the unknown Arctic region in an attempt to find a shipping route along the northern coast of North America, also called the Northwest Passage. The expedition to the North Pole begins in Murmansk. In Murmansk, on the Kola Gulf by the Barents Sea, travelers board one of the Russian nuclear-powered vessels. On the way to the North Pole, onboard helicopters scout the polar ice cap for open water routes. Helicopter sightseeing flights and shore excursions are available. Onboard Russian and American professors lecture on and discuss topics like geology, explorations, and arctic wildlife.

The vessel stops at the Russian islands of Northbrook Island and Franz Josef Land. Franz Josef Land is an archipelago of about eighty-five islands. The islands are covered almost entirely by glacial ice. In 1893, the Norwegian polar explorer Fridtjof Nansen headed for the North Pole but became trapped

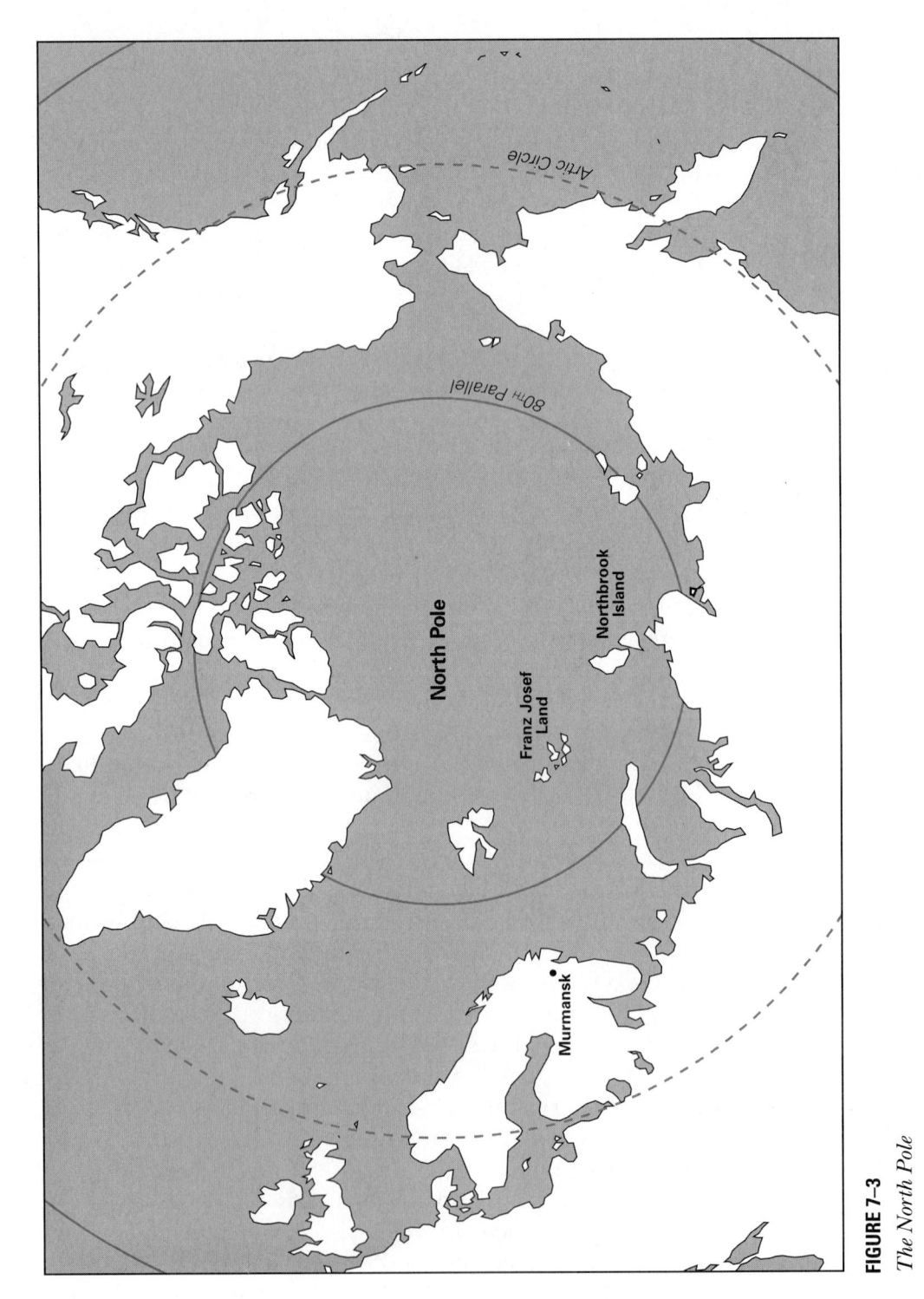

FIGURE 7-3
The North Pole

in the ice. He drifted to 84 degrees latitude. From there, he and a teammate reached 86 degrees on foot, the northernmost point ever reached at that time. The two wintered at Franz Josef Land for 7 months. The remnants of Nansen's hut, a famous Arctic monument, is of great historical value.

Upon reaching the North Pole, many passengers celebrate with champagne and a barbecue on the ice. An adventurous few take a quick polar swim in the Arctic Ocean.

TRAVELING WISELY

Travelers should take time to listen and observe instead of rushing and taking photographs of local people. People of many cultures are offended when their photographs are taken without permission.

SUMMARY

- In December 1991, the Soviet Union ceased to exist.
- The former Soviet Union's republics have reappeared as fifteen independent states.
- Eleven of the fifteen independent republics were established by the treaty of the Commonwealth of Independent States (CIS). The CIS is headquartered in Minsk, Belarus.
- Aeroflot is now divided into 320 smaller airlines. Of these, 286 are in the Russian Federation.
- The Trans-Siberian Railroad is the world's longest rail line. It spans eight time zones between Moscow and Vladivostok.
- The only ship able to make the trip to the North Pole is a Russian nuclear-powered vessel.

CHECK YOUR UNDERSTANDING 7–1

Discuss and assess the developments in the New Russia. Be sure to incorporate answers to the following:

- The advantages and disadvantages of the Commonwealth of Independent States (CIS)
- How the changes in the CIS affect a first-time visitor
- The historical aspects that eventually led to the break-up of the former Soviet Union
- The cultural changes throughout the CIS

CHECK YOUR UNDERSTANDING 7–2

Directions: Fill in the following blanks:

1. Name the fifteen independent states that were part of the former Soviet Union.

    _____
    _____
    _____
    _____

2. List the republics that created the Commonwealth of Independent States (CIS).

    _____
    _____
    _____
    _____

3. Give three examples of name changes in the CIS.

    _____
    _____
    _____
    _____

4. Describe the size of the Russian Federation.

    _____
    _____
    _____
    _____

5. Describe air travel in the CIS.

CHECK YOUR UNDERSTANDING 7–3

Directions: Fill in the following blanks:

1. What type of visitor would travel on the Trans-Siberian Railroad and why?

2. Describe the most important selling feature of the Trans-Siberian Railroad.

3. How does the Trans-Siberian Railroad compete with the European rail passes?

4. Identify some advantages of traveling by rail throughout the Russian Federation.

5. Identify some disadvantages of traveling by rail throughout the Russian Federation.

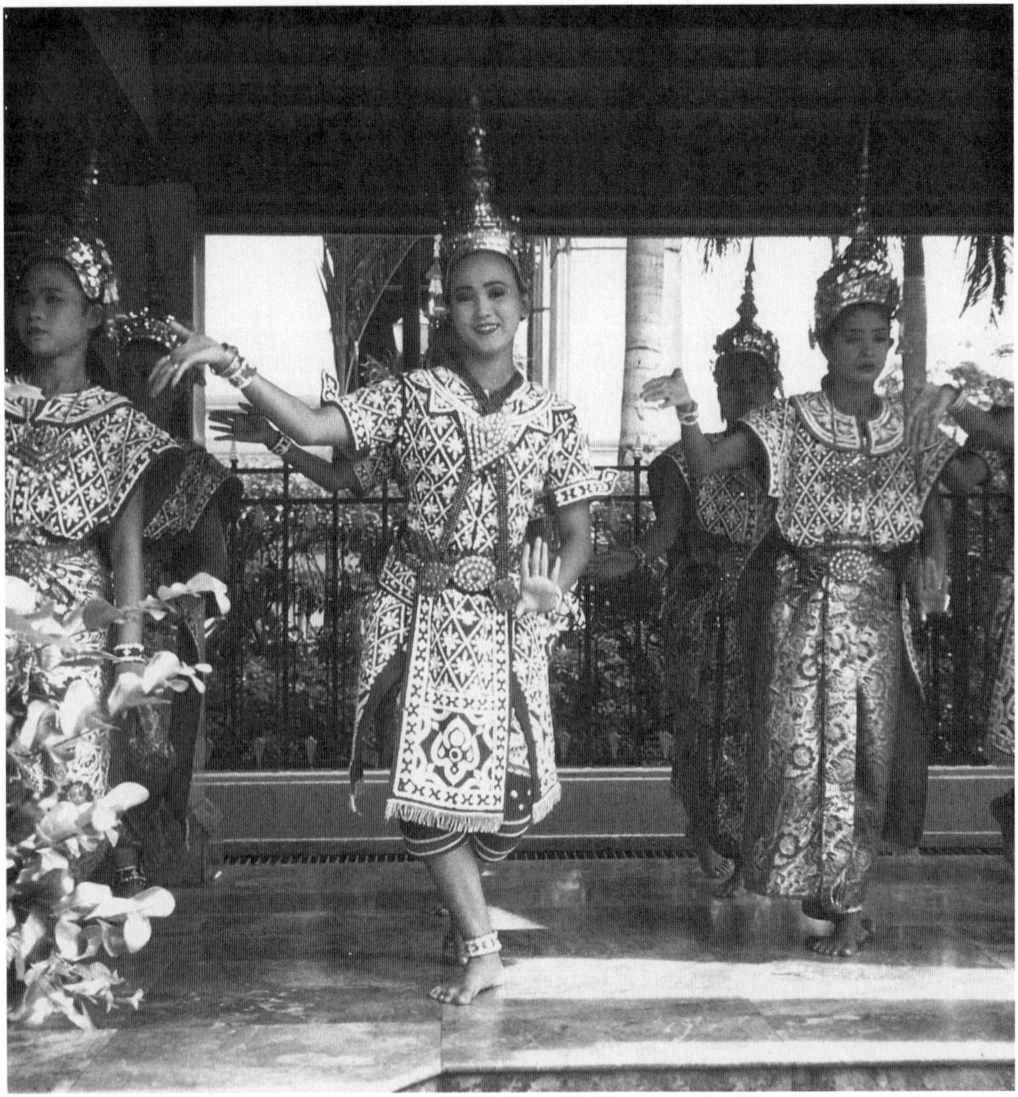

Chapter 8

Asia and the Pacific

The Eastern & Oriental Express
    Singapore
    Malaysia
    Ipoh and Butterworth
    Southern Thailand
    Bangkok
    Northern Thailand
Vietnam
    The Reunification Express
Australia
    Indian Pacific
    The Ghan
    The Queenslander
The South Pacific
    Tonga
    Fiji
    Easter Island
    Bora Bora
    American Samoa
    Tahiti
    Cook Islands
    New Zealand

OBJECTIVE

After completing Chapter 8, you should be able to:

- Identify and describe the variety of destinations and itineraries throughout Asia and the Pacific.

In a continent with the tallest mountain range in the world, the Himalayas, Asia boasts the second highest average elevation. With an average elevation of 3,150 feet, it is surpassed only by Antarctica, which has an average elevation of 6,500 feet. The eight highest peaks in the world, located in the Himalayan range, soar well over 26,000 feet; many others rise over 23,000 feet. The Tibetan plateau, at an elevation of 13,000 to 16,500 feet, dominates central Asia.

Asia is the largest continent in the world and home to 60 percent of the world's inhabitants. In fact, over half the world's population lives in the southern part of Asia. Eurasia, the northwestern extension of Asia, consists of Russia west of the Ural Mountains. Australasia, comprised of Australia, New Zealand, and the South Pacific, is the southeastern extension of Asia.

Tourists visiting Asia travel mostly throughout East Asia and the Pacific. Recently, this region has experienced amazing growth in international tourism. In 1995, this region reported its international tourist arrivals at 68.5 million, an increase of 11.8 percent from the previous year. As Figure 8–1, shows, at 22.8 percent Vietnam boasted the fastest annual growth of tourism in 1995.

A new and powerful political and financial region is being developed in the Pearl River delta of China. On June 30, 1997, after 99 years of British colonial rule, Hong Kong will be returned to China. After 448 years of Portuguese colonial rule, Macau will be returned to China in 1999. These cities, together with southern China's Guangdong Province is being developed in Asia and the cities of Shenzhen and Guangzhon, will blend into one region connected by a massive network of highways.

Macau's main attraction is gambling, and it has opened a new international airport. The construction of a $46 billion Chek Lap Kok airport complex in Hong Kong is astonishing.[1]

---

[1]Waters, S. (1995–1996). *The travel industry yearbook: The big picture.* New York: Child and Waters.

FIGURE 8–1

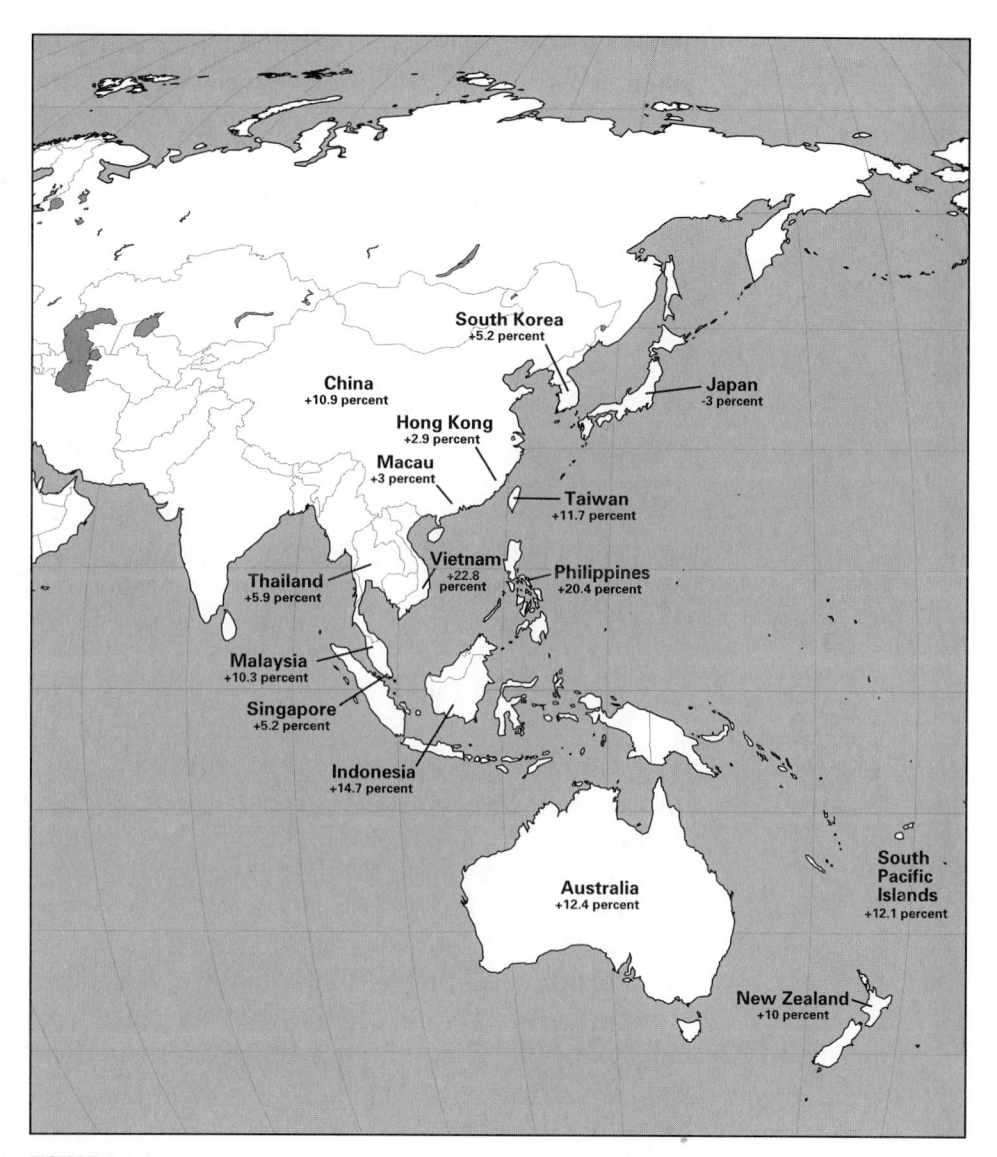

Annual percent increases in Asia and Pacific visitor totals for 1995. Source: Travel Weekly, June 10, 1996.

The complex is the largest infrastructure project to be undertaken in Asia in modern times. This huge project includes a new town, located just outside Hong Kong, complete with schools, police stations, firehouses, and shopping centers. Also included are two suspension bridges, a high-speed rail system from central Hong Kong, a six-lane highway connecting the new town's center and Hong Kong, and a third tunnel under Hong Kong's harbor. The town's population will be 20,000.

In 1995, according to the June 10, 1996 issue of *Travel Weekly*, China received 33,360 million tourists, the highest in Australasia, but it was only a 10.9 percent increase from the previous year (see Figure 8–1). The Philippines showed a remarkable annual growth of 20.4 percent in 1995. With Sydney hosting the 2000 Summer Olympics, Australia is now busy promoting tourism. Australia has already seen a sharp increase of foreign visitors, particularly from Japan. Few Americans visit Malaysia. Most of its tourist arrivals are from Europe and Asia. Thailand is an inexpensive and exotic destination.

Chinese invasions and immigrations have heavily influenced the ethnicity of Southeast Asia. Southeast Asia's blend of Hinduism, Buddhism, art, and architecture also bears strong Indian imprints. Thus, the French named the region "Indochina." Vietnam has developed into the cultural heartland of Indochina. Travelers to this region rediscover a Southeast Asia that has emerged from two decades of isolation.

The Malay Peninsula is crisscrossed by the long chain of the Central Range. East of the mountain range are miles of uncrowded, white-sand beaches, but most people live west of the range. Gunong Tahan is the highest peak in the north at 7,186 feet. Because this peninsula reaches within 90 miles of the Equator, the average temperature is 80 degrees year round. Thick jungle also bisects the peninsula. Over 70 percent of the area is covered in lush tropical rain forest.

The Eastern & Oriental Express

Southeast Asia's first luxury train, the **Eastern & Oriental Express,** traverses the Malay Peninsula between Singapore and

Bangkok (see Figure 8–2). Travelers on the 1,200-mile rail journey through one of the most mysterious and exotic regions of Southeast Asia are accompanied by delightful Thailander, Singaporean, and Malaysian staff. The Eastern & Oriental Express company also restored the Simplon Orient Express in Europe.

The Eastern & Oriental Express journey can be combined with an **open-jaw air ticket.** After travelers with open-jaw air tickets depart Los Angeles at 11:40 A.M. on Singapore Airlines, they cross the International Date Line and arrive at the lush and tropical garden city of Singapore at 11:05 P.M., 1 day later. From there they commence the "open-jaw" portion of their trip from Singapore to Bangkok on the Eastern & Oriental Express, the portion not traveled by air.

SINGAPORE

Singapore is a cluster of islands off the southern tip of the Malay Peninsula that is connected to the peninsula only by a road and a rail bridge across the Jahore Strait (see Figure 8–2). Singapore is the fourth busiest port in the world and the primary shipping route between the Pacific and Indian Oceans.

Singapore consists of one main island and fifty-four smaller ones. Sentosa, among the most popular of the resort islands, offers activities for the entire family, including an Asian village, an 18-hole golf course, a butterfly park, and an underwater world. Sentosa's Fantasy Island amusement park has thirteen water rides and is very popular. The island's great beaches offer a wide variety of water sports.

Averaging 6 million visitors a year, Singapore receives more tourists than its population of almost 3 million. That population represents a multitude of cultures. With 76 percent Chinese, 15 percent Malay, 7 percent Indian, and 2 percent other residents, Singapore vibrantly reflects its cultural diversity in its religions, structures, and festivals. A mixture of world cultures and a modern skyline can be found all over the island. Among Singapore's main attractions is the Sri Mariamman Temple, built between 1827 and 1843. It is the oldest Hindu temple in Singapore and the most photographed because its tower is colorful and spectacular.

FIGURE 8-2

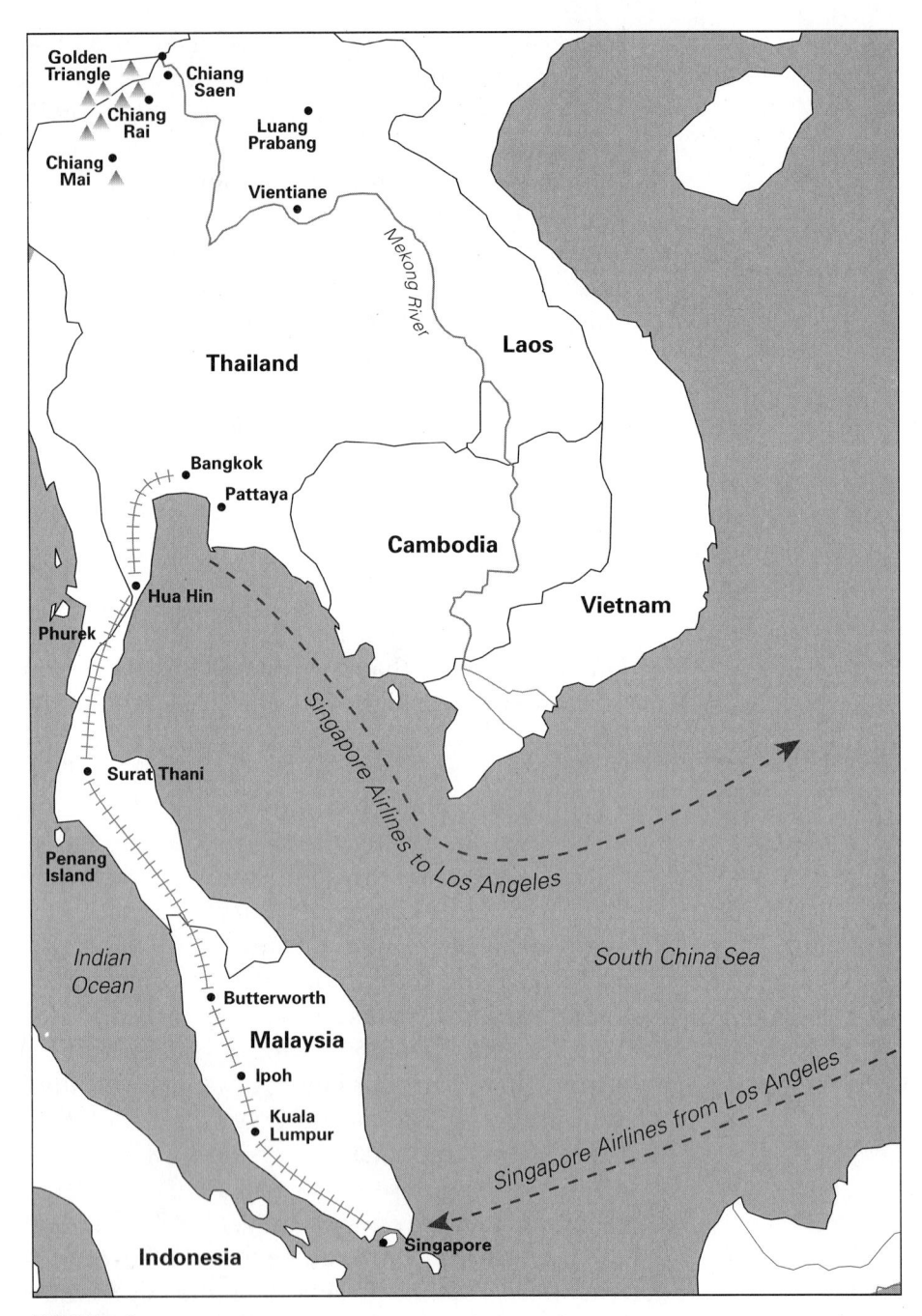

The Eastern & Oriental Express

The biggest Muslim mosque in Singapore, the Sultan Mosque, calls for prayer five times a day. Its massive golden dome is imposing. Inside another religious structure, the Temple of 1,000 Lights, a 50-foot-high statue of Buddha is surrounded by lights. Important events in Buddha's life are portrayed at the statue. The Taoist temple, Thian Hock Keng Temple, is decorated beautifully with wood carvings and ornamental stonework. The Gothic St. Andrew's Cathedral, built between 1856 and 1863, represents Christianity.

Singapore's colorful, ceremonial, and religious festivals occur throughout the year. On the island, New Year's Eve is celebrated on January 1, and the Chinese New Year is honored in late January or early February. The Hindu Malay celebrate the end of Ramadan (the month of fasting) toward the end of August, and, in late October, the Hindu Indians carry on festivities that symbolize the victory of good over evil. Also in late October, the Muslims celebrate completing their pilgrimage to Mecca, Hari Raya Haji.

Although Singapore covers only 225 square miles, it boasts many exotic parks and jungles. Jurong BirdPark, Southeast Asia's largest bird park, is home to over 600 species of birds from all over the world. The Bukit Timah Nature Reserve is a significant area of rain forest and contains more species of plants than the continent of North America.

MALAYSIA

Shortly after the train leaves Singapore every Sunday at 2:45 P.M., the Eastern & Oriental Express crosses the border to Malaysia (see Figure 8–2). The capital of Malaysia, Kuala Lumpur, is a charming and exotic city located in a lush, green valley with rugged mountain tops rising in the background. As the train nears Kuala Lumpur's palace-like railway station, a diverse Indian, Chinese, Malaysian, and European heritage becomes evident in the temples and architecture.

Near Kuala Lumpur's railway station is the National Mosque, which is surrounded by lawns adorned with fountains. Also near the station is the old Chinese temple, Chan See

Yuen, and the colorful Indian temple, Sri Mahamariaman. Within the Tasek Perdana Lake Gardens is the Parliament House. A few miles north of Kuala Lumpur are large natural caves, the Batu Caves, which house the Hindu shrine of Lord Subramaniam. Just a little farther north of the city is Templar Park. This rain forest is rich in waterfalls, lagoons, and exciting hiking paths.

IPOH AND BUTTERWORTH

The next stop on the Eastern & Oriental Express is the city of Ipoh. Ipoh lies in the tin-producing Kinta Valley, which has many famous cave temples. The next city is Butterworth, a short ferry ride from the lovely island of Penang, which has Malaysia's best sand beaches and most glorious sunsets. Penang's most unusual attraction is the Snake Temple. Heavily incense-drugged, poisonous snakes slither among the temple's ornaments. The 2,300-foot-high Penang Hill in the center of the island offers travelers great views and hike venues. Penang's only town, Georgetown, houses many European churches, Chinese temples, and Indian mosques.

Continuing north, the train passes through yellow paddy fields and enchanting countryside villages with houses raised on stilts.

SOUTHERN THAILAND

After the train crosses the border to Thailand, it stops at Surat Thani (see Figure 8–2). There the impressive Wat Phra Boromathat Monument from the Srivijaya Period is surrounded by walls and moats. Travelers can relax at Thailand's oldest beach resort, Hua Hin, which also has been the Thai royal family's summer residence since the 1920s. From Hua Hin the scenery changes as the train winds down the huge Chao Phraya river valley. The rice fields of the valley are surrounded by mountains. The next and final rail stop is Thailand's frenetic capital, Bangkok.

BANGKOK

Bangkok is also known as Krung Thep or the "City of Angels." With a blend of modern highrise buildings and the gilded spires of the Grand Palace, Bangkok is clearly an exciting mixture of old and new.

The richly adorned Grand Palace and the Wat Phra Keo, the Temple of the Emerald Buddha, are beautifully and brightly colored. The Temple of the Emerald Buddha contains a 500-year-old jasper image of Buddha. Bangkok has more than 400 Buddhist temples, the most famous of which is the Temple of the Reclining Buddha. At 46 feet, its statue is the largest in Thailand. Another remarkable temple in Bangkok is the 244-foot-high tower of the Wat Arun, the Temple of Dawn. This tower is decorated with colored, glazed earthenware and porcelain.

A favorite sidetrip from Bangkok is to Southeast Asia's most renowned beach resort, Pattaya (see Figure 8–2). Another favorite stop is the resort on the island of Phuket by the Indian Ocean.

NORTHERN THAILAND

Before they return to the United States, many visitors explore northern Thailand. Chiang Mai in the far north (see Figure 8–2) is the gateway to teak forests, waterfalls, and working elephants. The many tribal villages scattered in the hills retain their separate, traditional lives.

Chiang Rai is the famous gateway for exploring the Mekong and the Golden Triangle. The Golden Triangle is where the borders of Thailand, Laos, and Burma meet. Chiang Rai's jungle-covered mountains and rugged wilderness give the high-altitude, hill-tribe villages a special mystique. From Chiang Rai, travelers journey through river valleys to the ancient capital of Chiang Saen, where a mountaintop provides a spectacular view of Thailand, Burma, ancient temple ruins, and several Hmong hill-tribe villages.

The Hmong originally migrated from China, and today approximately 50,000 have settled in the mountains of northern Thailand. Roughly 200,000 Hmong live in northern Laos and

300,000 occupy northern Vietnam (see Figure 8–2). The many houses of a traditional Hmong village are built in a horseshoe arrangement. Pigs usually run free in the village. The Hmong are farmers and, therefore, spend most of their time in the rice fields. Because rice fields can only be used for 2 to 3 years, the Hmong burn forests to clear new areas for rice cultivation.

Beginning in Luang Prabang, a cruise westbound along the densely forested river plain terminates at the Golden Triangle in Chieng Khong, Thailand (see Figure 8–2). Once the capital of the first Lao kingdom, Luang Prabang is filled with striking historical architecture. The royal palace contains fine artwork of the former kings. There is a splendid view of the Royal Palace from the top of Mt. Phousi in the city. From Luang Prabang travelers can take an excursion to the Pak Ou Caves, which contain many statues of Buddha.

Vietnam

Since Vietnam reunified in 1975, this unspoiled destination has made a striking comeback in the international arena. It has emerged as a major political and economic force in Southeast Asia. Tourism in Vietnam has boomed since the United States lifted its trade embargo and improved diplomatic relations. To visit Vietnam it is no longer necessary to join a hosted tour with a prearranged itinerary. Vietnam is now open for independent travelers. As a result, according to the June 10, 1996 issue of *Travel Weekly*, Vietnam is experiencing explosive growth in international tourist arrivals. Visitor totals to Vietnam increased by 22.8 percent between 1994 and 1995. Major investments in tourism infrastructure, such as roads and hotels, are rapidly being made to keep pace with the influx of tourists. While Vietnam's infrastructure and buildings, particularly its hotels, do not meet American expectations, the incredible beauty and fascinating history of the country have captivated many visitors. Vietnam's stunning coastline, marvelous mountains, wonderful food, ancient temples, emerald-green rice fields, and sandy beaches are beguiling.

Vietnam is an affordable destination with bargain prices everywhere. Its markets offer products not seen since the fall of Communism. Indian, French, Portuguese, Chinese, and American influences have been absorbed into the already wonderful Vietnamese culture. French influence is most evident, particularly in Ho Chi Minh City and Hanoi.

Vietnam reveals itself on a rail journey up the crowded coastline, crossing the spectacular Hai Van mountain pass and traveling through numerous tunnels. The 1,036-mile rail trip on the Reunification Express links Ho Chi Minh City in southern Vietnam with Hanoi in the north (see Figure 8–3).

THE REUNIFICATION EXPRESS

The Reunification Express journey is an intriguing and cultural event. The **Reunification Express** is not a luxury train designed for tourists. It has few modern comforts and hard, wooden seats. It is a train where people share their sleeping compartments with locals. With a top speed of 25 miles per hour, the fastest Express makes its journey in 36 hours. The slowest takes about 48 hours. The 12-mile stretch over Hai Van mountain pass can alone take up to 2 hours.

HO CHI MINH CITY. As Figure 8–3 shows, Ho Chi Minh City is the departing point of the Reunification Express. The Saigon River flows through Ho Chi Minh City. One of the city's most interesting sights is the Cholon market with its Chinese temples. The tour through the Cu Chi network of tunnels built by the Vietcong to defeat the French and American occupiers is eerie. A visit to the Thien Hau Pagoda and the Cao Dai Great Temple is extraordinary. Just outside Ho Chi Minh City is the beach resort of Vung Tau.

NHA TRANG. Leaving Ho Chi Minh City, the Reunification Express slowly ascends a steep mountainside, still in view of mile after mile of white-sand beaches. The golden sand beaches near the quiet fishing village of Nha Trang (see Figure 8–3) and snorkeling at one of the off-shore tropical islands are popular

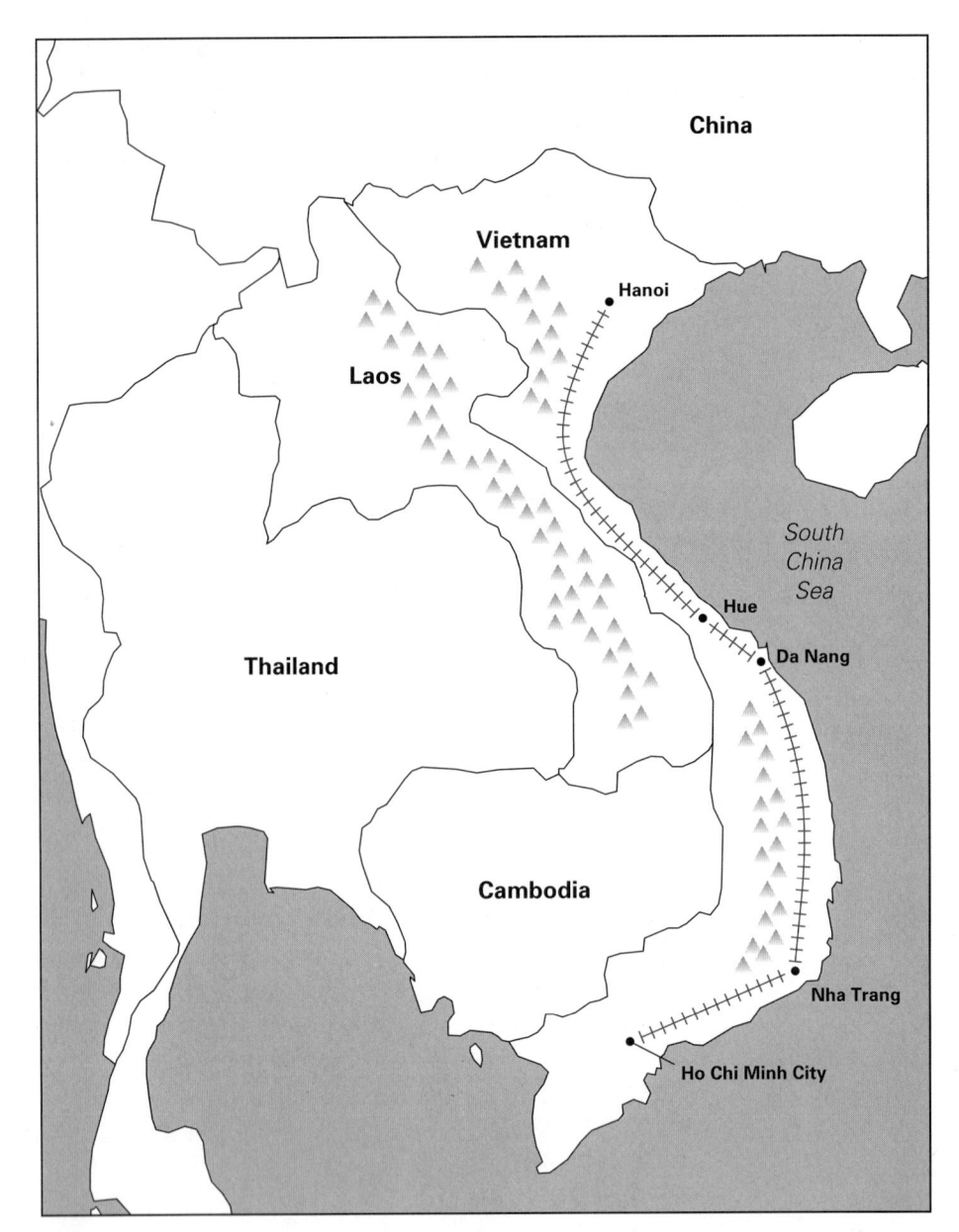

FIGURE 8-3
The Reunification Express

tourist attractions. There are many sacred seventh-century temples and monuments from the Cham culture in Nha Trang. The Champa towers, built in the eleventh century, are religious sanctuaries. These towers contain traditional artifacts symbolizing ancient legends. Stilt houses along the river banks and in the harbor add to the country's charm as the train heads north to the Hai Van mountain pass.

DA NANG. After the train crosses Hai Van Pass, it gently descends to Da Nang (see Figure 8–3). Surrounded by mountains, Da Nang's major attraction is the Cham Museum, which has an exceptional collection of Champa arts and crafts. From A.D. 200 to A.D. 1471, the Cham were a powerful people whose kingdom was called Champa. The kingdom flourished along the coastal area of Vietnam until the Annamese Emperor ultimately destroyed it in about A.D. 1471. The Cham people were nearly extinct by 1901 and fled to Cambodia.

Vietnamese mythology is alive deep in the heart of the Marble Mountains, just west of Da Nang. These mountains form five peaks made of marble. To the Vietnamese, these five peaks symbolize the five components of the universe: water, fire, metal, wood, and earth. Several natural caves in the largest marble peak hold Buddhist shrines, which followers believe watch over the country. On the other side of this peak is China Beach, which once hosted an international surfing competition.

HUE. When the Reunification Express arrives in Hue (see Figure 8–3), travelers may notice that the Imperial Palace inside Hue is a complete replica of the Forbidden City in Beijing. Hue was the capital of the Nguyen Dynasty from 1803 to 1883. The Perfume River forms the border between Hue and the "Forbidden City." In this city-within-a-city, magnificent palaces, tombs, and temples were built under the thirteen emperors of the Nguyen Dynasty. Travelers on a boat trip up the Perfume River pass the beautiful Thien Mu Pagoda and tombs of the Nyguyen emperors. Hue is also divided into distinct areas by the Hue River. North of the river is a section full of traditional culture. Sections south of the river are more modern.

HANOI. Just before the train reaches Hanoi (see Figure 8–3), an important industrial center, it passes rice fields tended by farmers wearing conical hats and plowing with teams of water buffalo. Hanoi features pagoda-studded lakes and tree-lined boulevards. The most famous pagoda in the city, the One Pillar Pagoda, was built in 1049 and is shaped like a lotus blossom. The One Pillar Pagoda, built in the eleventh century and constructed of wood, was devoted to the Bhuddist Goddess of Mercy, Quan Am. Hanoi is also home to Vietnam's first university, a fascinating eleventh-century Temple of Literature. Hanoi's markets are fun and interesting, as is strolling by the Lake of the Restored Sword.

For authentic cultural involvement, travelers take side trips to Sa Pa in the Fan Si Pan Mountains. The highest mountain in these highlands is the Fan Si Pan at 10,312 feet. Tours visit the remote hill-tribe villages of the Hmong people, deep in the forests and jungles. The Hmong still carry on their ethnic and traditional way of life.

Australia

Golden beaches, tropical forests, and vast deserts are among the attractions of the only continent entirely occupied by one nation with one government, Australia. Australia is so remote that from Sydney the nearest point in North America is San Francisco, 7,600 miles away. Australia is the smallest and driest continent but is the largest island in the world. Australia is a country where crocodile attack insurance is highly recommended, and highly modern cities contrast the stark Outback.

Railways run throughout Australia (see Figure 8–4). The best of Australia can be easily and economically accessed using a rail pass. Rail Australia offers Austrailpass with unlimited economy or first-class travel anywhere on the network for 14 to 90 consecutive days. The Austrail Flexipass also offers unlimited economy or first-class travel anywhere on the Australian rail network. It is valid for 8 to 29 consecutive days. Both passes must be purchased outside Australia, and travel must be completed within a 6-month period. Passes do not include sleeping berths or meals.

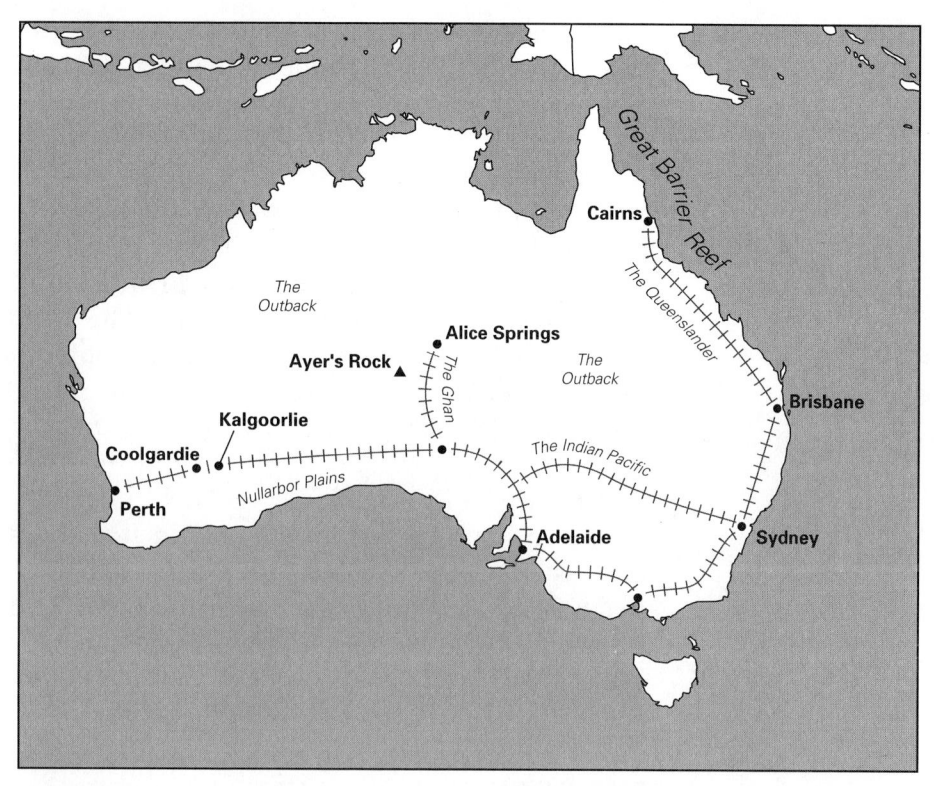

FIGURE 8–4
Australian railways

Australia's rail journeys abound. Some truly wondrous and spectacular rail itineraries include trips on the Indian Pacific, the Ghan, and the Queenslander.

INDIAN PACIFIC

It takes the famous Indian Pacific 3 days to travel the 2,700 miles from coast to coast across Australia, from Sydney on the Pacific Ocean to Perth on the Indian Ocean. The Indian Pacific makes five stops and departs twice weekly in both directions.

One of Australia's main attractions is Sydney (see Figure 8–4). This city is best known for its striking architectural landmark, the Sydney Opera House. The roof of this Danish-designed building symbolizes the sails of the boats in the beautiful harbor it overlooks. The Opera House holds world-famous opera, ballet, theater, and symphony orchestra performances. About 65 miles west of Sydney, the Indian Pacific heads over the rugged and dramatic cliffs and gorges of the Blue Mountains, where scenic attractions include waterfalls, limestone caverns, and bizarre rock formations.

The Indian Pacific continues through the vast red desert of the Outback and across the Nullarbor Plains (see Figure 8–4). Stretching over 200 kilometers, the Plains comprise the longest continuous rocky coast in the world. The Nullarbor finishes abruptly at a jagged rock wall. From this point the train travels the longest straight track section in the world, 297 miles. After the Indian Pacific passes through the thriving gold-mining towns of Kalgoorlie and Coolgardie, it finally arrives in Perth (see Figure 8–4).

Perth is noted for its year-round hot and sunny climate and its relatively isolated and uncrowded beaches. Because Perth is situated on the banks of the Swan River, visitors can go swimming. Southeast of Perth is the famous 2,700-million-year-old Wave Rock.

THE GHAN

Since 1929, the legendary desert train, the Ghan, has taken passengers the 966 miles from Adelaide to Alice Springs year round (see Figure 8–4). The Ghan is named for the Afghan camel trains of the late 1800s. Before the Ghan began operating, the desolate Red Center of Australia could be reached only by camel. The Ghan's 20-hour ride through the mountains, across the inhospitable red desert, and through bleak outback towns ends at the sparsely populated and flat heart of Australia, Red Center.

The frontier town of Alice Springs in Red Center is the only town for hundreds of miles in any direction. It is a popular base for Outback excursions. The landscape outside Alice Springs is full of dramatic gorges. With its ancient rock engravings, the N'Dhala Gorge is the town's most famous. The Stanley Chasm west of Alice Springs is also wondrous.

Most travelers visit Alice Springs to view and climb the nearby grooved, wrinkled, and windswept Uluru or Ayers Rock, which is 280 miles southwest (see Figure 8–4). Measuring 2 miles long, 1 mile wide, and rising 1,099 feet, this majestic rock is the largest monolith on Earth. The rock's surface provides an extraordinary color show at sunset and sunrise. The colors change from flaming orange to fiery red.

The Uluru is sacred to the Aborigines, with its many fine rock paintings inscribed by the Aborigines over 35,000 years ago in the 230-million-year-old caves at its base. Much of the Red Center is also sacred to the Aborigines, who still inhabit this remote region. The Uluru is a vital part of Aboriginal mythology, which says the Uluru was formed by Aboriginal ancestors. The Aboriginal people still follow a traditional tribal lifestyle. They have no written language and, therefore, still pass their history orally from generation to generation. On an Aboriginal desert cultural tour, bush rangers highlight the Aboriginal people playing Australia's original instrument, the didgeridoo.

THE QUEENSLANDER

The Queenslander travels the breathtaking sun, surf, and, sand coastal route between Brisbane and Cairns for 34 hours and 1,045 miles (see Figure 8–4). The Queenslander travels only once a week from April to January. Brisbane is a charming city that flourished from a primitive 1824 convict settlement. The colonial days are still evident in the city's architecture. The Brisbane River winds and twists for 13 miles through the center of the city. Surrounded by hills and rain forests, Brisbane is a city of parks and gardens. A famous attraction is the Lone Pine Koala Sanctuary.

On the way to Cairns, the Queenslander offers many unspoiled glimpses of the Sunshine Coast's white surfing beaches, mountains, and wilderness. The Sunshine Coast offers some of the world's most beautiful offshore tropical island resorts. The Sunshine Coast is also a lively place filled with casinos, restaurants, and theme parks.

With its 40 miles of tropical beaches, lakes, mountain winterlands, and daily cruise departures to the Great Barrier Reef, Cairns is a major vacation area (see Figure 8–4). The Great Barrier Reef, the world's longest and largest coral reef, stretches an enormous 1,250 miles. The reef is the largest living organism on Earth with over 1,000 species of tropical fish. The Great Barrier Reef is considered the best and most expensive diving spot in the world. With a visibility of up to 200 feet, the reef offers an unparalleled view of animal, plant, and coral life. Glass-bottom boats also offer splendid views of the reef.

Twice a week Queenslander passengers can party and rock and roll nonstop on the train's disco car, Club Loco. This unusual rail car is complete with a sound and lighting system, a smoke machine, music videos, and a dance floor. Some tourists complete their Australian visits by dancing and drinking their way to Cairns.

The South Pacific

It is easy to be overwhelmed by the Pacific Ocean. With an estimated area of 70 million square miles, the Pacific Ocean is larger than the world's total landmass combined. At its broadest stretch between Panama and the Malay Peninsula, the Pacific Ocean measures 19,000 kilometers, or nearly half the earth's circumference. One could easily fall in love with the timeless and pleasant life of the South Pacific. This is true paradise.

It is peculiar how one region of the largest ocean on earth, the South Pacific, can hold such an enormous concentration of tiny islands (see Figure 8–5). The South Pacific contains more islands per square mile than any other ocean region. There are two geological answers for this phenomenon. First, some of the islands are of volcanic origin. A chain of mountains under the ocean runs through the South Pacific. The chain's highest peaks rise above the surface of the ocean, creating islands, like Tahiti. Second, other islands are built by corals.

Most islands in the South Pacific depend heavily on tourism as their main source of income. The thousands of tropical and unpolluted islands have unspoiled and uncrowded beaches that are protected by reef corals. The islands' forests, rivers, and mountains are also very inviting to travelers. More active travelers swim, snorkel, sail, or take diving lessons. Whitewater rafting, glacier walks, volcanic hikes, caving, and rain forest treks are also available to the more adventurous.

FIGURE 8–5

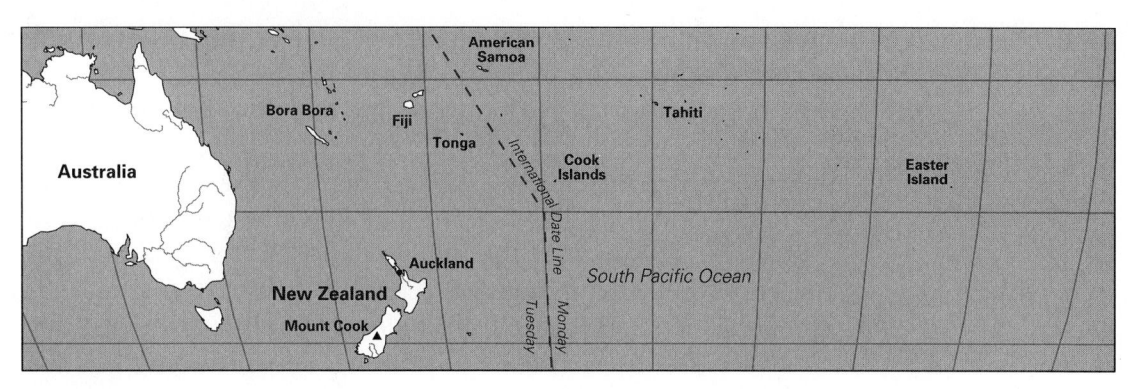

The South Pacific

Traveling between the South Pacific islands can be confusing when crossing the International Date Line. Tonga, just west of the International Date Line, is the first nation in the world to begin a new day (see Figure 8–5). American Samoa is located just east of the International Date Line. While the clock hour in American Samoa is the same as in Tonga, the two islands experience a 24-hour difference (1 day). When it is noon Monday in American Samoa, for example, it is noon Tuesday in nearby Tonga.

For thousands of years the world's first island cultures were isolated by miles of ocean. These fascinating cultures, including their myths and legends, remain virtually unchanged. Although there are over a thousand languages throughout the South Pacific, each island has managed to retain its own unique culture. This is quite evident in the 172 islands of Tonga.

TONGA

Tonga is a lush group of islands with caves carved by the sea. Tonga's capital, Nuku'alofa, is on Tongatapu Island. Other major island groups include 'Eua, VaVa'u, and Ha'apai. These islands are lush and hilly with caves carved by the sea.

The royal family of the Kingdom of Tonga has been traced back over 1,000 years. The Polynesian King Taufa'ahau Tupou IV still reigns from the Victorian-style Royal Palace. Tonga's fantastic natural harbor, Port of Refuge, is a perfect setting for yachting and sailing.

Tonga's islands are spread out and form two parallel chains. The western islands are high volcanic forms; the eastern islands are low coral forms. Tonga islands have several active volcanoes. Tonga's coral reefs spread over a 100,000 square miles. One impressive attraction of the reefs are the "blow holes," holes in the coral reefs through which sea water bursts 60 feet into the air. The "blow holes" are found along the coast 10 miles from Nuku'alofa on the Tongatapu island group. On the other side of the island are the Terraced Tombs. The tombstones, rising in terraces to a height of 13 feet, were built of coral about A.D. 1,200. The stone arch Ha'amonga Trilithon from the same era is also made of coral. Each coral stone weighs about 40 tons.

FIJI

The main islands of Fiji's 320 islands are of volcanic origin, surrounded by ½ million square miles of coral reef (see Figure 8–5). Fiji offers exciting ethnic variety. Suva, the capital of Fiji, offers colorful native markets and Fijian, Indian, and Chinese cultures. Visitors are fascinated by exotic treks in landscapes with dramatic and rugged volcanic peaks, spectacular waterfalls, lush forests, yellow grasslands, and tropical vegetation. The two largest Fijian islands are extinct volcanoes that rise abruptly from the sea.

EASTER ISLAND

Easter Island was discovered Easter Day in 1722 and is often considered to be one of the most isolated places on earth. The island, which is of volcanic origin, has three extinct craters rising to 1,765 feet each. Tours to the crater of the volcano Rano Kao can be arranged. The weather on Easter Island is unusual because it has no rivers or trees and thus is subject to strong winds.

On Easter Island a mysterious culture once flourished. Followers worshipped spirits through huge enigmatic stone statues of humans called Moai. The island is famous for these 600 statues, of which only the elongated heads rise about

30 feet above the ground. Built of compressed ash and weighing an average of 50 tons, these gigantic statues stand like quiet guards along the coast. One of the largest statues weighs 400 tons.

BORA BORA

For the traveler seeking a smaller, less crowded, beautiful island in the South Pacific, Bora Bora is a good choice. It has jagged volcanic peaks, blue lagoons, and secluded beaches. Climbs up the island's two mountains of Otemanu and Pahia can be arranged for more active travelers.

AMERICAN SAMOA

The city of Pago Pago on American Samoa has interesting jungle-like vegetation and Mt. Alava and Mt. Piao, the "Rainmaker" as great backdrops. The five inhabited islands of American Samoa are volcanic in origin.

TAHITI

Tahiti was born of two volcanic masses that grew together and are now connected by a narrow isthmus. The two Tahiti islands have it all, including towering volcanic peaks, rugged terrain, spectacular waterfalls, and gorgeous beaches beckoning to be explored. Tahiti's rugged landscape of tropical vegetation and lagoons protected by coral reefs make it the most sought-after South Pacific destination. Accommodations range from rustic thatched-roof country cottages to posh hotels.

COOK ISLANDS

The Cook Islands are scattered over a large area. The northern group of islands are coral atolls (reefs surrounding lagoons); the southern group are volcanic in origin. Many of the larger Cook Islands have gorgeous lagoons surrounded by volcanic hills. The Cook Islands are a true "get-away-from-it-all" destination. No television and miles of perfect white-sand beaches await world-weary travelers. Rarotonga is the largest Cook Island. Its highest peak, Te Manga, rises to 2,140 feet. Places of interest include Pa's Palace, which is built of coral and lime.

NEW ZEALAND

New Zealand consists of two major islands, the North Island and the South Island (see Figure 8–5). Much of the country is mountainous and scattered with volcanoes. The islands offer white-water-rafting-type rivers and high alpine lakes. There are many small beach areas throughout the North Island. Also known as the "City of Sails," Auckland sits on the peninsula of North Island and is a famous stopover and popular beach area.

Auckland's Waitemata Harbor is an important yachting center. In its backdrop are many extinct volcanoes that protect the harbor from the Pacific Ocean. Rotorua, which is south of Auckland, has raging geysers that send boiling mud and water violently into the air. Rotorua is the best place to experience the 1,000-year-old native Maori culture. Here the traditional Maori wood and stone carving can be seen.

The city of Queenstown on the South Island is a major ski center between June and August. The highest peak, Mount Cook, stands at 12,349 feet. With its awesome fjords, the island's scenery is breathtaking.

TRAVELING WISELY

The United States State Department issues travel advisories to inform and sometimes warn travelers of problems in a certain area of a country. The country may still be safe to visit, but precautions are recommended. For example, in 1995, the State Department announced that a consular office had opened in Salzburg, Austria. The State Department also recommended limited road travel at night in eastern Turkey because of terrorist activities. Travel advisories can be obtained from most computer reservation systems.

SUMMARY

- The best way to explore Australia is to purchase one of its many rail passes.
- The Eastern & Oriental Express is a luxury rail service between Singapore and Bangkok.
- The Reunification Express follows the Vietnamese coastline between Hanoi and Ho Chi Minh City.
- The railways of Australia travel throughout the world's smallest continent and largest island.
- In the South Pacific, which boasts thousands of tropical and unpolluted islands with unspoiled and uncrowded beaches, each island retains its own unique culture.

CHECK YOUR UNDERSTANDING 8–1

Discuss and assess international tourism to Asia and the Pacific while considering the following:

- What type of visitor would travel to this region and why?
- What role does the travel professional play in the successful outcome of a trip to Asia and the Pacific?
- What problems does this region face in attracting more visitors?
- Assess and discuss why Vietnam has experienced an enormous growth of tourist arrivals over the last few years.

CHECK YOUR UNDERSTANDING 8–2

Directions: Fill in the following blanks:

1. Define *Austrailpass*.

   _____
   _____
   _____
   _____

2. Differentiate between the Queenslander and the Indian Pacific.

   _____
   _____
   _____
   _____

3. Outline the Ghan rail services.

   _____
   _____
   _____
   _____

4. Identify a typical buyer of an Austrailpass.

   _____
   _____
   _____
   _____

5. Identify the advantages and disadvantages of traveling by rail in Australia.

   _____
   _____
   _____
   _____

CHECK YOUR UNDERSTANDING 8–3

Directions: Fill in the following blanks:

1. What type of visitor to Asia would travel with the Reunification Express and why?

   _____
   _____
   _____
   _____

2. Describe the most important selling feature of the Eastern & Orient Express.

3. How does the Eastern & Orient Express compare with Rail Australia?

4. How does a South Pacific cruise compete with a Mediterranean cruise?

5. What type of visitor would travel to Southeast Asia and why?

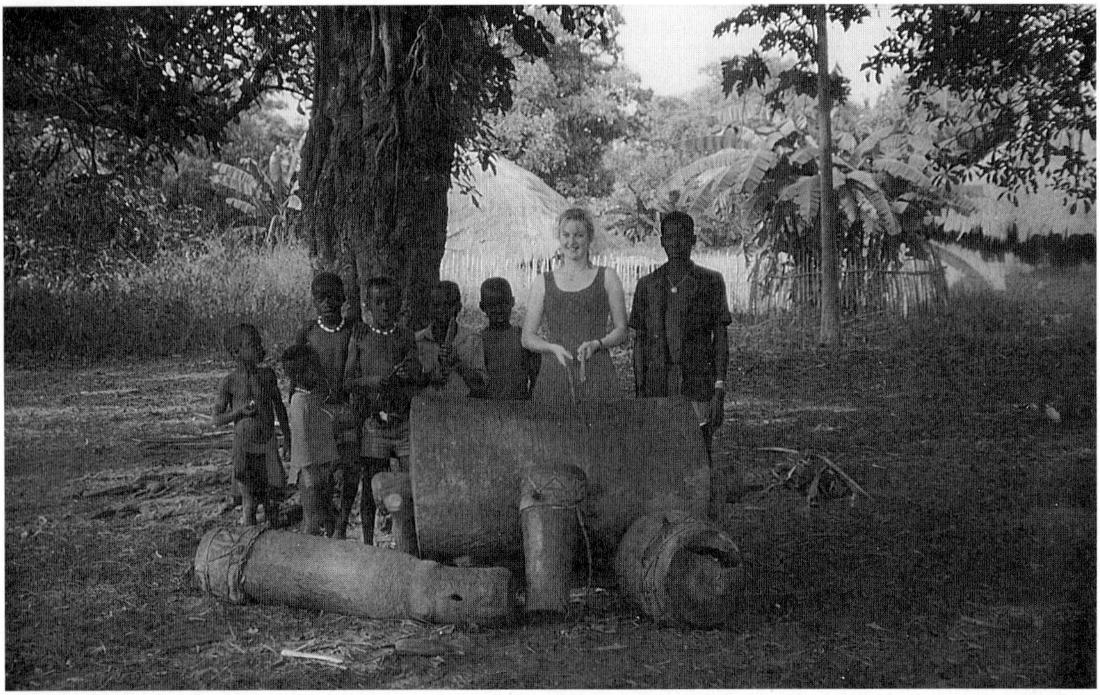

Chapter 9

Developing Nations

Southern Africa
    The Blue Train
    Zimbabwe
    Zambia
    Tanzania
The Nile River
    Egypt
    Sudan
    Ethiopia
The Zambezi River Valley
South America
    Quito
    Ambato
    Riobamba
    Cuenca
    Guayaquil
Argentina and Chile
    Patagonia
    Tierra del Fuego
    Ushuaia
    Punta Arenas
    Puerto Montt
Antarctica

OBJECTIVES

After completing Chapter 9, you should be able to:

- Identify and describe the variety of destinations throughout the developing nations.
- Identify the tourism trends in the developing nations.
- Understand the importance of proper preparation for visiting the developing nations.

Unfortunately for the tourism business, the media tend to focus on accidents, natural disasters, famine, and revolutions in developing nations. Tourism in developing nations suffers particularly from these negative and distorted pictures. Developing nations receive only 4 percent of international tourist arrivals. For example, when a traveler in Zambia is killed by the most dangerous creature in Africa, the hippopotamus, the media makes the entire nation of Zambia appear unsafe. The media exaggerate a tiny percentage of tourist fatalities, and travelers should not be dissuaded from experiencing the wonders of developing nations.

Many developing nations are former European colonies. Many are located in the Southern Hemisphere. Since they gained their independence, these developing nations have been unable to develop stable economic and political situations. These 120 nations, predominantly in Asia, Africa, and Central/South Americas, are making economic gains, but about 70 percent of the world's poorest nations are found in Africa. The underdeveloped nations are grouped as agricultural societies with limited industrial development. The quality of life in these nations is low because they have more than 75 percent of the world's population. The explosive population growth in developing nations has resulted in high rates of illiteracy, high infant mortality, widespread disease, and low life expectancies. International tourism carries far wider effects for developing nations than developed ones because it transfers much-needed skills and professional labor.

Much can be done to prepare properly for an exciting vacation in developing nations. First, the developing nations are not for the inexperienced traveler. Those expecting clean, private bathrooms with functional plumbing will often be disappointed. There are many insects and much pollution in the warmer countries. Travelers must understand that they are offered the best conditions available. Travelers must also understand that crowded cities can be noisy and dusty. Flexibility is critical because many difficult travel conditions prevail. Jeep safaris, for example, commonly become stuck in the mud for hours. Impatience is not an asset in these situations.

While they present some challenges to the traveler, many developing nations offer unparalleled scenic beauty, cultural richness, and historical treasures. Figure 9–1 shows the nine most-visited nations on the African continent in 1995. The most remarkable statistic comes from South Africa. This nation soared to the top of the chart with an annual visitor increase of 20 percent.

Some of the northern African nations hugging the Mediterranean Coast are extremely popular among European tourists. Europeans are attracted to the fabulous beaches, mountains, and remnants of Roman, Berber, and Arab cultures. In addition, this region is far less expensive than other Mediterranean nations.

The volcanic islands of Mauritius (see Figure 9–1) and Reunion are other increasingly popular vacation retreats for Europeans. According to the *Travel Industry World Yearbook: The Big Picture, 1994–1995*, published by Child & Waters, Inc., Europeans account for about 50 percent of the islands' international tourist arrivals. Africans make up the other half.

There is no place like Kenya, Botswana, and Zimbabwe for the excitement of safaris and wildlife viewing. Much of the wildlife on these trips can only be found in Africa. This region of Africa also provides the spectacle of the tallest waterfall in Africa, Victoria Falls.

Tunisia has managed to become a leading North African tourist destination (see Figure 9–1). Its neighboring countries of Algeria and Morocco have not.

In contrast to popular spots, some developing nations such as Morocco, Algeria, and Tunisia suffer economic turmoil, escalating terrorism, and massive demonstrations. Rebellious outbursts are sometimes targeted toward foreigners and have led tourists to flee and stay away from the better-known beach resorts. As a result, tourism in such regions has declined heavily over the last few years.

FIGURE 9-1

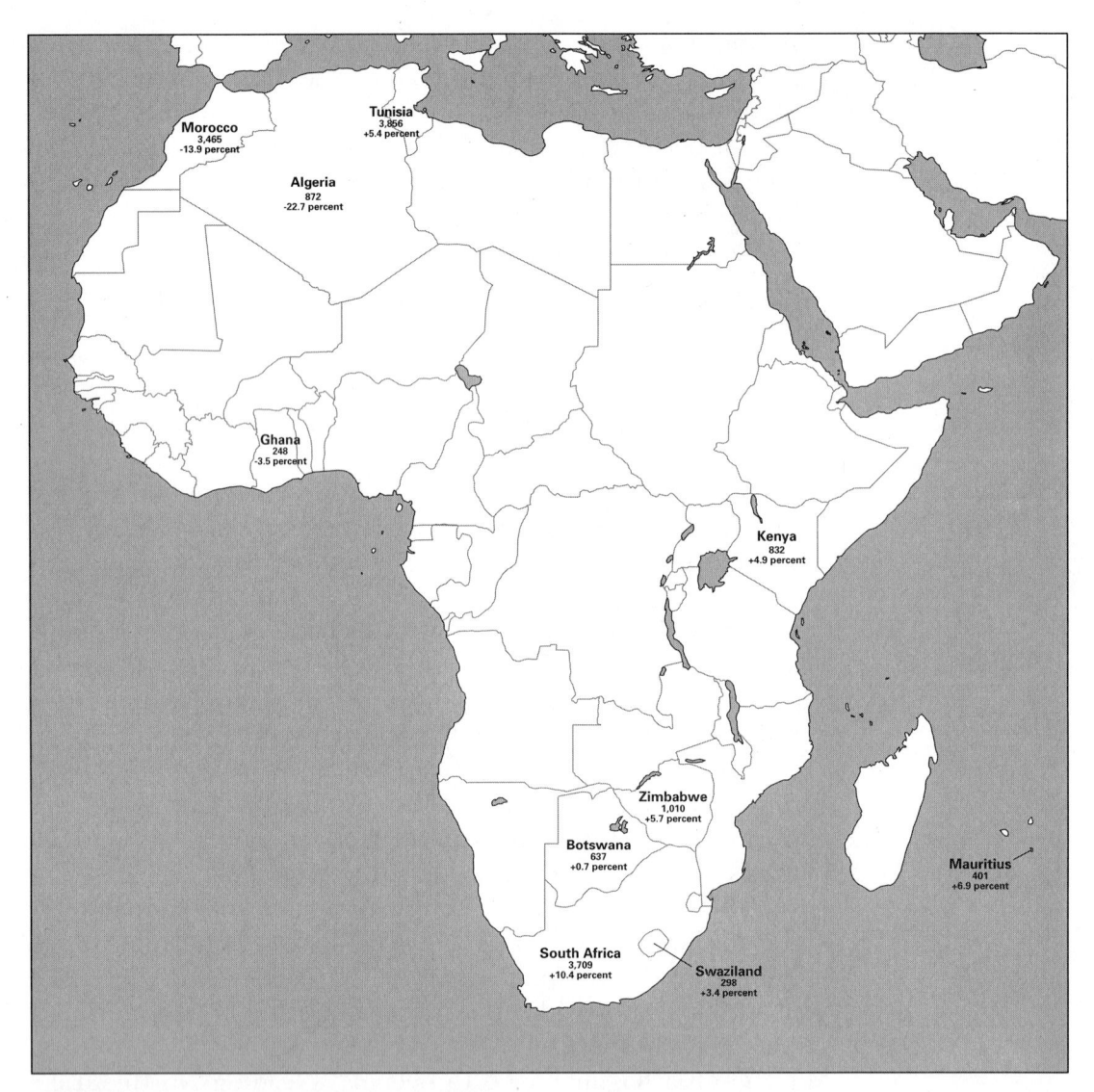

1995 Visitor arrivals to Africa. Source: Travel Weekly, *April 29, 1996.*

Southern Africa

Since Nelson Mandela declared South Africa "free at last" in 1994, the country has experienced an explosion of international tourist arrivals. As was mentioned earlier, annual tourist arrivals to South Africa increased 20 percent in 1995 (see Figure 9–1). Tourism is now the nation's fourth largest industry.

South Africa is known as "a world in one country" because it truly has it all, including rich vineyards, high plateaus, varied wildlife, and tribal village life. Travelers fall in love with the nation's gorgeous white-sand beaches, rocky shore lines, vast deserts, deep canyons, and marvelous mountains.

South Africa is also one of the most culturally diverse nations in the world. Settlers came from all over the world to live there. South Africa's multiculturalism is evident in its overwhelming choice of international restaurants and theatrical and musical repertoires. Walking down almost any city street, the traveler will find an interesting mix of Malaysian, Indian, Zulu, French, Portuguese, German, Chinese, Japanese, and Dutch ethnicities.

South Africa's population has been divided into four main ethnic groups. The blacks are the original population. Most are Zulu or Xhosa. The Zulu are the largest language group in South Africa. They total approximately 30 million, or 74 percent of the population. Originally *Zulu* was the name of the Bantu-speaking tribal cultures. Each tribe was independent and had its own chief. Today many Zulu have resettled permanently in towns and cities.

The whites, who are mostly of Dutch, British, German, and French descent, total about 5 million, or 14 percent of the population. About 9 percent of the population, or 3 million, is of a mixed race of blacks, whites, and Asians called "coloreds." The smallest group in South Africa is Asian. They total about 1 million, or 3 percent of the population and come predominantly from India. These statistics are taken from the 1993 *The Countries of the World and Their Leaders Yearbook,* volume 2, published by Gale Research, Inc.

Racial disparity in South Africa has created one of the most controversial problems in the world. After South Africa's black leader, Nelson Mandela, was imprisoned in 1962, South Africa's white minority-rule government practiced apartheid. *Apartheid* is a Dutch word meaning "separateness." The white government completely controlled the four main racial groups and kept them segregated in all aspects of life.

During apartheid, blacks were not allowed to vote. Nonwhites were told where to go to school, live, and work. Nonwhites had their own beaches, busses, restaurants, hotels, and so on. During the 30 years of apartheid, the black population organized many demonstrations and riots, leading to bloody clashes with the white police. South Africa had been under a state of emergency for many years. When Mandela was released from prison in 1990 and reelected president of South Africa, major and drastic changes occurred, of which the abolishment of apartheid was most important.

This historic event has led to the wonderful rediscovery of a country ranked one of the most scenic and beautiful in the world. South Africa is also the most modern nation on the African continent with its highly developed infra- and suprastructures.

Nonstop air service between New York and Johannesburg, South Africa (see Figure 9–2), has been established. Because there is a limited number of nonstop and direct flights, reservations must be made at least 8 months in advance. South Africa is so popular that all flights fill quickly. Reservations on South Africa's famous Blue Train must be made at least 12 months in advance.

THE BLUE TRAIN

South Africa's luxurious and stylish **Blue Train** is indeed blue. The new Blue Trains were put into service in 1972. The train's main route is between Cape Town and Pretoria (see Figure 9–2). It departs every other day from September to April. Between May and August it departs every fourth day of the month. The 2-day journey includes stops in Kimberley and Johannesburg.

CAPE TOWN. In one of the most beautiful cities in the world, Cape Town (see Figure 9–2), a cable car travels up a 3,000-foot-high landmark, Table Mountain. From its flat top is one of the most far-reaching views in the world. Table Bay sits just below the city, boasting a beautiful harbor. A cruise around the harbor provides a great view of lazy sea lions sunbathing. South of Cape Town a spectacle occurs at the tip of the rocky, 850-foot-high cliff, Cape of Good Hope. Here the Atlantic Ocean clashes with the Indian Ocean, creating some of the best surfing conditions and the most bedazzling beaches in the world.

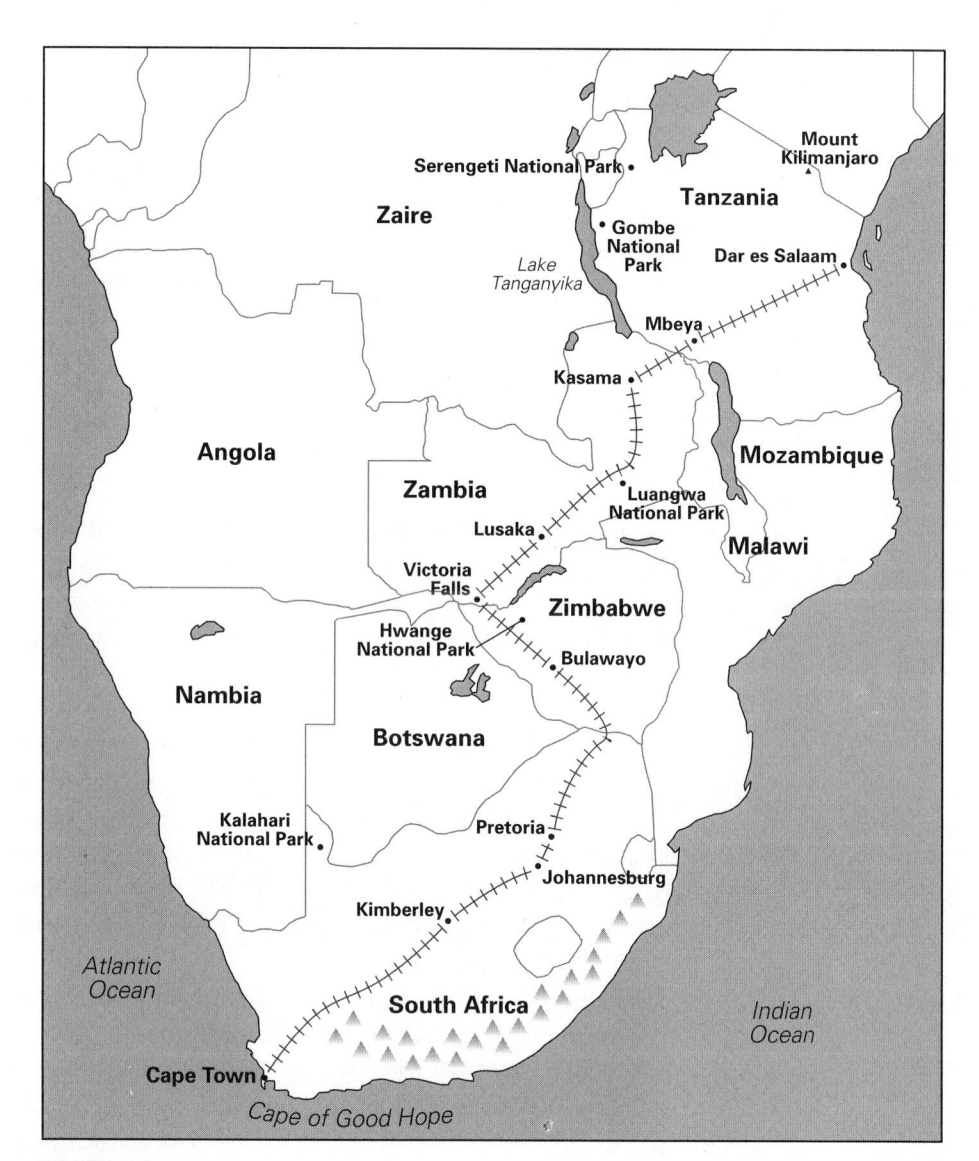

FIGURE 9–2

The Blue Train

KIMBERLEY. On its way to Kimberley (see Figure 9–2), the Blue Train passes through the Hex River Valley and Hex River Pass. The town of Kimberley, founded in 1871, has retained its Victorian charm. Here diamonds were first discovered in 1866, when a 21-carat stone was found on the banks of the Orange River. In 1869, an 83-carat diamond was found. Soon after, Kimberley became the world's diamond capital and home to the largest diamond specialist in the world, de Beers. In Kimberley, the largest excavation in the world, the Big Hole, produced 2,722 kilos of diamonds during the 43 years of the town's heyday. People from all over the world came to the site in search of diamonds.

A new era began in South Africa when gold and diamonds were discovered in the second half of the nineteenth century. South Africa now accounts for about two thirds of world gold production. When travelers buy diamonds in Johannesburg, they enjoy discounts of up to 13 percent by presenting their passports and airline tickets.

JOHANNESBURG. Johannesburg, the next stop on the Blue Train (see Figure 9–2), is the gold capital of the world. The entire city is built on a mine. The mine produces almost 700,000 kilos of gold per year. The highlight of Johannesburg is a tour of the reconstructed Gold Reef City, a gold-rush-era city built around an old gold mine. Here Zulu, Xhosa, and Sotho tribal mine dancers perform.

From Johannesburg guided tours go to Kalahari National Park. Covering an impressive 79,000 square miles, the Kalahari is the largest nature conservation area in Southern Africa. The park is also one of the largest unspoiled ecosystems in the world. Its variety of flora and fauna here is overwhelming.

From Johannesburg, the Blue Train continues to Pretoria, the capital of South Africa (see Figure 9–2). Pretoria is known as the "Jacaranda City" because of the flowering trees lining the streets. The 16-mile long Church Street is one of the longest straight streets in the world. Pretoria has many fine museums, including the Museum of Geological Survey and the Pretoria Art Museum. Once a year travelers can extend their itineraries and travel from South Africa through Zimbabwe, Zambia, and Tanzania to the Indian Ocean. This annual journey takes 11 days one way.

ZIMBABWE

The 17,254 square miles of Zimbabwe have been reserved for national parks. Hwange National Park, Zimbabwe's largest park (see Figure 9–2), has the largest variety of animals in Zimbabwe. Hwange is home to over 100 species of animals and over 400 species of birds. Hwange is also one of the last elephant sanctuaries in Africa. Huge herds of up to 100 elephants can be seen at the park's water holes.

ZAMBIA

The Blue Train's next stop is one of the most spectacular attractions in Africa, Victoria Falls, Zambia (see Figure 9–2). The third largest in the world in volume, Victoria Falls is just over 1 mile wide in April, May, and June when the water flow is at its maximum. Not far from Victoria Falls is Lusaka, the capital of Zambia.

The Zambian government limits the number of participants in a safari from six to eight people, thereby allowing travelers to fully experience African wildlife as it roams its unspoiled, natural habitat. Entire herds of elephants, zebras, and antelope are often seen. The river banks of the Luangwa National Park (see Figure 9–2) are home to hundreds of species of birds. This park also houses one of the largest elephant concentrations left in Africa. Over 100,000 elephants live in the park's valley. The Sumbu National Park offers year-round beach resorts. The Kasaba is the most famous.

TANZANIA

Dar es Salaam is the gateway to the highlights of Tanzania (see Figure 9–2). On the border between Tanzania and Kenya, the snow-covered, 19,340-foot volcanic Mt. Kilimanjaro is the highest in Africa. Tour companies guide trekkers, climbers, and mountaineers from all over the world during the 5-day ascent of Kilimanjaro.

Tanzania is also home to eleven exciting national parks that cover 13,000 square miles. The 5,000 square miles of the

Serengeti National Park (see Figure 9–2) is one of the finest and most-visited game parks in Africa. It is home to 35 species of animals, including the wildebeest and a large variety of birds. A collapsed volcano, the Ngorongo Crater, rises above the Serengeti. This 100-square-mile area is home to different species of animals, including the leopard. Another park of interest in Tanzania is the Ruaha National Park, which holds the largest elephant sanctuary in the world. About 200 chimpanzees can be seen in their natural habitat in Gombe National Park, which is on the shores of Lake Tanganyika. The largest game reserve in the world, Selous Game Reserve, is particularly attractive to travelers because it houses one of the largest elephant populations in the world. Adventurous travelers go on safaris past lions, hippopotami, and crocodiles with armed rangers.

The Nile River

The opportunity to explore the ancient cultures that have remained over the centuries makes the Nile among the most sought-after river cruises in the world (see Figure 9–3). Modern cruise ships, as well as elegant felucca sailing boats, explore the overwhelming immensity of the longest river in the world. No roads run parallel to the Nile, so the impressive temples and tombs along the shores of the Nile Valley are best discovered on a Nile River cruise. The Nile Valley is often described as "the world's largest outdoor museum."

The Nile is the heart of Egypt. In desert Egypt, people, animals, and agriculture depend totally on the Nile. The Nile is the Sahara Desert's biggest oasis. The Nile Valley makes up only 3 percent of Egypt's landmass, but it holds 95 percent of the population. Some of the world's earliest civilizations and most ancient and mysterious cultures developed in the Nile Valley over 7,000 years ago.

The 4,160-mile-long Nile River originates deep in the African highlands of Burundi, by Lake Tanganyika just south of the Equator (see Figure 9–3). It flows from the lakes of the Rift Valley through Lake Victoria. In southern Sudan the river changes its name to the White Nile and continues north to

FIGURE 9–3

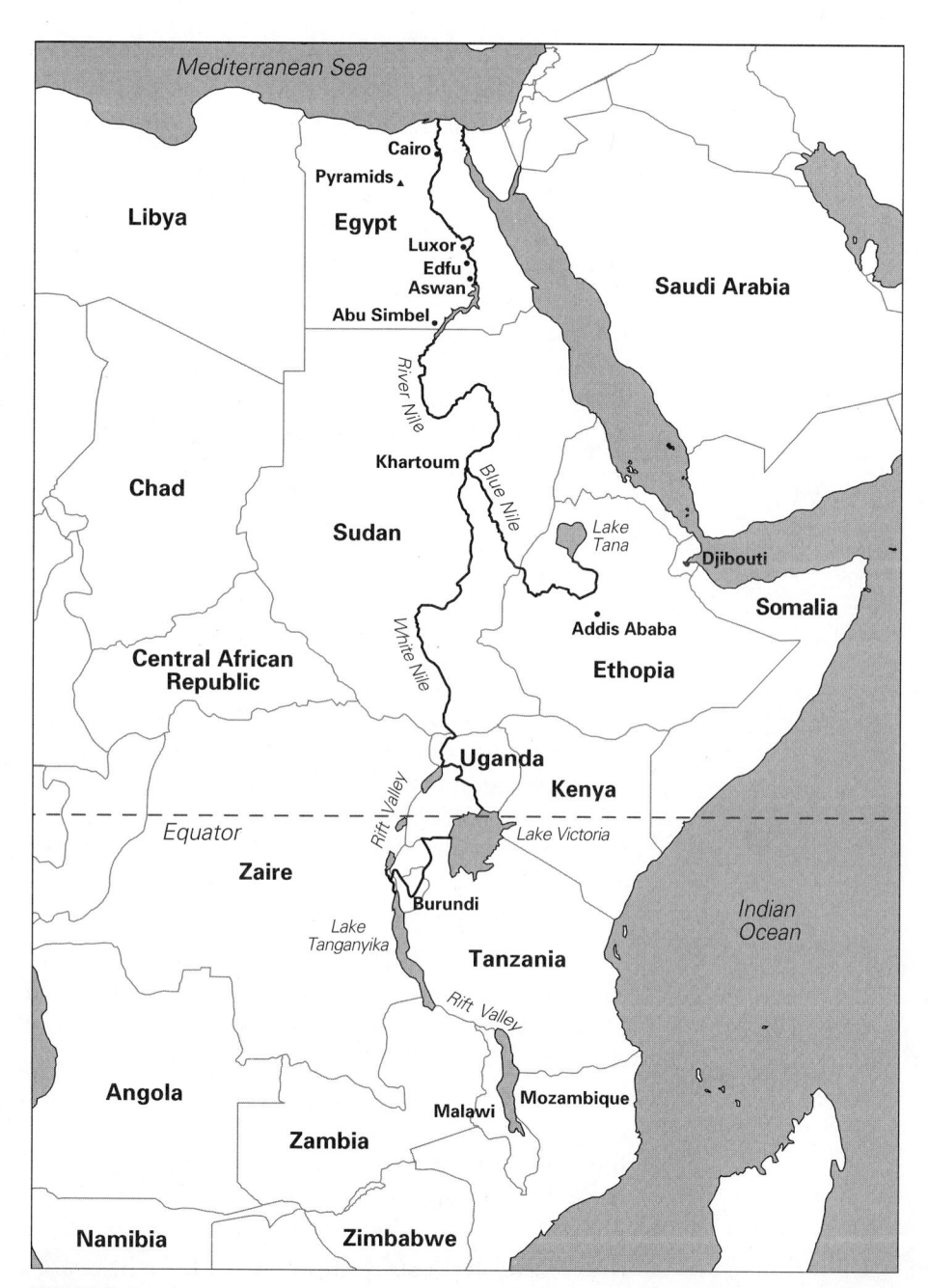

The Nile River

Cairo, Egypt, where it starts to form a 100-mile-wide delta that empties into the Mediterranean Sea. In Khartoum, Sudan, the White Nile is joined by its major tributary, the Blue Nile, which originates at 6,000 feet in Lake Tana in Ethiopia. The water of the White Nile appears white, while the water in the Blue Nile looks blue. For several miles outside Khartoum, the waters do not mix, and the blue and white waters remain distinct.

Too many cataracts in southern Egypt and waterfalls around the Equator make sailing the entire Nile impossible. The most popular portion of the Nile is the portion through the eastern edge of the Sahara Desert. A 1-week journey between Cairo and Aswan reveals a multitude of historic sites along the Nile's banks, including pyramids, statues, monuments, and temples.

EGYPT

Before many travelers begin a Nile cruise, they explore Cairo, the capital of Egypt. Cairo's 14 million inhabitants are sprawled around the Nile River. An astonishing art and sculpture collection from the Pharaohnic and Byzantine eras can be seen in the city's Egyptian Museum. The Cairo Tower sits on an island in the Nile River, offering a grand view of the city. The narrow, winding streets of the Khan-el-Khalil Bazaar are filled with stalls and stores. Cairo's ancient 1,000 mosques mix with modern casinos and luxury hotels.

The main attraction for travelers is just south of Cairo. A 5-mile ride by camel or Arabian horse from Giza into the Sahara Desert leads to three 5,000-year-old pyramids that appear through the desert heat (see Figure 9–3). The largest is 450 feet high. It has been speculated that these pyramids have been used to tell time for thousands of years. The pyramids have also been used for astronomical purposes. They stand untouched and unchanged. These awesome and wondrous pyramids were built as tombs for the ancient rulers of Egypt, the Pharaohs, using about 3 million limestone blocks, each weighing 2 to 3 tons. It took 100,000 slave workers approximately 25 years to complete their construction. It is almost more impressive that the Pyramids have endured. Of the original Seven Wonders of the Ancient World, the Pyramids are the only one left.

Not far from the three pyramids is a low hill carved in the shape of a lion with a human head. Between its paws lies a small temple. This enormous 69-foot-high, 243-foot-long Sphinx guards the pyramids. Throughout Egypt there are about 100 pyramids, all west of the Nile River.

As the Nile heads upstream and southbound toward Luxor through irrigated lands, it becomes evident why 95 percent of Egypt's population live as fishers, farmers, and cattle-raising nomads along the Nile. Ancient Egyptian cities consisted of two parts, one for the living and one for the dead. At fascinating riverside Luxor, clearly the east bank of the Nile was for the living during Pharaohnic times because of the enormous Karnak Temples, built in the twelfth century B.C. and covering 50,000 square feet, are found there.

The largest Karnak Temple is the Temple of Amon. For 2,000 years, many Pharaohs built extensions to and carved tales of their deeds in the walls, columns, and pillars of the Temple. As a result, all remaining columns and pillars are adorned impressively with hieroglyphs.

Almost completely hidden behind a steep and rocky coastline on the west side of the Nile lies the ancient burial place of Thebes, called the Valley of the Kings. In this valley, mummified Pharaohs were placed in burial chambers carved into the rock wall. The last burial took place 3,000 years ago. Today, the valley contains over sixty tombs of Pharaohs.

The city of Edfu reveals the Temple of Horus, dedicated to the falcon-headed sun god and built from 237 B.C. to 212 B.C. In Kom Ombo, the Temple of Sebok, the crocodile-headed god, houses a chamber of mummified crocodiles.

SUDAN

The 1,000-mile portion of the Nile between Aswan and Khartoum (see Figure 9–3) has many rapids and waterfalls. The

Nile has been dammed at Lake Nasser, one of the world's largest artificial lakes, for irrigation and electrical power purposes. At 2½ miles long and 365 feet high, the Aswan High Dam is the world's largest.

Along the shores of Lake Nasser, Pharaoh Ramses II built two temples. The most famous is dedicated to the sun god Amon Ra. In front of this temple are four colossal statues of Ramses II. Among these colossal statues is an entrance that reaches far into the rock wall. Inside are beautifully decorated mummies and statues and paintings of Ramses II and his beautiful Queen Nefertari.

ETHIOPIA

From Sudan, many travelers take a spectacular side trip to the source of the Blue Nile at Lake Tana in Ethiopia (see Figure 9–3). The lake is surrounded by historic monasteries and castles. Twenty miles downstream, in the town of Bahir Dar, the Blue Nile plunges over the impressive Tissisat Falls, the second largest waterfall in Africa. Below the falls, the Blue Nile cuts through some of the most dangerous gorges and rapids in Africa.

The Zambezi River Valley

The Zambezi River Valley in Central Africa is one of the few remaining areas that is still true wilderness (see Figure 9–4). The spectacular, mountainous Zambezi River Valley delivers Africa and its raw nature right to the traveler.

The Zambezi, Africa's least spoiled river, is the fourth longest in Africa. It flows about 1,650 miles on a winding and dramatic course. The Zambezi begins in Angola at an altitude of 4,500 feet, forms part of the Zambia/Zimbabwe border, and continues through Mozambique to the Indian Ocean. Zambia got its name from the Zambezi River.

At its upper reaches, the Zambezi River is calm and slow moving, but at the border of Zambia and Zimbabwe it suddenly

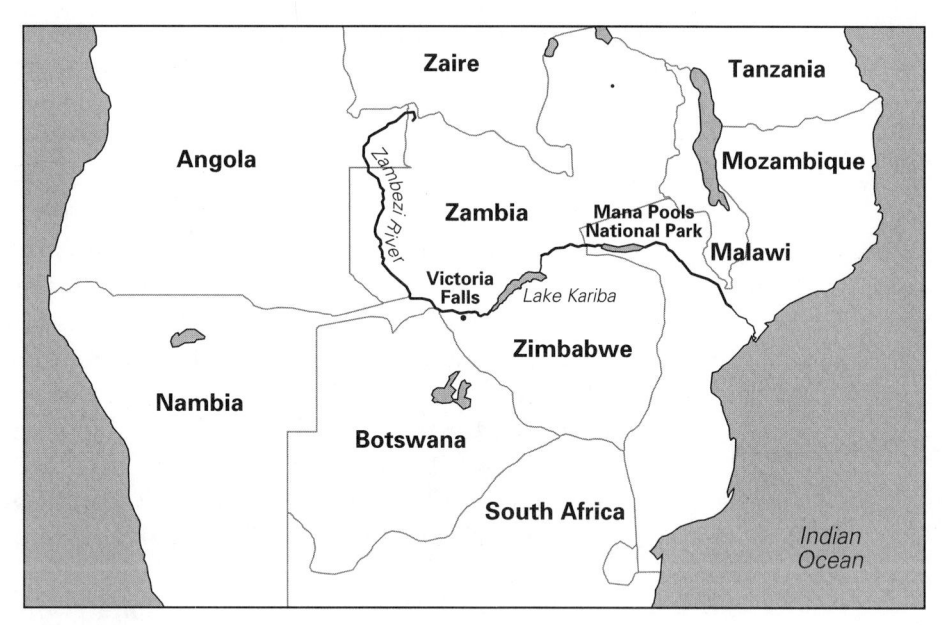

FIGURE 9–4
The Zambezi River Valley

plummets 350 feet into a sheer-sided and narrow abyss, kicking voluminous spray clouds 1,200 feet into the air and forming Victoria Falls. The spray and mist can be seen up to 20 miles away. The falls are the most famous site of the valley. Scottish explorer David Livingstone visited the falls, called the "Smoke that Thunders," in 1855 and named it after Queen Victoria of England.

The Flight of Angels, a helicopter tour, provides the greatest view of Victoria Falls, the river upstream and the gorges downstream. A spectacular hike through the rain forest below the falls also offers great views of the falls.

Rafting vacations of the Zambezi from Victoria Falls to Lake Kariba are becoming quite popular (see Figure 9–4). Below the falls the water tumbles down the Batoka Gorge for 60 miles, creating dangerous and tumultuous rapids. These rapids are infamous for furnishing a thrilling white-water rafting experience that is unmatched anywhere in the world. The Songwe Gorge joins the Batoka Gorge for a few miles before turning into the

Chimamba Rapids. Sixty miles after the rapids, the Zambezi becomes considerably wider and deepens up to 800 feet. It then suddenly expands into the wide Gwembe Valley.

Farther downstream, the river was dammed in 1958, to create Lake Kariba (see Figure 9–4). The dam changed the Kariba gorge region from a wilderness area to a 2,500-square-mile lake, thus creating one of the largest man-made lakes in the world. The main goal was to create one of Africa's largest power stations. Lake Kariba provides Zimbabwe with 80 percent of its electricity. The lake is also used for fishing and watering crops.

Lake Kariba, fringed by the majestic Matusadona Mountains and forests, abounds with wildlife, including crocodiles, rhinoceroses, elephants, buffalo, waterbuck, and hippopotami. The shores of Lake Kariba offer numerous camping and game viewing opportunities. Water activities, such as fishing, water skiing, and sailing, also abound.

Downstream from Lake Kariba, Mana Pools National Park is far from civilization (see Figure 9–4). Mana Pools National Park is a beautiful forest-type park. Its bird life along the Zambezi River is astonishing, as are its enormous animal populations of rhinoceros and buffalo. The park is also home to a startling quantity of zebra, kudu, and waterbuck. This is one of the last places on Earth where the black rhinoceros can still be found. A canoe safari through Mana Pools National Park reveals many small waterways that become little pools during the wet months.

South America

The "main street" of South America, the Pan American Highway, extends 16,000 miles from the United States/Canadian border, through Quito, Ecuador to Santiago, Chile. It leads to some of the most fascinating and scenic locations on the South American continent. For example, the barren Andean mountain range in Ecuador sits on the Pan American Highway and used to be a busy highway for the Inca Indians. As a result, it is also called the Inca Road. The dramatic mountains and snow-ringed volcanoes of the Andes make for one of the most spectacular train rides in the Western Hemisphere.

QUITO

With a San Francisco-like terrain and at an altitude of 9,350 feet, Quito sits at the foot of the snowcapped Pichincha Volcano (see Figure 9–5). Quito is one of South America's oldest cities,

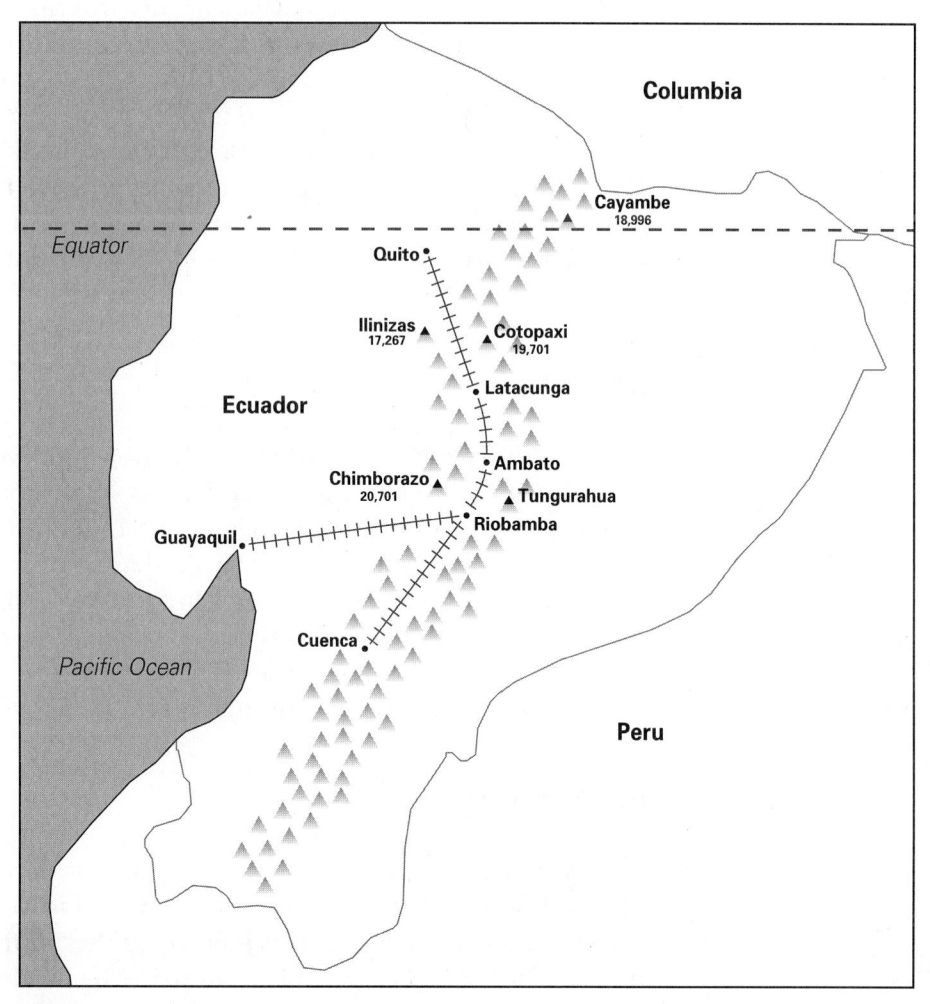

FIGURE 9–5

Ecuadorian rail lines

full of historical and spacious plazas and narrow cobblestoned streets. Outside Quito, travelers hike across fields of lava to Cotopaxi Mountain.

From Quito, Ecuador Rail runs south over the Andes and through lush valleys to small villages with colorful native markets. Many of these markets are found along a route called the "Avenue of the Volcanoes," which is the same route the train runs. This route also follows much of the Pan American Highway. Some of the highest peaks along this route are Chimborazo at 20,561 feet, Cotopaxi at 19,347 feet (the highest active volcano in the world), Cayambe at 18,996 feet, and Ilinizas at 17,267 feet. Skiing is nearly impossible in the Ecuadoran Andes. The volcanic peaks are too steep and filled with dangerous crevasses.

Just north of Quito, some travelers enjoy walking along the Equator and placing one foot in each hemisphere, North and South. The Equatorial Monument is located on the Equator at the middle of the world. From the top of the monument, the view of the Andes is striking. *Ecuador* is the Spanish word for Equator.

AMBATO

The train ride from Quito to Riobamba is marvelously scenic (see Figure 9–5). The route skirts steep slopes, passes through tunnels, climbs mountain passes at 11,841 feet, stops briefly in Ambato, and drops to Riobamba. Ambato is the site of one of South America's largest markets. On Mondays, plaza after plaza is filled with brightly colored fruits, vegetables, flowers, blankets, ponchos, and panama hats. The towering Tungurahua and Chimborazo volcanoes are in full view.

RIOBAMBA

The ancient capital city of Riobamba is located at an altitude of 9,000 feet and sits just below the snow-clad volcano, Chimborazo (see Figure 9–5). This volcano is the highest mountain in Ecuador and the second highest in the Andes. Riobamba is a popular base for trekking the Chimborazo glacier fields. Adventurous travelers may wish to hike southbound toward Cuenca along the 12,000 miles of Inca Road network that follows the path of the "Royal Road" used by the Inca rulers. Riobamba's Saturday market, which spreads over nine plazas filled with Indians from all over Ecuador, is one of Ecuador's largest Indian markets.

CUENCA

Tucked away in a valley rimmed by the Andes, elegant cobblestoned streets and charming tree-lined, flowered plazas make Cuenca Ecuador's most beautiful city (see Figure 9–5). Founded in 1577, Cuenca sits on the Pan American Highway that once connected Quito with Cuzco, Peru.

GUAYAQUIL

A narrow line from Riobamba leads from the spectacular Andes to the Devil's Nose and drops dramatically to the "Pearl of the Pacific," Guayaquil (see Figure 9–5). The city is located on the Guayas River 50 miles inland from the Pacific Ocean. There is no better way to end an Ecuadorean vacation than by relaxing at the popular beach resort of Playas, 60 miles south of the city. Playas has exceptional deep-sea fishing.

Argentina and Chile

Chile is an unusually shaped country: 2610 miles long and not more than 115 miles wide. The northern region of Chile contains the driest desert in the world, the Atacama Desert. The Andes run from north to south and take up almost half of the Chile's width.

Argentina, the third largest country in the Southern Hemisphere and the eighth largest in the world, boasts a wide range of geographical features. In the Andes Mountains in the west, Mount Aconcagua towers 23,000 feet and the waterfalls at Iguazu thunder 230 feet into the Parana River below. The southwest part of the country resembles Switzerland with many beautiful lakes surrounded by mountains.

PATAGONIA

The southernmost region of South America, Patagonia, which includes Argentina south of the Rio Colorado and Chile south of the Bio Bio Rio, is 300,000 square miles of barren land (see Figure 9–6). This region offers the sheer, natural beauty of the smoking and snow-covered Andean volcanoes and massive glaciers caving and crashing into the ocean. Patagonia draws hundreds of whales to the Valdez Peninsula to breed between May and September. The Valdez Peninsula also houses the largest concentration of penguins in the world. Thousands of penguins arrive from the sea to raise their young before returning to the sea in March.

TIERRA DEL FUEGO

The southern tip of the immense island of Tierra del Fuego points to the end of the world (see Figure 9–6). This mountainous island boasts glacial landscapes, canyons, and waterfalls. Since 1520, Tierra del Fuego has also been known as the "Land of Fire" because many native Indians burn fires along its coasts.

USHUAIA

The rustic town of Ushuaia (see Figure 9–6), or "Bay to the West," is located amid soaring and snow-covered mountains, dramatic waterfalls, and massive glaciers. This southernmost town in the world, which has steep streets, beautifully overlooks the Beagle Channel. The channel is named after the British vessel *Beagle* that sailed around the world between 1831 and 1836. The Beagle Channel is a historic passage through the Strait of Magellan and was traversed by Charles Darwin. The Strait of Magellan separates Tierra del Fuego from the southern tip of the South American mainland.

PUNTA ARENAS

Punta Arenas, the southernmost city in the world (see Figure 9–6), is easily accessed through the famous Strait of Magellan.

Chapter 9 Developing Nations 253

FIGURE 9–6

Argentina and Antarctica

This route is hundreds of miles shorter than sailing around Cape Horn. In 1520, the Portuguese explorer Ferdinand Magellan discovered this passage connecting the Atlantic and Pacific Oceans. According to local legend, the statue of Magellan brings good luck to all who kiss its foot.

PUERTO MONTT

Puerto Montt is a small town snuggled in a bay plied by fishing boats and island-hopping ferries (see Figure 9–6). It serves as the departure point for sailing trips along Chile's breathtaking coast of giant glaciers, icy fjords, and little fishing villages. The Andes provide a spectacular scenic backdrop. After 2 days of sailing south, ships docks at the small village of Puerto Natales. This village serves as a gateway for further inland exploration of Chile.

Antarctica

In the frozen desert of Antarctica (see Figure 9–6), a 1,400-mile-long mountain range of ice appears in the whiteness. Behind the range lies a valley drier than the Sahara Desert where it has not rained, or even snowed, in 2 million years. On Deception Island, it is possible to sail into the crater of an active volcano, swim in hot springs, or walk black-sand beaches.

In the summer months, Antarctica's thousands of miles of beaches are busier and noisier than Miami Beach. Millions of animals breed along the coast, including the famous penguin. The most common penguin, the Adelie, can be seen in the ice-free areas of Antarctica's many surrounding islands, such as King George Island and Hope Bay. The emperor penguin lives on ice floes and goes to land only to lay eggs and raise its young. The Gerlache Strait is home to thousands of the famous gentoo and chin-strap penguins. An estimated 20 million seals can also be found on the packed ice. Many species of whales are also found here. The humpback whale is the most frequent visitor. With 200 species of fish, the Antarctic waters are full of life.

With the entire continent of Antarctica inside the Antarctic Circle, 6 months of winter darkness begin in April. During these months, Antarctica nearly doubles in size as the ice extends 1,000 miles to the sea. With temperatures rarely above freezing, Antarctica is the coldest place in the world. Despite the cold and merciless 200-mile-per-hour winds, explorers have come to Antarctica from all over the world. The very heart of Antarctica, the South Pole, was the last region in the world to be explored. Two men, Roald Amundsen from Norway and Robert Scott from Great Britain, wanted to be the first to discover it. With four companions and fifty-four team dogs, Amundsen set out 14 days before Scott. He reached the South Pole 32 days before Scott. Scott and his four companions died on the return trip.

Reaching Antarctica can be an excruciating endeavor. The shortest route is through Drake's Passage (see Figure 9–6), the most dangerous waterway in the world. In the 600-mile-long Drake's Passage, the turbulent Atlantic Ocean joins the calm Pacific Ocean, creating the stormiest wind tunnels in the world. Only a few cruise ships sail beyond this point.

Today, thousands of men and women from different nationalities live in Antarctica during the summer months (October through February). Scientists and students from many different nations live on its scientific bases to study ice conditions and their effects on global weather, climates, and ecosystems.

Seven nations each claim a part of Antarctica: Argentina, Australia, Chile, France, New Zealand, Norway, and Great Britain. In 1959, thirty-four nations signed the Antarctic Treaty Agreement, which required Antarctica to be used for scientific and peaceful purposes only and prohibited the hunting of seals and whales. Nuclear testing on the continent was also banned. In 1991, mining was banned in Antarctica.

TRAVELING WISELY

International tourism generally spreads and transfers Western values and modern concepts to developing societies. This Westernization can be seen readily in the emulation of Western clothes, the popularity of McDonald's, and the proliferation of cellular phones.

SUMMARY

- The Blue Train is a rail link through southern Africa.
- Ecuador Rail travels over the Andes, through small villages with colorful Indian markets to the Pacific coast.
- A cruise on the Nile River reveals some of the world's earliest civilizations and most mysterious cultures.
- Rafting vacations on the Zambezi-River from Victoria Falls to Lake Kariba are becoming quite popular.
- Patagonia is an enormous barren area that offers a spectacular landscape of fjords, glaciers, mountains, and icebergs.
- Antarctica is a frozen desert with a 1,400-mile-long mountain range of ice.

CHECK YOUR UNDERSTANDING 9–1

Discuss and assess the possibilities of expanding tourism to the developing nations while considering the following:

- What type of visitor would travel to developing nations and why?
- What role does the travel professional play in ensuring that a trip to developing nations has a successful outcome?
- What problems do developing nations face in attracting visitors?
- What can governments in developing nations do to attract more tourists? Should they do anything?
- Assess and discuss why South Africa has experienced an enormous growth of tourist arrivals over the last few years.

CHECK YOUR UNDERSTANDING 9–2

Directions: Fill in the following blanks:

1. What type of visitor would travel on the Blue Train and why?

   _____

   _____

2. Describe the most important selling feature of Ecuador Rail.

3. How does the Blue Train compare with Ecuador Rail?

4. How does Ecuador as a destination compare with Southern Africa?

5. What type of visitor would travel throughout Southern Africa?

CHECK YOUR UNDERSTANDING 9–3

Directions: Fill in the following blanks:

1. What type of visitor would travel to Egypt and why?

2. Name the most important selling feature of a Nile River cruise.
   _____
   _____
   _____
   _____

3. How does a Nile River cruise compare with Mediterranean cruises?
   _____
   _____
   _____
   _____

4. How does a rafting experience on the Zambezi River compare with rafting in the United States?
   _____
   _____
   _____
   _____

5. What type of visitor would travel to Antarctica and why?
   _____
   _____
   _____
   _____

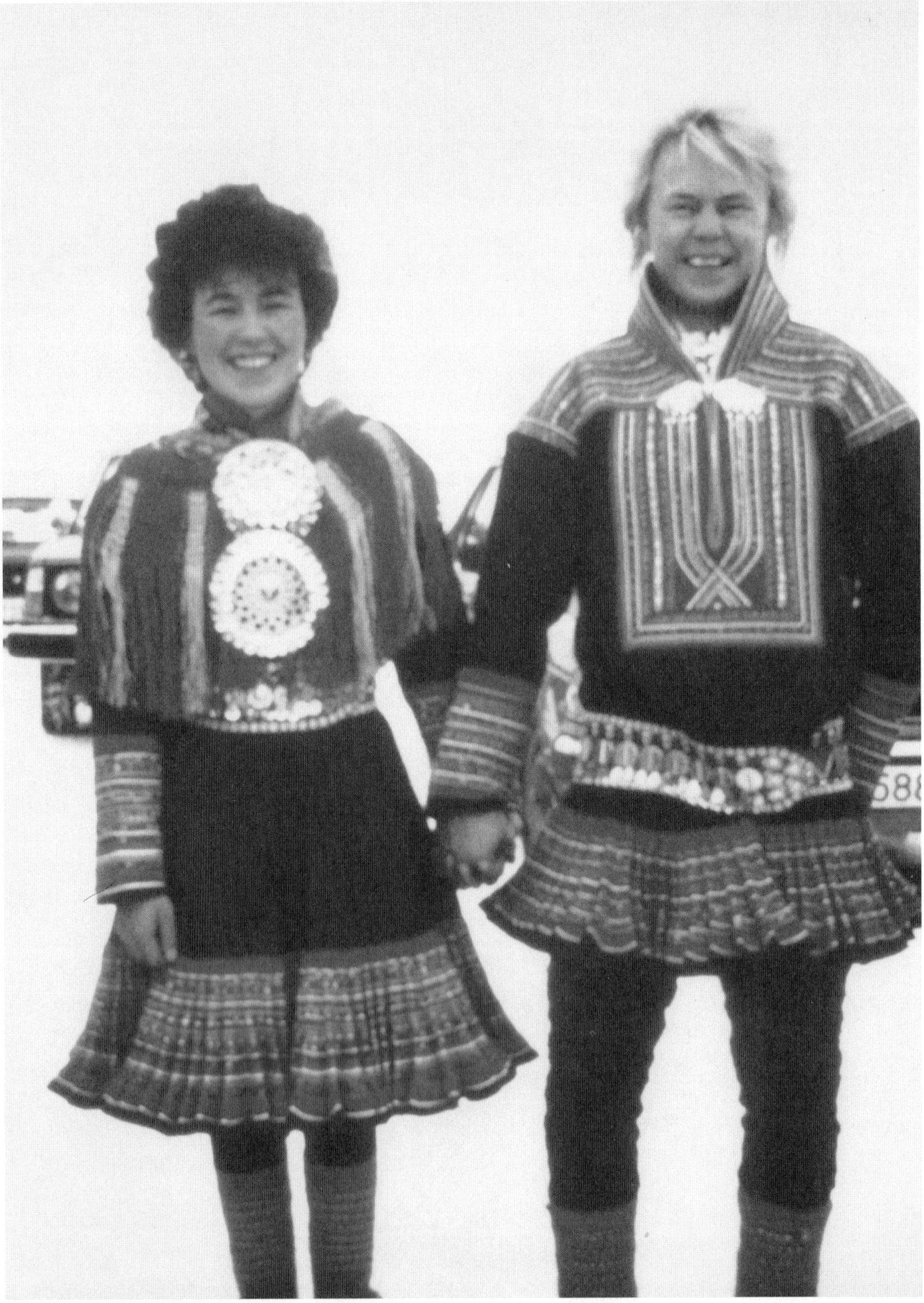

Chapter 10

A Sustainable Future

Sustainable Tourism
    Embracing International Values
    Selling Sustainable Tourism
Ecotourism
    Defining Ecotourism
    Understanding Ecotourism
Adventure Travel
Maintaining Environmental Welfare
    The Amazon
    Protecting the Rain Forest
Preserving Social Structures
Protecting Animal Habitats

OBJECTIVES

After completing Chapter 10, you should be able to:

- Discuss the effects of international tourism on sociocultural and environmental survival
- Define and discuss *ecotourism*
- Define and discuss *adventure travel*

Today's international traveler is adventurous, highly educated, and aware of the activities and various new destinations that exist. Today's travelers seek to interact with a destination and its people by using all the senses. Contemporary travelers want to look deeper into cultures, listen to foreign languages and music, smell different surroundings, taste exotic foods, and touch other people. These discoveries reward travelers with the enriching, educational, and quality experiences they seek. Travel products, and the travel professionals that market and sell these products, are adapting to this new and rapidly growing market by emphasizing environmental, social, and cultural issues. International tourism can broaden horizons, expand cultural awareness, and lead to new understandings.

Sustainable Tourism

As the world becomes smaller each day, saving the environment and preserving indigenous cultures are growing concerns in the fight to protect the quality of life. For example, the loss of the Amazonian rain forest presents a complex environmental problem and greatly affects the local populace.

Sustainable tourism is a form of tourism that supports and encourages the continued survival of indigenous cultures while impacting the environment as little as possible. Travel professionals play a major role in the success of this new form of tourism. First, travel professionals must thoroughly know and understand new products such as ecotourism and adventure travel products. Without a sound product knowledge base, travel professionals cannot educate the traveling public about sustainable tourism. Second, to successfully market and sell these new products requires travel professionals to interact with their clients in an educated way. Educated interaction includes a sound understanding of the product and its objectives and a geographic knowledge of the destination. Travel professionals may be intimidated at the prospect of venturing into this unknown industry without any clearly marked paths, but they must carve the way and be open to evolving from mass tourism to the new, low-impact tourism.

EMBRACING INTERNATIONAL VALUES

Travel professionals enter the enormous new field of sustainable tourism by opening and reframing their minds. Because the world keeps growing smaller, multiculturalism, diversity, and globalization are inevitable. To work, live, and compete successfully in this intermixed atmosphere, travel professionals must embrace international values. It is also time for travel professionals to consciously and deliberately assess new points of view. Being open-minded helps others to become open to differences.

Prospective travelers interested in sustainable tourism must also learn not to "travel blindfolded down a one-way street." "Traveling down a two-way street" means being actively involved with a destination and its locals. Sustainable tourists show a sincere and genuine interest in a destination by living like the locals, enduring what the locals endure, and participating in the lifestyle of the locals. This is the best way to fully understand, respect, and appreciate another culture and its diversity.

One way travelers can minimize misunderstanding, indifference, and opposition is to simply respect the conditions of their destinations. In nations with no air conditioning, limited hot water, and crude plumbing, travelers must endure the conditions without complaint. Successful tourism can be a cultural exchange if, instead of expecting foreign visitors to adapt to our ways, we also adapt to theirs.

Whether traveling for pleasure or business, all travelers, including travel professionals, are the best ambassadors for their country. Their attitudes and codes of ethics paint the picture for the rest of their fellow nationals. For example, much has been said about "ugly Americans," but not much is said about "ugly Japanese" or "ugly Norwegians." One crucial responsibility of the travel professional is to match the prospective traveler with the right product and the right destination. For example, a four-wheel drive camping safari in the interior of Australia's desert is designed for those who want to experience nature and to get away from the modern world. The participants may get involved in various camp activities such as helping to raise the tents. This tour is not designed to accommodate hair driers or high heels.

SELLING SUSTAINABLE TOURISM

Successfully selling a sustainable travel product requires the travel professional to identify a potential buyer. Therefore, it is vital that travel professionals ask all the so-called *wh* qualifying questions. In addition to asking *wh*ere travelers want to go, travel professionals must discuss *wh*at travelers expect and, most importantly, *why* the travelers want to travel in order to obtain a good traveler-product match. The Adventure Travel Society in Engelewood, Colorado, reported that in the past the adventure traveler was considered a low-income male, 20 to 40 years old, experienced in the outdoors, who traveled solo. The Adventure Travel Society is a public relations and marketing firm that specializes in assisting countries, regions, and companies in promoting adventure travel. The Adventure Travel Society also organizes the annual International World Congress on Adventure Travel and Ecotourism.

Demographics have changed drastically in the last 20 to 30 years, and aging has been redefined. Now men and women retire much earlier and are more health conscious than their parents were. Today, adventurous travelers who are well into their 60s and 70s are common. The most striking fact the Adventure Travel Society reported in a September 1996 interview with Jerry Mallett, president of the society, was that women, single and married, have entered the adventure travel market at such a tremendous rate that they now play a major role in this area.

Ecotourism

Ecotourism, a term that sprung from *ecology*, the study of interactions between people and their environments, animals, and plants, is the newest travel concept. Ecotourism has become the ideal in the travel world, protecting the quality of the earth and the rapidly vanishing traditional societies and cultures, including wildlife in their natural habitats. Ecotourism suggests an ethical form of tourism that is socioculturally and environmentally responsible. Ecotourism is meant to improve destinations. However, because ecotourism is a new concept, it currently lacks a clear mission statement and well-defined objectives.

The 1991 edition of the *Oxford Encyclopedic English Dictionary* defines *tourism* as "the organization and operation of (especially foreign) holidays, especially as a commercial enterprise." It defines *holiday* as "an extended period of recreation." Therefore, a tourist may not necessarily be an ecologist and may not care about ecological issues, because the purpose of travel is recreation, or "mass tourism." The word *ecotraveler* may be a better fit.

DEFINING ECOTOURISM

The Ecotourism Society is an international nonprofit organization dedicated to making tourism a viable tool for conserving and sustaining development. As the Ecotourism Society defines it, ecotourism is responsible travel that conserves natural environments and sustains the well-being of local people.

Therefore, ecotourism is ideally multiculturalism, awareness, open-mindedness, challenge, diversity, and a strong educational component. To be responsible to the environment and its sociocultures, ecotourists must benefit local societies through genuine and sincere interest. Ecotourists must also be involved directly with the objectives of ecotourism. One way ecotourists become involved is by working as volunteers on projects that study or help preserve the sociocultural and/or environmental surroundings. This style of tourism is becoming increasingly popular. The travel industry has entered a new era.

Because ecotourism is involvement in a protection project, consider how the concept can be applied to tourism. For example, is ecotourism an educational project in which participants learn about ecological issues? Is ecotourism conventional tourism? Should ecotourism mix luxury and Western comforts with traditional cultures? Is ecotourism traveling with a large group on an air-conditioned and luxurious cruise ship? Is ecotourism a photographic safari of diminishing species? Is ecotourism traveling in an air-conditioned, polluting, toilet-equipped motorcoach on a paved road in a national park?

It is well-known that Mount Everest base camps in Nepal and Tibet have been completely destroyed. Oxygen tanks are scattered everywhere, and human waste and food disposal have left distinct marks. Imagine the disappointment at having endured the conditions of 17,000-plus feet altitude through weeks of climbing and trekking, only to find the goal is a dump. Michael Knakkergard Jorgensen, the first Dane to climb this mountain, revealed in June 1995, that some of the climbers in his expedition group may not have ascended Mount Everest successfully (see Figure 10–1) without aid from the polluted camps. Jorgensen's group avoided starvation and was able to continue its expedition because it ate food left from previous attempts. These remnants allowed members of Jorgensen's group to conserve just enough energy to successfully complete their expedition and reach the summit. The remains of earlier expeditions also created a sense of security and comfort. The group strongly needed a psychological boost on this ultimate test of survival.

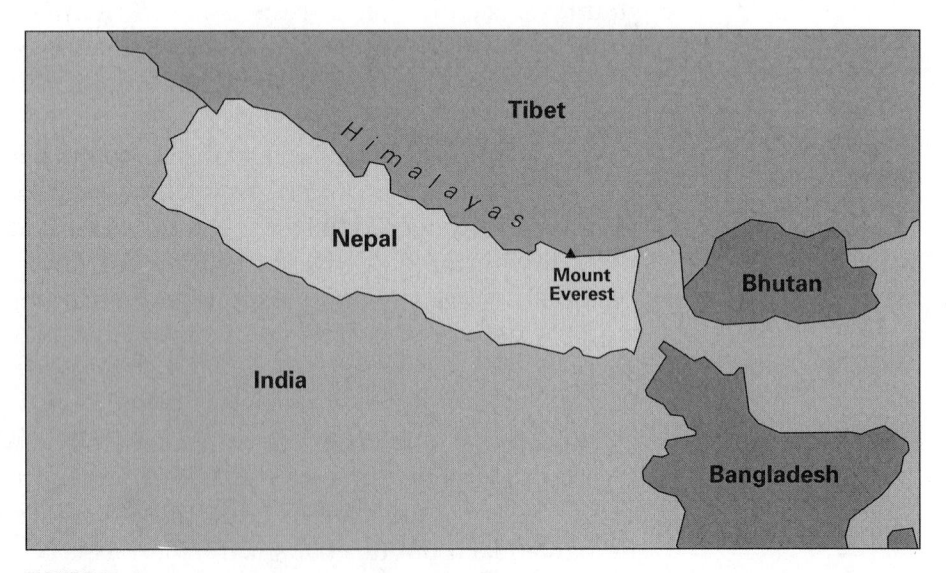

FIGURE 10–1

Mount Everest Region

Clearly, a closer look at ecotourism is needed. Because ecotourism is a new concept, it is still confusing. In an interview conducted in May 1996, Marylin Staff, vice president and cofounder of Bolder Adventures in Boulder, Colorado, said, "I almost never use the word *ecotourism,* because it has been used and abused by so many. We do not call ourselves an 'ecotourism company,' even though we may fall into that category in terms of the small-group nature of our programs and our caring of the environment, particularly the cultural environment." Although more and more travel products include cultural, social, ethical, and environmental components in their itineraries, they do not necessarily reflect the concepts of ecotourism. As Jerry Mallett, president of Adventure Travel Society, explained in a September 1996 interview, "The whole idea of ecotourism is a paradox, because we are trying to protect the very thing we are trying to sell. Sustainability is increasingly difficult given [that] the population continues to increase."

UNDERSTANDING ECOTOURISM

Because it is often difficult to understand what a real ecotourist project is, some travel products hide under the name *ecotourism.* Some travel companies equate ecotourism to "green tourism," and consequently problems arise. The ecological aspect of ecotourism should not only be "green," because there would have to be "white tourism" for Antarctica and "blue tourism" for the coral reefs. In reality, such programs may offer environmentally friendly adventure programs, which is fine, because they take a big step toward true ecotourism.

True ecotourism products are extremely difficult to sell successfully. As Staff said, "You cannot be too weird and too remote in the itineraries. Unless people have heard of the destination or read about it in a guidebook, they won't buy it. Travelers need to have a smattering of the places they have heard of. Travelers need and want the unique and the familiar."

Organizations like Earthwatch and the National Audubon Society are among the few that involve the tourist in ecological activities. **Earthwatch,** founded in 1972, sponsors scientists, teachers, students, and artists to document a changing world.

Members of this international organization have the opportunity to assist scientists in their research work.

The **National Audubon Society** was founded in 1905, and works to conserve natural ecosystems, particularly those of birds and other wildlife. The National Audubon Society has developed a travel ethic to which all its tour operators must adhere:[1]

1. Wildlife and their habitat must not be disturbed.
2. Audubon tourism to natural areas will be sustainable.
3. Waste disposal must have neither environmental nor aesthetic impacts.
4. The experience tourists gain in traveling with Audubon must enrich their appreciation of nature, conservation, and the environment.
5. Audubon tours must strengthen the conservation effort and enhance the natural integrity of places visited.

If all ecotourist companies were to follow Audubon's basic guidelines, however, there may be problems, because, for instance, most cruise ships dump garbage in the ocean.

Adventure Travel

The next challenge, then, is to define adventure travel. Mallett defined **adventure travel** as "... participatory, exciting travel that offers unique challenges to the individual in an outdoor setting." Adventure travel has always been around, and even though its form has changed somewhat, it is still based on human curiosity. Therefore, the outlook for adventure travel is excellent. Travelers all over the world continue to leave the beaten path in record numbers. Humans are the only species who would climb to the top of a mountain solely to see what was on the other side or travel to another continent to explore.

---

[1] Whelan, T. (1991). *Nature tourism.* National Audubon Society: Island Press.

People have always been interested in new cultures, outstanding scenery, and the great unknown. Adventure travel is not new, and it will remain an ever-increasing part of many lifestyles.[2] Almost half the travel industry, nearly $220 billion, is already in this niche, including the revenue from local travelers.

Because adventure travel is a lifestyle, it means different things to different people. The level of adventure is a reflection of the self, the personality, and the sociocultural environment. Adventure is a feeling. For some, just boarding an international flight may require a great deal of courage. Some travelers perceive adventure as going without showers, hair dryers, and toilet facilities for 1 day, while others love the challenge of being without them for weeks or months. Staff defined adventure travel as "... the quality of the experience at being close to the people and the natural environment while at the same time always staying within the desires of the individual person."

Maintaining Environmental Welfare

The two most fragile, vulnerable, and important ecosystems for human survival are being destroyed intentionally and rapidly by the human race. These two ecosystems are the tropical rain forest and the coral reef. Both suffer greatly from pollution, disease, modern technology, overpopulation, agricultural damages, land development, and climatic changes. It is important to protect and preserve the world's ecosystems that are essential for human survival to ensure that future generations survive. The growing number of travelers seeking unspoiled wilderness areas ironically may end up threatening those wilderness areas.

---

[2]Mallett, J. (1994). *Proceedings of the 1994 World Congress on adventure travel and ecotourism.* Englewood, Colorado: Adventure Travel Society.

Although ecotourism often is a cover for "environmentally friendly" tours, it could carry many low-impact benefits to protect the scarce environment.

THE AMAZON

One popular, environmentally friendly tour is to the Amazon. As Figure 10–2 shows, the Amazon flows from the Andes in Peru, only 100 miles from the Pacific Ocean, then makes its way through Colombia and Brazil before emptying into the Atlantic Ocean. At about 4,080 miles, the Amazon is the second longest river in the world. It has over 1,000 tributaries, 14,000 miles of navigable waterways, and millions of miles of hidden swamp thoroughfares that are navigable only by dugout canoe. The Amazon contributes 220 thousand cubic meters of fresh water per second to the Atlantic Ocean, which is 20 percent of the world's total.

The Amazon is navigable from Iquitos, Peru, which is very isolated. Here the Amazon is narrow, slow moving, and less trafficked. River cruises are most popular here during the Peruvian rain forest's low water season, which is from June through November. During this dry season, the Amazon's water level can be as much as 45 feet lower than normal. This is the best time for rain forest hiking. Many trails lead to Quechua Indian villages. From Iquitos, cruises depart weekly to Leticia, Colombia, the major gateway to the Amazon.

Most Amazon cruises begin in Manaus, 900 miles upstream from the Atlantic Ocean. The true highlight of Manaus is the famed "Meeting of the Waters" where the reddish-brown waters of Rio Negro merge with the muddy-brown waters of the Amazon. The rivers flow side-by-side without mixing for about 3 miles. Sailing in dugout canoes down hidden tribuaries and deeper into the swamps of the rain forest is a popular event among travelers. Indigenous Indian tribes still inhabit these remote regions of the Amazon. Santarem lies at the mouth of the bluish-green Rio Tapajos, which flows into the Amazon. The hill above town provides an impressive view of the meeting of these two grandiose rivers, which run parallel for many miles before blending. An Amazon cruise terminates at the river's impressive

Chapter 10 A Sustainable Future *271*

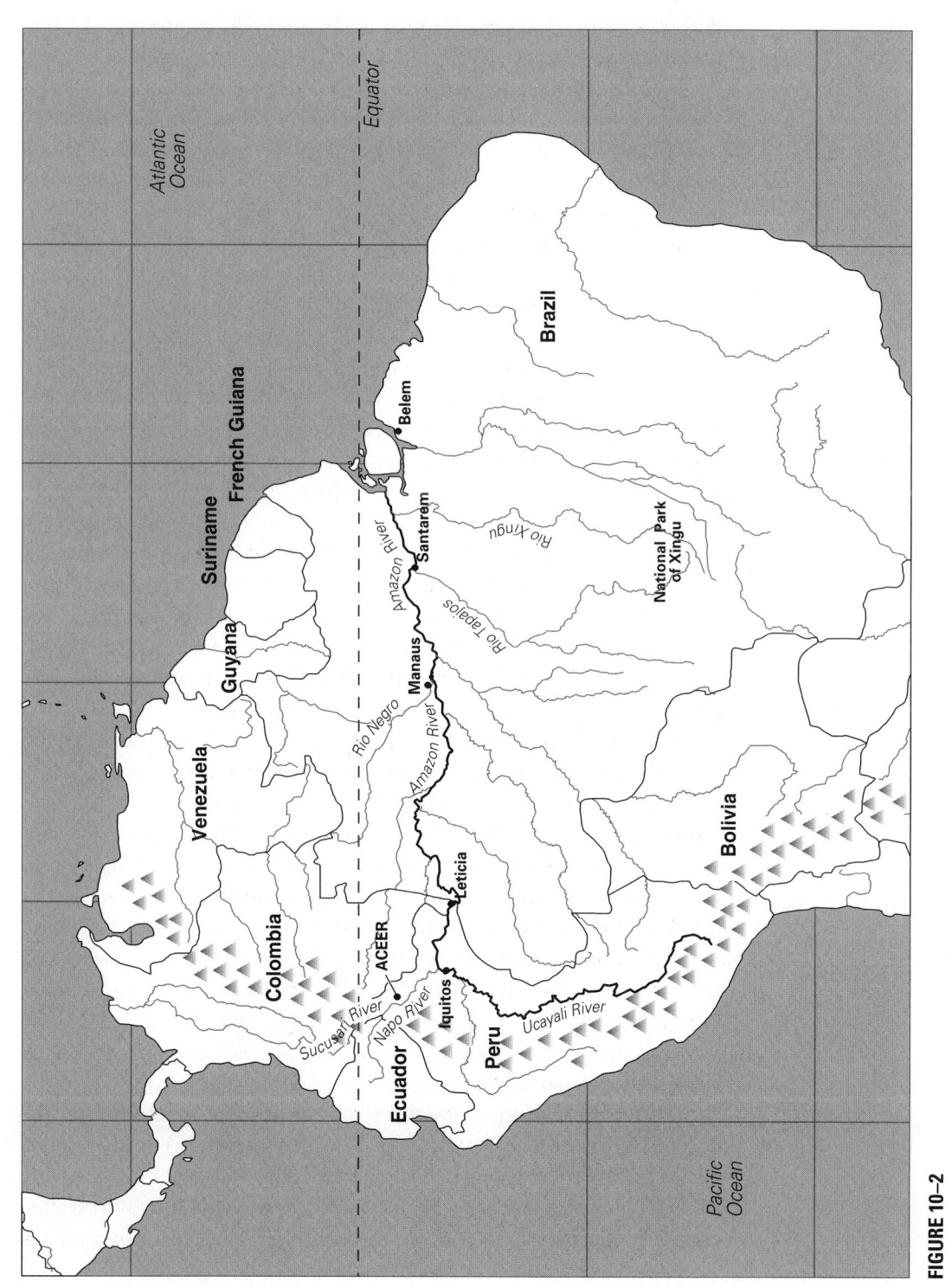

FIGURE 10–2
Amazonia

200-mile-wide delta at the city of Belem, 75 miles inland from the Atlantic Ocean.

The rain forest surrounding the Amazon River, called Amazonia, covers an area of over 2.5 million square miles. About 70 percent of Amazonia, approximately the size of the United States west of the Mississippi, is in Brazil. Nearly 30 percent extends through Bolivia, Colombia, Ecuador, French Guyana, Guyana, Peru, Surinam, and Venezuela. Amazonia is home to the Amazon rain forest, which holds the richest, most complex, and most fragile ecosystem on Earth. A wider variety of animal and plant life cannot be found in any other region on Earth. How many species there are in Amazonia is still disputed. Scientists debate that there are anywhere from 800,000 to 5 million biological organisms, or about 50 percent of the world's species. This incredible biodiversity can be seen in the region's 1,800 species of birds (nearly half the world's), 25,000 species of plants, and 2,000 species of fish (more than are contained in the entire Atlantic Ocean). An additional 300 species of mammals, 2 million species of insects, and 4,000 species of trees have also been identified so far. The Amazon rain forest supplies the entire world with one third of its oxygen. The forest affects the weather patterns worldwide. Brazilian Amazonia possesses 75 percent of the largest rain forests on Earth.

It is, therefore, ironic that humanity destroys such an incredible biodiversity as the rain forest. Tropical deforestation carries tremendous consequences. One problem is the economic situation in developing nations. With population exploding in developing regions, including Amazonia, large areas are being cleared to make room for agriculture and cattle ranches. The "slash-and-burn" method is used in Amazonia and continues at an alarmingly unregulated rate. In this method, trees are cleared by "slashing" then burning entire sections. The ecological damage is devastating, because thick forest cover prevents soil erosion. Without trees, heavy downpours wash soil away quickly.

Although the agricultural slash-and-burn method has destroyed parts of the jungle, much of Amazonia's rain forest remains. Remote areas of the river basin beg discovery. One such program in Amazonia is an 8-day itinerary offered by International Expeditions, a company from Helena, Alabama. This company takes visitors on a boat ride from the isolated city of Iquitos, Peru down the Amazon and up the major tributary of the Napo River to the Sucusari River.

PROTECTING THE RAIN FOREST

International Expeditions has established the nonprofit Amazon Center for Environmental Education and Research (ACEER), an educational and research base for scientists and visitors to enhance understanding of the rain forest. Tourist dollars support ACEER. ACEER has completed a canopy walkway system, which is an aerial pathway in the treetops. From this walkway, visitors can view and study the wildlife that lives at treetop level. According to the International Expeditions Amazon brochure, the walkway opens doors to ". . . an unexplored world where over 2,000 epiphytic plants may cling to the branches of a single tree. In the forest canopy it is estimated that 20 million insects species may exist, 80 percent as yet unknown to science."

Preserving Social Structures

In over 200 nations, thousands of cultures are represented, and 6,000 languages are spoken, translated, interpreted, and misunderstood. Nothing defines a nation more than its languages, ethnicity, cultures, and religions. Etiquette is deeply rooted in cultural heritage, carried on throughout the centuries and generations.

Each culture has its own set of **norms,** that behavior which is socially acceptable. Norms are sometimes unwritten and include values, customs, and food habits. Many of these codes of conduct are detailed in books, and the travel professional should educate travelers as to the resources available. The hope is travelers will be prepared for seemingly rude behavior. For example, Tibetan women customarily stick out their tongues several times as a sign of respect. This behavior is unacceptable in some other cultures.

Nothing defines a tourist like offensive dress. A tight and low-cut T-shirt may be an affront in a traditional and conservative society like Egypt. It may sometimes be difficult to understand or agree with local customs and cultures, but it is important to always respect them.

Many cultural differences are rooted in religion. Festivals, ceremonies, dress codes, marriage ceremonies, and death procedures are just a few examples. Ceremonies are a true expression of ethnic heritage. Cultural events, like music, dance, and theatrical performances and food, art, and sports shows help preserve cultures and are popular among tourists. Being culturally aware expands global understanding and broadens the traveler's horizon.

International tourism can even help preserve traditional local cultures. Tourism encourages local people to take pride in their national heritage. Even though many cultural events are for the tourist only, culture may be preserved only through such events. Tribal communities and other ancient traditional societies coexist with nature. Their lifestyles are under enormous pressure from the outside influences that clearly differ from their heritage.

It is challenging to evaluate how international tourism impacts societies. The impacts depend on the travel itinerary, its components, and how it relates to the local area. The growing number of travelers into remote areas often changes the native society. Commercialization, for example, can be seen in beach bungalows in Thailand and Indonesia. Even a small group of visitors will always leave a trace on a destination.

Since 1972, Cultural Survival has promoted and protected the rights of indigenous peoples and ethnic groups throughout the world. Through projects and research, the organization's Special Projects Program supports ethnic groups in maintaining their cultures by providing promotional support, helping to manage funds, managing bookkeeping, and helping to raise money. As a nonprofit organization, Cultural Survival depends on donations. About 80 percent of all donations go directly to an individual project. All projects are individually run and operated.

One group struggling to survive is the Australian Aborigines. These natives boast one of the longest unbroken cultures in the world. The Aborigines have always lived in complete harmony with their environment. The Aborigines believe that man, animal, and Earth are one. Their many stories of the creation, which they call Dreamtime, are interesting. During Dreamtime, a man could change into an animal, and an animal could change into a man. Dreamtime created the land. To preserve their unity with nature, Aborigines believe they must take care of their country. The group's art and singing show how they remain with the Dreamtime spirits. Dreamtime is powerful. Spirits join Dreamtime when the physical body dies.

Only fully initiated, old male Aborigines know how to preserve their country and their traditions. Obeying Aboriginal law ensures that unity with all living things will continue. Only the elders are wise and know the secret rites. This wisdom of tradition and tribal law is passed on orally and musically. Wisdom can only be passed on to fully initiated men. Traditionally, a very sharp stone knife is used in initiation ceremonies to pierce the nose and to cut a design on a young man's shoulder and chest. Currently, only a few newly initiated men are following these important Aboriginal rituals. The new generation is often growing up away from its culture. The Aborigines did not build impressive monuments, nor have they developed any new thoughts and ideas. Their entire lives are centered around repeating and adapting ancient tribal ways. Some work as park rangers, for example. The elders may be the last traditional inhabitants because more and more Aboriginal cultures are vanishing.

Ironically, Aboriginal law in Kakadu calls for followers to burn their land. To Aborigines, the law is in the rock and the earth. During the burning the land is cleansed. It is necessary to burn the grassland because the intense heat makes the new seed shells pop. New shoots grow through the ashes. The elders are given the trusted task of burning the grasslands so fires do not rage out of control. The Aboriginal law of burning, such as how and when the fires may be lit, must be strictly followed. The right season is when the animals of the grassland have matured and can escape the fire. This is also a cool time of the year. The soil beneath the dry grass is damp then. Because it is Aboriginal law, the burning is fully regulated and controlled. If the laws of burning are broken, there will be a great loss of animal life and severe ecological damages. Note how beneficial the burning is for one ecosystem, but harmful to another (Amazonia).

Until 200 years ago, only Aborigines inhabited Australia. Today, only a few groups live on their traditional lands. One of these lands is called Kakadu where the Aborigines own the tourism infrastructure, such as accommodation (see Figure 10–3). Aborigines have lived on Kakadu lands for more than 40,000 years. The Australian government manages Kakadu as a national park and preserves the interests and needs of the Aborigines. A 5-day Aboriginal Culture Tour is offered by Adventure Terra Safari Tours. This tour takes visitors to meet local Aborigines and learn about their culture by hearing tales of their Dreamtime, seeing traditional hunting methods, experiencing their handicrafts, and learning about their food. With its many paintings in the caverns and overhangs, Aborigine art is beautifully admired at Ubirr Rock.

A sustainable model that has proven successful is the Uluru National Park. Penelope Figgis at the 1993 World Congress on Adventure Travel and Ecotourism in Manaus, Brazil presented the story. Figgis described the Uluru model as follows:

> The Aboriginal people living in the vicinity of the Uluru Rock call themselves Anangu. The land in the Uluru National Park still carries great spiritual importance to the Anangu. In 1985, the Uluru Park was returned to the Anangu under joint management. Despite superficial changes, like Western clothes and the adoption of vehicles and other technology, the community remains deeply traditional. All speak their traditional language, Pitjanjatjara; few have total command of English. Traditional laws remain paramount guiding forces.
>
> Figgis further explained that joint management ensures the Anangu a strong, ongoing role in maintaining the values of their culture and determining the management of the park. Uluru, as Aboriginal land, should place Aboriginal imperatives foremost. Figgis observed how the model has benefited the Anangu. She contended having the dominant culture

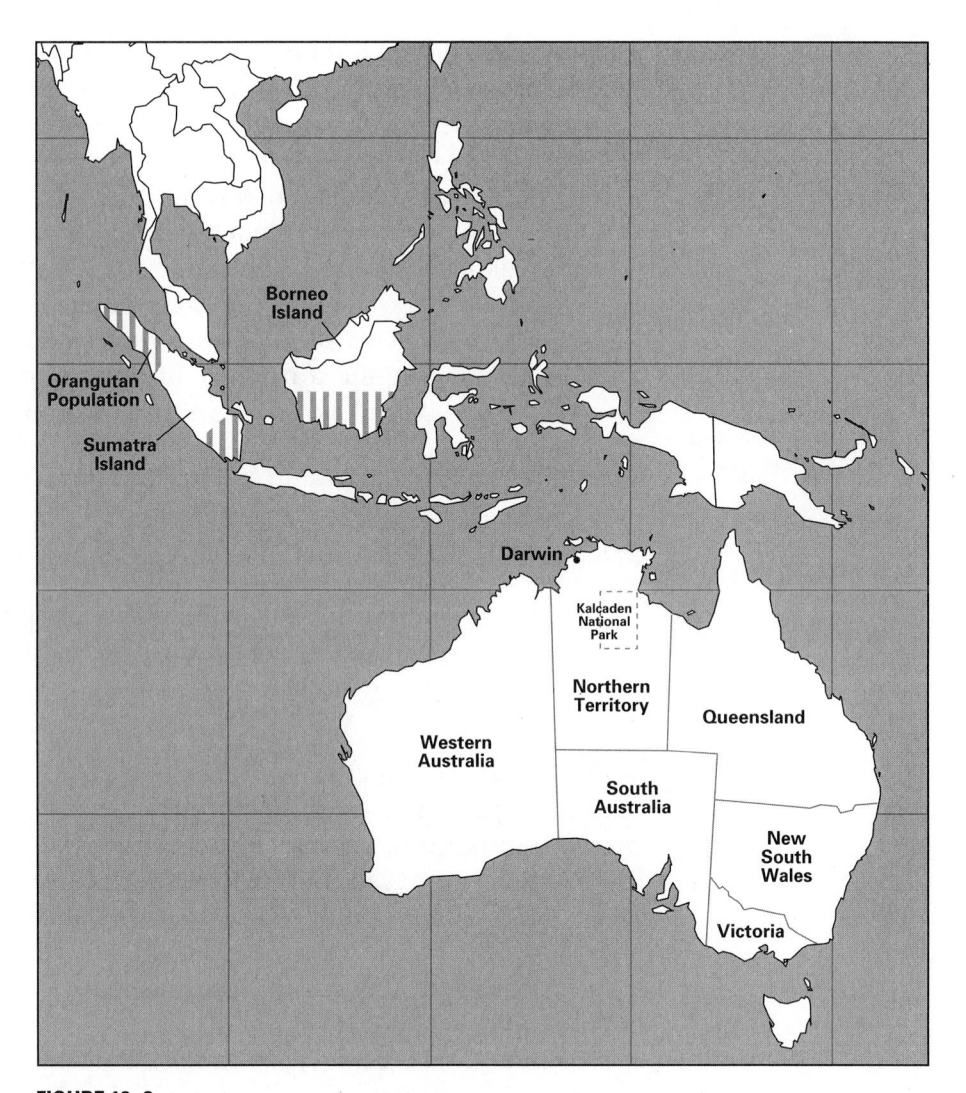

FIGURE 10–3
Australia and Indonesia

recognize that this is their land, their special place, is very important psychologically. Given the history of dispossession, discrimination, and denial, the emotional importance of this fact cannot be overstressed. The simple pride of the community in their place is moving, as is their willingness to share it.

Greater pride will not heal the social damage of the past but it is an important foundation for any improvements. In particular, the young can see that their elders' traditional knowledge earns both respect and dollars. This gives them greater incentive to accumulate such knowledge and to respect their elders. Naming a prominent park Aboriginal Place, along with making symbolic gestures like adapting the Aboriginal flag as the park symbol, positively impacted the pride of other Aboriginal people. The Anangu have also been able to close access to quite a number of important law sites and reroute whole roads to avoid culturally important sites. On at least one occasion, they closed the entire park to conduct an important ceremony. Their beliefs also prevented a permanent toilet from being constructed at the base of the climb, despite continued lobbying by tourist operators.

This small community of 150 to 200 shy people are sharing their land with over 260,000 visitors each year. The Aborigines do not prefer this way of life but have compromised.

The negative effect of white people's presence in indigenous societies can be examined in the case of the Indian tribes and 180 ethnic groups spread throughout the area of the Xingu River in the Xingu National Park in Brazil. Covering an area of about 11,500 square miles of jungle, river, lake, and savannah, this oasis in the jungle was created by the Brazilian government in the 1960s to protect the indigenous tribes and the environment (see Figure 10–2).

Not much has changed in the self-contained culture and customs of the natives of the isolated Xingu region. The tribes inhabiting the region in the northern part of the Xingu Park speak different languages, yet they live in complete cultural harmony, sharing beliefs, habits, festivals, ceremonies, and traditions, especially the Kuarup, the Festival of the Dead. These northern tribes do not eat red meat. During the dry season, the Indians fish with a poisonous liana that drugs the fish. The culture of the tribes inhabiting the region in the southern part of the Xingu Park differs completely from that in the north.

During the last 50 years, the Xingu Indians have experienced a significant reduction in their population due to infectious diseases like influenza and dysentery. The diseases were brought by the white people, but the Indians also contracted them during trading visits into towns outside the Xingu region. The Indians do not have the medicinal plants needed to fight such diseases.

Compared to the Aborigines, the Xingu Indians do not live in complete harmony. Both cultures face extinction, even though tourism seems to benefit the Aborigines. Megaron Txucarramae, director of the Xingu Indian Park, explained at the 1993 World Congress on Adventure Travel and Ecotourism that according to the Indian Statement (Law #6001) tourism is prohibited on Indian reserves. Before Portuguese settlement in Brazil in 1500, more than 6 million people of different Indian populations were living in Brazil. Today, little more than 300 came from their original lands.

The Xingu Indians appear hostile and may thereby be contributing to their extinction. Intertribal war is a game, a sports event in which war heroes receive awards. With painted bodies and sharp arrows, the Xingu ambush, capture, and kill their enemies. To them, death is exciting. In the middle of a war, a tribe may perform a dance festival in the enemy's village to provoke them.

It is questionable whether tourism should enter indigenous areas at all. For a culture to preserve its ancient traditions and minimize the risk of vanishing, such cultures should not be exposed to any Western-style values. Contact with Western societies will inevitably modify customs and traditions. The challenge is whether two cultures can adapt to each other with positive results. Could ecotourism help them survive?

Protecting Animal Habitats

Most Africans do not see wildlife as tourists do. **Game reserves** are located in isolated areas, and motor vehicles are required to reach them. Most Africans do not own motor vehicles. In fact, most Kenyans have never seen a lion. Such an experience is designed for Westerners who can afford it.

Many environmental changes have caused the threat of animal extinction. One such change is land clearing to build towns and roads. Such projects reduce the animal habitat and thereby reduce and destroy ecosystems. Other environmental changes, including making space for tourism infrastructure, make animal habitats suffer greatly. Animal extinction is also caused by poaching. With an ever-increasing world population, food demand is climbing. Animals are also hunted for their fur or hides.

A game reserve is unique in that it contains a variety of animal habitats. For example, the zebra and the lion live in a savannah habitat, while the hippopotamus lives in a water habitat. Studying wildlife in its natural habitats can also take place outside game reserves. With the Orangutan Foundation International, Bolder Adventures in Boulder, Colorado offers an 11-day research/study tour to Kalimantan, the Indonesian part of the island of Borneo. The research efforts of participants provide valuable data to ensure species survival.

Orangutans, for example, are extremely endangered. There used to be several million throughout Indonesia. Today, only three small pockets of orangutans are left in the wild: northern Sumatra, southern Sumatra, and southern Borneo. As the 1994 edition of the *Encyclopedia of Endangered Species* published by Gale Research reported, the most recent population count in 1993 estimated about 20,000 in Borneo and 9,000 in Sumatra. The habitat of the orangutan is eroding because the entire area is being logged. However, the biggest threat is that the orangutan is a very fasionable, popular, and common pet throughout Asia. Rich Asians buy thousands of orangutans on the black market. To capture a baby orangutan to be used as a pet, its mother must be killed. There are huge poaching rings all throughout southeast Asia, particularly in Taiwan. According to Staff, there are more orangutans in Taipei per square mile than there are in the jungles of Borneo.

Unfortunately, the orangutan makes a wonderful pet. Having a baby orangutan as a pet is like having a child. A baby orangutan is cute, cuddly, and very intelligent. It has a mild temper and a high level of curiosity and can even be diaper-trained. The problem is that baby orangutans grow large and strong and experience puberty at about age 10. The Taiwanese can no longer keep them in their small apartments. Many people abandon the animals to the streets. The authorities do their best to return them to the jungle, but the challenge is to help them readapt to the jungle environment. The orangutans must learn what to eat and how to interact with the native orangutan population. They still crave human attention and often approach and touch the travelers.

As difficult working and living conditions prevail, participating in such fieldwork is for the true ecotourist. Perhaps only an ecotourist can appreciate the reward of observing a wild orangutan up close in its jungle environment while directly supporting the survival of the species. Participants work with the indigenous people of Borneo, the Dayaks, while tracking the orangutans through the jungle.

As another example, do not make the saltwater crocodile a pet. This ferocious monster is common throughout Southeast Asia, but it suffers severely from depletion. In South Africa, for example, poachers sell crocodile bones to Zulu witch-doctors. Australia faces a different dilemma.

For hundreds of years the Australian crocodile was hunted for its skin. By World War II, the crocodile was nearly extinct. Twenty years ago, a new law prohibited crocodile hunting, and the first crocodile farm started in Australia. Instead of shooting the crocodile for its skin, farmers are now raising crocodiles with support from the government. The farm-raised crocodiles will be used to make leather products.

Since the government ban, the crocodile has made an impressive comeback in the region between Queensland and the Northern Territory (see Figure 10–3). As the number of people and crocodiles attempting to coexist has risen, predicaments have risen dramatically. The large Australian saltwater crocodile has existed for over 200 million years. This species is the largest and most dangerous of its kind. It can remain submerged and motionless for hours, completely concealed, then suddenly attack a nearby, unsuspecting animal, including a person.

The Australian crocodile is quite large. A mature male can measure up to 21 feet and weigh as much as 3,000 pounds. Even at the relatively young age of 16 years, this crocodile may measure 11 feet and weigh 500 pounds. Females are much smaller, measuring only about 9 to 10 feet. A crocodile has sixty-four teeth. Each tooth is replaced forty-four times during a crocodile's lifetime. The crocodile drowns its prey, including divers, swimmers, and fishers, or crushes it in its powerful jaws. The crocodile only hunts in or near water. Crocodiles are unlikely to attack a person unless that person is around their water domain.

Today, there are an estimated 60,000 crocodiles. The waters of the Northern Territory and Queensland now belong to the crocodile. The city of Darwin is surrounded by swamps, which is an excellent crocodile habitat. Just outside Darwin are fabulous white-sand beaches. However, these waters are invaded by crocodiles and safe swimming is not possible.

Tourists travel to the north to see a crocodile bite or attack. Some tourists, and even some locals, ignore the danger. In Australia, people swim seemingly fearlessly in the crocodile's habitat. The fear of being torn to pieces by this huge monster is not always apparent. In reality, fewer and fewer places are safe for swimming.

One challenge that remains is an issue we all face. Western values contradict the values of the natural environment. The question remains whether we impose those values upon others.

TRAVELING WISELY

Traveling abroad, even within the Western world, takes common sense and logic. Traveling with an open mind provides a wonderful opportunity to mix with all kinds of people and to learn about their country and culture. Flexibility and patience yield a relaxing and enriching experience.

SUMMARY

- International tourism can broaden horizons, expand cultural awareness, and lead to new understandings.
- Ecotourism has become the new ideal in the travel industry, protecting the quality of the Earth and the rapidly vanishing traditional societies and cultures, including wildlife in its natural habitat.
- To be responsible to the environment and its sociocultures, ecotourists must benefit local societies by becoming actively involved in the customs and traditions of cultures and their environments.

- Adventure travel, as defined by the Adventure Travel Society, is participatory, exciting travel that offers unique challenges to the traveler in an outdoor setting.
- The two most fragile, vulnerable, and important ecosystems for human survival, the tropical rain forest and the coral reef, are being destroyed intentionally and rapidly by the human race.
- Many cultural differences are rooted in religion.
- International tourism can help preserve traditional, local cultures.
- Many environmental changes have caused the threat of animal extinction.

CHECK YOUR UNDERSTANDING 10–1

On the blank map following, record the location of tropical rain forests.

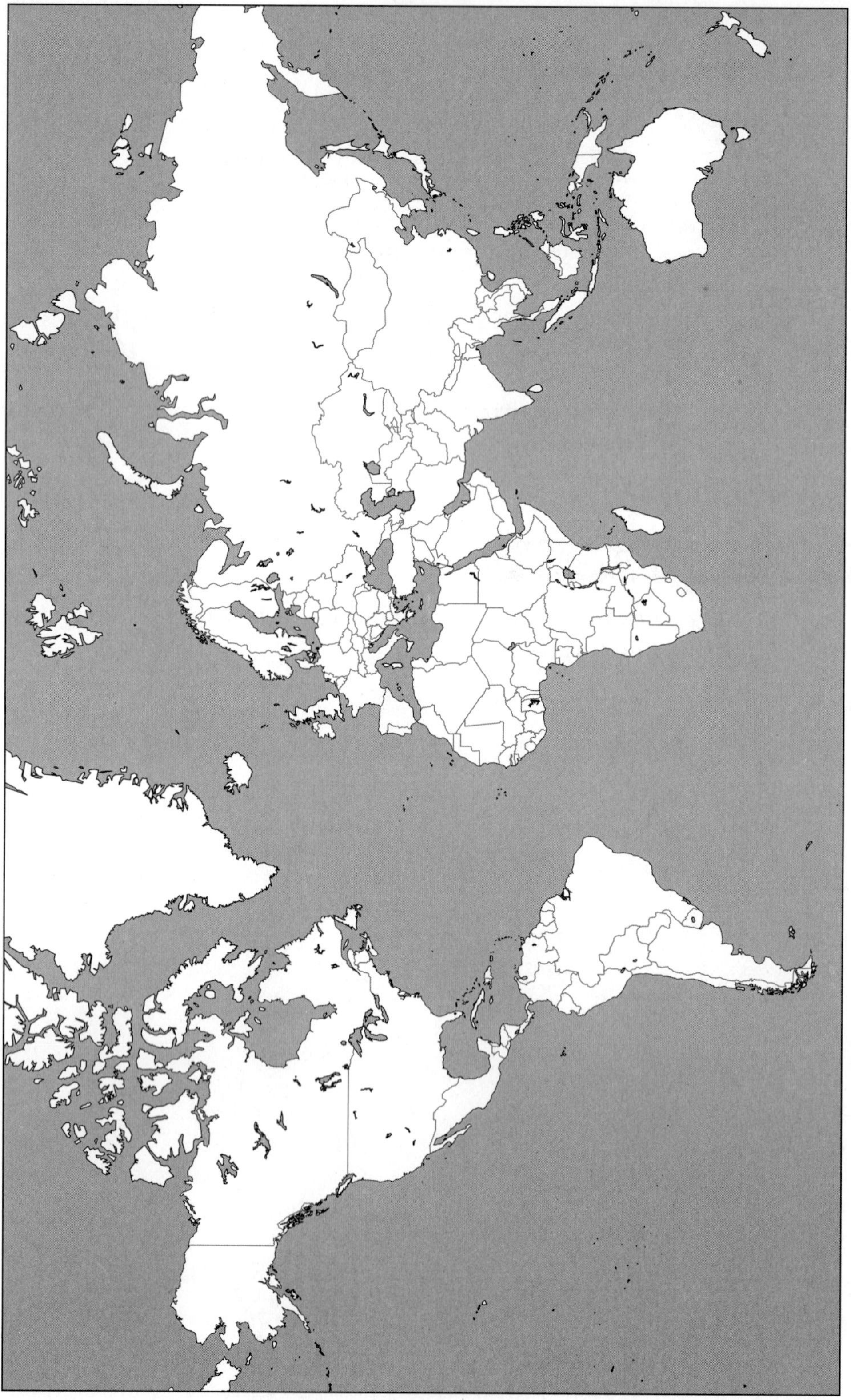

CHECK YOUR UNDERSTANDING 10-2

Write a report discussing and analyzing the following questions:

- What is the difference between ecotourism and adventure travel?
- What should ecotourism be?
- What should adventure travel be?
- What should the objectives of ecotourism be?
- What purpose does ecotourism achieve, if it is designed only for the tourist?
- Do the goals of ecology and tourism match?

CHECK YOUR UNDERSTANDING 10-3

Create an ecotour, reflecting on how you perceive ecotourism should be, while paying particular attention to the following components. Draw the itinerary on the blank map provided.

- Number of participants
- Transportation methods
- Accommodations
- Activities
- Educational components
- Sensitivity to sociocultures and the environment
- Gear list
- Duration of trip

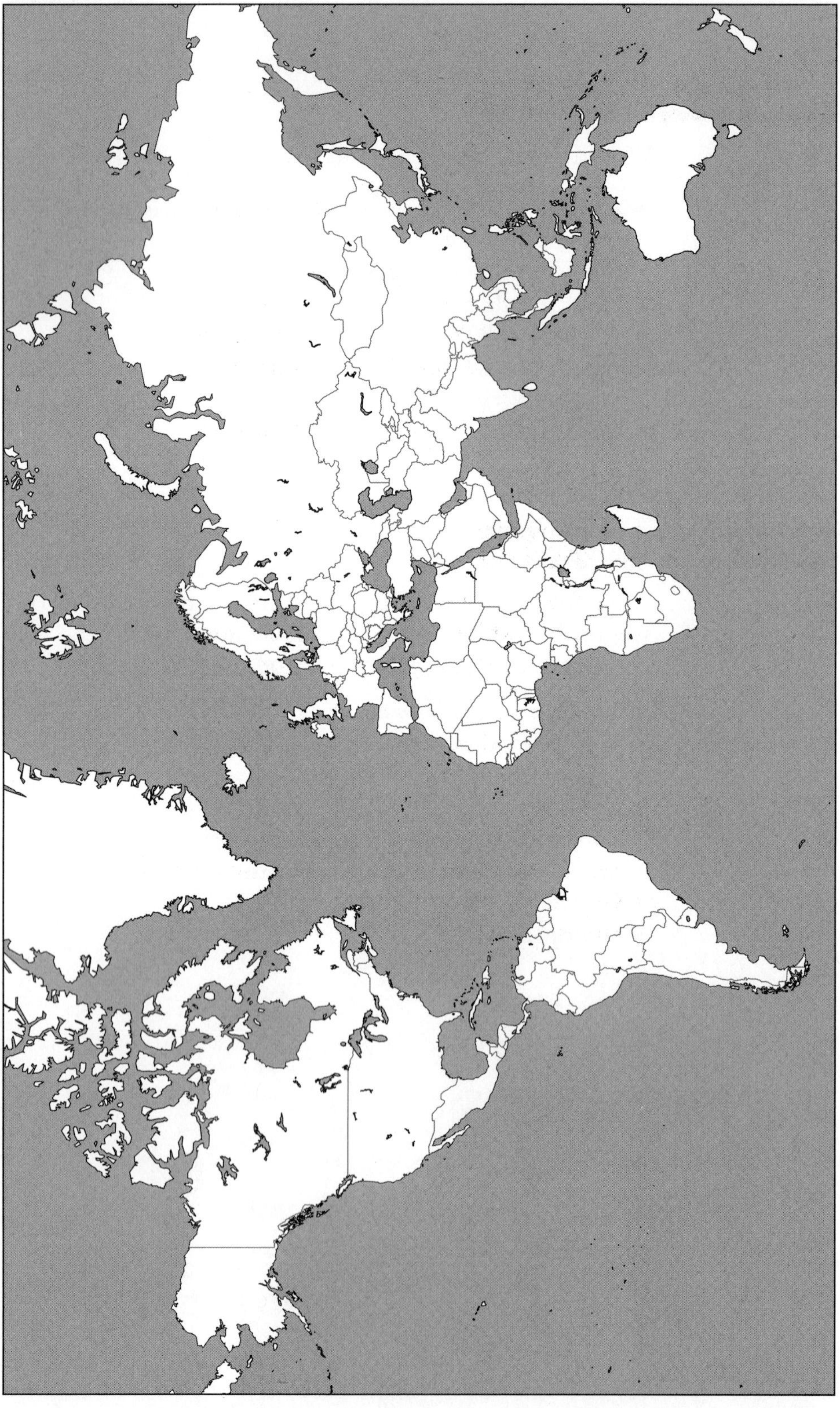

Appendix A
IATA Areas with City Codes

288 International Travel and Tourism

AREA 1

CITY	CODE	CITY	CODE	CITY	CODE
Anchorage	ANC	Honolulu	HNL	Quito	UIO
Asuncion	ASU	Houston	HOU		
Atlanta	ATL			Rio de Janeiro	RIO
		Kingston	KIN		
Bogota	BOG			San Francisco	SFO
Buenos Aires	BUE	La Paz	LPB	San Jose	SJO
		Lima	LIM	San Juan	SJU
Calgary	YYC	Los Angeles	LAX	Santiago	SCL
Caracas	CCS			Seattle	SEA
Cayenne	CAY	New York	NYC	Sao Paulo	SAO
Chicago	CHI				
		Mexico City	MEX	Toronto	YYZ
Dallas	DFW	Montevideo	MVD		
Denver	DEN	Montreal	YUL	Vancouver	YVR
Edmonton	YEG	Panama City	PTY	Washington, DC	WAS
		Paramaribo	PBM		
Georgetown	GEO	Philadelphia	PHL		
Godhaven	JGO				
Guatemala City	GUA				

AREA 2

Appendix A IATA Areas with City Codes

CITY	CODE	CITY	CODE	CITY	CODE
Abidjan	ABJ	Frankfurt	FRA	Nairobi	NBO
Abu Dhabi	AUH				
Accra	ACC	Harare	HRE	Oslo	OSL
Amsterdam	AMS	Helsinki	HEL		
Ankara	ANK			Paris	PAR
Athens	ATH	Johannesburg	JNB	Prague	PRG
Bamako	BKO	Khartoum	KRT	Reykjavik	REK
Berlin	BER	Kiev	IEV	Riyadh	RUH
Brussels	BRU	Kinshasa	FIH	Rome	ROM
Budapest	BUD				
Bucharest	BUH	Lagos	LOS	Sanaa	SAH
		Lisbon	LIS	St. Petersburg	LED
Cairo	CAI	London	LON	Sofia	SOF
Capetown	CPT	Luanda	LAD	Stockholm	STO
Casablanca	CAS	Lusaka	LUN		
Copenhagen	CPH			Tehran	THR
		Madrid	MAD		
Dakar	DKR	Minsk	MSQ	Vienna	VIE
Damascus	DAM	Moscow	MOW		
Dar es Salaam	DAR	Munich	MUC	Warsaw	WAW
		Muscat	MCT		

International Travel and Tourism

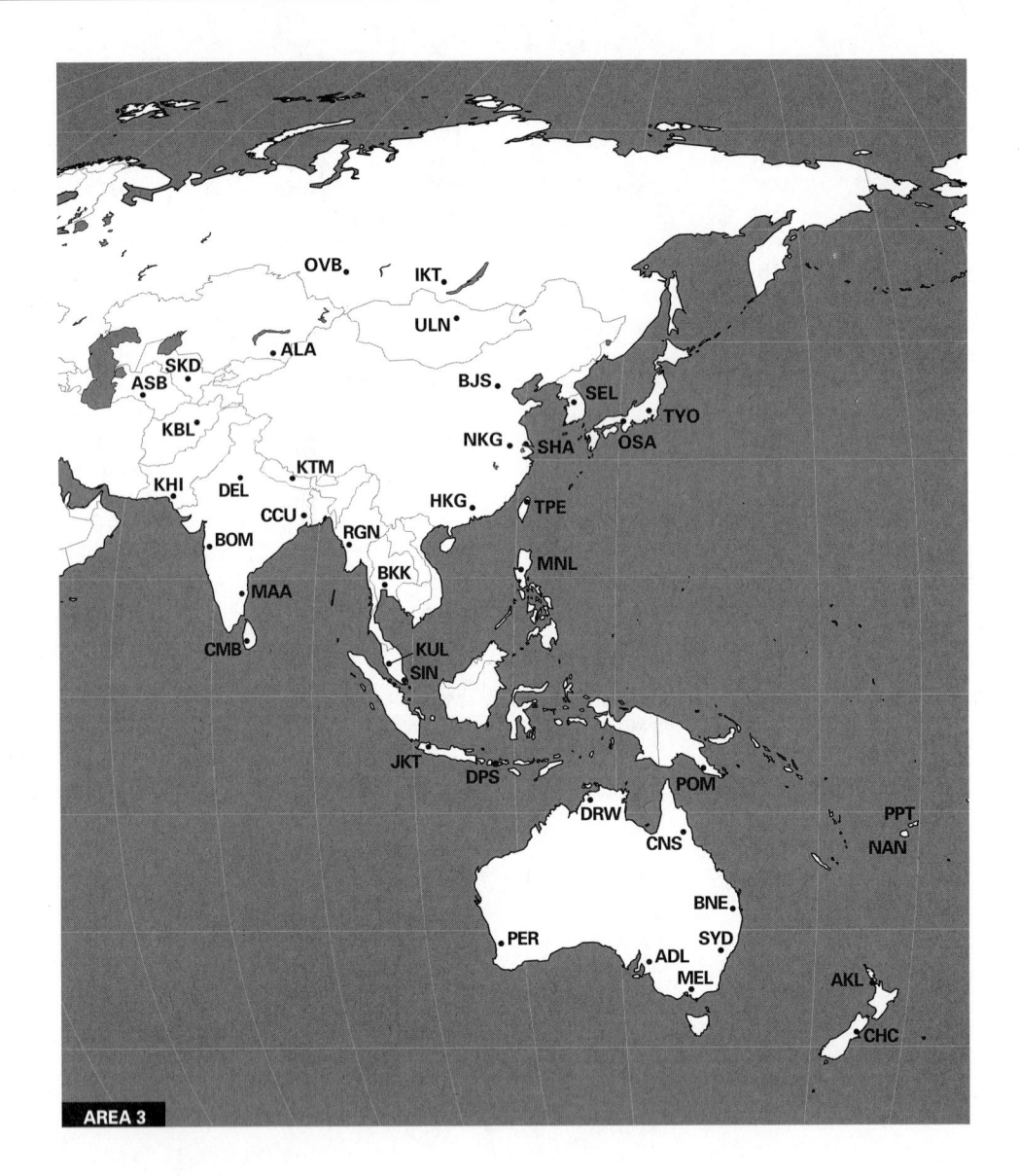

AREA 3

Appendix A IATA Areas with City Codes

CITY	CODE	CITY	CODE	CITY	CODE
Adelaide	ADL	Hong Kong	HKG	Osaka	OSA
Alma Ata	ALA				
Ashkhabad	ASB	Irkutsk	IKT	Papeete	PPT
Auckland	AKL			Perth	PER
		Jakarta	JKT	Port Moresby	POM
Bangkok	BKK				
Beijing	BJS	Kabul	KBL	Samarkand	SKD
Bombay	BOM	Karachi	KHI	Seoul	SEL
Brisbane	BNE	Katmandu	KTM	Shanghai	SHA
		Kuala Lumpur	KUL	Singapore	SIN
Cairns	CNS			Sydney	SYD
Calcutta	CCU	Madras	MAA		
Christchurch	CHC	Manila	MNL	Taipei	TPE
Colombo	CMB	Melbourne	MEL	Tokyo	TYO
Darwin	DRW	Nadi	NAN	Ulan Bator	ULN
Delhi	DEL	Nanjing	NKG		
Denpasar	DPS	Novosibirsk	OVB	Yangon	RGN

Appendix B

City and Airport Codes Listed Alphabetically by Code

A
AAC	Al Arish, Egypt
AAE	Annaba, Algeria
AAK	Aranuka, Kiribati
AAL	Aalborg, Denmark
AAN	Al Ain, United Arab Emirates
AAQ	Anapa, Russian Fed.
AAR	Aarhus, Denmark
AAT	Altay, P. R. China
AAW	Abbottabad, Pakistan
AAY	Al Ghaydah, Republic of Yemen
ABA	Abakan, Russian Fed.
ABD	Abadan, Iran
ABE	Allentown, Pennsylvania, USA
ABF	Abaiang, Kiribati
ABI	Abilene, Texas, USA
ABJ	Abidjan, Cote D'Ivoire
ABK	Kabri Dar, Ethiopia
ABL	Ambler, Alaska, USA
ABM	Bamaga, QLD, Australia
ABQ	Albuquerque, New Mexico, USA
ABR	Aberdeen, South Dakota, USA
ABS	Abu Simbel, Egypt
ABT	Al-Baha, Saudi Arabia
ABV	Abuja, Nigeria
ABX	Albury, NSW, Australia
ABY	Albany, Georgia, USA
ABZ	Aberdeen, United Kingdom
ACA	Acapulco, Mexico
ACC	Accra, Ghana
ACE	Lanzarote, Canary Is.
ACH	Altenrhein, Switzerland
ACI	Alderney, United Kingdom
ACK	Nantucket, MA, USA
ACR	Araracuara, Colombia
ACT	Waco, Texas, USA
ACV	Eureka/Arcata, California, USA
ACY	Atlantic City International, New Jersey, USA
ADA	Adana, Turkey
ADB	Izmir Adnan Menderes Apt, Turkey
ADD	Addis Ababa, Ethiopia
ADE	Aden, Republic of Yemen
ADK	Adak Island, Alaska, USA
ADL	Adelaide, SA, Australia
ADQ	Kodiak, Alaska, USA
ADU	Ardabil, Iran
ADZ	San Andres Island, Colombia
AEA	Abemama Atoll, Kiribati
AEH	Abecher, Chad
AEO	Aioun El Atrouss, Mauritania
AEP	Jorge Newbery, BA, Argentina
AER	Adler/Sochi, Russian Fed.
AES	Aalesund, Norway
AET	Allakaket, Alaska, USA
AEY	Akureyri, Iceland
AFA	San Rafael, MD, Argentina
AFL	Alta Floresta, MT, Brazil
AFT	Afutara, Solomon Is.
AGA	Agadir, Morocco
AGB	Munich/Augsburg Apt., Germany
AGF	Agen, France
AGH	Helsingborg, Sweden
AGJ	Aguni, Japan
AGL	Wanigela, Papua New Guinea
AGN	Angoon, Alaska, USA
AGP	Malaga, Spain
AGR	Agra, India
AGS	Augusta, Georgia, USA
AGT	Ciudad Del Este, Paraguay
AGU	Aguascalientes, Mexico
AGV	Acarigua, Venezuela
AGX	Agatti Island, India
AHB	Abha, Saudi Arabia
AHN	Athens, Georgia, USA
AHO	Alghero, Italy
AHU	Al Hoceima, Morocco
AIA	Alliance, Nebraska, USA
AIC	Airok, Marshall Islands
AID	Anderson, Indiana, USA
AIE	Aiome, Papua New Guinea
AIM	Ailuk Island, Marshall Islands
AIN	Wainwright, Alaska, USA
AIR	Aripuana, MT, Brazil
AIS	Arorae Island, Kiribati
AIT	Aitutaki, Cook Is., S. Pacific

Reprinted by special permission from the February 1996 issue of the OAG Desktop Guide-Worldwide Edition. *All rights Reserved. Copyright 1996, Reed Travel Group.*

City and Airport Codes, cont.

AIU	Atiu Island, Cook Is., S. Pacific
AIY	Atlantic City, New Jersey, USA
AJA	Ajaccio, France
AJF	Jouf, Saudi Arabia
AJN	Anjouan, Comoros
AJR	Arvidsjaur, Sweden
AJU	Aracaju, SE, Brazil
AKA	Ankang, P. R. China
AKB	Atka, Alaska, USA
AKC	Akron, Fulton International Apt., Ohio, USA
AKE	Akieni, Gabon
AKI	Akiak, Alaska, USA
AKJ	Asahikawa, Japan
AKK	Akhiok, Alaska, USA
AKL	Auckland, New Zealand
AKN	King Salmon, Alaska, USA
AKO	Akron, Colorado, USA
AKP	Anaktuvuk Pass, Alaska, USA
AKS	Auki, Solomon Is.
AKU	Aksu, P. R. China
AKV	Akulivik, Quebec, Canada
AKX	Aktyubinsk, Kazakhstan
AKY	Sittwe, Myanmar
ALA	Almaty, Kazakhstan
ALB	Albany, New York, USA
ALC	Alicante, Spain
ALE	Alpine, Texas, USA
ALF	Alta, Norway
ALG	Algiers, Algeria
ALH	Albany, WA, Australia
ALJ	Alexander Bay, S. Africa
ALM	Alamogordo, New Mexico, USA
ALO	Waterloo, Iowa, USA
ALP	Aleppo, Syria
ALS	Alamosa, Colorado, USA
ALW	Walla Walla, Washington, USA
ALY	Alexandria, Egypt
AMA	Amarillo, Texas, USA
AMD	Ahmedabad, India
AMH	Arba Mintch, Ethiopia
AMI	Mataram, Indonesia
AMM	Amman, Jordan
AMQ	Ambon, Indonesia
AMS	Amsterdam, Netherlands
ANB	Anniston, Alabama, USA
ANC	Anchorage, Alaska, USA
ANF	Antofagasta, Chile
ANG	Angouleme, France
ANI	Aniak, Alaska, USA
ANK	Ankara, Turkey
ANM	Antalaha, Madagascar
ANR	Antwerp, Belgium
ANS	Andahuaylas, Peru
ANU	Antigua, West Indies
ANV	Anvik, Alaska, USA
ANX	Andenes, Norway
AOB	Annanberg, Papua New Guinea
AOG	Anshan, P. R. China
AOI	Ancona, Italy
AOJ	Aomori, Japan
AOK	Karpathos, Greece
AOO	Altoona, Pennsylvania, USA
AOR	Alor Setar, Malaysia
APF	Naples, Florida, USA
API	Apjay, Colombia
APL	Nampula, Mozambique
APN	Alpena, Michigan, USA
APO	Apartado, Colombia
APP	Asapa, Papua New Guinea
APW	Apia, Samoa
AQG	Anqing, P. R. China
AQI	Qaisumah, Saudi Arabia
AQJ	Aqaba, Jordan
AQP	Arequipa, Peru
ARC	Arctic Village, Alaska, USA
ARD	Alor Island, Indonesia
ARH	Arkhangelsk, Russian Fed.
ARI	Arica, Chile
ARM	Armidale, NSW, Australia
ARN	Arlanda, Sweden
ARP	Aragip, Papua New Guinea
ART	Watertown, New York, USA
ARU	Aracatuba, SP, Brazil
ARV	Minocqua, Wisconsin, USA
ARW	Arad, Romania
ARZ	N'zeto, Angola
ASA	Assab, Eritrea
ASB	Ashkhabad, Turkmenistan
ASD	Andros Town, Bahamas
ASE	Aspen, Colorado, USA
ASF	Astrakhan, Russian Fed.
ASJ	Amami O. Shima, Japan
ASK	Yamoussoukro, Cote D'Ivoire
ASM	Asmara, Eritrea
ASO	Asosa, Ethiopia
ASP	Alice Springs, NT, Australia
ASR	Kayseri, Turkey
ASU	Asuncion, Paraguay
ASV	Amboseli, Kenya
ASW	Aswan, Egypt
ATB	Atbara, Sudan
ATC	Arthur's Town, Bahamas
ATD	Atoifi, Solomon Is.
ATH	Athens, Greece
ATK	Atqasuk, Alaska, USA
ATL	Atlanta, Georgia, USA
ATM	Altamira, PA, Brazil
ATN	Namatanai, Papua New Guinea
ATP	Aitape, Papua New Guinea
ATQ	Amritsar, India
ATR	Atar, Mauritania
ATT	Atmautluak, Alaska, USA
ATW	Appleton, Wisconsin, USA
ATY	Watertown, South Dakota, USA
AUA	Aruba, Aruba
AUC	Arauca, Colombia
AUG	Augusta, Maine, USA
AUH	Abu Dhabi, United Arab Emirates
AUK	Alakanuk, Alaska, USA
AUL	Aur Island, Marshall Islands
AUP	Agaun, Papua New Guinea
AUQ	Atuona, Marquesas Islands
AUR	Aurillac, France
AUS	Austin, Texas, USA
AUV	Aumo, Papua New Guinea
AUW	Wausau, Wisconsin, USA
AUX	Araguaina, TO, Brazil
AUY	Aneityum, Vanuatu
AVI	Ciego de Avila, Cuba
AVL	Asheville, North Carolina, USA
AVN	Avignon, France
AVP	Wilkes-Barre/Scranton, Pennsylvania, USA
AVU	Avu Avu, Solomon Is.
AWD	Aniwa, Vanuatu
AWH	Awareh, Ethiopia
AWZ	Ahwaz, Iran
AXA	Anguilla, Leeward Is.
AXD	Alexandroupolis, Greece
AXK	Ataq, Republic of Yemen
AXM	Armenia, Colombia
AXP	Spring Point, Bahamas
AXT	Akita, Japan
AXU	Axum, Ethiopia
AYK	Arkalyk, Kazakhstan
AYP	Ayacucho, Peru
AYQ	Ayers Rock, NT, Australia
AYT	Antayla, Turkey
AYU	Aiyura, Papua New Guinea
AZB	Amazon Bay, Papua New Guinea
AZD	Yazd, Iran
AZN	Andizhan, Uzbekistan
AZO	Kalamazoo, Michigan, USA
AZR	Adrar, Algeria

B

BAA	Bialla, Papua New Guinea
BAG	Baguio, Philippines

City and Airport Codes, cont.

BAH	Bahrain, Bahrain
BAJ	Bali, Papua New Guinea
BAK	Baku, Azerbaijan
BAL	Batman, Turkey
BAQ	Barranquilla, Colombia
BAS	Balalae, Solomon Is.
BAU	Bauru, SP, Brazil
BAV	Baotou, P. R. China
BAX	Barnaul, Russian Fed.
BAY	Baia Mare, Romania
BBA	Balmaceda, Chile
BBG	Butaritari, Kiribati
BBI	Bhubaneswar, India
BBK	Kasane, Botswana
BBM	Battambang, Cambodia
BBN	Bario, Malaysia
BBO	Berbera, Somalia
BBQ	Barbuda, West Indies
BBR	Basse Terre, French Antilles
BBU	Baneasa, Romania
BCA	Baracoa, Cuba
BCD	Bacolod, Philippines
BCE	Bryce Canyon, Utah, USA
BCI	Barcaldine, QLD, Australia
BCL	Barra Colorado, Costa Rica
BCN	Barcelona, Spain
BCO	Jinka, Ethiopia
BCV	Belmopan, Belize
BCX	Beloreck, Russian Fed.
BDA	Bermuda, Atlantic Ocean
BDB	Bundaberg, QLD, Australia
BDH	Bandar Lengeh, Iran
BDJ	Banjarmasin, Indonesia
BDK	Bondoukou, Cote D'Ivoire
BDL	Bradley International Apt., CT, USA
BDO	Bandung, Indonesia
BDP	Bhadrapur, Nepal
BDQ	Vadodara, India
BDR	Bridgeport, CT, USA
BDS	Brindisi, Italy
BDT	Gbadolite, Zaire
BDU	Bardufoss, Norway
BEB	Benbecula, United Kingdom
BEF	Bluefields, Nicaragua
BEG	Belgrade, Yugoslavia
BEH	Benton Harbor, Michigan, USA
BEI	Beica, Ethiopia
BEJ	Berau, Indonesia
BEL	Belem, PA, Brazil
BEO	Belmont, NSW, Australia
BER	Berlin, Germany
BES	Brest, France
BET	Bethel, Alaska, USA
BEU	Bedourie, QLD, Australia
BEW	Beira, Mozambique
BEY	Beirut, Lebanon
BEZ	Beru, Kiribati
BFD	Bradford, Pennsylvania, USA
BFE	Bielefeld, Germany
BFF	Scottsbluff, Nebraska, USA
BFI	Boeing Field International Apt., Washington, USA
BFL	Bakersfield, California, USA
BFN	Bloemfontein, S. Africa
BFO	Buffalo Range, Zimbabwe
BFS	Belfast, United Kingdom
BFU	Bengbu, P. R. China
BGA	Bucaramanga, Colombia
BGF	Bangui, Central African Republic
BGI	Barbados, Barbados
BGJ	Borgarfjordur Eystri, Iceland
BGK	Big Creek, Belize
BGM	Binghampton, New York, USA
BGO	Bergen, Norway
BGR	Bangor, Maine, USA
BGX	Bage, RS, Brazil
BGY	Orio Al Serio, Italy
BHA	Bahia de Caraquez, Ecuador
BHB	Bar Barbor, Maine, USA
BHD	Belfast City, United Kingdom
BHE	Blenheim, New Zealand
BHH	Bisha, Saudi Arabia
BHI	Bahia Blanca, BA, Argentina
BHJ	Bhuj, India
BHK	Bukhara, Uzbekistan
BHM	Birmingham, Alabama, USA
BHO	Bhopal, India
BHQ	Broken Hill, NSW, Australia
BHR	Bharatpur, Nepal
BHS	Bathurst, NSW, Australia
BHU	Bhavnagar, India
BHV	Bahawalpur, Pakistan
BHX	Birmingham, United Kingdom
BHY	Beihai, P. R. China
BHZ	Belo Horizonte, MG, Brazil
BIA	Bastia, France
BID	Block Island, Rhode Island, USA
BII	Bikini Atoll, Marshall Islands
BIK	Biak, Indonesia
BIL	Billings, Montana, USA
BIM	Bimini, Bahamas
BIO	Bilbao, Spain
BIQ	Biarritz, France
BIR	Biratnagar, Nepal
BIS	Bismarck, North Dakota, USA
BIY	Bisho, S. Africa
BJA	Bejaia, Algeria
BJD	Bakkafijordur, Iceland
BJF	Batsfjord, Norway
BJI	Bemidji, Minnesota, USA
BJL	Banjul, Gambia
BJM	Bujumbura, Burundi
BJR	Bahar Dar, Ethiopia
BJS	Beijing, P. R. China
BJW	Bajawa, Indonesia
BJX	Leon/Guanajuato, Mexico
BJZ	Badajoz, Spain
BKA	Bykovo, Russian Fed.
BKC	Buckland, Alaska, USA
BKI	Kota Kinabalu, Malaysia
BKK	Bangkok, Thailand
BKM	Bakalalan, Malaysia
BKO	Bamako, Mali
BKQ	Blackall, QLD, Australia
BKS	Bengkulu, Indonesia
BKW	Beckley, West Virginia, USA
BKX	Brookings, South Dakota, USA
BKY	Bukavu, Zaire
BLA	Barcelona, Venezuela
BLE	Borlange, Sweden
BLF	Bluefield, West Virginia, USA
BLG	Belaga, Malaysia
BLI	Bellingham, Washington, USA
BLK	Blackpool, United Kingdom
BLL	Billund, Denmark
BLP	Bellavista, Peru
BLQ	Bologna, Italy
BLR	Bangalore, India
BLT	Blackwater, QLD, Australia
BLZ	Blantyre, Malawi
BMA	Bromma, Sweden
BME	Broome, WA, Australia
BMG	Bloomington, Indiana, USA
BMI	Bloomington, Illinois, USA
BMM	Bitam, Gabon
BMO	Bhamo, Myanmar
BMP	Brampton Island, QLD, Australia
BMU	Bima, Indonesia
BMV	Ban Me Thuot, Vietnam
BMW	Bordj Badji Mokhtar, Algeria
BMY	Belep Island, New Caledonia
BNA	Nashville, Tennessee, USA
BND	Bandar Abbas, Iran
BNE	Brisbane, QLD, Australia
BNJ	Bonn, Germany
BNK	Ballina, NSW, Australia
BNN	Bronnoysund, Norway

City and Airport Codes, cont.

BNP	Bannu, Pakistan	BSD	Baoshan, P. R. China	BYW	Blakely Island, Washington, USA
BNS	Barinas, Venezuela	BSG	Bata, Equatorial Guinea	BZA	Bonanza, Nicaragua
BNT	Bundi, Papua New Guinea	BSK	Biskra, Algeria	BZE	Belize City, Belize
BNU	Blumenau, SC, Brazil	BSL	Basel, Switzerland	BZN	Bozeman, Montana, USA
BNY	Bellona, Solomon Is.	BTH	Batu Besar, Indonesia	BZR	Beziers, France
BOB	Bora Bora, Society Islands	BTI	Barter Island, Alaska, USA	BZV	Brazzaville, Congo
BOD	Bordeaux, France	BTJ	Banda Aceh, Indonesia	BZZ	Brize Norton, United Kingdom
BOG	Bogota, Colombia	BTM	Butte, Montana, USA		
BOI	Boise, Idaho, USA	BTR	Baton Rouge, Louisiana, USA	**C**	
BOJ	Bourgas, Bulgaria	BTS	Bratislava, Slovakia	CAB	Cabinda, Angola
BOM	Bombay, India	BTT	Bettles, Alaska, USA	CAC	Cascavel, PR, Brazil
BON	Bonaire, Netherlands Antilles	BTU	Bintulu, Malaysia	CAE	Columbia, South Carolina, USA
BOO	Bodo, Norway	BTV	Burlington, Vermont, USA	CAF	Carauari, AM, Brazil
BOS	Boston, MA, USA	BUA	Buka, Papua New Guinea	CAG	Cagliari, Italy
BOV	Boang, Papua New Guinea	BUC	Burketown, QLD, Australia	CAI	Cairo, Egypt
BOX	Borroloola, NT, Australia	BUD	Budapest, Hungary	CAJ	Canaima, Venezuela
BOY	Bobo Dioulasso, Burkina Faso	BUE	Buenos Aires, BA, Argentina	CAK	Akron/Canton, Ohio, USA
BPF	Batuna, Solomon Is.	BUF	Buffalo, New York, USA	CAL	Campbeltown, United Kingdom
BPG	Barra Do Garcas, MT, Brazil	BUG	Benguela, Angola	CAN	Guangzhou, P. R. China
BPN	Balikpapan, Indonesia	BUH	Bucharest, Romania	CAP	Cap Haitien, Haiti
BPS	Porto Seguro, BA, Brazil	BUK	Albuq, Republic of Yemen	CAQ	Caucasia, Colombia
BPT	Beaumont/Pt. Arthur, Texas, USA	BUL	Bulolo, Papua New Guinea	CAS	Casablanca, Morocco
BQE	Bubaque, Guinea-Bissau	BUO	Burao, Somalia	CAW	Campos, RJ, Brazil
BQH	Biggin Hill, United Kingdom	BUQ	Bulawayo, Zimbabwe	CAY	Cayenne, French Guiana
BQK	Glynon Jetport, Georgia, USA	BUR	Burbank, California, USA	CAZ	Cobar, NSW, Australia
BQL	Boulia, QLD, Australia	BUS	Batumi, Georgia	CBB	Cochabamba, Bolivia
BQN	Aguadilla, Puerto Rico	BUZ	Bushehr, Iran	CBE	Cumberland, Maryland, USA
BQO	Bouna, Cote D'Ivoire	BVB	Boa Vista, RR, Brazil	CBG	Cambridge, United Kingdom
BQS	Blagoveschensk, Russian Fed.	BVC	Boa Vista, Cape Verde	CBH	Bechar, Algeria
BQT	Brest, Belarus	BVE	Brive-la-Gaillarde, France	CBL	Ciudad Bolivar, Venezuela
BQU	Port Elizabeth, Windward Islands	BVG	Berlevag, Norway	CBO	Cotabato, Philippines
BRA	Barreiras, BA, Brazil	BVH	Vihena, RO, Brazil	CBQ	Calabar, Nigeria
BRC	S.C. Bariloch, RN, Argentina	BVI	Birdsville, QLD, Australia	CBR	Canberra, ACT, Australia
BRD	Brainerd, Minnesota, USA	BVR	Brava, Cape Verde	CCC	Cayo Coco, Cuba
BRE	Bremen, Germany	BVS	Breves, PA, Brazil	CCF	Carcassonne, France
BRI	Bari, Italy	BWA	Bhairawa, Nepal	CCJ	Calicut, India
BRK	Bourke, NSW, Australia	BWD	Brownwood, Texas, USA	CCK	Cocos Islands, Cocos Islands
BRL	Burlington, Iowa, USA	BWE	Braunschweig, Germany	CCM	Crisciuma, SC, Brazil
BRM	Barquisimeto, Venezuela	BWI	Baltimore, Maryland, USA	CCO	Carimagua, Colombia
BRN	Berne, Switzerland	BWN	Bandar Seri Begawan, Brunei	CCP	Concepcion, Chile
BRO	Brownsville, Texas, USA	BWO	Balakovo, Russian Fed.	CCS	Caracas, Venezuela
BRQ	Brno, Czech Republic	BWQ	Brewarrina, NSW, Australia	CCU	Calcutta, India
BRR	Barra, United Kingdom	BWT	Burnie, Tasmania, Australia	CCV	Craig Cove, Vanuatu
BRS	Bristol, United Kingdom	BXH	Balkhash, Kazakhstan	CDB	Cold Bay, Alaska, USA
BRT	Bathurst Island, NT, Australia	BXI	Boundiali, Cote D'Ivoire	CDC	Cedar City, Utah, USA
BRU	Brussels, Belgium	BXN	Bodrum, Turkey	CDG	Charles de Gaulle, France
BRW	Barrow, Alaska, USA	BXU	Butuan, Philippines	CDJ	Conceicao Do Araguaia, PA, Brazil
BSA	Bossaso, Somalia	BXV	Breiddalsvik, Iceland	CDL	Candle, Alaska, USA
BSB	Brasilia, DF, Brazil	BXX	Borama, Somalia	CDR	Chadron, Nebraska, USA
BSC	Bahia Solano, Colombia	BYA	Boundary, Alaska, USA	CDV	Cordova, Alaska, USA
		BYB	Dibaa, Oman	CEB	Cebu, Philippines
		BYK	Bouake, Cote D'Ivoire		
		BYM	Bayamo, Cuba		
		BYU	Bayreuth, Germany		

City and Airport Codes, cont.

CEC	Crescent City, California, USA
CED	Ceduna, SA, Australia
CEI	Chiang Rai, Thailand
CEK	Chelyabinsk, Russian Fed.
CEM	Central, Alaska, USA
CEN	Ciudad Obregon, Mexico
CEO	Waco Kungo, Angola
CEQ	Cannes, France
CER	Cherbourg, France
CEZ	Cortez, Colorado, USA
CFE	Clermont-Ferrand, France
CFN	Donegal, Republic of Ireland
CFO	Confreza, MT, Brazil
CFR	Caen, France
CFS	Coffs Harbour, NSW, Australia
CFU	Kerkyra, Greece
CGA	Craig, Alaska, USA
CGB	Cuiaba, MT, Brazil
CGC	Cape Gloucester, Papua New Guinea
CGH	Congonhas, SP, Brazil
CGI	Cape Girardeau, Missouri, USA
CGK	Soekarno-Hatta Intl. Apt., Indonesia
CGN	Cologne/Bonn, Germany
CGO	Zhengzhou, P. R. China
CGP	Chittagong, Bangladesh
CGQ	Changchun, P. R. China
CGR	Campo Grande, MS, Brazil
CGX	Meigs Field, Illinois, USA
CGY	Cagayan de Oro, Philippines
CHA	Chattanooga, Tennessee, USA
CHC	Christchurch, New Zealand
CHH	Chachapoyas, Peru
CHI	Chicago, Illinois, USA
CHM	Chimbote, Peru
CHO	Charlottesville, Virginia, USA
CHP	Circle Hot Springs, Alaska, USA
CHQ	Chania, Greece
CHS	Charleston, South Carolina, USA
CHT	Chatham Island, New Zealand
CHU	Chuathbaluk, Alaska, USA
CHX	Changuinola, Panama
CHY	Choiseul Bay, Solomon Is.
CIA	Ciampino, Italy
CIC	Chico, California, USA
CID	Cedar Rapids/Iowa City, Iowa, USA
CIJ	Cobija, Bolivia
CIK	Chalkyitsik, Alaska, USA
CIT	Shimkent, Kazakhstan
CIU	Chippewa County, Michigan, USA
CIW	Canouan Island, Windward Islands
CIX	Chiclayo, Peru
CJA	Cajamarca, Peru
CJB	Coimbatore, India
CJC	Calama, Chile
CJL	Chitral, Pakistan
CJS	Ciudad Juarez, Mexico
CJU	Cheju, Republic of Korea
CKB	Clarksburg, West Virginia, USA
CKD	Crooked Creek, Alaska, USA
CKG	Chongqing, P. R. China
CKS	Carajas, PA, Brazil
CKX	Chicken, Alaska, USA
CKY	Conakry, Guinea
CKZ	Canakkale, Turkey
CLD	Carlsbad, California, USA
CLE	Cleveland, Ohio, USA
CLJ	Cluj, Romania
CLL	College Station, Texas, USA
CLM	Port Angeles, Washington, USA
CLO	Cali, Colombia
CLP	Clarks Point, Alaska, USA
CLQ	Colima, Mexico
CLT	Charlotte, North Carolina, USA
CLV	Caldas Novas, GO, Brazil
CLY	Calvi, France
CMA	Cunnamulla, QLD, Australia
CMB	Colombo, Sri Lanka
CMD	Cootamundra, NSW, Australia
CME	Ciudad Del Carmen, Mexico
CMF	Chambery, France
CMG	Corumba, MS, Brazil
CMH	Columbus, Ohio, USA
CMI	Champaign, Illinois, USA
CMJ	Chi Mei, Taiwan
CMK	Club Makokola, Malawi
CMN	Mohamed V, Morocco
CMP	Santana Do Araguaia, PA, Brazil
CMQ	Clermont, QLD, Australia
CMU	Kundiawa, Papua New Guinea
CMW	Camaguey, Cuba
CMX	Hancock, Michigan, USA
CNB	Coonamble, NSW, Australia
CNF	Tancredo Neves Intl. Apt., MG, Brazil
CNJ	Cloncurry, QLD, Australia
CNM	Carlsbad, New Mexico, USA
CNP	Neerlerit Inaat, Greenland
CNQ	Corrientes, CR, Argentina
CNS	Cairns, QLD, Australia
CNX	Chiang Mai, Thailand
CNY	Moab, Utah, USA
COD	Cody, Wyoming, USA
COG	Condoto, Colombia
COJ	Coonabarabran, NSW, Australia
COK	Cochin, India
COO	Cotonou, Benin
COR	Cordoba, CD, Argentina
COS	Colorado Springs, Colorado, USA
COU	Columbia, Missouri, USA
CPB	Capurgana, Colombia
CPC	San Martin de Los An, NE, Argentina
CPD	Coober Pedy, SA, Australia
CPE	Campeche, Mexico
CPH	Copenhagen, Denmark
CPO	Copiapo, Chile
CPQ	Campinas, SP, Brazil
CPR	Casper, Wyoming, USA
CPT	Cape Town, S. Africa
CPV	Campina Grande, PB, Brazil
CPX	Culebra, Puerto Rico
CRD	Comodoro Rivadavia, CB, Argentina
CRI	Crooked Island, Bahamas
CRP	Corpus Christi, Texas, USA
CRQ	Caravelas, BA, Brazil
CRU	Carriacou, Windward Islands
CRW	Charleston, West Virginia, USA
CSG	Columbus, Georgia, USA
CSI	Casino, NSW, Australia
CSK	Cap Skirring, Senegal
CSL	San Luis Obispo, California, USA
CST	Castaway, Fiji
CSU	Santa Cruz Do Sul, RS, Brazil
CSX	Changsha, P. R. China
CSY	Cheboksary, Russian Fed.
CTA	Catania, Italy
CTC	Catamarca, CA, Argentina
CTG	Cartagena, Colombia
CTL	Charleville, QLD, Australia
CTM	Chetumal, Mexico
CTN	Cooktown, QLD, Australia
CTS	Chitose, Japan
CTU	Chengdu, P. R. China
CUC	Cucuta, Colombia
CUE	Cuenca, Ecuador
CUG	Cudal, NSW, Australia

City and Airport Codes, cont.

CUK	Caye Caulker, Belize	DAL	Love Field, Dallas, Texas, USA	DKI	Dunk Island, QLD, Australia
CUL	Culiacan, Mexico			DKR	Dakar, Senegal
CUM	Cumana, Venezuela	DAM	Damascus, Syria	DLA	Douala, Cameroon
CUN	Cancun, Mexico	DAR	Dar Es Salaam, Tanzania	DLC	Dalian, P. R. China
CUP	Carupano, Venezuela	DAT	Datong, P. R. China	DLD	Geilo, Norway
CUR	Curacao, Netherlands Antilles	DAU	Daru, Papua New Guinea	DLG	Dillingham, Alaska, USA
		DAV	David, Panama	DLH	Duluth, Minnesota, USA
CUT	Cutral, NE, Argentina	DAY	Dayton, Ohio, USA	DLI	Dalat, Vietnam
CUU	Chihuahua, Mexico	DBA	Dalbandin, Pakistan	DLM	Dalaman, Turkey
CUY	Cue, WA, Australia	DBM	Debra Marcos, Ethiopia	DLO	Dolomi, Alaska, USA
CUZ	Cuzco, Peru	DBO	Dubbo, NSW, Australia	DLU	Dali City, P. R. China
CVB	Chungribu, Papua New Guinea	DBQ	Dubuque, Iowa, USA	DLY	Dillons Bay, Vanuatu
		DBT	Debre Tabor, Ethiopia	DMB	Zhambyl, Kazakhstan
CVC	Cleve, SA, Australia	DBV	Dubrovnik, Croatia	DMD	Doomadgee Mission, QLD, Australia
CVG	Cincinnati, Ohio, USA	DCA	Washington National, District of Columbia, USA	DME	Domodedovo, Russian Fed.
CVJ	Cuernavaca, Mexico				
CVL	Cape Vogel, Papua New Guinea	DCF	Cane Field, West Indies	DMU	Dimapur, India
		DCM	Castres, France	DND	Dundee, United Kingdom
CVM	Cuidad Victoria, Mexico	DDC	Dodge City, Kansas, USA	DNH	Dunhuang, P. R. China
CVN	Clovis, New Mexico, USA	DDG	Dandong, P. R. China	DNM	Denham, WA, Australia
CVQ	Carnarvon, WA, Australia	DDI	Daydream Island, QLD, Australia	DNQ	Deniliquin, NSW, Australia
CVU	Corvo Island, Portugal (Azores)			DNR	Dinard, France
		DDM	Dodoima, Papua New Guinea	DNV	Danville, Illinois, USA
CWA	Central Wisconsin, Wisconsin, USA			DNZ	Denizli, Turkey
		DEC	Decatur, Illinois, USA	DOF	Dora Bay, Alaska, USA
CWB	Curitiba, PR, Brazil	DEL	Delhi, India	DOG	Dongola, Sudan
CWC	Chernovtsy, Ukraine	DEM	Dembidollo, Ethiopia	DOH	Doha, Qatar
CWL	Cardiff, United Kingdom	DEN	Denver, Colorado, USA	DOK	Donetsk, Ukraine
CWS	Center Island, Washington, USA	DER	Derim, Papua New Guinea	DOL	Deauville, France
		DEZ	Deirezzor, Syria	DOM	Dominica, West Indies
CWT	Cowra, NSW, Australia	DFW	Dallas/Fort Worth, Texas, USA	DOP	Dolpa, Nepal
CXB	Cox's Bazar, Bangladesh			DPL	Dipolog, Philippines
CXH	Coal Harbour, BC, Canada	DGA	Dangriga, Belize	DPO	Devonport, Tasmania, Australia
CXJ	Caxias Do Sul, RS, Brazil	DGE	Mudgee, NSW, Australia		
CXP	Cilacap, Indonesia	DGO	Durango, Mexico	DPS	Denpasar Bali, Indonesia
CYB	Cayman Brac, West Indies	DGT	Dumaguete, Philippines	DRB	Derby, WA, Australia
CYF	Chefornak, Alaska, USA	DHA	Dhahran, Saudi Arabia	DRG	Deering, Alaska, USA
CYI	Chiayi, Taiwan	DHI	Dhangarhi, Nepal	DRO	Durango, Colorado, USA
CYO	Cayo Largo Del Sur, Cuba	DHN	Dothan, Alabama, USA	DRS	Dresden, Germany
CRY	Colonia, Uruguay	DIB	Dibrugarh, India	DRT	Del Rio, Texas, USA
CYS	Cheyenne, Wyoming, USA	DIE	Antsiranana, Madagascar	DRW	Darwin, NT, Australia
CZA	Chichen Itza, Mexico	DIJ	Dijon, France	DSD	La Desirade, French Antilles
CZE	Coro, Venezuela	DIK	Dickinson, North Dakota, USA	DSE	Dessie, Ethiopia
CZH	Corozal, Belize			DSK	Dera Ismail Khan, Pakistan
CZL	Constantine, Algeria	DIL	Dili, Indonesia	DSM	Des Moines, Iowa, USA
CZM	Cozumel, Mexico	DIN	Dien Bien Phu, Vietnam	DTM	Dortmund, Germany
CZN	Chisana, Alaska, USA	DIO	Little Diomede Island, Alaska, USA	DTR	Decatur Island, Washington, USA
CZS	Cruzeiro Do Sul, AC, Brazil				
		DIQ	Divinopolis, MG, Brazil	DTT	Detroit, Michigan, USA
CZU	Corozal, Colombia	DIR	Dire Dawa, Ethiopia	DTW	Metro Wayne County Apt., Michigan, USA
CZX	Changzhou, P. R. China	DIS	Loubomo, Congo		
		DIY	Diyarbakir, Turkey	DUB	Dublin, Republic of Ireland
D		DJB	Jambi, Indonesia	DUD	Dunedin, New Zealand
DAB	Daytona Beach, Florida, USA	DJE	Djerba, Tunisia	DUE	Dundo, Angola
		DJG	Djanet, Algeria	DUJ	Dubois, Pennsylvania, USA
DAC	Dhaka, Bangladesh	DJJ	Jayapura, Indonesia	DUR	Durban, S. Africa
DAD	Da Nang, Vietnam	DJN	Delta Junction, Alaska, USA	DUS	Duesseldorf, Germany

City and Airport Codes, cont.

DUT	Dutch Harbor, Alaska, USA
DVL	Devils Lake, North Dakota, USA
DVO	Davao, Philippines
DXB	Dubai, United Arab Emirates
DYA	Dysart, QLD, Australia
DYG	Dayong, P. R. China
DYR	Anadyr, Russian Fed.
DYU	Dushanbe, Tajikistan
DZA	Dzaoudzi, Mayotte
DZN	Zhezkazgan, Kazakhstan

E

EAA	Eagle, Alaska, USA
EAE	Emae, Vanuatu
EAM	Nejran, Saudi Arabia
EAR	Kearney, Nebraska, USA
EAS	San Sebastian, Spain
EAT	Wenatchee, Washington, USA
EAU	Eau Claire, Wisconsin, USA
EBB	Entebbe/Kampala, Uganda
EBD	EL Obeid, Sudan
EBG	El Bagre, Colombia
EBJ	Esbjerg, Denmark
EBO	Ebon, Marshall Islands
EBU	St. Etienne, France
ECN	Ercan, Cyprus
EDA	Edna Bay, Alaska, USA
EDB	Eldebba, Sudan
EDI	Edinburgh, United Kingdom
EDR	Edward River, QLD, Australia
EEK	Eek, Alaska, USA
EEN	Keene, New Hampshire, USA
EFD	Ellington Field, Texas, USA
EFL	Kefallinia, Greece
EGC	Bergerac, France
EGE	Vail, Colorado, USA
EGM	Sege, Solomon Is.
EGN	El Geneina, Sudan
EGP	Eagle Pass, Texas, USA
EGS	Egilsstadir, Iceland
EGV	Eagle River, Wisconsin, USA
EGX	Egegik, Alaska, USA
EIA	Eia, Papua New Guinea
EIN	Eindhoven, Netherlands
EIS	Tortola, British Virgin Islands
EJA	Barrancabermeja, Colombia
EJH	Wedjh, Saudi Arabia
EKB	Ekibastuz, Kazakhstan
EKO	Elko, Nevada, USA
ELC	Elcho Island, NT, Australia
ELD	El Dorado, Arkansas, USA
ELE	El Real, Panama
ELF	El Fasher, Sudan
ELG	El Golea, Algeria
ELH	North Eleuthera, Bahamas
ELI	Elim, Alaska, USA
ELM	Elmira/Corning, New York, USA
ELP	El Paso, Texas, USA
ELQ	Gassim, Saudi Arabia
ELS	East London, S. Africa
ELU	El Oued, Algeria
ELV	Elfin Cove, Alaska, USA
ELY	Ely, Nevada, USA
EMA	East Midlands, United, Kingdom
EMD	Emerald, QLD, Australia
EMI	Emirau, Papua New Guinea
EMK	Emmonak, Alaska, USA
EMN	Nema, Mauritania
EMO	Emo, Papua New Guinea
EMS	Embessa, Papua New Guinea
ENA	Kenai, Alaska, USA
ENE	Ende, Indonesia
ENF	Enontekio, Finland
ENH	Enshi, P. R. China
ENO	Encarnacion, Paraguay
ENS	Enschede, Netherlands
ENT	Eniwetok Island, Marshall Islands
ENU	Enugu, Nigeria
ENV	Wendover, Utah, USA
ENY	Yan'an, P. R. China
EOH	Enrique Olaya Herrerra, Colombia
EPL	Epinal, France
EPR	Esperance, WA, Australia
EQS	Esquel, CB, Argentina
ERA	Erigavo, Somalia
ERC	Erzincan, Turkey
ERE	Erave, Papua New Guinea
ERF	Erfurt, Germany
ERH	Errachidia, Morocco
ERI	Erie, Pennsylvania, USA
ERM	Erechim, RS, Brazil
ERN	Elrunepe, AM, Brazil
ERS	Eros, Namibia
ERZ	Erzurum, Turkey
ESA	Esa'ala, Papua New Guinea
ESB	Esenboga, Turkey
ESC	Escanaba, Michigan, USA
ESD	Eastsound, Washington, USA
ESF	Alexandria, Louisiana, USA
ESM	Esmeraldas, Ecuador
ESR	El Salvador, Chile
ESS	Essen, Germany
ETH	Elat, Israel
ETZ	Metz/Nancy, France
EUA	Eua, Tonga Is., S. Pacific
EUG	Eugene, Oregon, USA
EUN	Laayoune, Morocco
EUX	St. Eustatius, Netherlands Antilles
EVE	Evenes, Norway
EVG	Sveg, Sweden
EVN	Yerevan, Armenia
EVV	Evansville, Indiana, USA
EWB	New Bedford, MA, USA
EWN	New Bern, North Carolina, USA
EWR	Newark International Apt., New Jersey, USA
EXI	Excursion Inlet, Alaska, USA
EXT	Exeter, United Kingdom
EYL	Yelimane, Mali
EYP	El Yopal, Colombia
EYW	Key West, Florida, USA
EZE	Ministro Pistarini, BA, Argentina
EZS	Elazig, Turkey

F

FAE	Faroe Islands, Faroe Islands
FAI	Fairbanks, Alaska, USA
FAJ	Fajardo, Puerto Rico
FAK	False Island, Alaska, USA
FAO	Faro, Portugal
FAR	Fargo, North Dakota, USA
FAT	Fresno, California, USA
FAV	Fakarava, Tuamotu Islands
FAY	Fayetteville, North Carolina, USA
FBM	Lubumbashi, Zaire
FBU	Fornebu, Norway
FCA	Kalispell/Glacier Ntl. Pk., Montana, USA
FCO	Leonardo Da Vinci (Fiumicino), Italy
FDE	Forde, Norway
FDF	Fort de France, Martinique
FDH	Friedrichshafen, Germany
FEG	Fergana, Uzbekistan
FEN	Fernando de Noronha, FN, Brazil
FEZ	Fez, Morocco
FFM	Fergus Falls, Minnesota, USA
FGI	Fagali'i, Samoa
FHU	Fort Huachuca/Sr. Vista, Arizona, USA
FIC	Fire Cove, Alaska, USA
FID	Fishers Island, New York, USA
FIE	Fair Isle, United Kingdom
FIH	Kinshasa, Zaire

City and Airport Codes, cont.

FIN	Finschhafen, Papua New Guinea
FJR	Al-Fujairah, United Arab Emirates
FKI	Kisangani, Zaire
FKL	Franklin, Pennsylvania, USA
FKQ	Fak Fak, Indonesia
FKS	Fukushima, Japan
FLA	Florencia, Colombia
FLG	Flagstaff, Arizona, USA
FLL	Ft. Lauderdale, Florida, USA
FLN	Florianopolis, SC, Brazil
FLO	Florence, South Carolina, USA
FLR	Florence, Italy
FLS	Flinders Island, Tasmania, Australia
FLW	Santa Cruz, Flores, Portugal (Azores)
FMA	Formosa, FO, Argentina
FMN	Farmington, New Mexico, USA
FMO	Muenster, Germany
FMY	Fort Myers, Florida, USA
FNA	Freetown, Sierra Leone
FNC	Funchal, Portugal (Madeira)
FNE	Fane, Papua New Guinea
FNI	Nimes, France
FNJ	Pyongyang, Dem. People's Rep. Korea
FNL	Fort Collins/Loveland, Colorado, USA
FNT	Flint, Michigan, USA
FOC	Fuzhou, P. R. China
FOD	Fort Dodge, Iowa, USA
FOE	Topeka Forbes AFB, Kansas, USA
FOO	Numfoor, Indonesia
FOR	Fortaleza, CE, Brazil
FOU	Fougamou, Gabon
FPO	Freeport, Bahamas
FRA	Frankfurt, Germany
FRB	Forbes, NSW, Australia
FRC	Franca, SP, Brazil
FRD	Friday Harbor, Washington, USA
FRE	Fera Island, Solomon Is.
FRG	Long Island Republic, New York, USA
FRM	Fairmont, Minnesota, USA
FRO	Floro, Norway
FRS	Flores, Guatemala
FRU	Bishkek, Kyrgyzstan
FRW	Francistown, Botswana
FSC	Figari, France
FSD	Souix Falls, South Dakota, USA
FSM	Fort Smith, Arkansas, USA
FSP	St. Pierre, St. Pierre & Miquelon
FTA	Futuna Island, Vanuatu
FTU	Fort Dauphin, Madagascar
FTW	Meacham Field, Ft. Worth, Texas, USA
FUB	Fulleborn, Papua New Guinea
FUE	Fuerteventura, Canary Is.
FUJ	Fukue, Japan
FUK	Fukuoka, Japan
FUN	Funafuti Atoll, Tuvalu Is.
FOU	Fuoshan, P. R. China
FUT	Futuna, Wallis and Futuna Is.
FWA	Forth Wayne, Indiana, USA
FYN	Fuyun, P. R. China
FYU	Fort Yukon, Alaska, USA
FYV	Fayetteville, Arkansas, USA

G

GAJ	Yamagata, Japan
GAL	Galena, Alaska, USA
GAM	Gambell, Alaska, USA
GAN	Gan Island, Maldives
GAO	Guantanamo, Cuba
GAQ	Gao, Mali
GAR	Garaina, Papua New Guinea
GAS	Garissa, Kenya
GAU	Gauahati, India
GAX	Gamba, Gabon
GAZ	Guasopa, Papua New Guinea
GBD	Great Bend, Kansas, USA
GBE	Gaborone, Botswana
GBG	Galesburg, Illinois, USA
GBJ	Marie Galante, French Antilles
GBZ	Great Barrier Island, New Zealand
GCC	Gillette, Wyoming, USA
GCI	Guernsey, United Kingdom
GCK	Garden City, Kansas, USA
GCM	Grand Cayman Island, West Indies
GCN	Grand Canyon, Arizona, USA
GDE	Gode, Ethiopia
GDL	Guadalajara, Mexico
GDN	Gdansk, Poland
GDQ	Gondar, Ethiopia
GDT	Grand Turk, Turks & Caicos Is.
GDV	Glendive, Montana, USA
GDX	Magadan, Russian Fed.
GDZ	Gelendzik, Russian Fed.
GEA	Magenta, New Caledonia
GEF	Geva, Solomon Is.
GEG	Spokane, Washington, USA
GEL	Santo Angelo, RS, Brazil
GEO	Georgetown, Guyana
GER	Nueva Gerona, Cuba
GET	Geraldton, WA, Australia
GEV	Gallivare, Sweden
GEW	Gewoya, Papua New Guinea
GFF	Griffith, NSW, Australia
GFK	Grand Forks, North Dakota, USA
GFN	Grafton, NSW, Australia
GGG	Longview, Texas, USA
GGT	George Town, Bahamas
GGW	Glasgow, Montana, USA
GHA	Ghardaia, Algeria
GHB	Governors Harbour, Bahamas
GHC	Great Harbour Cay, Bahamas
GHD	Ghimbi, Ethiopia
GHE	Garachine, Panama
GIB	Gibraltar, Gibraltar
GIG	Internacional, RJ, Brazil
GIL	Gilgit, Pakistan
GIS	Gisborne, New Zealand
GIZ	Gizan, Saudi Arabia
GJA	Guanaja, Honduras
GJL	Jijel, Algeria
GJT	Grand Junction, Colorado, USA
GKA	Goroka, Papua New Guinea
GKL	Great Keppel Island, QLD, Australia
GLA	Glasgow, United Kingdom
GLD	Goodland, Kansas, USA
GLF	Golfito, Costa Rica
GLH	Greenville, Mississippi, USA
GLI	Glen Innes, NSW, Australia
GLS	Galveston, Texas, USA
GLT	Gladstone, QLD, Australia
GLV	Golovin, Alaska, USA
GMA	Gemena, Zaire
GMB	Gambela, Ethiopia
GME	Gomel, Belarus
GMI	Gasmata, Papua New Guinea
GNB	Grenoble, France
GND	Grenada, Windward Islands
GNI	Green Island, Taiwan
GNM	Guanambi, BA, Brazil
GNR	General Roca, RN, Argentina
GNU	Goodnews Bay, Alaska, USA
GNV	Gainesville, Florida, USA
GOA	Genoa, Italy
GOB	Goba, Ethiopia
GOC	Gora, Papua New Guinea

City and Airport Codes, cont.

GOE	Gonalia, Papua New Guinea
GOH	Nuuk, Greenland
GOI	Goa, India
GOJ	Nizhniy Novgorod, Russian Fed.
GOM	Goma, Zaire
GON	New London/Groton, CT, USA
GOR	Gore, Ethiopia
GOT	Gothenburg, Sweden
GOU	Garoua, Cameroon
GOV	Gove, NT, Australia
GPI	Guapi, Colombia
GPN	Garden Point, NT, Australia
GPS	Galapagos Islands, Ecuador
GPT	Gulfport/Biloxi, Mississippi, USA
GPZ	Grand Rapids, Minnesota, USA
GRB	Green Bay, Wisconsin, USA
GRI	Grand Island, Nebraska, USA
GRJ	George, S. Africa
GRL	Garasa, Papua New Guinea
GRP	Gurupi, GO, Brazil
GRQ	Groningen, Netherlands
GRR	Grand Rapids, Michigan, USA
GRU	Guarulhos International Apt., SP, Brazil
GRW	Graciosa Island, Portugal (Azores)
GRX	Granada, Spain
GRZ	Graz, Austria
GSA	Long Pasia, Malaysia
GSA	Gothenburg Saeve Apt., Sweden
GSO	Greensboro/H.Pt./Win-Salem, North Carolina, USA
GSP	Greenville/Spartanburg, South Carolina, USA
GST	Gustavus, Alaska, USA
GTA	Gatokae, Solomon Is.
GTE	Groote Eylandt, NT, Australia
GTF	Great Falls, Montana, USA
GTO	Gorontalo, Indonesia
GTR	Golden Triangle Rgnl, Columbus, Mississippi, USA
GUA	Guatemala City, Guatemala
GUB	Guerrero Negro, Mexico
GUC	Gunnison, Colorado, USA
GUD	Goundam, Mali
GUH	Gunnedah, NSW, Australia
GUM	Guam, Guam
GUP	Gallup, New Mexico, USA
GUR	Alotau, Papua New Guinea
GUW	Atyrau, Kazakhstan
GUZ	Guarapari, ES, Brazil
GVA	Geneva, Switzerland
GVR	Governador Valadares, MG, Brazil
GVX	Gavle, Sweden
GWD	Gwadar, Pakistan
GWL	Gwalior, India
GWT	Westerland, Germany
GWY	Galway, Republic of Ireland
GXF	Seiyun, Republic of Yemen
GXQ	Coyhaique, Chile
GYA	Guayaramerin, Bolivia
GYE	Guayaquil, Ecuador
GYM	Guaymas, Mexico
GYN	Goiania, GO, Brazil
GYY	Chicago Gary Regional Apt., Indiana, USA
GZM	Gozo, Malta
GZO	Gizo, Solomon Is.
GZT	Gaziantep, Turkey

H

HAA	Hasvik, Norway
HAC	Hachijo Jima, Japan
HAD	Halmstad, Sweden
HAE	Havasupai, Arizona, USA
HAH	Hahaya Aeroport International, Comoros
HAJ	Hanover, Germany
HAK	Haikou, P. R. China
HAM	Hamburg, Germany
HAN	Hanoi, Vietnam
HAP	Long Island, QLD, Australia
HAQ	Hanimaadhoo, Maldives
HAR	Harrisburg, Pennsylvania, USA
HAS	Hail, Saudi Arabia
HAU	Haugesund, Norway
HAV	Havana, Cuba
HBA	Hobart, Tasmania, Australia
HBH	Hobart Bay, Alaska, USA
HCR	Holy Cross, Alaska, USA
HDB	Heidelberg, Germany
HDD	Hyderabad, Pakistan
HDN	Steamboat Springs/Hayden, Colorado, USA
HDY	Hat Yai, Thailand
HEH	Heho, Myanmar
HEK	Heihe, P. R. China
HEL	Helsinki, Finland
HER	Heraklion, Greece
HET	Hohhot, P. R. China
HFA	Haifa, Israel
HFD	Hartford, CT, USA
HFE	Hefei, P. R. China
HFN	Hornafijordur, Iceland
HFS	Hagfors, Sweden
HFT	Hammerfest, Norway
HGA	Hargeisa, Somalia
HGD	Hughenden, QLD, Australia
HGH	Hangzhou, P. R. China
HGN	Mae Hong Son, Thailand
HGO	Korhogo, Cote D'Ivoire
HGR	Hagerstown, Maryland, USA
HGU	Mount Hagen, Papua New Guinea
HHA	Huanghua, P. R. China
HHH	Hilton Head Island, South Carolina, USA
HHQ	Hua Hin, Thailand
HIB	Hibbing/Chisholm, Minnesota, USA
HID	Horn Island, QLD, Australia
HII	Lake Havasu City, Arizona, USA
HIJ	Hiroshima, Japan
HIL	Shillavo, Ethiopia
HIN	Chinju, Republic of Korea
HIR	Honiara, Solomon Is.
HIS	Hayman Island, QLD, Australia
HJR	Khajuraho, India
HKB	Healy Lake, Alaska, USA
HKD	Hakodate, Japan
HKG	Hong Kong, Hong Kong
HKK	Hokitika, New Zealand
HKN	Hoskins, Papua New Guinea
HKT	Phuket, Thailand
HKY	Hickory, North Carolina, USA
HLD	Hailar, P. R. China
HLF	Hultsfred, Sweden
HLN	Helena, Montana, USA
HLP	Halim Perdana Kusuma, Indonesia
HLZ	Hamilton, New Zealand
HMA	Malmo City Hvc, Sweden
HME	Hassi Messaoud, Algeria
HMO	Hermosillo, Mexico
HMV	Hemavan, Sweden
HNA	Morioka, Japan
HND	Haneda, Japan
HNH	Hoonah, Alaska, USA
HNL	Honolulu, Oahu, Hawaii, USA
HNM	Hana, Maui, Hawaii, USA
HNS	Haines, Alaska, USA
HOB	Hobbs, New Mexico, USA
HOD	Hodeidah, Republic of Yemen
HOE	Houeisay, Laos
HOF	Hofuf, Saudi Arabia
HOG	Holguin, Cuba

City and Airport Codes, cont.

HOK	Hooker Creek, NT, Australia	HYA	Hyannis, MA, USA	IMK	Simikot, Nepal
HOM	Homer, Alaska, USA	HYD	Hyderabad, India	IMP	Imperatriz, MA, Brazil
HON	Huron, South Dakota, USA	HYG	Hydaburg, Alaska, USA	IMT	Iron Mountain, Michigan, USA
HOQ	Hof, Germany	HYL	Hollis, Alaska, USA		
HOR	Horta, Portugal (Azores)	HYN	Huangyan, P. R. China	INC	Yinchuan, P. R. China
HOS	Chos Malal, NE, Argentina	HYS	Hays, Kansas, USA	IND	Indianapolis, Indiana, USA
HOT	Hot Springs, Arkansas, USA	HZG	Hanzhong, P. R. China	INF	In Guezzam, Algeria
HOU	Houston, Texas, USA	HZK	Husavik, Iceland	ING	Lago Argentino, SC, Argentina
HOV	Orsta-Volda, Norway				
HPA	Ha'apai, Tonga Is., S. Pacific	**I**		INL	International Falls, Minnesota, USA
		IAA	Igarka, Russian Fed.		
HPB	Hooper Bay, Alaska, USA	IAD	Dulles International Apt., District of Columbia, USA	INN	Innsbruck, Austria
HPH	Haiphong, Vietnam			INQ	Inisheer, Republic of Ireland
HPN	Westchester County, New York, USA	IAH	Intercontinental, Texas, USA	INU	Nauru Island, Nauru Island
		IAM	In Amenas, Algeria	INV	Inverness, United Kingdom
HPV	Princeville, Kauai, Hawaii, USA	IAN	Kiana, Alaska, USA	INZ	In Salah, Algeria
		IAS	Iasi, Romania	IOA	Ioannina, Greece
HRB	Harbin, P. R. China	IBE	Ibague, Colombia	IOK	Iokea, Papua New Guinea
HRE	Harare, Zimbabwe	IBI	Iboki, Papua New Guinea	IOM	Isle of Man, United Kingdom
HRG	Hurghada, Egypt	IBZ	Ibiza, Spain	IOP	Ioma, Papua New Guinea
HRK	Kharkov, Ukraine	ICK	Nieuw Nickerie, Suriname	IOR	Inishmore, Republic of Ireland
HRL	Harlingen, Texas, USA	ICT	Wichita, Kansas, USA		
HRO	Harrison, Arkansas, USA	IDA	Idaho Falls, Idaho, USA	IOS	Ilheus, BA, Brazil
HSH	Henderson Sky Harbor, Nevada, USA	IDB	Idre, Sweden	IPA	Ipota, Vanuatu
		IDN	Indagen, Papua New Guinea	IPC	Easter Island, Chile
HSI	Hastings, Nebraska, USA			IPG	Ipiranga, AM, Brazil
HSL	Huslia, Alaska, USA	IDR	Indore, India	IPH	Ipoh, Malaysia
HSV	Huntsville/Decatur, Alabama, USA	IEV	Kiev, Ukraine	IPI	Ipiales, Colombia
		IFJ	Isafjordur, Iceland	IPL	El Centro/Imperial, California, USA
HTA	Chita, Russian Fed.	IFN	Isfahan, Iran		
HTI	Hamilton Island, QLD, Australia	IFO	Ivano-Frankovsk, Ukraine	IPN	Ipatinga, MG, Brazil
		IFP	Bullhead City, Arizona, USA	IPT	Williamsport, Pennsylvania, USA
HTN	Hotan, P. R. China	IGA	Inagua, Bahamas		
HTO	East Hampton, New York, USA	IGG	Igiugig, Alaska, USA	IQM	Qiemo, P. R. China
		IGM	Kingman, Arizona, USA	IQQ	Iquique, Chile
HTR	Hateruma, Japan	IGO	Chigorodo, Colombia	IQT	Iquitos, Peru
HTS	Huntington, West Virginia, USA	IGR	Iguazu, MI, Argentina	IRA	Kirakira, Solomon Islands
		IGU	Iguassu Falls, PR, Brazil	IRC	Circle, Alaska, USA
HUE	Humera, Ethiopia	IHU	Ihu, Papua New Guinea	IRD	Ishurdi, Bangladesh
HUF	Terre Haute, Indiana, USA	IIA	Inishmaan, Republic of Ireland	IRJ	La Rioja, LR, Argentina
HUH	Huahine Island, Society Islands			IRK	Kirksville, Missouri, USA
		IIS	Nissan Island, Papua New Guinea	IRP	Isiro, Zaire
HUI	Hue, Vietnam			ISA	Mount Isa, QLD, Australia
HUN	Hualien, Taiwan	IJK	Izhevsk, Russian Fed.	ISB	Islamabad, Pakistan
HUS	Hughes, Alaska, USA	IKO	Nikolski, Alaska, USA	ISC	Isles of Scilly, United Kingdom
HUU	Huanuco, Peru	IKS	Tiksi, Russian Fed.		
HUV	Hudiksvall, Sweden	IKT	Irkutsk, Russian Fed.	ISG	Ishigaki, Japan
HUX	Huatulco, Mexico	ILE	Killeen, Texas, USA	ISN	Williston, North Dakota, USA
HUY	Humberside, United Kingdom	ILI	Iliamna, Alaska, USA		
		ILM	Wilmington, North Carolina, USA	ISO	Kinston, North Carolina, USA
HUZ	Huizhou, P. R. China				
HVB	Hervey Bay, QLD, Australia	ILO	Iloilo, Philippines	ISP	Long Island MacArthur, New York, USA
HVG	Honningsvag, Norway	ILP	Ile Des Pins, New Caledonia		
HVN	New Haven, CT, USA	ILQ	Ilo, Peru	ISS	Wiscasset, Maine, USA
HVR	Havre, Montana, USA	ILY	Islay, United Kingdom	IST	Istanbul, Turkey
HWN	Hwange National Park, Zimbabwe	IMF	Imphal, India	ITB	Itaituba, PA, Brazil
		IMI	Ine Island, Marshall Islands	ITH	Ithaca, New York, USA

City and Airport Codes, cont.

ITK	Itokama, Papua New Guinea
ITM	Itami, Japan
ITN	Itabuna, BA, Brazil
ITO	Hilo, Hawaii, Hawaii, USA
IUE	Niue, Niue
IVC	Invercargill, New Zealand
IVL	Ivalo, Finland
IVR	Inverell, NSW, Australia
IWD	Ironwood, Michigan, USA
IWJ	Iwami, Japan
IXA	Agartala, India
IXB	Bagdogra, India
IXC	Chandigarh, India
IXD	Allahabad, India
IXE	Mangalore, India
IXI	Lilabari, India
IXJ	Jammu, India
IXK	Keshod, India
IXL	Leh, India
IXM	Madurai, India
IXR	Ranchi, India
IXS	Silchar, India
IXU	Aurangabad, India
IXY	Kandla, India
IXZ	Port Blair, Andaman Islands
IYK	Inyokern, California, USA
IZM	Izmir, Turkey
IZO	Izumo, Japan

J

JAC	Jackson Hole, Wyoming, USA
JAG	Jacobabad, Pakistan
JAI	Jaipur, India
JAN	Jackson, Mississippi, USA
JAQ	Jacquinot Bay, Papua New Guinea
JAT	Jabat, Marshall Islands
JAV	Ilulissat, Greenland
JAX	Jacksonville, Florida, USA
JBR	Jonesboro, Arkansas, USA
JCA	Cannes Croisette H/P, France
JCH	Qasigiannguit, Greenland
JCK	Julia Creek, QLD, Australia
JDF	Juiz de Fora, MG, Brazil
JDH	Jodhpur, India
JDO	Juazeiro Do Norte, CE, Brazil
JED	Jeddah, Saudi Arabia
JEG	Aasiaat, Greenland
JEJ	Jeh, Marshall Islands
JER	Jersey, United Kingdom
JFK	Kennedy International Apt., New York, USA
JFR	Paamiut, Greenland
JGA	Jamnagar, India
JGC	Grand Canyon Heliport, Arizona, USA
JGN	Jiayuguan, P. R. China
JGO	Qeqertarsuaq, Greenland
JGR	Groennedal, Greenland
JHB	Johor Bahru, Malaysia
JHE	Heliport, Sweden
JHG	Jinghong, P. R. China
JHM	Kapalua, Maui, Hawaii, USA
JHQ	Shute Harbour, QLD, Australia
JHS	Sisimiut, Greenland
JHW	Jamestown, New York, USA
JIA	Juina, MT, Brazil
JIB	Djibouti, Djibouti
JIK	Ikaria Island, Greece
JIL	Jilin, P. R. China
JIM	Jimma, Ethiopia
JIU	Jiujiang, P. R. China
JIW	Jiwani, Pakistan
JJI	Juanjui, Peru
JJU	Qaqortoq, Greenland
JKG	Jonkoping, Sweden
JKH	Chios, Greece
JKR	Janakpur, Nepal
JKT	Jakarta, Indonesia
JLN	Joplin, Missouri, USA
JLR	Jabalpur, India
JMK	Mikonos, Greece
JMM	Malmo Harbour Heliport, Sweden
JMO	Jomsom, Nepal
JMS	Jamestown, North Dakota, USA
JMU	Jiamusi, P. R. China
JNB	Johannesburg, S. Africa
JNG	Jining, P. R. China
JNN	Nanortalik, Greenland
JNS	Narsaq, Greenland
JNU	Juneau, Alaska, USA
JNX	Naxos, Cyclades Islands, Greece
JNZ	Jinzhou, P. R. China
JOE	Joensuu, Finland
JOG	Yogyakarta, Indonesia
JOI	Joinville, SC, Brazil
JOK	Joshkar-Ola, Russian Fed.
JON	Johnston Island, Johnston Island
JOP	Joephstaal, Papua New Guinea
JOS	Jos, Nigeria
JPA	Joao Pessoa, PB, Brazil
JPR	Ji-Parana, RO, Brazil
JQE	Jaque, Panama
JRH	Jorhat, India
JRN	Juruena, MT, Brazil
JRO	Kilimanjaro, Tanzania
JRS	Jerusalem,
JSH	Sitia, Greece
JSI	Skiathos, Greece
JSR	Jessore, Bangladesh
JST	Johnstown, Pennsylvania, USA
JSU	Maniitsoq, Greenland
JSY	Syros Island, Greece
JTI	Jatai, GO, Brazil
JTR	Santorini, Thira Is., Greece
JTY	Astypalaia Island, Greece
JUA	Juara, MT, Brazil
JUJ	Jujuy, PJ, Argentina
JUL	Juliaca, Peru
JUM	Jumla, Nepal
JUO	Jurado, Colombia
JUV	Upernavik, Greenland
JUZ	Juzhou, P. R. China
JYV	Jyvaskyla, Finland

K

KAB	Kariba, Zimbabwe
KAC	Kameshli, Syria
KAD	Kaduna, Nigeria
KAE	Kake, Alaska, USA
KAG	Kangnung, Republic of Korea
KAJ	Kajaani, Finland
KAK	Kar, Papua New Guinea
KAL	Kaltag, Alaska, USA
KAN	Kano, Nigeria
KAO	Kuusamo, Finland
KAT	Kaitaia, New Zealand
KAX	Kalbarri, WA, Australia
KBC	Birch Creek, Alaska, USA
KBJ	Kings Canyon, NT, Australia
KBM	Kabwum, Papua New Guinea
KBP	Borispol, Ukraine
KBR	Kota Bharu, Malaysia
KBT	Kaben, Marshall Islands
KBZ	Kaikoura, New Zealand
KCA	Kuqa, P. R. China
KCC	Coffman Cove, Alaska, USA
KCG	Fisheries, Alaska, USA
KCH	Kuching, Malaysia
KCL	Chignik, Alaska, USA
KCQ	Chignik, Alaska, USA
KCZ	Kochi, Japan
KDA	Kolda, Senegal
KDD	Khuzdar, Pakistan
KDI	Kendari, Indonesia
KDL	Kardla, Estonia
KDM	Kaadedhdhoo, Maldives
KDN	N'dende, Gabon

City and Airport Codes, cont.

KDO	Kadhdhoo, Maldives
KDR	Kandrian, Papua New Guinea
KDU	Skardu, Pakistan
KDV	Kandavu, Fiji
KED	Kaedi, Mauritania
KEF	Keflavik International Apt., Iceland
KEJ	Kemerovo, Russian Fed.
KEK	Ekwok, Alaska, USA
KEL	Kiel, Germany
KEM	Kemi/Tornio, Finland
KEO	Odienne, Cote D'Ivoire
KEP	Nepalganj, Nepal
KER	Kerman, Iran
KET	Kengtung, Myanmar
KEX	Kanabea, Papua New Guinea
KFA	Kiffa, Mauritania
KFG	Kalkurung, NT, Australia
KFP	False Pass, Alaska, USA
KGA	Kananga, Zaire
KGB	Konge, Papua New Guinea
KGC	Kingscote, SA, Australia
KGD	Kaliningrad, Russian Fed.
KGF	Karaganda, Kazakhstan
KGG	Kedougou, Senegal
KGI	Kalgoorlie, WA, Australia
KGK	Koliganek, Alaska, USA
KGL	Kigali, Rwanda
KGS	Kos, Greece
KGX	Grayling, Alaska, USA
KHG	Kashi, P. R. China
KHH	Kaohsiung, Taiwan
KHI	Karachi, Pakistan
KHN	Nanchang, P. R. China
KHS	Khasab, Oman
KHV	Khabarovsk, Russian Fed.
KIB	Ivanof Bay, Alaska, USA
KID	Kristianstad, Sweden
KIF	Kingfisher Lake, Ontario, Canada
KIJ	Niigata, Japan
KIM	Kimberley, S. Africa
KIN	Kingston, Jamaica
KIO	Kili Island, Marshall Islands
KIQ	Kira, Papua New Guinea
KIR	Kerry County, Republic of Ireland
KIS	Kisumu, Kenya
KIT	Kithira, Greece
KIV	Kishinev, Moldova
KIX	Kansai Intl. Apt., Japan
KJA	Krasnoyarsk, Russian Fed.
KJP	Kerama, Japan
KKA	Koyuk, Alaska, USA
KKC	Khon Kaen, Thailand
KKD	Kokoda, Papua New Guinea
KKE	Kerikeri, New Zealand
KKH	Kongiganak, Alaska, USA
KKI	Akiachak, Alaska, USA
KKJ	Kita Kyushu, Japan
KKN	Kirkenes, Norway
KKR	Kaukura Atoll, Tuamotu Islands
KKU	Ekuk, Alaska, USA
KKX	Kikaiga Shima, Japan
KKZ	Koh Kong, Cambodia
KLG	Kalskag, Alaska, USA
KLL	Levelock, Alaska, USA
KLN	Larsen Bay, Alaska, USA
KLO	Kalibo, Philippines
KLR	Kalmar, Sweden
KLT	Kaiserslauter Off-Line Point, Germany
KLU	Klagenfurt, Austria
KLW	Klawock, Alaska, USA
KLX	Kalamata, Greece
KLZ	Kleinzee, S. Africa
KMA	Kerema, Papua New Guinea
KMF	Kamina, Papua New Guinea
KMG	Kunming, P. R. China
KMI	Miyazaki, Japan
KMJ	Kumamoto, Japan
KMO	Manokotak, Alaska, USA
KMP	Keetmanshoop, Namibia
KMQ	Komatsu, Japan
KMV	Kalemyo, Myanmar
KND	Kindu, Zaire
KNE	Kanainj, Papua New Guinea
KNG	Kaimana, Indonesia
KNH	Kinmen, Taiwan
KNK	Kakhonak, Alaska, USA
KNQ	Kone, New Caledonia
KNS	King Island, Tasmania, Australia
KNV	Knights Inlet, BC, Canada
KNW	New Stuyahok, Alaska, USA
KNX	Kununurra, WA, Australia
KNZ	Kenieba, Mali
KOA	Kona, Hawaii, Hawaii, USA
KOC	Koumac, New Caledonia
KOE	Kupang, Indonesia
KOI	Kirkwall, Orkney Is., Scotland, United Kingdom
KOJ	Kagoshima, Japan
KOK	Kokkola/Pietarsaari, Finland
KOP	Nakhon Phanom, Thailand
KOS	Sihanoukville, Cambodia
KOT	Kotlik, Alaska, USA
KOU	Koulamoutou, Gabon
KOV	Kokshetau, Kazakhstan
KOW	Ganzhou, P. R. China
KOZ	Ouzinkie, Alaska, USA
KPB	Point Baker, Alaska, USA
KPC	Port Clarence, Alaska, USA
KPI	Kapit, Malaysia
KPN	Kipnuk, Alaska, USA
KPO	Pohang, Republic of Korea
KPS	Kempsey, NSW, Australia
KPV	Perryville, Alaska, USA
KQA	Akutan, Alaska, USA
KRB	Karumba, QLD, Australia
KRF	Kramfors, Sweden
KRI	Kikori, Papua New Guinea
KRK	Krakow, Poland
KRL	Korla, P. R. China
KRN	Kiruna, Sweden
KRO	Kurgan, Russian Fed.
KRP	Karup, Denmark
KRR	Krasnodar, Russian Fed.
KRS	Kristiansand, Norway
KRT	Khartoum, Sudan
KRX	Kar Kar, Papua New Guinea
KRY	Karamay, P. R. China
KSA	Kosrae, Caroline Is., Pac. Ocean
KSC	Kosice, Slovakia
KSD	Karlstad, Sweden
KSH	Kermanshah, Iran
KSJ	Kasos Island, Greece
KSM	St. Marys, Alaska, USA
KSN	Kostanay, Kazakhstan
KSO	Kastoria, Greece
KSQ	Karshi, Uzbekistan
KSU	Kristiansund, Norway
KSW	Kiryat Shmona, Israel
KSY	Kars, Turkey
KTA	Karratha, WA, Australia
KTB	Thorne Bay, Alaska, USA
KTD	Kitadaito, Japan
KTE	Kerteh, Malaysia
KTG	Ketapang, Indonesia
KTM	Kathmandu, Nepal
KTN	Ketchikan, Alaska, USA
KTP	Tinson, Jamaica
KTR	Katherine, NT, Australia
KTS	Brevig Mission, Alaska, USA
KTT	Kittila, Finland
KTW	Katowice, Poland
KUA	Kuantan, Malaysia
KUC	Kuria, Kiribati
KUD	Kudat, Malaysia
KUE	Kukundu, Solomon Is.
KUF	Samara, Russian Fed.
KUH	Kushiro, Japan
KUK	Kasigluk, Alaska, USA
KUL	Kuala Lumpur, Malaysia
KUM	Yakushima, Japan
KUN	Kaunas, Lithuania
KUO	Kuopio, Finland

City and Airport Codes, cont.

KUQ	Kuri, Papua New Guinea
KUS	Kulusuk Island, Greenland
KUU	Kulu, India
KUV	Kunsan, Republic of Korea
KVA	Kavala, Greece
KVB	Skovde, Sweden
KVG	King Cove, Alaska, USA
KVE	Kitava, Papua New Guinea
KVG	Kavieng, Papua New Guinea
KVL	Kivalina, Alaska, USA
KVX	Kirov, Russian Fed.
KWA	Kwajalein, Marshall Islands
KWE	Guiyang, P. R. China
KWF	Waterfall, Alaska, USA
KWI	Kuwait, Kuwait
KWJ	Kwangju, Republic of Korea
KWK	Kwigillingok, Alaska, USA
KWL	Guilin, P. R. China
KWM	Kowanyama, QLD, Australia
KWN	Quinhagak, Alaska, USA
KWO	Kawito, Papua New Guinea
KWS	Kwailabesi, Solomon Is.
KWT	Kwethluk, Alaska, USA
KWY	Kiwayu, Kenya
KXA	Kasaan, Alaska, USA
KXF	Koro Island, Fiji
KYK	Komsomolsk Na Amure, Russian Fed.
KYD	Orchid Island, Taiwan
KYK	Karluk, Alaska, USA
KYP	Kyaukpyu, Myanmar
KYS	Kayes, Mali
KYU	Koyukuk, Alaska, USA
KYX	Yalumet, Papua New Guinea
KZF	Kaintiba, Papua New Guinea
KZI	Kozani, Greece
KZN	Kazan, Russian Fed.
KZS	Kastelorizo, Greece

L

LAA	Lamar, Colorado, USA
LAB	Lablab, Papua New Guinea
LAD	Luanda, Angola
LAE	Lae, Papua New Guinea
LAF	Lafayette, Indiana, USA
LAI	Lannion, France
LAJ	Lages, SC, Brazil
LAN	Lansing, Michigan, USA
LAO	Laoag, Philippines
LAP	La Paz, Mexico
LAR	Laramie, Wyoming, USA
LAS	Las Vegas, Nevada, USA
LAU	Lamu, Kenya
LAW	Lawton, Oklahoma, USA
LAX	Los Angeles, California, USA
LAZ	Bom Jesus Da Lapa, BA, Brazil
LBA	Leeds/Bradford, United Kingdom
LBB	Lubbock, Texas, USA
LBE	Latrobe, Pennsylvania, USA
LBF	North Platte, Nebraska, USA
LBJ	Labuan Bajo, Indonesia
LBL	Liberal, Kansas, USA
LBP	Long Banga, Malaysia
LBQ	Lambarene, Gabon
LBS	Labasa, Fiji
LBU	Labuan, Malaysia
LBV	Libreville, Gabon
LCA	Larnaca, Cyprus
LCE	La Ceiba, Honduras
LCG	La Coruna, Spain
LCH	Lake Charles, Louisiana, USA
LCR	La Chorrera, Colombia
LCY	London City, United Kingdom
LDB	Londrina, PR, Brazil
LDE	Lourdes/Tarbes, France
LDH	Lord Howe Island, NSW, Australia
LDI	Lindi, Tanzania
LDK	Lidkoping, Sweden
LDN	Lamidanda, Nepal
LDU	Lahad Datu, Malaysia
LDY	Londonderry, United Kingdom
LEA	Learmonth, WA, Australia
LEB	Lebanon, New Hampshire, USA
LED	St. Petersburg, Russian Fed.
LEH	Le Havre, France
LEI	Almeria, Spain
LEJ	Leipzig, Germany
LEK	Labe, Guinea
LEL	Lake Evella, NT, Australia
LEQ	Lands End, United Kingdom
LER	Leinster, WA, Australia
LET	Leticia, Colombia
LEV	Bureta, Fiji
LEX	Lexington, Kentucky, USA
LFT	Lafayette, Louisiana, USA
LFW	Lome, Togo
LGA	La Guardia, New York, USA
LGB	Long Beach, California, USA
LGG	Liege, Belgium
LGH	Leigh Creek, SA, Australia
LGI	Deadmans Cay, Long Is., Bahamas
LGK	Langkawi, Malaysia
LGL	Long Lellang, Malaysia
LGP	Legaspi, Philippines
LGQ	Lago Agrio, Ecuador
LGS	Malargue, MD, Argentina
LGW	Gatwick, United Kingdom
LGZ	Leguizamo, Colombia
LHE	Lahore, Pakistan
LHG	Lightning Ridge, NSW, Australia
LHK	Guanghua, P. R. China
LHR	Heathrow, United Kingdom
LHW	Lanzhou, P. R. China
LIF	Lifou, Loyalty Islands
LIG	Limoges, France
LIH	Lihue, Kauai, Hawaii, USA
LIK	Likiep Island, Marshall Islands
LIL	Lille, France
LIM	Lima, Peru
LIN	Linate, Italy
LIR	Liberia, Costa Rica
LIS	Lisbon, Portugal
LIT	Little Rock, Arkansas, USA
LIW	Loikaw, Myanmar
LJG	Lijang City, P. R. China
LJU	Ljubljana, Slovenia
LKA	Larantuka, Indonesia
LKB	Lakeba, Fiji
LKE	Lake Union Spb, Washington, USA
LKL	Lakselv, Norway
LKN	Leknes, Norway
LKO	Lucknow, India
LLA	Lulea, Sweden
LLI	Lalibela, Ethiopia
LLW	Lilongwe, Malawi
LMA	Lake Minchumina, Alaska, USA
LMC	Lamacarena, Colombia
LML	Lae Island, Marshall Islands
LMM	Los Mochis, Mexico
LMN	Limbang, Malaysia
LMP	Lampedusa, Italy
LMT	Klamath Falls, Oregon, USA
LNB	Lamen Bay, Vanuatu
LNE	Lonorore, Vanuatu
LNG	Lese, Papua New Guinea
LNK	Lincoln, Nebraska, USA
LNO	Leonora, WA, Australia
LNS	Lancaster, Pennsylvania, USA
LNV	Londolovit, Papua New Guinea
LNY	Lanai City, Lanai, Hawaii, USA
LNZ	Linz, Austria
LOD	Longana, Vanuatu
LOF	Loen, Marshall Islands
LOH	Loja, Ecuador
LON	London, United Kingdom
LOS	Lagos, Nigeria

City and Airport Codes, cont.

LOV	Monclova, Mexico	LUO	Luena, Angola	MAU	Maupiti Island, Society Islands
LPA	Gran Canarla, Canary Is.	LUP	Kalaupapa, Molokai, Hawaii, USA	MAV	Maloelap Island, Marshall Islands
LPB	La Paz, Bolivia	LUQ	San Luis, SL, Argentina	MAY	Mangrove Cay, Bahamas
LPD	La Pedrera, Colombia	LUV	Langgur, Indonesia	MAZ	Mayaguez, Puerto Rico
LPE	La Primavera, Colombia	LUW	Luwuk, Indonesia	MBA	Mombasa, Kenya
LPI	Linkoping, Sweden	LUX	Luxembourg, Luxembourg	MBC	M'bigou, Gabon
LPK	Lipetsk, Russian Fed.	LVB	Livramento, RS, Brazil	MBD	Mmabatho, S. Africa
LPL	Liverpool, United Kingdom	LVD	Lime Village, Alaska, USA	MBE	Monbetsu, Japan
LPM	Lamap, Vanuatu	LVI	Livingstone, Zambia	MBH	Maryborough, QLD, Australia
LPP	Lappeenranta, Finland	LVO	Laverton, WA, Australia	MBJ	Montego Bay, Jamaica
LPQ	Luang Prabang, Laos	LWB	Greenbrier, West Verginia, USA	MBL	Manistee, Michigan, USA
LPS	Lopez Island, Washington, USA	LWE	Lewoleba, Indonesia	MBP	Moyobamba, Peru
LPT	Lampang, Thailand	LWK	Lerwick/Tingwall, United Kingdom	MBS	Saginaw, Michigan, USA
LPW	Little Port Walter, Alaska, USA	LWN	Leninakan, Armenia	MBU	Mbambanakira, Solomon Is.
LPY	Le Puy, France	LWO	Lvov, Ukraine	MBW	Moorabbin, Victoria, Australia
LRD	Laredo, Texas, USA	LWS	Lewiston, Idaho, USA	MBZ	Maues, AM, Brazil
LRE	Longreach, QLD, Australia	LWT	Lewistown, Montana, USA	MCE	Merced, California, USA
LRH	La Rochelle, France	LWY	Lawas, Malaysia	MCG	Mcgrath, Alaska, USA
LRL	Lama-Kara/Niamtougou, Togo	LXA	Lhasa, P. R. China	MCH	Machala, Ecuador
LRM	Casa de Campo, Dominican Rep.	LXG	Luang Namtha, Laos	MCI	International, Missouri, USA
LRS	Leros, Greece	LXR	Luxor, Egypt	MCK	McCook, Nebraska, USA
LRT	Lorient, France	LXS	Lemnos, Greece	MCM	Monte Carlo, Monaco
LRU	Las Cruces, New Mexico, USA	LYA	Luoyang, P. R. China	MCN	Macon, Georgia, USA
LSA	Losuia, Papua New Guinea	LYB	Little Cayman, West Indies	MCO	Orlando International Apt., Florida, USA
LSC	La Serena, Chile	LYC	Lycksele, Sweden	MCP	Macapa, AP, Brazil
LSE	La Crosse, Wisconsin, USA	LYG	Lianyungang, P. R. China	MCT	Muscat, Oman
LSH	Lashio, Myanmar	LYH	Lynchburg, Virginia, USA	MCU	Montlucon, France
LSI	Sumburgh, United Kingdom	LYP	Faisalabad, Pakistan	MCV	Mac Arthur River, NT, Australia
LSM	Long Semado, Malaysia	LYR	Longyearbyen, Norway	MCW	Mason City, Iowa, USA
LSP	Las Piedras, Venezuela	LYS	Lyon, France	MCX	Makhachkala, Russian Fed.
LSQ	Los Angeles, Chile	LZC	Lazaro Cardenas, Mexico	MCY	Sunshine Coast, QLD, Australia
LSS	Terre-De-Haut, French Antilles	LZH	Liuzhou, P. R. China	MCZ	Maceio, AL, Brazil
LST	Launceston, Tasmania, Australia	LZO	Luzhou, P. R. China	MDC	Manado, Indonesia
LSY	Lismore, NSW, Australia	LZR	Lizard Island, QLD, Australia	MDE	Medellin, Colombia
LTK	Latakia, Syria	**M**		MDG	Mudanjiang, P. R. China
LTL	Lastourville, Gabon	MAA	Madras, India	MDH	Carbondale, Illinois, USA
LTN	Luton International Apt., United Kingdom	MAB	Maraba, PA, Brazil	MDI	Makurdi, Nigeria
LTO	Loreto, Mexico	MAD	Madrid, Spain	MDK	Mbandaka, Zaire
LTQ	Le Touquet, France	MAF	Midland/Odessa, Texas, USA	MDL	Mandalay, Myanmar
LUA	Lukla, Nepal	MAG	Madang, Papua New Guinea	MDQ	Mar Del Plata, BA, Argentina
LUD	Lüderitz, Namibia	MAH	Menorca, Spain	MDS	Middle Caicos, Turks & Caicos Is.
LUG	Lugano, Switzerland	MAJ	Majuro, Marshall Islands	MDT	Harrisburg International Apt., Pennsylvania, USA
LUH	Ludhiana, India	MAL	Mangole, Indonesia	MDU	Mendl, Papua New Guinea
LUK	Lunken Field, Ohio, USA	MAM	Matamoros, Mexico	MDW	Midway, Illinois, USA
LUL	Laurel/Hattiesburg, Mississippi, USA	MAN	Manchester, United Kingdom	MDZ	Mendoza, MD, Argentina
LUM	Luxi, P. R. China	MAO	Manaus, AM, Brazil	MEC	Manta, Ecuador
LUN	Lusaka, Zambia	MAQ	Mae Sot, Thailand		
		MAR	Maracaibo, Venezuela		
		MAS	Manus Island, Papua New Guinea		

City and Airport Codes, cont.

MED	Madinah, Saudi Arabia
MEE	Mare, Loyalty Islands
MEG	Malange, Angola
MEH	Mehamn, Norway
MEI	Meridian, Mississippi, USA
MEL	Melbourne, Victoria, Australia
MEM	Memphis, Tennessee, USA
MES	Medan, Indonesia
MEU	Monte Dourado, PA, Brazil
MEX	Mexico City, Mexico
MEY	Meghauli, Nepal
MFE	Mcallen, Texas, USA
MFF	Moanda, Gabon
MFG	Muzaffarabad, Pakistan
MFJ	Moala, Fiji
MFM	Macau, Macau
MFN	Milford Sound, New Zealand
MFO	Manguna, Papua New Guinea
MFR	Medford, Oregon, USA
MFT	Machu Picchu, Peru
MFU	Mfuwe, Zambia
MGA	Managua, Nicaragua
MGB	Mount Gambier, SA, Australia
MGD	Magdalena, Bolivia
MGF	Maringa, PR, Brazil
MGH	Margate, S. Africa
MGM	Montgomery, Alabama, USA
MGP	Manga, Papua New Guinea
MGQ	Mogadishu, Somalia
MGS	Mangaia Island, Cook Is., S. Pacific
MGT	Milingimbi, NT, Australia
MGW	Morgantown, West Virginia, USA
MGX	Moabi, Gabon
MGZ	Myeik, Myanmar
MHD	Mashad, Iran
MHE	Mitchell, South Dakota, USA
MHG	Mannheim, Germany
MHH	Marsh Harbour, Bahamas
MHK	Manhattan, Kansas, USA
MHQ	Mariehamn, Finland
MHT	Manchester, New Hampshire, USA
MHX	Manihiki Island, Cook Is., S. Pacific
MIA	Miami, Florida, USA
MID	Merida, Mexico
MIE	Muncie, Indiana, USA
MII	Marilia, SP, Brazil
MIJ	Mili Island, Marshall Islands
MIK	Mikkeli, Finland
MIL	Milan, Italy
MIM	Merimbula, NSW, Australia
MIR	Monastir, Tunisia
MIS	Misima Island, Papua New Guinea
MIU	Maiduguri, Nigeria
MJB	Mejit Island, Marshall Islands
MJC	Man, Cote D'Ivoire
MJD	Mohenjodaro, Pakistan
MJE	Majkin, Marshall Islands
MJF	Mosjoen, Norway
MJJ	Moki, Papua New Guinea
MJK	Monkey Mia, WA, Australia
MJL	Mouila, Gabon
MJM	Mbuji-Mayi, Zaire
MJN	Majunga, Madagascar
MJO	Mount Etjo Lodge, Namibia
MJT	Mytilene, Greece
MJV	Murcia, Spain
MJZ	Mirnyj, Russian Fed.
MKB	Mekambo, Gabon
MKC	Kansas City, Missouri, USA
MKE	Milwaukee, Wisconsin, USA
MKG	Muskegon, Michigan, USA
MKK	Molokai/Hoolehua, Hawaii, USA
MKL	Jackson, Tennessee, USA
MKM	Mukah, Malaysia
MKN	Malekolon, Papua New Guinea
MKQ	Merauke, Indonesia
MKR	Meekatharra, WA, Australia
MKS	Mekane Selam, Ethiopia
MKT	Mankato, Minnesota, USA
MKU	Makokou, Gabon
MKW	Manokwari, Indonesia
MKY	Mackay, QLD, Australia
MKZ	Malacca, Malaysia
MLA	Malta, Malta
MLB	Melbourne, Florida, USA
MLE	Male, Maldives
MLG	Malang, Indonesia
MLH	Mulhouse, France
MLI	Moline, Illinois, USA
MLL	Marshall, Alaska, USA
MLM	Morelia, Mexico
MLN	Melilla, Spain
MLO	Milos, Greece
MLQ	Malalaua, Papua New Guinea
MLS	Miles City, Montana, USA
MLU	Monroe, Louisiana, USA
MLW	Monrovia, Liberia
MLX	Malatya, Turkey
MLY	Manley Hot Springs, Alaska, USA
MMA	Malmo, Sweden
MMB	Memambetsu, Japan
MMD	Minami Daito, Japan
MME	Teesside, United Kingdom
MMG	Mount Magnet, WA, Australia
MMJ	Matsumoto, Japan
MMK	Murmansk, Russian Fed.
MMM	Middlemount, QLD, Australia
MMO	Maio, Cape Verde
MMX	Sturup, Sweden
MMY	Miyako Jima, Japan
MNA	Melangguane, Indonesia
MNF	Mana Island, Fiji
MNG	Maningrida, NT, Australia
MNI	Montserrat, Montserrat
MNJ	Mananjary, Madagascar
MNK	Maiana, Kiribati
MNL	Manila, Philippines
MNM	Menominee, Michigan, USA
MNT	Minto, Alaska, USA
MNU	Maulmyine, Myanmar
MNY	Mono, Solomon Islands
MOA	Moa, Cuba
MOB	Mobile, Alabama, USA
MOC	Montes Claros, MG, Brazil
MOD	Modesto, California, USA
MOF	Maumere, Indonesia
MOG	Mong Hsat, Myanmar
MOI	Mitiaro Island, Cook Is., S. Pacific
MOL	Molde, Norway
MON	Mount Cook, New Zealand
MOQ	Morondava, Madagascar
MOT	Minot, North Dakota, USA
MOU	Mountain Village, Alaska, USA
MOV	Moranbah, QLD, Australia
MOW	Moscow, Russian Fed.
MOZ	Moorea, Society Islands
MPA	Mpacha, Namibia
MPB	Spb, Florida, USA
MPD	Mirpur Khas, Pakistan
MPK	Mokpo, Republic of Korea
MPL	Montpellier, France
MPM	Maputo, Mozambique
MPN	Mount Pleasant, Falkland Is.
MPU	Mapua, Papua New Guinea
MQF	Magnitogorsk, Russian Fed.
MQH	Minacu, GO, Brazil
MQL	Mildura, Victoria, Australia
MQN	Mo I. Rana, Norway
MQQ	Moundou, Chad
MQS	Mustique, Windward Islands
MQT	Marquette, Michigan, USA
MQX	Makale, Ethiopia
MRD	Merida, Venezuela

City and Airport Codes, cont.

Code	Location	Code	Location	Code	Location
MRE	Mara Lodges, Kenya	MVT	Mataiva, Tuamotu Islands	NAW	Narathiwat, Thailand
MRO	Masterton, New Zealand	MVX	Minvoul, Gabon	NAY	Nanyuan, P. R. China
MRS	Marseille, France	MVY	Martha's Vineyard, MA, USA	NBB	Barrancominas, Colombia
MRU	Mauritius, Mauritius	MVZ	Masvingo, Zimbabwe	NBC	Naberevnye Chelny, Russian Fed.
MRV	Mineralnye Vody, Russian Fed.	MWA	Marion, Illinois, USA	NBO	Nairobi, Kenya
MRY	Monterey, California, USA	MWE	Merowe, Sudan	NBX	Nabire, Indonesia
MRZ	Moree, NSW, Australia	MWF	Maewo, Vanuatu	NCA	North Caicos, Turks & Caicos Is.
MSA	Muskrat Dam, Ontario, Canada	MWH	Moses Lake, Washington, USA	NCE	Nice, France
MSH	Masirah, Oman	MWI	Maramuni, Papua New Guinea	NCI	Necocli, Colombia
MSJ	Misawa, Japan	MWU	Mussau, Papua New Guinea	NCL	Newcastle, United Kingdom
MSL	Muscle Shoals, Alabama, USA	MWZ	Mwanza, Tanzania	NCR	San Carlos, Nicaragua
MSN	Madison, Wisconsin, USA	MXB	Masamba, Indonesia	NCU	Nukus, Uzbekistan
MSO	Missoula, Montana, USA	MXH	Moro, Papua New Guinea	NCY	Annecy, France
MSP	Minneapolis/St. Paul, Minnesota, USA	MXL	Mexicali, Mexico	NDA	Bandanaira, Indonesia
MSQ	Minsk, Belarus	MXM	Morombe, Madagascar	NDB	Nouadhibou, Mauritania
MSR	Mus, Turkey	MXP	Malpensa, Italy	NDE	Mandera, Kenya
MSS	Massena, New York, USA	MXS	Maota, Savail Island, Samoa	NDG	Qiqihar, P. R. China
MST	Maastricht, Netherlands	MXX	Mora, Sweden	NDI	Namudi, Papua New Guinea
MSU	Maseru, Lesotho	MXZ	Meixian, P. R. China	NDJ	Ndjamena, Chad
MSY	New Orleans, Louisiana, USA	MYA	Moruya, NSW, Australia	NDK	Namorik Island, Marshall Islands
MSZ	Namibe, Angola	MYB	Mayoumba, Gabon	NDM	Mendi, Ethiopia
MTH	Marathon, Florida, USA	MYD	Malindi, Kenya	NDU	Rundu, Namibia
MTI	Mosteiros, Cape Verde	MYE	Miyake Jima, Japan	NEC	Necochea, BA, Argentina
MTJ	Montrose, Colorado, USA	MYG	Mayaguana, Bahamas	NEF	Neftekamsk, Russian Fed.
MTK	Makin Island, Kiribati	MYJ	Matsuyama, Japan	NEG	Negril, Jamaica
MTL	Maitland, NSW, Australia	MYR	Myrtle Beach, South Carolina, USA	NEJ	Nejjo, Ethiopia
MTM	Metlakatla, Alaska, USA	MYT	Myitkyina, Myanmar	NER	Neryungri, Russian Fed.
MTO	Mattoon, Illinois, USA	MYU	Mekoryuk, Alaska, USA	NEV	Nevis, Leeward Islands
MTR	Monteria, Colombia	MYW	Mtwara, Tanzania	NFG	Nefteyugansk, Russian Fed.
MTS	Manzini, Swaziland	MYX	Menyamya, Papua New Guinea	NFO	Niuafo'ou, Tonga Is., S. Pacific
MTT	Minatitlan, Mexico	MYY	Miri, Malaysia	NGA	Young, NSW, Australia
MTV	Mota Lava, Vanuatu	MZC	Mitzic, Gabon	NGB	Ningbo, P. R. China
MTY	Monterrey, Mexico	MZG	Makung, Taiwan	NGE	Ngaoundere, Cameroon
MTZ	Masada, Israel	MZI	Mopti, Mali	NGI	Ngau Island, Fiji
MUA	Munda, Solomon Is.	MZK	Marakei, Kiribati	NGO	Nagoya, Japan
MUB	Maun, Botswana	MZL	Manizales, Colombia	NGS	Nagasaki, Japan
MUC	Munich, Germany	MZO	Manzanillo, Cuba	NGX	Manang, Nepal
MUE	Kamuela, Hawaii, USA	MZP	Motueka, New Zealand	NHA	Nha-Trang, Vietnam
MUK	Mauke Island, Cook Is., S. Pacific	MZT	Mazatlan, Mexico	NHV	Nuku Hiva, Marquesas Islands
MUN	Maturin, Venezuela	MZV	Mulu, Malaysia	NIB	Nikolai, Alaska, USA
MUR	Marudi, Malaysia	**N**		NIG	Nikunau, Kiribati
MUW	Mascara, Algeria	NAA	Narrabri, NSW, Australia	NIM	Niamey, Niger
MUX	Multan, Pakistan	NAG	Nagpur, India	NIX	Nioro, Mali
MUZ	Musoma, Tanzania	NAH	Naha, Indonesia	NJC	Nizhnevartovsk, Russian Fed.
MVB	Franceville, Gabon	NAK	Nakhon Ratchasima, Thailand	NKC	Nouakchott, Mauritania
MVD	Montevideo, Uruguay	NAN	Nadi, Fiji	NKG	Nanjing, P. R. China
MVM	Kayenta, Arizona, USA	NAO	Nanchong, P. R. China	NKI	Naukiti, Alaska, USA
MVN	Mt. Vernon, Illinois, USA	NAP	Naples, Italy	NKN	Nankina, Papua New Guinea
MVP	Mitu, Colombia	NAR	Nare, Colombia	NKY	Nkayi, Congo
MVR	Maroua, Cameroon	NAS	Nassau, Bahamas	NLA	Ndola, Zambia
MVS	Mucuri, BA, Brazil	NAT	Natal, RN, Brazil	NLD	Nuevo Laredo, Mexico

City and Airport Codes, cont.

NLG	Nelson Lagoon, Alaska, USA
NLK	Norfolk Island, Norfolk Island
NLP	Nelspruit, S. Africa
NLV	Nikolaev, Ukraine
NMA	Namangan, Uzbekistan
NME	Nightmute, Alaska, USA
NMG	San Miguel, Panama
NNB	Santa Ana Island, Solomon Is.
NNG	Nanning, P. R. China
NNK	Naknek, Alaska, USA
NNL	Nondalton, Alaska, USA
NNT	Nan, Thailand
NNY	Nanyang, P. R. China
NOB	Nosara Beach, Costa Rica
NOC	Connaught, Republic of Ireland
NOJ	Nojabrxsk, Russian Fed.
NON	Nonouti, Kiribati
NOS	Nossi-Be, Madagascar
NOU	Noumea, New Caledonia
NOV	Huambo, Angola
NOZ	Novokuznetsk, Russian Fed.
NPE	Napier, New Zealand
NPL	New Plymouth, New Zealand
NQL	Niquelandia, GO, Brazil
NQN	Neuquen, NE, Argentina
NQU	Nuqui, Colombia
NQY	Newquay, United Kingdom
NRA	Narrandera, NSW, Australia
NRK	Norrkoping, Sweden
NRT	Narita, Japan
NSB	Bimini North Spb, Bahamas
NSI	Nsimalen, Cameroon
NSK	Norilsk, Russian Fed.
NSN	Nelson, New Zealand
NSO	Scone, NSW, Australia
NST	Nakhon Si Thammarat, Thailand
NTE	Nantes, France
NTG	Nantong, P. R. China
NTL	Newcastle, NSW, Australia
NTN	Normanton, QLD, Australia
NTO	Santo Antao, Cape Verde
NTT	Niuatoputapu, Tonga Is., S. Pacific
NTY	Sun City, S. Africa
NUB	Numbulwar, NT, Australia
NUE	Nuremberg, Germany
NUI	Nuiqsut, Alaska, USA
NUL	Nulato, Alaska, USA
NUP	Nunapitchuk, Alaska, USA
NUS	Norsup, Vanuatu
NUX	Novyj Urengoj, Russian Fed.
NVA	Neiva, Colombia
NVG	Nueva Guinea, Nicaragua
NVK	Narvik, Norway
NVT	Navegantes, SC, Brazil
NWA	Moheli, Comoros
NWI	Norwich, United Kingdom
NWT	Nowata, Papua New Guinea
NYC	New York, New York, USA
NYK	Nanyuki, Kenya
NYM	Nadym, Russian Fed.
NYN	Nyngan, NSW, Australia
NYU	Nyaung-U, Myanmar

O

OAG	Orange, NSW, Australia
OAJ	Jacksonville, North Carolina, USA
OAK	Oakland, California, USA
OAL	Cacoal, TO, Brazil
OAX	Oaxaca, Mexico
OBO	Obihiro, Japan
OBU	Kobuk, Alaska, USA
OCC	Coca, Ecuador
OCJ	Ocho Rios, Jamaica
OCV	Ocana, Colombia
ODE	Odense, Denmark
ODN	Long Seridan, Malaysia
ODS	Odessa, Ukraine
ODW	Oak Harbor, Washington, USA
ODY	Oudomxay, Laos
OER	Ornskoldsvik, Sweden
OES	San Antonio Oesta, RN, Argentina
OFK	Norfolk, Nebraska, USA
OFU	Ofu, American Samoa
OGG	Kahului, Maui, Hawaii, USA
OGN	Yonaguni Jima, Japan
OGS	Ogdensburg, New York, USA
OGX	Ouargla, Algeria
OGZ	Vladikavkaz, Russian Fed.
OHD	Ohrid, MacEdonia
OIM	Oshima, Japan
OIT	Oita, Japan
OKA	Okinawa, Japan
OKC	Oklahoma City, Oklahoma, USA
OKD	Okadama, Japan
OKE	Okino Erabu, Japan
OKI	Oki Island, Japan
OKJ	Okayama, Japan
OKK	Kokomo, Indiana, USA
OKN	Okondja, Gabon
OKT	Oktiabrskij, Russian Fed.
OKU	Mokuti Lodge, Namibia
OLB	Olbia, Italy
OLF	Wolf Point, Montana, USA
OLH	Old Harbor, Alaska, USA
OLJ	Olpoi, Vanuatu
OLP	Olympic Dam, SA, Australia
OMA	Omaha, Nebraska, USA
OMB	Omboue, Gabon
OMD	Oranjemund, Namibia
OME	Nome, Alaska, USA
OMH	Urmieh, Iran
OMR	Oradea, Romania
OMS	Omsk, Russian Fed.
ONB	Ononge, Papua New Guinea
OND	Ondangwa, Namibia
ONG	Mornington Island, QLD, Australia
ONT	Ontario, California, USA
ONX	Colon, Panama
OOK	Toksook Bay, Alaska, USA
OOL	Gold Coast, QLD, Australia
OOM	Cooma, NSW, Australia
OOT	Onotoa, Kiribati
OPB	Open Bay, Papua New Guinea
OPO	Porto, Portugal
OPS	Sinop, MT, Brazil
OPU	Balimo, Papua New Guinea
ORB	Orebro, Sweden
ORD	O'hare International Apt., Illinois, USA
ORF	Norfold/Va. Bch/Wmbg, Viriginia, USA
ORG	Zorg En Hoop, Suriname
ORH	Worcester, MA, USA
ORI	Port Lions, Alaska, USA
ORK	Cork, Republic of Ireland
ORL	Orlando, Florida, USA
ORN	Oran, Algeria
ORV	Noorvik, Alaska, USA
ORW	Ormara, Pakistan
ORY	Orly, France
OSA	Osaka, Japan
OSD	Ostersund, Sweden
OSH	Oshkosh, Wisconsin, USA
OSK	Oskarshamn, Sweden
OSL	Oslo, Norway
OSR	Ostrava, Czech Republic
OSS	Osh, Kyrgyzstan
OSY	Namsos, Norway
OTD	Contadora, Panama
OTH	North Bend, Oregon, USA
OTM	Ottumwa, Iowa, USA
OTP	Otopeni, Romania
OTR	Coto 47, Costa Rica
OTS	Anacortes, Washington, USA
OTU	Otu, Colombia
OTZ	Kotzebue, Alaska, USA
OUA	Ouagadougou, Burkina Faso
OUD	Oujda, Morocco

City and Airport Codes, cont.

OUE	Ouesso, Congo
OUL	Oulu, Finland
OUZ	Zouerate, Mauritania
OVB	Novosibirsk, Russian Fed.
OVD	Asturias, Spain
OWB	Owensboro, Kentucky, USA
OXB	Bissau, Guinea-Bissau
OXR	Oxnard, California, USA
OYE	Oyem, Gabon
OYK	Oiapoque, AP, Brazil
OZH	Zaporozhye, Ukraine
OZZ	Ouarzazate, Morocco

P

PAC	Paitilla, Panama
PAD	Paderborn, Germany
PAH	Paducah, Kentucky, USA
PAJ	Para Chinar, Pakistan
PAP	Port au Prince, Haiti
PAR	Paris, France
PAS	Paros, Greece
PAT	Patna, India
PAV	Paulo Afonso, BA, Brazil
PAZ	Poza Rica, Mexico
PBC	Puebla, Mexico
PBD	Porbandar, India
PBE	Puerto Berrio, Colombia
PBH	Paro, Bhutan
PBI	West Palm Beach, Florida, USA
PBJ	Paama, Vanuatu
PBM	Paramaribo, Suriname
PBO	Paraburdoo, WA, Australia
PBP	Punta Islita, Costa Rica
PBU	Putao, Myanmar
PBZ	Plettenberg Bay, S. Africa
PCA	Portage Creek, Alaska, USA
PCH	Palacios, Honduras
PCL	Pucallpa, Peru
PCM	Playa Del Carmen, Mexico
PCP	Principe Island, Principe Island
PCR	Puerto Carreno, Colombia
PDA	Puerto Inirida, Colombia
PDB	Pedro Bay, Alaska, USA
PDG	Padang, Indonesia
PDL	Ponta Delgada, Portugal (Azores)
PDP	Punta Del Este, Uruguay
PDT	Pendleton, Oregon, USA
PDX	Portland, Oregon, USA
PEC	Pelican, Alaska, USA
PEE	Perm, Russian Fed.
PEG	Perugia, Italy
PEI	Pereira, Colombia
PEK	Capital, P. R. China
PEM	Puerto Maldonado, Peru
PEN	Penang, Malaysia
PER	Perth, WA, Australia
PES	Petrozavodsk, Russian Fed.
PET	Pelotas, RS, Brazil
PEU	Puerto Lempira, Honduras
PEW	Peshawar, Pakistan
PFB	Passo Fundo, RS, Brazil
PFJ	Patreksfjordur, Iceland
PFN	Panama City, Florida, USA
PFO	Paphos, Cyprus
PGA	Page, Arizona, USA
PGF	Perpignan, France
PGK	Pangkalpinang, Indonesia
PGV	Greenville, North Carolina, USA
PGX	Perigueux, France
PGZ	Ponta Grossa, PR, Brazil
PHB	Parnaiba, PI, Brazil
PHC	Port Harcourt, Nigeria
PHE	Port Hedland, WA, Australia
PHF	Newport News/Wmbg, Virginia, USA
PHL	Philadelphia, Pennsylvania, USA
PHO	Point Hope, Alaska, USA
PHS	Phitsanulok, Thailand
PHW	Phalaborwa, S. Africa
PHX	Phoenix, Arizona, USA
PIA	Peoria, Illinois, USA
PIB	Laurel Pine Belt Regional Apt., Mississippi, USA
PID	Nassau Paradise Island, Bahamas
PIE	St. Petersburg International Apt., Florida, USA
PIF	Pingtung, Taiwan
PIH	Pocatello, Idaho, USA
PIK	Prestwick, United Kingdom
PIN	Parintins, AM, Brazil
PIP	Pilot Point, Alaska, USA
PIR	Pierre, South Dakota, USA
PIS	Poitiers, France
PIT	Pittsburgh, Pennsylvania, USA
PIU	Piura, Peru
PIX	Pico Island, Portugal (Azores)
PIZ	Point Lay, Alaska, USA
PJC	Pedro Juan Caballero, Paraguay
PJG	Panjgur, Pakistan
PJM	Puerto Jimenez, Costa Rica
PKA	Napaskiak, Alaska, USA
PKB	Parkersburg, West Virginia, USA
PKC	Petropavlovsk, Russian Fed.
PKE	Parkes, NSW, Australia
PKN	Pangkalanbun, Indonesia
PKR	Pokhara, Nepal
PKU	Pekanbaru, Indonesia
PKY	Palangkaraya, Indonesia
PKZ	Pakse, Laos
PLB	Plattsburgh, New York, USA
PLH	Plymouth, United Kingdom
PLJ	Placencia, Belize
PLM	Palembang, Indonesia
PLN	Pellston, Michigan, USA
PLO	Port Lincoln, SA, Australia
PLP	La Palma, Panama
PLQ	Palanga, Lithuania
PLS	Providenciales, Turks & Caicos Is.
PLU	Pamphula, MG, Brazil
PLW	Palu, Indonesia
PLX	Semipalatinsk, Kazakhstan
PLZ	Port Elizabeth, S. Africa
PMA	Pemba, Tanzania
PMC	Puerto Montt, Chile
PMD	Palmdale/Lancaster, California, USA
PMF	Parma, Italy
PMG	Ponta Pora, MS, Brazil
PMI	Palma Mallorca, Spain
PML	Port Moller, Alaska, USA
PMN	Pumani, Papua New Guinea
PMO	Palermo, Italy
PMR	Palmerston North, New Zealand
PMV	Porlamar, Venezuela
PMW	Palmas, TO, Brazil
PMZ	Palmar, Costa Rica
PNA	Pamplona, Spain
PNB	Porto Nacional, TO, Brazil
PNC	Ponca City, Oklahoma, USA
PND	Punta Gorda, Belize
PNG	Paranagua, PR, Brazil
PNH	Phnom Penh, Cambodia
PNI	Pohnpei, Caroline Is., Pac. Ocean
PNK	Pontianak, Indonesia
PNL	Pantelleria, Italy
PNP	Popondetta, Papua New Guinea
PNQ	Poona, India
PNR	Pointe Noire, Congo
PNS	Pensacola, Florida, USA
PNZ	Petrolina, PE, Brazil
POA	Porto Alegre, RS, Brazil
POG	Port Gentil, Gabon
POL	Pemba, Mozambique
POM	Port Moresby, Papua New Guinea
POP	Puerto Plata, Dominican Rep.

City and Airport Codes, cont.

POR	Pori, Finland
POS	Port of Spain, Trinidad & Tobago
POT	Port Antonio, Jamaica
POU	Poughkeepsie, New York, USA
POX	Pontoise, France
POZ	Poznan, Poland
PPB	President Prudente, SP, Brazil
PPG	Pago Pago, American Samoa
PPK	Petropavlovsk, Kazakhstan
PPL	Phaplu, Nepal
PPN	Popayan, Colombia
PPP	Proserpine, QLD, Australia
PPQ	Paraparaumu, New Zealand
PPS	Puerto Princesa, Philippines
PPT	Papeete, Tahiti
PPV	Port Protection, Alaska, USA
PPY	Pouso Alegre, MG, Brazil
PQC	Phuquoc, Vietnam
PQI	Presque Isle, Maine, USA
PQQ	Port MacQuarie, NSW, Australia
PQS	Pilot Station, Alaska, USA
PRC	Prescott, Arizona, USA
PRG	Prague, Czech Republic
PRH	Phrae, Thailand
PRI	Praslin Is., Seychelles Is. Indian Ocean
PRS	Parasi, Solomon Is.
PSA	Pisa, Italy
PSC	Pasco, Washington, USA
PSE	Ponce, Puerto Rico
PSG	Petersburg, Alaska, USA
PSI	Pasni, Pakistan
PSJ	Poso, Indonesia
PSM	Portsmouth, New Hampshire, USA
PSO	Pasto, Colombia
PSP	Palm Springs, California, USA
PSR	Pescara, Italy
PSS	Posadas, MI, Argentina
PSZ	Puerto Suarez, Bolivia
PTA	Port Alsworth, Alaska, USA
PTD	Port Alexander, Alaska, USA
PTF	Malololailal, Fiji
PTG	Pietersburg, S. Africa
PTH	Port Heiden, Alaska, USA
PTJ	Portland, Victoria, Australia
PTL	Port Armstrong, Alaska, USA
PTP	Pointe-A-Pitre, French Antilles
PTU	Platinum, Alaska, USA
PTY	Panama City, Panama
PUB	Pueblo, Colorado, USA
PUD	Puerto Deseado, SC, Argentina
PUF	Pau, France
PUG	Port Augusta, SA, Australia
PUJ	Punta Cana, Dominican Rep.
PUM	Pomala, Indonesia
PUQ	Punta Arenas, Chile
PUS	Pusan, Republic of Korea
PUT	Puttaparthi, India
PUU	Puerto Asis, Colombia
PUV	Poum, New Caledonia
PUW	Pullman, Washington, USA
PUY	Pula, Croatia
PUZ	Puerto Cabezas, Nicaragua
PVA	Providencia, Colombia
PVC	Provincetown, MA, USA
PVD	Providence, Rhode Island, USA
PVH	Porto Velho, RO, Brazil
PVK	Preveza/Lefkas, Greece
PVO	Portoviejo, Ecuador
PVR	Puerto Vallarta, Mexico
PWE	Pevek, Russian Fed.
PWK	Pal-Waukee, Illinois, USA
PWM	Portland, Maine, USA
PWQ	Pavlodar, Kazakhstan
PXM	Puerto Escondido, Mexico
PXO	Porto Santo, Portugal (Madeira)
PXU	Pleiku, Vietnam
PYE	Penrhyn Island, Cook Is., S. Pacific
PYH	Puerto Ayacucho, Venezuela
PYJ	Polyarnyj, Russian Fed.
PZA	Paz de Ariporo, Colombia
PZB	Pietermaritzburg, S. Africa
PZE	Penzance, United Kingdom
PZH	Zhob, Pakistan
PZO	Puerto Ordaz, Venezuela
PZU	Port Sudan, Sudan

Q

QBC	Bella Coola, BC, Canada
QBF	Vail Van Service Off Line Point, Colorado, USA
QDU	Main Railroad Station, Germany
QKL	Main Railroad Station, Germany
QLE	Leeton, NSW, Australia
QRA	Randgermiston, S. Africa
QRO	Queretaro, Mexico

R

RAB	Rabaul, Papua New Guinea
RAE	Arar, Saudi Arabia
RAF	Ras An Naqb, Egypt
RAH	Rafha, Saudi Arabia
RAI	Praia, Cape Verde
RAJ	Rajkot, India
RAK	Marrakech, Morocco
RAM	Ramingining, NT, Australia
RAO	Ribeirao Preto, SP, Brazil
RAP	Rapid City, South Dakota, USA
RAR	Rarotonga, Cook Is., S. Pacific
RAS	Rasht, Iran
RAT	Raduzhnyi, Russian Fed.
RAV	Cravo Norte, Colombia
RAW	Arawa, Papua New Guinea
RAZ	Rawala Kot, Pakistan
RBA	Rabat, Morocco
RBE	Ratanankiri, Cambodia
RBM	Straubing, Germany
RBP	Rabaraba, Papua New Guinea
RBR	Rio Branco, AC, Brazil
RBY	Ruby, Alaska, USA
RCB	Richards Bay, S. Africa
RCE	Roche Harbor, Washington, USA
RCH	Riohacha, Colombia
RCL	Redcliffe, Vanuatu
RCM	Richmond, QLD, Australia
RCU	Rio Cuarto, CD, Argentina
RDC	Redencao, PA, Brazil
RDD	Redding, California, USA
RDG	Reading, Pennsylvania, USA
RDM	Redmond, Oregon, USA
RDS	Rincon de Los Sauces, NE, Argentina
RDU	Raleigh/Durham, North Carolina, USA
RDV	Red Devil, Alaska, USA
RDZ	Rodez, France
REC	Recife, PE, Brazil
REG	Reggio Calabria, Italy
REK	Reykjavik, Iceland
REL	Trelew, CB, Argentina
REN	Orenburg, Russian Fed.
REP	Siem Reap, Cambodia
RES	Resistencia, CH, Argentina
RET	Rost, Norway
REU	Reus, Spain
REX	Reynosa, Mexico
RFD	Rockford, Illinois, USA
RFP	Raiatea Island, Society Islands
RFS	Rosita, Nicaragua

City and Airport Codes, cont.

RGA	Rio Grande, TF, Argentina
RGE	Porgera, Papua New Guinea
RGI	Rangiroa Island, Tuamotu Islands
RGL	Rio Gallegos, SC, Argentina
RGN	Yangon, Myanmar
RHE	Reims, France
RHI	Rhinelander, Wisconsin, USA
RHO	Rhodes, Greece
RHP	Ramechhap, Nepal
RIA	Santa Maria, RS, Brazil
RIB	Riberalta, Bolivia
RIC	Richmond/Wmbg, Virginia, USA
RIG	Rio Grande, RS, Brazil
RIJ	Rioja, Peru
RIK	Carrillo, Costa Rica
RIN	Ringi Cove, Solomon Islands
RIO	Rio de Janeiro, RJ, Brazil
RIW	Riverton, Wyoming, USA
RIX	Riga, Latvia
RIY	Riyan Mukalla, Republic of Yemen
RJH	Rajshahi, Bangladesh
RJK	Rjieka, Croatia
RKD	Rockland, Maine, USA
RKS	Rock Springs, Wyoming, USA
RKT	Ras Al Khaimah, United Arab Emirates
RKU	Yule Island, Papua New Guinea
RKV	Reykjavik Domestic, Iceland
RLG	Rostock-Laage, Germany
RMA	Roma, QLD, Australia
RMK	Renmark, SA, Australia
RMP	Rampart, Alaska, USA
RNB	Ronneby, Sweden
RNE	Roanne, France
RNI	Corn Island, Nicaragua
RNJ	Yoronjima, Japan
RNL	Rennell, Solomon Islands
RNN	Bornholm, Denmark
RNO	Reno, Nevada, USA
RNS	Rennes, France
ROA	Roanoke, Virginia, USA
ROC	Rochester, New York, USA
ROK	Rockhampton, QLD, Australia
ROM	Rome, Italy
RON	Rondon, Colombia
ROO	Rondonopolis, MT, Brazil
ROP	Rota, Mariana Islands
ROR	Koro, Palau Island, Pacific Ocean
ROS	Rosario, SF, Argentina
ROT	Rotorua, New Zealand
ROV	Rostov, Russian Fed.
ROW	Roswell, New Mexico, USA
RPM	Ngukurr, NT, Australia
RPN	Rosh Pina, Israel
RPR	Raipur, India
RRG	Rodrigues Island, Mauritius
RRS	Roros, Norway
RSA	Santa Rosa, LP, Argentina
RSD	Rock Sound, Bahamas
RSH	Russian Mission, Alaska, USA
RSJ	Rosario, Washington, USA
RST	Rochester, Minnesota, USA
RSU	Yosu, Republic of Korea
RSW	Southwest Florida Regional Apt., Florida, USA
RTA	Rotuma Island, Fiji
RTB	Roatan, Honduras
RTG	Ruteng, Indonesia
RTI	Roti, Indonesia
RTM	Rotterdam, Netherlands
RTS	Rottnest Island, WA, Australia
RTW	Saratov, Russian Fed.
RUG	Rugao, P. R. China
RUH	Riyadh, Saudi Arabia
RUI	Ruidoso, New Mexico, USA
RUM	Rumjatar, Nepal
RUN	St. Denis de la Reunion, Indian Ocean
RUR	Rurutu, Tubuai Islands
RUS	Marau Island, Solomon Is.
RUT	Rutland, Vermont, USA
RVA	Farafangana, Madagascar
RVE	Saravena, Colombia
RVH	Rzhevka, Russian Fed.
RVK	Roervik, Norway
RVN	Rovaniemi, Finland
RWB	Rowan Bay, Alaska, USA
RWI	Rocky Mount/Wilson, North Carolina, USA
RXS	Roxas, Philippines
RYK	Rahim Yar Khan, Pakistan

S

SAB	Saba, Netherlands Antilles
SAC	Sacramento, California, USA
SAF	Santa Fe, New Mexico, USA
SAH	Sanaa, Republic of Yemen
SAK	Saudarkrokur, Iceland
SAL	San Salvador, El Salvador
SAM	Salamo, Papua New Guinea
SAN	San Diego, California, USA
SAO	Sao Paulo, SP, Brazil
SAP	San Pedro Sula, Honduras
SAQ	San Andros, Bahamas
SAT	San Antonio, Texas, USA
SAU	Sawu, Indonesia
SAV	Savannah, Georgia, USA
SAX	Sambu, Panama
SBA	Santa Barbara, California, USA
SBH	St. Barthelemy, French Antilles
SBK	St. Brieuc, France
SBN	South Bend, Indiana, USA
SBP	San Luis Obispo County, California, USA
SBS	Steamboat Springs, Colorado, USA
SBU	Springbok, S. Africa
SBW	Sibu, Malaysia
SBY	Salisbury, Maryland, USA
SBZ	Sibiu, Romania
SCC	Prudhoe Bay/Deadhorse, Alaska, USA
SCE	State College, Pennsylvania, USA
SCJ	Smith Cove, Alaska, USA
SCL	Santiago, Chile
SCM	Scammon Bay, Alaska, USA
SCN	Saarbrucken, Germany
SCO	Aktau, Kazakhstan
SCQ	Santiago de Compostela, Spain
SCU	Santiago, Cuba
SCV	Suceava, Romania
SCW	Syktyvkar, Russian Fed.
SCX	Salina Cruz, Mexico
SCZ	Santa Cruz Island, Solomon Islands
SDD	Lubango, Angola
SDE	Santiago Del Estero, SE, Argentina
SDF	Louisville, Kentucky, USA
SDI	Saidor, Papua New Guinea
SDJ	Sendai, Japan
SDK	Sandakan, Malaysia
SDL	Sundsvall, Sweden
SDN	Sandane, Norway
SDP	Sand Point, Alaska, USA
SDQ	Santo Domingo, Dominican Rep.
SDR	Santander, Spain
SDT	Saidu Sharif, Pakistan
SDU	Santos Dumont, RJ, Brazil
SDV	Sde Dov, Israel
SDY	Sidney, Montana, USA
SDZ	Shetland Islands, United Kingdom
SEA	Seattle/Tacoma, Washington, USA

City and Airport Codes, cont.

SEL	Seoul, Republic of Korea
SEY	Selibaby, Mauritania
SEZ	Mahe Island, Seychelles Is. Indian Ocean
SFA	Sfax, Tunisia
SFD	San Fernando de Apure, Venezuela
SFG	St. Martin, French Antilles
SFJ	Kangerlussauq, Greenland
SFN	Santa Fe, SF, Argentina
SFO	San Francisco, California, USA
SFQ	Sanliurfa, Turkey
SFT	Skelleftea, Sweden
SFU	Safia, Papua New Guinea
SGC	Surgut, Russian Fed.
SGD	Sonderborg, Denmark
SGF	Springfield, Missouri, USA
SGK	Sangapi, Papua New Guinea
SGN	Ho Chi Minh City, Vietnam
SGO	St. George, QLD, Australia
SGU	St. George, Utah, USA
SGY	Skagway, Alaska, USA
SHA	Shanghai, P. R. China
SHB	Nakashibetsu, Japan
SHC	Indaselassie, Ethiopia
SHD	Shenandoah Valley, Virginia, USA
SHE	Shenyang, P. R. China
SHG	Shungnak, Alaska, USA
SHH	Shishmaref, Alaska, USA
SHJ	Sharjah, United Arab Emirates
SHM	Nanki Shirahama, Japan
SHO	Sokcho, Republic of Korea
SHP	Qinhuangdao, P. R. China
SHR	Sheridan, Wyoming, USA
SHS	Shashi, P. R. China
SHV	Shreveport, Louisiana, USA
SHW	Sharurah, Saudi Arabia
SHX	Shageluk, Alaska, USA
SIA	Xi An, P. R. China
SID	Sal, Cape Verde
SIF	Simra, Nepal
SIG	Isla Grande, Puerto Rico
SIL	Sila, Papua New Guinea
SIM	Simbai, Papua New Guinea
SIN	Singapore, Singapore
SIP	Simferopol, Ukraine
SIT	Sitka, Alaska, USA
SIU	Siuna, Nicaragua
SIX	Singleton, NSW, Australia
SJB	San Joaquin, Bolivia
SJC	San Jose, California, USA
SJD	Los Cabos, Mexico
SJI	San Jose, Philippines
SJK	Sao Jose Dos Campos, SP, Brazil
SJL	Sao Gabriel, RS, Brazil
SJO	San Jose, Costa Rica
SJP	Sao Jose Do Rio Preto, SP, Brazil
SJT	San Angelo, Texas, USA
SJU	San Juan, Puerto Rico
SJW	Shijiazhuang, P. R. China
SJY	Seinajoki, Finland
SJZ	Sao Jorge Island, Portugal (Azores)
SKB	St. Kitts, Leeward Islands
SKD	Samarkand, Uzbekistan
SKE	Skien, Norway
SKG	Thessaloniki, Greece
SKH	Surkhet, Nepal
SKK	Shaktoolik, Alaska, USA
SKN	Stokmarknes, Norway
SKO	Sokoto, Nigeria
SKP	Skopje, MacEdonia
SKS	Vojens, Denmark
SKU	Skiros, Greece
SKX	Saransk, Russian Fed.
SKZ	Sukkur, Pakistan
SLA	Salta, SA, Argentina
SLC	Salt Lake City, Utah, USA
SLH	Sola, Vanuatu
SLK	Saranac Lake, New York, USA
SLL	Salalah, Oman
SLM	Salamanca, Spain
SLN	Salina, Kansas, USA
SLP	San Luis Potosi, Mexico
SLQ	Sleetmute, Alaska, USA
SLU	St. Lucia, West Indies
SLV	Simla, India
SLW	Saltillo, Mexico
SLX	Salt Cay, Turks & Caicos Is.
SLY	Salehard, Russian Fed.
SLZ	Sao Luiz, MA, Brazil
SMA	Santa Maria, Portugal (Azores)
SMF	Sacrametno Metropolitan Apt., California, USA
SMI	Samos, Greece
SMK	St. Michael, Alaska, USA
SML	Stella Maris, Long Island, Bahamas
SMM	Semporna, Malaysia
SMR	Santa Marta, Colombia
SMS	Sainte Marie, Madagascar
SMX	Santa Maria, California, USA
SNA	Orange County, California, USA
SNB	Snake Bay, NT, Australia
SNE	Sao Nicolau, Cape Verde
SNN	Shannon, Republic of Ireland
SNO	Sakon Nakhon, thailand
SNP	St. Paul Island, Alaska, USA
SNV	Santa Elena, Venezuela
SNW	Thandwe, Myanmar
SOC	Solo City, Indonesia
SOF	Sofia, Bulgaria
SOG	Sogndal, Norway
SOI	South Molle Island, QLD, Australia
SOJ	Sorkjosen, Norway
SOM	San Tome, Venezuela
SON	Espiritu Santo, Vanuatu
SOO	Soderhamn, Sweden
SOP	Pinehurst, North Carolina, USA
SOQ	Sorong, Indonesia
SOT	Sodankyla, Finland
SOU	Southampton, United Kingdom
SOW	Show Low, Arizona, USA
SOX	Sogamoso, Colombia
SPB	Seaplane Base, Virgin Islands
SPC	Santa Cruz de la Palma, Canary Is.
SPD	Saidpur, Bangladesh
SPI	Springfield, Illinois, USA
SPK	Sapporo, Japan
SPN	Saipan, Mariana Islands
SPP	Menongue, Angola
SPR	San Pedro, Belize
SPS	Wichita Falls, Texas, USA
SPU	Split, Croatia
SPW	Spencer, Iowa, USA
SPY	San Pedro, Cote D'Ivoire
SQC	Southern Cross, WA, Australia
SQI	Sterling/Rock Falls, Illinois, USA
SQJ	Shehdi, Ethiopia
SQO	Storuman, Sweden
SQR	Soroako, Indonesia
SQS	San Ignacia, Belize
SQU	Saposoa, Peru
SQW	Skive, Denmark
SRA	Santa Ros, RS, Brazil
SRD	San Ramon, Bolivia
SRE	Sucre, Bolivia
SRG	Semarang, Indonesia
SRH	Sarh, Chad
SRI	Samarinda, Indonesia
SRJ	San Borja, Bolivia
SRN	Strahan, Tasmania, Australia

City and Airport Codes, cont.

SRP	Stord, Norway
SRQ	Sarasota/Bradenton, Florida, USA
SRV	Stony River, Alaska, USA
SRY	Sary, Iran
SRZ	Santa Cruz, Bolivia
SSA	Salvador, BA, Brazil
SSB	Seaplane Base, Virgin Islands
SSG	Malabo, Equatorial Guinea
SSH	Sharm El Sheikh, Egypt
SSI	Brunswick, Georgia, USA
SSJ	Sandnessjoen, Norway
SSL	Santa Rosalia, Colombia
SSM	Sault Sainte Marie, Michigan, USA
SSR	Sara, Vanuatu
SSX	Samsun, Turkey
SSY	M'banza Congo, Angola
STB	Santa Barbara Zulia, Venezuela
STC	Saint Cloud, Minnesota, USA
STD	Santo Domingo, Venezuela
STG	St. George Island, Alaska, USA
STI	Santiago, Dominican Rep.
STL	St. Louis, Missouri, USA
STM	Santarem, PA, Brazil
STN	Stansted, United Kingdom
STO	Stockholm, Sweden
STR	Stuttgart, Germany
STS	Santa Rosa, California, USA
STT	St. Thomas, Virgin Islands
STW	Stavropol, Russian Fed.
STX	St. Croix, Virgin Islands
STZ	Santa Terezinha, MT, Brazil
SUB	Surabaya, Indonesia
SUE	Sturgeon Bay, Wisconsin, USA
SUF	Lamezia Terme, Italy
SUH	Sur, Oman
SUJ	Satu Mare, Romania
SUL	Sui, Pakistan
SUN	Sun Valley, Idaho, USA
SUR	Summer Beaver, Ontario, Canada
SUV	Suva, Fiji
SUX	Sioux City, Iowa, USA
SVA	Savoonga, Alaska, USA
SVB	Sambava, Madagascar
SVD	St. Vincent, St. Vincent
SVG	Stavanger, Norway
SVI	San Vicente Del Caguan, Colombia
SVJ	Svolvaer, Norway
SVL	Savonlinna, Finland
SVO	Sheremetyevo, Russian Fed.
SVP	Kuito, Angola
SVQ	Sevilla, Spain
SVS	Stevens Village, Alaska, USA
SVU	Savusavu, Fiji
SVX	Ekaterinburg, Russian Fed.
SVZ	San Antonio, Venezuela
SWA	Shantou, P. R. China
SWD	Seward, Alaska, USA
SWF	Newburgh, New York, USA
SWG	Satwag, Papua New Guinea
SWJ	South West Bay, Vanuatu
SWP	Swakopmund, Namibia
SWQ	Sumbawa, Indonesia
SWR	Silur, Papua New Guinea
SWT	Strzhewoi, Russian Fed.
SXB	Strasbourg, France
SXE	Sale, Victoria, Australia
SXF	Schonefeld, Germany
SXH	Sehulea, Papua New Guinea
SXL	Sligo, Republic of Ireland
SXM	St Maarten, Netherlands Antilles
SXO	Sao Felix Do Araguaia, MT, Brazil
SXP	Sheldon Point, Alaska, USA
SXR	Srinagar, India
SXS	Sahabat 16, Malaysia
SXW	Sauren, Papua New Guinea
SXX	Sao Felix Do Xingu, PA, Brazil
SXZ	Siirt, Turkey
SYD	Sydney, NSW, Australia
SYM	Simao, P. R. China
SYO	Shonai, Japan
SYR	Syracuse, New York, USA
SYX	Sanya, P. R. China
SYY	Stornoway, United Kingdom
SYZ	Shiraz, Iran
SZA	Soyo, Angola
SZG	Salzburg, Austria
SZK	Skukuza, S. Africa
SZS	Stewar Island, New Zealand
SZV	Suzhou, P. R. China
SZX	Shenzhen, P. R. China
SZZ	Szczecin, Poland

T

TAB	Tobago, Trinidad & Tobago
TAC	Tacloban, Philippines
TAE	Taegu, Republic of Korea
TAG	Tagbilaran, Philippines
TAH	Tanna, Vanuatu
TAI	Taiz, Republic of Yemen
TAJ	Aitape Tadji Apt., Papua New Guinea
TAK	Takamatsu, Japan
TAL	Tanana, Alaska, USA
TAM	Tampico, Mexico
TAO	Qingdao, P. R. China
TAP	Tapachula, Mexico
TAS	Tashkent, Uzbekistan
TAT	Tatry/Poprad, Slovakia
TAV	Tau, American Samoa
TBF	Tabiteuea, North, Kiribati
TBG	Tabubil, Papua New Guinea
TBI	The Bight, Bahamas
TBN	Fort Leonard Wood, Missouri, USA
TBO	Tabora, Tanzania
TBP	Tumbes, Peru
TBS	Tbilisi, Georgia
TBT	Tabatinga, AM, Brazil
TBU	Tongatapu, Tonga, Is., S. Pacific
TBW	Tambov, Russian Fed.
TBZ	Tabriz, Iran
TCA	Tennant Creek, NT, Australia
TCB	Treasure Cay, Bahamas
TCH	Tchibanga, Gabon
TCI	Tenerife, Canary Islands
TCL	Tuscaloosa, Alabama, USA
TCO	Tumaco, Colombia
TCQ	Tacna, Peru
TCT	Takotna, Alaska, USA
TDB	Tetabedi, Papua New Guinea
TDD	Trinidad, Bolivia
TDL	Tandil, BA, Argentina
TED	Thisted, Denmark
TEE	Tbessa, Algeria
TEF	Telfer, WA, Australia
TEH	Tetlin, Alaska, USA
TEO	Terapo, Papua New Guinea
TEP	Teptep, Papua New Guinea
TER	Terceira, Portugal (Azores)
TET	Tete, Mozambique
TEU	Te Anau, New Zealand
TEX	Telluride, Colorado, USA
TEY	Thingeyri, Iceland
TEZ	Texpur, India
TFF	Tefe, AM, Brazil
TFI	Tufi, Papua New Guinea
TFM	Telefomin, Papua New Guinea
TFN	Norte Los Rodeos, Canary Is.
TFS	Sur Reina Sofia, Canary Is.
TGG	Kuala Terengganu, Malaysia
TGH	Tongoa, Vanuatu
TGI	Tingo Maria, Peru
TGJ	Tiga, Loyalty Islands
TGM	Tigru Mures, Romania
TGN	Traralgon, Victoria, Australia

City and Airport Codes, cont.

TGR	Touggourt, Algeria
TGT	Tanga, Tanzania
TGU	Tegucigalpa, Honduras
TGZ	Tuxtla Gutierrez, Mexico
THE	Teresina PI, Brazil
THF	Tempelhof, Germany
THG	Thangool, QLD, Australia
THK	Thakhek, Laos
THL	Tachilek, Myanmar
THN	Trollhattan, Sweden
THR	Tehran, Iran
THU	Pituffik, Greenland
TIA	Tirana, Albania
TIC	Tinak Island, Marshall Islands
TID	Tiaret, Algeria
TIE	Tippi, Ethiopia
TIF	Taif, Saudi Arabia
TIH	Tikehau Atoll, Tuamotu Islands
TIJ	Tijuana, Mexico
TIM	Tembagapura, Indonesia
TIN	Tindouf, Algeria
TIQ	Tinian, Mariana Islands
TIS	Thursday Island, QLD, Australia
TIU	Timaru, New Zealand
TIY	Tidjikja, Mauritania
TIZ	Tari, Papua New Guinea
TJA	Tarija, Bolivia
TJH	Toyooka, Japan
TJK	Tokat, Turkey
TJM	Tyumen, Russian Fed.
TJQ	Tanjung Pandan, Indonesia
TKB	Tekadu, Papua New Guinea
TKE	Tenakee, Alaska, USA
TKG	Bandar Lampung, Indonesia
TKI	Tokeen, Alaska, USA
TKJ	Tok, Alaska, USA
TKK	Truk, Caroline Is., Pac. Ocean
TKN	Tokunoshima, Japan
TKP	Takapoto, Tuamotu Islands
TKQ	Kigoma, Tanzania
TKS	Tokushima, Japan
TKU	Turku, Finland
TKX	Takaroa, Tuamotu Islands
TLA	Teller, Alaska, USA
TLE	Tulear, Madagascar
TLH	Tallahassee, Florida, USA
TLI	Tolitoli, Indonesia
TLJ	Tatalina, Alaska, USA
TLL	Tallinn, Estonia
TLM	Tlemcen, Algeria
TLN	Toulon, France
TLO	Tol, Papua New Guinea
TLS	Toulouse, France
TLT	Tuluksak, Alaska, USA
TLV	Tel Aviv, Israel
TMC	Tambolaka, Indonesia
TME	Tame, Colombia
TMG	Tomanggong, Malaysia
TMI	Tumlingtar, Nepal
TMJ	Termez, Uzbekistan
TMM	Tamatave, Madagascar
TMN	Tamana Island, Kiribati
TMP	Tampere, Finland
TMR	Tamanrasset, Algeria
TMS	Sao Tome Island, Sao Tome Is.
TMT	Trombetas, PA, Brazil
TMU	Tambor, Costa Rica
TMW	Tamworth, NSW, Australia
TMX	Timimoun, Algeria
TNA	Jinan, P. R. China
TNC	Tin City, Alaska, USA
TNE	Tanegashima, Japan
TNF	Toussus-Le-Noble, France
TNG	Tangier, Morocco
TNH	Tonghua, P. R. China
TNJ	Tanjung Pinang, Indonesia
TNK	Tununak, Alaska, USA
TNN	Tainan, Taiwan
TNO	Tamarindo, Costa Rica
TNR	Antananarivo, Madagascar
TNX	Stung Treng, Cambodia
TOD	Tioman, Malaysia
TOE	Tozeur, Tunisia
TOF	Tomsk, Russian Fed.
TOG	Tojiak, Alaska, USA
TOH	Torres, Vanuatu
TOK	Torokina, Papua New Guinea
TOL	Toledo, Ohio, USA
TOM	Tombouctou, Mali
TON	Tonu, Papua New Guinea
TOP	Topeka, Kansas, USA
TOS	Tromso, Norway
TOU	Touho, New Caledonia
TOW	Toledo, PR, Brazil
TOY	Toyama, Japan
TOZ	Touba, Cote D'Ivoire
TPA	Tampa/St. Petersburg, Florida, USA
TPE	Taipei, Taiwan
TPI	Tapini, Papua New Guinea
TPJ	Taplejung, Nepal
TPP	Tarapoto, Peru
TPQ	Tepic, Mexico
TPR	Tom Price, WA, Australia
TPS	Trapani, Italy
TRA	Taramajima, Japan
TRB	Turbo, Colombia
TRC	Torreon, Mexico
TRD	Trondheim, Norway
TRE	Tireeisland, Scotland, United Kingdom
TRF	Sandefjord, Norway
TRG	Tauranga, New Zealand
TRI	Tri-City Airport, Tennessee, USA
TRK	Tarakan, Indonesia
TRN	Turin, Italy
TRO	Taree, NSW, Australia
TRS	Trieste, Italy
TRU	Trujillo, Peru
TRV	Trivandrum, India
TRW	Tarawa, Kiribati
TRZ	Tiruchirapally, India
TSA	Sung Shan, Taiwan
TSB	Tsumeb, Namibia
TSE	Akmola, Kazakhstan
TSJ	Tsushima, Japan
TSN	Tianjin, P. R. China
TSO	Tresco, United Kingdom
TSR	Timisoara, Romania
TSS	East 34th Street Heliport, New York, USA
TST	Trang, Thailand
TSU	Tabiteuea South, Kiribati
TSV	Townsville, QLD, Australia
TTA	Tan Tan, Morocco
TTE	Ternate, Indonesia
TTJ	Tottori, Japan
TTN	Trenton, New Jersey, USA
TTQ	Tortuquero, Costa Rica
TTR	Tana Toraja, Indonesia
TTT	Taitung, Taiwan
TTU	Tetuan, Morocco
TUA	Tulcan, Ecuador
TUB	Tubuai, Tubuai Islands
TUC	Tucuman, TU, Argentina
TUD	Tambacounda, Senegal
TUF	Tours, France
TUG	Tuguegarao, Philippines
TUI	Turaif, Saudi Arabia
TUJ	Tum, Ethiopia
TUK	Turbat, Pakistan
TUL	Tulsa, Oklahoma, USA
TUN	Tunis, Tunisia
TUO	Taupo, New Zealand
TUP	Tupelo, Mississippi, USA
TUR	Tucurui, PA, Brazil
TUS	Tucson, Arizona, USA
TUU	Tabuk, Saudi Arabia
TUZ	Tucuma, PA, Brazil
TVC	Traverse City, Michigan, USA
TVF	Thief River Falls, Minnesota, USA
TVL	Lake Tahoe, California, USA
TVU	Taveuni, Fiji

City and Airport Codes, cont.

TVY	Dawe, Myanmar	UKK	Ust-Kamenogorsk, Kazakhstan	VAN	Van, Turkey
TWA	Twin Hills, Alaska, USA			VAO	Suavanao, Solomon Is.
TWB	Toowoomba, QLD, Australia	ULB	Ulei, Vanuatu	VAR	Varna, Bulgaria
TWF	Twin Falls, Idaho, USA	ULE	Sule, Papua New Guinea	VAS	Sivas, Turkey
TWU	Tawau, Malaysia	ULG	Ulgii, Mongolia	VAV	Vava'u, Tonga Is., S. Pacific
TXF	Teixeira de Freitas, BA, Brazil	ULN	Ulan Bator, Mongolia	VAW	Vardoe, Norway
		ULP	Quilpie, QLD, Australia	VBV	Vanuabalavu, Fiji
TXG	Taichung, Taiwan	ULY	Ulyanovsk, Russian Fed.	VBY	Visby, Sweden
TXK	Texarkana, Arkansas, USA	UMD	Uummannaq, Greenland	VCD	Victoria River Downs, NT, Australia
TXL	Tegel, Germany	UME	Umea, Sweden		
TXN	Tunzi, P. R. China	UMR	Woomera, SA, Australia	VCE	Venice, Italy
TYF	Torsby, Sweden	UNG	Kiung, Papua New Guinea	VCT	Victoria, Texas, USA
TYL	Talara, Peru	UNI	Union Island, Windward Islands	VDA	Ovda, Israel
TYN	Taiyuan, P. R. China			VDB	Fagernes, Norway
TYO	Tokyo, Japan	UNK	Unalakleet, Alaska, USA	VDC	Vitoria Da Conquista, BA, Brazil
TYR	Tyler, Texas, USA	UNN	Ranong, Thailand		
TYS	Knoxville, Tennessee, USA	UNT	Unst, Shetland Is., Scotland, United Kingdom	VDM	Viedma, RN, Argentina
TZA	Municipal, Belize			VDS	Vadso, Norway
TZN	South Andros, Bahamas	UOL	Buol, Indonesia	VDZ	Valdez, Alaska, USA
TZX	Trabzon, Turkey	UPG	Ujung Pandang, Indonesia	VEE	Venetie, Alaska, USA
		UPN	Uruapan, Mexico	VEL	Vernal, Utah, USA
U		URA	Uralsk, Kazakhstan	VER	Veracruz, Mexico
UAK	Narsarsuaq, Greenland	URC	Urumqi, P. R. China	VEV	Barakoma, Solomon Islands
UAQ	San Juan, SJ, Argentina	URG	Uruguaiana, RS, Brazil	VEY	Vestmannaeyjar, Iceland
UAS	Samburu, Kenya	URJ	Uraj, Russian Fed.	VFA	Victoria Falls, Zimbabwe
UBA	Uberaba, MG, Brazil	URO	Rouen, France	VGO	Vigo, Spain
UBI	Buin, Papua New Guinea	URR	Urrao, Colombia	VGT	North Air Terminal, Nevada, USA
UBJ	Ube, Japan	URT	Surat Thani, Thailand		
UBP	Ubon Ratchathani, Thailand	URY	Gurayat, Saudi Arabia	VHC	Saurimo, Angola
UBS	Columbus/Strkville/West Pt. Mississippi, USA	USH	Ushuaia, TF, Argentina	VHM	Vilhelmina, Sweden
		USK	Usinsk, Russian Fed.	VIA	Videira, SC, Brazil
UCA	Utica, New York, USA	USL	Useless Loop, WA, Australia	VIE	Vienna, Austria
UCT	Ukhta, Russian Fed.	USM	Koh Samui, Thailand	VIG	El Vigia, Venezuela
UDI	Uberlandia, MG, Brazil	USN	Ulsan, Republic of Korea	VII	Vinh City, Vietnam
UDJ	Uzhgorod, Ukraine	UTH	Udon Thani, Thailand	VIJ	Virgin Gorda, British Virgin Islands
UDR	Udaipur, India	UTK	Utirik Island, Marshall Islands		
UEE	Queenstown, Tasmania, Australia			VIL	Dakhla, Morocco
		UTN	Upington, S. Africa	VIS	Visalia, California, USA
UEL	Quelimane, Mozambique	UTO	Utopia Creek, Alaska, USA	VIT	Vitoria, Spain
UEO	Kume Jima, Japan	UTP	Utapao, Thailand	VIU	Viru, Solomon Islands
UET	Quetta, Pakistan	UTT	Umtata, S. Africa	VIV	Vivigani, Papua New Guinea
UFA	Ufa, Russian Fed.	UUD	Ulan-Ude, Russian Fed.	VIX	Vitoria, ES, Brazil
UGB	Ugashik Bay, Alaska, USA	UUS	Yyzhno-Sakhalinsk, Russian Fed.	VKG	Rachgia, Vietnam
UGC	Urgench, Uzbekistan			VKO	Vnukovo, Russian Fed.
UGO	Uige, Angola	UVE	Ouvea, Loyalty Islands	VKT	Vorkuta, Russian Fed.
UIB	Quibdo, Colombia	UVF	Hewanorra, West Indies	VLC	Valencia, Spain
UIH	Quinhon, Vietnam	UVL	New Valley, Egypt	VLD	Valdosta, Georgia, USA
UII	Utila, Honduras	UVO	Uvol, Papua New Guinea	VLG	Villa Gesell, BA, Argentina
UIK	Ust-Ilimsk, Russian Fed.	UYL	Nyala, Sudan	VLI	Port Vila, Vanuatu
UIN	Quincy, Illinois, USA	UYN	Yulin, P. R. China	VLL	Valladolid, Spain
UIO	Quito, Ecuador			VLN	Valencia, Venezuela
UIP	Quimper, France	**V**		VLP	Vila Rica, MT, Brazil
UIT	Jaluit Island, Marshall Islands	VAA	Vaasa, Finland	VLS	Valesdir, Vanuatu
		VAG	Varginha, MG, Brazil	VLV	Valera, Venezuela
UJE	Ujae Island, Marshall Islands	VAI	Vanimo, Papua New Guinea	VME	Villa Mercedes, SL, Argentina
		VAK	Chevak, Alaska, USA		

City and Airport Codes, cont.

VMU	Baimuru, Papua New Guinea
VNA	Saravane, Laos
VNO	Vilnius, Lithuania
VNS	Varanasi, India
VOG	Volgograd, Russian Fed.
VOH	Vohemar, Madagascar
VOZ	Voronezh, Russian Fed.
VPN	Vopnafjordur, Iceland
VPS	Ft. Walton Beach, Florida, USA
VQS	Vieques, Puerto Rico
VRA	Varadero, Cuba
VRB	Vero Beach, Florida, USA
VRK	Varkaus, Finland
VRN	Verona, Italy
VRY	Vaeroy, Norway
VSA	Villahermosa, Mexico
VSG	Lugansk, Ukraine
VST	Vasteras, Sweden
VTE	Vientiane, Laos
VTU	Las Tunas, Cuba
VTZ	Vishakhapatnam, India
VUP	Valledupar, Colombia
VVC	Villavicencio, Colombia
VVI	Viru Viru International Apt., Bolivia
VVO	Vladivostok, Russian Fed.
VVZ	Illizi, Algeria
VXC	Lichinga, Mozambique
VXE	Sao Vicente, Cape Verde
VXO	Vaxjo, Sweden

W

WAA	Wales, Alaska, USA
WAE	Wadi Ad Dawasir, Saudi Arabia
WAG	Wanganui, New Zealand
WAS	Washington, District of Columbia, USA
WAT	Waterford, Republic of Ireland
WAW	Warsaw, Poland
WBB	Stebbins, Alaska, USA
WBM	Wapenamanda, Papua New Guinea
WBQ	Beaver, Alaska, USA
WDG	Enid, Oklahoma, USA
WDH	Windhoek, Namibia
WED	Wedau, Papua New Guinea
WEF	Weifang, P. R. China
WEH	Weihai, P. R. China
WEI	Weipa, QLD, Australia
WFI	Fianarantsoa, Madagascar
WFK	Frenchville, Maine, USA
WGA	Wagga Wagga, NSW, Australia
WGE	Walgett, NSW, Australia
WGP	Waingapu, Indonesia
WHD	Hyder, Alaska, USA
WHK	Whakatane, New Zealand
WHU	Wuhu, P. R. China
WIC	Wick, United Kingdom
WIL	Wilson, Kenya
WIN	Winton, QLD, Australia
WIU	Witu, Papua New Guinea
WJA	Woja, Marshall Islands
WJR	Wajir, Kenya
WKA	Wanaka, New Zealand
WKJ	Wakkanai, Japan
WKK	Aleknagik, Alaska, USA
WKN	Wakunai, Papua New Guinea
WKR	Walkers Cay, Bahamas
WLB	Labouchere Bay, Alaska, USA
WLG	Wellington, New Zealand
WLH	Walaha, Vanuatu
WLK	Selawik, Alaska, USA
WLS	Wallis Island, Wallis Island
WME	Mount Keith, WA, Australia
WMH	Mountain Home, Arkansas, USA
WMK	Meyers Chuck, Alaska, USA
WMN	Maroantsetra, Madagascar
WMO	White Mountain, Alaska, USA
WMR	Mananara, Madagascar
WMX	Wamena, Indonesia
WNA	Napakiak, Alaska, USA
WNN	Wunnummin Lake, Ontario, Canada
WNR	Windorah, QLD, Australia
WNS	Nawabshah, Pakistan
WNU	Wanuma, Papua New Guinea
WNZ	Wenzhou, P. R. China
WRE	Whangarei, New Zealand
WRG	Wrangell, Alaska, USA
WRL	Worland, Wyoming, USA
WRO	Wroclaw, Poland
WSN	South Naknek, Alaska, USA
WSP	Waspam, Nicaragua
WST	Westerly, Rhode Island, USA
WSU	Wasu, Papua New Guinea
WSX	Westsound, Washington, USA
WSY	Airlie Beach, QLD, Australia
WSZ	Westport, New Zealand
WTE	Wotje Island, Marshall Islands
WTK	Noatak, Alaska, USA
WTL	Tuntutuliak, Alaska, USA
WTO	Wotho Island, Marshall Islands
WTP	Woitape, Papua New Guinea
WUD	Wudinna, SA, Australia
WUG	Wau, Papua New Guinea
WUH	Wuhan, P. R. China
WUN	Wiluna, WA, Australia
WUS	Wuyishan, P. R. China
WUX	Wuxi, P. R. China
WUZ	Wuzhou, P. R. China
WVB	Walvis Bay, Namibia
WVK	Manakara, Madagascar
WWK	Wewak, Papua New Guinea
WWP	Whale Pass, Alaska, USA
WWT	Newtok, Alaska, USA
WWY	West Wyalong, NSW, Australia
WXN	Wanxian, P. R. China
WYA	Whyalla, SA, Australia
WYN	Wyndham, WA, Australia

X

XAP	Chapeco, SC, Brazil
XBE	Bearskin Lake, Ontario, Canada
XBN	Biniguni, Papua New Guinea
XCH	Christmas Island, Australia
XDT	C. de Gaulle/Tgv Railway Service, France
XFN	Xiangfan, P. R. China
XGR	Kangiqsualujjuaq, Quebec, Canada
XIC	Xichang, P. R. China
XIY	Xianyang, P. R. China
XKH	Xieng Khouang, Laos
XKS	Kasabonika, Ontario, Canada
XLB	Lac Brochet, Manitoba, Canada
XLS	Saint Louis, Senegal
XMG	Mahendranagar, Nepal
XMH	Manihi, Tuamotu Islands
XMN	Xiamen, P. R. China
XMS	Macas, Ecuador
XNN	Xining, P. R. China
XNT	Xingtai, P. R. China
XPK	Pukatawagan, Manitoba, Canada
XQP	Quepos, Costa Rica
XQU	Qualicum, BC, Canada
XRY	Jerez de la Frontera, Spain

City and Airport Codes, cont.

XSC	South Caicos, Turks & Caicos Is.
XSI	South Indian Lake, Manitoba, Canada
XSP	Seletar, Singapore
XTG	Thargomindah, QLD, Australia
XTL	Tadoule Lake, Manitoba, Canada
XUZ	Xuzhou, P. R. China
XYA	Yandina, Solomon Is.

Y

YAA	Anahim Lake, BC, Canada
YAB	Arctic Bay, NWT, Canada
YAC	Cat Lake, Ontario, Canada
YAG	Fort Frances, Ontario, Canada
YAI	Chillan, Chile
YAJ	Lyall Harbour, BC, Canada
YAK	Yakutat, Alaska, USA
YAL	Alert Bay, BC, Canada
YAM	Sault Sainte Marie, Ontario, Canada
YAO	Yaounde, Cameroon
YAP	Yap, Caroline Is., Pacific Ocean
YAQ	Maple Bay, BC, Canada
YAT	Attawapiskat, Ontario, Canada
YAV	Miner's Bay, BC, Canada
YAX	Angling Lake, Ontario, Canada
YAY	St. Anthony, Nfld, Canada
YBA	Banff, Alberta, Canada
YBB	Townsite, NWT, Canada
YBC	Baie Comeau, Quebec, Canada
YBE	Uranium City, Sask, Canada
YBG	Bagotville, Quebec, Canada
YBI	Black Tickle, Nfld, Canada
YBK	Baker Lake, NWT, Canada
YBL	Campbell River, BC, Canada
YBP	Yibin, P. R. China
YBQ	Telegraph Harbour, BC, Canada
YBR	Brandon, Manitoba, Canada
YBT	Brochet, Manitoba, Canada
YBV	Berens River, Manitoba, Canada
YBW	Bedwell Harbor, BC, Canada
YBX	Blanc Sablon, Quebec, Canada
YCB	Cambridge Bay, NWT, Canada
YCD	Nanaimo, BC, Canada
YCG	Castlegar, BC, Canada
YCH	Chatham, NB, Canada
YCK	Colville Lake, NWT, Canada
YCL	Charlo, NB, Canada
YCN	Cochrane, Ontario, Canada
YCO	Coppermine, NWT, Canada
YCR	Cross Lake, Manitoba, Canada
YCS	Chesterfield Inlet, NWT, Canada
YCY	Clyde River, NWT, Canada
YDA	Dawson City, YT, Canada
YDF	Deer Lake, Nfld, Canada
YDI	Davis Inlet, Nfld, Canada
YDL	Dease Lake, BC, Canada
YDN	Dauphin, Manitoba, Canada
YDP	Nain, Nfld, Canada
YDQ	Dawson Creek, BC, Canada
YEA	Edmonton, Alberta, Canada
YEC	Yechon, Republic of Korea
YEG	Edmonton International Apt., Alberta, Canada
YEK	Arviat, NWT, Canada
YEL	Elliot Lake, Ontario, Canada
YER	Fort Severn, Ontario, Canada
YEV	Inuvik, NWT, Canada
YFA	Fort Albany, Ontario, Canada
YFB	Iqaluit, NWT, Canada
YFC	Fredericton, NB, Canada
YFH	Fort Hope, Ontario, Canada
YFO	Flin Flon, Manitoba, Canada
YFR	Fort Resolution, NWT, Canada
YFS	Fort Simpson, NWT, Canada
YFX	Fox Harbour, Nfld, Canada
YGB	Gillies Bay, BC, Canada
YGG	Ganges Harbor, BC, Canada
YGH	Fort Good Hope, NWT, Canada
YGJ	Yonago, Japan
YGK	Kingston, Ontario, Canada
YGL	La Grande, Quebec, Canada
YGN	Greenway Sound, BC, Canada
YGO	Gods Narrows, Manitoba, Canada
YGP	Gaspe, Quebec, Canada
YGQ	Geraldton, Ontario, Canada
YGR	Iles de la Madeleine, Quebec, Canada
YGT	Igloolik, NWT, Canada
YGV	Havre Saint Pierre, Quebec, Canada
YGW	Kuujjuarapik, Quebec, Canada
YGX	Gillam, Manitoba, Canada
YGZ	Grise Fiord, NWT, Canada
YHA	Port Hope Simpson, Nfld, Canada
YHD	Dryden, Ontario, Canada
YHF	Hearst, Ontario, Canada
YHG	Charlottetown, Nfld, Canada
YHH	Campbell River Harbor Spb, BC, Canada
YHI	Holman Island, NWT, Canada
YHK	Gjoa Haven, NWT, Canada
YHM	Hamilton, Ontario, Canada
YHN	Hornepayne, Ontario, Canada
YHO	Hopedale, Nfld, Canada
YHP	Poplar Hill, Ontario, Canada
YHR	Chevery, Quebec, Canada
YHS	Sechelt, BC, Canada
YHY	Hay River, NWT, Canada
YHZ	Halifax, NS, Canada
YIF	Pakuashipi, Quebec, Canada
YIK	Ivujivik, Quebec, Canada
YIN	Yining, P. R. China
YIO	Pond Inlet, NWT, Canada
YIV	Island Lake/Garden Hill, Manitoba, Canada
YIW	Yiwu, P. R. China
YJP	Jasper Hinton, Alberta, Canada
YJT	Stephenville, Nfld, Canada
YKA	Kamloops, BC, Canada
YKG	Kangirsuk, Quebec, Canada
YKK	Kitkatla, BC, Canada
YKL	Schefferville, Quebec, Canada
YKM	Yakima, Washington, USA
YKN	Yankton, South Dakota, USA
YKQ	Waskaganish, Quebec, Canada
YKS	Yakutsk, Russian Fed.
YKU	Chisasibi, Quebec, Canada
YKX	Kirkland Lake, Ontario, Canada
YLC	Lake Harbour, NWT, Canada
YLD	Chapleau, Ontario, Canada
YLE	Lac la Martre, NWT, Canada
YLH	Lansdowne House, Ontario, Canada
YLL	Lloydminster, Alberta, Canada
YLR	Leaf Rapids, Manitoba, Canada
YLW	Kelowna, BC, Canada
YMG	Manitouwadge, Ontario, Canada
YMH	Mary's Harbour, Nfld, Canada

City and Airport Codes, cont.

YML	Murray Bay, Quebec, Canada
YMM	Fort McMurray, Alberta, Canada
YMN	Makkovik, Nfld, Canada
YMO	Moosonee, Ontario, Canada
YMP	Port McNeil, BC, Canada
YMQ	Montreal, Quebec, Canada
YMS	Yurimaguas, Peru
YMT	Chibougamau, Quebec, Canada
YMX	Mirabel, Quebec, Canada
YNA	Natashquan, Quebec, Canada
YNB	Yanbu, Saudi Arabia
YNC	Wemindji, Quebec, Canada
YND	Gatineau/Hull, Quebec, Canada
YNE	Norway House, Manitoba, Canada
YNG	Youngstown, Ohio, USA
YNJ	Yanji, P. R. China
YNL	Points North Landing, Sask, Canada
YNO	North Spirit Lake, Ontario, Canada
YNS	Nemiscau, Quebec, Canada
YNT	Yantai, P. R. China
YNZ	Yancheng, P. R. China
YOC	Old Crow, YT, Canada
YOH	Oxford House, Manitoba, Canada
YOJ	High Level, Alberta, Canada
YOL	Yola, Nigeria
YOP	Rainbow Lake, Alberta, Canada
YOW	Ottawa, Ontario, Canada
YPA	Prince Albert, Sask, Canada
YPB	Port Alberni, BC, Canada
YPC	Paulatuk, NWT, Canada
YPE	Peace River, Alberta, Canada
YPH	Inukjuak, Quebec, Canada
YPI	Port Simpson, BC, Canada
YPJ	Aupaluk, Quebec, Canada
YPL	Pickle Lake, Ontario, Canada
YPM	Pikangikum, Ontario, Canada
YPN	Port Menier, Quebec, Canada
YPO	Peawanuck, Ontario, Canada
YPQ	Peterborough, Ontario, Canada
YPR	Prince Rupert, BC, Canada
YPW	Powell River, BC, Canada
YPX	Povungnituk, Quebec, Canada
YPY	Fort Chipewyan, Alberta, Canada
YQB	Quebec, Quebec, Canada
YQC	Quaqtaq, Quebec, Canada
YQD	The Pas, Manitoba, Canada
YQG	Windsor, Ontario, Canada
YQH	Watson Lake, YT, Canada
YQI	Yarmouth, NS, Canada
YQK	Kenora, Ontario, Canada
YQL	Lethbridge, Alberta, Canada
YQM	Moncton, NB, Canada
YQQ	Comox, BC, Canada
YQR	Regina, Sask, Canada
YQT	Thunder Bay, Ontario, Canada
YQU	Grande Prairie, Alberta, Canada
YQX	Gander, Nfld, Canada
YQY	Sydney, NS, Canada
YQZ	Quesnel, BC, Canada
YRA	Rae Lakes, NWT, Canada
YRB	Resolute, NWT, Canada
YRD	Dean River, BC, Canada
YRF	Cartwright, Nfld, Canada
YRG	Rigolet, Nfld, Canada
YRJ	Roberval, Quebec, Canada
YRL	Red Lake, Ontario, Canada
YRS	Red Sucker Lake, Manitoba, Canada
YRT	Rankin Inlet, NWT, Canada
YSB	Sudbury, Ontario, Canada
YSF	Stony Rapids, Sask, Canada
YSG	Snowdrift, NWT, Canada
YSJ	Saint John, NB, Canada
YSK	Sanikiluaq, NWT, Canada
YSL	St. Leonard, NB, Canada
YSM	Fort Smith, NWT, Canada
YSN	Salmon Arm, BC, Canada
YSO	Postville, Nfld, Canada
YSP	Marathon, Ontario, Canada
YSR	Nanisivik, NWT, Canada
YST	Sainte Therese Point, Manitoba, Canada
YSY	Sachs Harbour, NWT, Canada
YTA	Pembroke, Ontario, Canada
YTB	Hartley Bay, BC, Canada
YTE	Cape Dorset, NWT, Canada
YTF	Alma, Quebec, Canada
YTG	Sullivan Bay, BC, Canada
YTH	Thompson, Manitoba, Canada
YTL	Big Trout Lake, Ontario, Canada
YTO	Toronto, Ontario, Canada
YTQ	Tasiujuaq, Quebec, Canada
YTS	Timmins, Ontario, Canada
YTZ	Toronto Island, Ontario, Canada
YUB	Tuktoyaktuk, NWT, Canada
YUD	Umiujaq, Quebec, Canada
YUF	Pelly Bay, NWT, Canada
YUL	Dorval, Quebec, Canada
YUM	Yuma, Arizona, USA
YUT	Repulse Bay, NWT, Canada
YUX	Hall Beach, NWT, Canada
YUY	Rouyn-Noranda, Quebec, Canada
YVA	Moroni, Comoros
YVB	Bonaventure, Quebec, Canada
YVC	La Ronge, Sask, Canada
YVM	Broughton Island, NWT, Canada
YVO	Val D'Or, Quebec, Canada
YVP	Kuujjuaq, Quebec, Canada
YVQ	Norman Wells, NWT, Canada
YVR	Vancouver, BC, Canada
YVZ	Deer Lake, Ontario, Canada
YWB	Kangiqsujuaq, Quebec, Canada
YWG	Winnipeg, Manitoba, Canada
YWH	Victoria Inner Harbor, BC, Canada
YWJ	Deline, NWT, Canada
YWK	Wabush, Nfld, Canada
YWL	Williams Lake, BC, Canada
YWP	Webequie, Ontario, Canada
YWS	Whistler, BC, Canada
YXC	Cranbrook, BC, Canada
YXD	Edmonton Municipal Apt., Alberta, Canada
YXE	Saskatoon, Sask, Canada
YXH	Medicine Hat, Alberta, Canada
YXJ	Fort St. John, BC, Canada
YXK	Rimouski, Quebec, Canada
YXL	Sioux Lookout, Ontario, Canada
YXN	Whale Cove, NWT, Canada
YXP	Pangnirtung, NWT, Canada
YXR	Earlton, Ontario, Canada
YXS	Prince George, BC, Canada
YXT	Terrace, BC, Canada
YXU	London, Ontario, Canada
YXX	Abbotsford, BC, Canada
YXY	Whitehorse, YT, Canada
YXZ	Wawa, Ontario, Canada
YYB	North Bay, Ontario, Canada
YYC	Calgary, Alberta, Canada

City and Airport Codes, cont.

YYD	Smithers, BC, Canada
YYE	Fort Nelson, BC, Canada
YYF	Penticton, BC, Canada
YYG	Charlottetown, PEI, Canada
YYH	Taloyak, NWT, Canada
YYJ	Victoria, BC, Canada
YYL	Lynn Lake, Manitoba, Canada
YYQ	Churchill, Manitoba, Canada
YYR	Goose Bay, Nfld, Canada
YYT	St. Johns, Nfld, Canada
YYU	Kapuskasing, Ontario, Canada
YYY	Mont Joli, Quebec, Canada
YYZ	Pearson International Apt., Ontario, Canada
YZE	Gore Bay, Ontario, Canada
YZF	Yellowknife, NWT, Canada
YZG	Salluit, Quebec, Canada
YZP	Sandspit, BC, Canada
YZR	Sarnia, Ontario, Canada
YZS	Coral Harbour, NWT, Canada
YZT	Port Hardy, BC, Canada
YZV	Sept-Iles, Quebec, Canada

Z

ZAC	York Landing, Manitoba, Canada
ZAD	Zadar, Croatia
ZAG	Zagreb, Croatia
ZAH	Zahedan, Iran
ZAL	Valdivia, Chile
ZAM	Zamboanga, Philippines
ZAT	Zhaotong, P. R. China
ZAZ	Zaragoza, Spain
ZBF	Bathurst, NB, Canada
ZBR	Chah-Bahar, Iran
ZBY	Sayaboury, Laos
ZCL	Zacatecas, Mexico
ZCO	Temuco, Chile
ZDJ	Rr Station, Switzerland
ZEL	Bella Bella, BC, Canada
ZEM	East Main, Quebec, Canada
ZFD	Fond du Lac, Sask, Canada
ZFN	Fort Norman, NWT, Canada
ZGI	Gods River, Manitoba, Canada
ZGS	Gethsemani, Quebec, Canada
ZGU	Gaua, Vanuatu
ZHA	Zhanjiang, P. R. China
ZIG	Zigunchor, Senegal
ZIH	Ixtapa/Zihuatanejo, Mexico
ZJG	Jenpeg, Manitoba, Canada
ZJN	Swan River, Manitoba, Canada
ZKE	Kaschechewan, Ontario, Canada
ZKG	Kegaska, Quebec, Canada
ZLO	Manzanillo, Mexico
ZLT	La Tabatiere, Quebec, Canada
ZMT	Masset, BC, Canada
ZNA	Harbour, BC, Canada
ZNE	Newman, WA, Australia
ZNZ	Zanzibar, Tanzania
ZOS	Osorno, Chile
ZPB	Sachigo Lake, Ontario, Canada
ZQN	Queenstown, New Zealand
ZQS	Queen Charlotte Is., BC, Canada
ZRG	Bratislava Bus Station, Slovakia
ZRH	Zurich, Switzerland
ZRI	Serui, Indonesia
ZRJ	Round Lake, Ontario, Canada
ZRM	Sarmi, Indonesia
ZSA	San Salvador, Bahamas
ZSJ	Sandy Lake, Ontario, Canada
ZSW	Seal Cove, BC, Canada
ZTB	Tete-A-La Baleine, Quebec, Canada
ZTH	Zakinthos, Greece
ZTM	Shamattawa, Manitoba, Canada
ZUH	Zhuhai, P. R. China
ZUM	Churchill Falls, Nfld, Canada
ZVK	Savannakhet, Laos
ZWL	Wollaston Lake, Sask, Canada
ZYL	Sylhet, Bangladesh
ZZU	Mzuzu, Malawi

Appendix C

Airline Codes and Abbreviations

Airline Codes

    AA   **American Airlines, Inc.**

    AA★   **American Airlines, Inc.** (Flight Numbers 6001-6002 South African Airways (SA); 6100-6118 Qantas Airways Ltd. (QF); 6520-6976 Canadian Airlines International Ltd. (CP))

    AA★   **American Eagle** (Flight numbers 3200-5839 American Eagle ■)

\# AB   **Aaron Airlines Pty. Ltd.**

    AC   **Air Canada**

    AC★   **Air Canada** (Flight Numbers 1003-1004 Royal Jordanian (RJ); 1025-1031, 1051-1069, 1090-1099 British Midland (BD); 1041-1042 Swissair (SR); 1071-1072 Korean Air (KE); 1075-1078 Iberia (IB); 1080-1081 Air France (AF); 1200-1497 Air Ontario; 1500-1991 AirBC, Ltd. (ZX); 5000-5025 United Air Lines, Inc. (UA); 8101-8197 Air Alliance (3J); 8800-8899 Air Nova Inc. (QK); 8951-8982 Northwest Territorial Airways Ltd. (NV); 9000-9003 Continental Airlines (CO))

    AD   **Lone Star Airlines** ■

    AE   **Mandarin Airlines Ltd.**

    AE★   **Mandarin Airlines Ltd.** (Flight Numbers 067-068 China Airlines (CI); 506 Canadian Airlines International Ltd. (CP); 821-822 Air New Zealand Limited (NZ))

    AF   **Air France**

    AF★   **Air France** (Flight Numbers 048-051 Air Canada (AC); 130-139 Aeromexico-Aerovias de Mexico S.A. de C.V. (AM); 293-294 Japan Airlines (JL); 494-495 Air Seychelles Ltd. (HM); 1053, 1057, 1513, 1536, 1540-1544, 1547-1550, 1552, 1555, 1566 Eurowings Luftverkehrs AG (EW); 2911, 2914, 2916-2917, 2920-2921, 2924-2927, 2930-2938 Sabena Belgian World Airlines (SN))

∞ AG   **Interprovincial Airlines**

    AH   **Air Algerie**

    AI   **Air India**

    AI★   **Air India** (Flight Numbers 967-968 SAS-Scandinavian Airlines Systems (SK); 3001-3002 United Air Lines, Inc. (UA); 3051-3061 Kuwait Airways (KU))

\# AK   **Island Air**

\# AL   **Alsair S.A.**

    AM   **Aeromexico**

    AM★   **Aeromexico** (Flight Numbers 134-135, 4300-4349, 4351-4635 Aeromar Airlines (VW); 1028-1444 America West Airlines, Inc. (HP); 2168-2330, 2333-2446, 2476-2770 Aerolitoral-Servicos Aereos Litoral; 5384-5770 Delta Air Lines, Inc. (DL); 8035-8038 Air France (AF); 9619-9620 Aeroperu (PL))

    AN   **Ansett Australia**

    AN★   **Ansett Australia** (Flight Numbers 6200-6457 Kendell Airlines (KD); 6501-6598, 7800-7815 Skywest Airlines (YT); 6620-6661 Aeropelican Air Services, Pty. Ltd. (PO); 6714-6719, 6803-6808, 6824-6836, 6839-6885, 6887-6888 Tranzair; 7101-7461 Impulse Airlines (VQ); 7501-7588 Hazelton Airlines (ZL); 8311-8312 EVA Airways Corporation (BR); 8820-8833 Malaysia Airlines (MH))

    AO   **Aviaco**

    AP   **Aliadriatica**

    AQ   **Aloha Airlines, Inc.**

    AQ★   **Aloha Airlines, Inc.** (Flight Numbers 1003-1645 Aloha Islandair, Inc. (WP) ■)

Reprinted by special permission from the February 1996 issue of the OAG Desktop Guide-Worldwide Edition. *All rights Reserved. Copyright 1996, Reed Travel Group.*

Airline Codes and Abbreviations, cont.

AR	**Aerolineas Argentinas**
AS	**Alaska Airlines**
AS★	**Alaska Airlines** (Flight Numbers 2001-2903 Horizon Air (QX); 4203-4265 Peninsula Airways, Inc. (KS); 4500-4527 Harbor Airlines, Inc. (HG) ■; 4800-4897 ERA Aviation (7H); 5587-5958 Northwest Airlines, Inc. (NW))
AT	**Royal Air Maroc**
AU	**Austral Lineas Aereas S.A.**
AV	**Avianca**
AY	**Finnair**
AY★	**Finnair** (Flight Numbers 819 Lufthansa German Airlines (LH))
AZ	**Alitalia**
AZ★	**Alitalia** (Flight Numbers 522-535 Malev-Hungarian Airlines (MA); 640-641 Continental Airlines (CO); 650-651 Canadian Airlines International Ltd. (CP); 7021-7025 Gulf Air Company (GF); 7688-7689 Korean Air (KE))
A7	**Air 21, Inc.**
A8	**Aerolineas Paraguayas (ARPA)**
BA	**British Airways**
BA★	**British Airways** (Flight Numbers 025-026 British Asia Airways; 998-999 Qantas Airways Ltd. (QF); 3120-3265 TAT European Airlines (IJ); 3300-3475 DEUTSCHE BA (DI); 7001-7002, 7014, 7121-7128, 7140-7144, 7152, 7185 USAir Express; 7004-7013, 7017-7120, 7130-7132, 7146-7151, 7154-7174, 7189-7500 USAir (US); 7600-7896 Manx Airlines (JE); 8011-8129 Cityflyer Express (FD); 8300-8397 Maersk Air Ltd. (VB); 8700-8825 Loganair Ltd. (LC); 8901-8993 GB Airways Ltd. (GT))
BC	**Air Jet**
BD	**British Midland**
BE	**Centennial Airlines S.A.**
BG	**Biman Bangladesh**
# BH	**Augusta Airways Pty. Ltd.**
BI	**Royal Brunei Airlines**
BL	**Pacific Airlines**
BM	**Air Sicilia**
# BO	**PT Bouraq Indonesia Airlines**
BP	**Air Botswana Pty. Ltd.**
BP★	**Air Botswana Pty. Ltd.** (Flight Numbers 385-386 Air Zimbabwe (UM))
∞ BQ	**Eurobelgian Airlines**
BR	**EVA Airways Corporation**
BR★	**EVA Airways Corporation** (Flight Numbers 235-236 Garuda Indonesia (GA); 301-302 Ansett Australia (AN); 2101-2102 Air Nippon Co. Ltd. (EL))
BT	**Air Baltic Corporation (ABC) (LATSABIA)**
BU	**Braathens S.A.F.E. Airtransport**
# BV	**Sun Air**
BV★	**Sun Air** (Flight Numbers 190-193 Airlink Airline (Pty) Ltd. (5T))
BW	**BWIA International**
# BX	**Coast Air K/S**
# BZ	**Keystone Air Service Ltd.**
B2	**Belavia**
B3	**K.D. Air Corporation**
B4	**Bhoja Airlines (Pvt.) Ltd.**
B6	**Top Air**
B7	**Makung Airlines**
B9	**Carib Air**
CA	**Air China**
CA★	**Air China** (Flight Numbers 121-122 Finnair (AY); 965-966 Austrian Airlines (OS))
∞ CB	**Suckling Airways**
# CE	**Care Airlines**
CF	**Compania de Aviacion Faucett**
∞ CG	**Milne Bay Air Pty. Ltd.**
# CH	**Bemidji Airlines** ■
CI	**China Airlines**
CI★	**China Airlines** (Flight Numbers 924-929 Vietnam Airlines (VN))
# CJ	**China Northern Airlines**
CK	**Gambia Airways**
CM	**Copa**
∞ CN	**Islands Nationair**
CO	**Continental Airlines**
CO★	**Continental Airlines** (Flight Numbers 4-5, 25-35 Transavia Airlines (HV); 40-41 Alitalia; 42-43 Alitalia (AZ); 821-822, 900-996 Continental Micronesia, Inc. (CS); 863-874, 5873 Air Micronesia, Inc.; 2110-2499 GP Express Airlines, Inc. (8G) ■; 7012-7990 America West Airlines, Inc. (HP); 8024-8077, 8120-8125, 8166-8169 Air Canada (AC); 8110, 8131 Air Alliance (3J); 8191-8198 Air Nova, Inc. (QK))
CO★	**Continental Express** (Flight Numbers 2502-3812, 9403-9479 Continental Express)
CP	**Canadian Airlines International Ltd.**
CP★	**Canadian Airlines International Ltd. Canadian Partners** (Flight Numbers 1010-1011, 1014-1015 Varig, S.A. (RG); 1025-1026, 1035-1036, 6080-6083 Qantas Airways Ltd. (QF); 1027-1028, 1037-1048, 6060-6065 Air New Zealand Limited (NZ); 1091-1097 Air St. Pierre; 1100-1386, 1601-1717, 1900-1999 Canadian Regional; 1401-1488 Air Atlantic Ltd.; 1550-1596 Calm Air International Ltd.; 1731-1744 Air Alma, Inc.; 6017-6018 Mandarin Airlines Ltd. (AE); 6020-6031 Lufthansa German Airlines (LH); 6097-6098 Malaysia Airlines (MH); 6100-6105 Brewster Bus; 6181-6220, 6222-6299 American Airlines, Inc. (AA))
# CQ	**Air Alpha, Inc.** ■
CU	**Cubana Airlines**
∞ CV	**Air Chathams**
CW	**Air Marshall Islands**
CX	**Cathay Pacific Airways Ltd.**
CX★	**Cathay Pacific Airways** (Flight Numbers 764-765, 791 Vietnam Airlines (VN))

Airline Codes and Abbreviations, cont.

	CY	Cyprus Airways	D7	Dinar Lineas Aereas S.A.
	CY★	Cyprus Airways, (Flight Numbers 033-034 Gulf Air Company (GF))	D9	Joint Stock Aviation Company Donavia
	CZ	China Southern Airlines	∞ ED	CCAir, Inc. ■
	C2	Air Caribbean Ltd.	# EF	Far Eastern Air Transport Corp.
	C4	Airlines of Carriacou Ltd.	EG	Japan Asia Airways Co. Ltd.
#	C6	Hageland Aviation Services, Inc.	EH	SAETA
	C8	Chicago Express Airlines, Inc. ■	EH★	SAETA (Flight Numbers 800-821, 827-832 SAN-Servicios Aereos Nacionales S.A. (WB))
	C9	Compagnie Aeronautique Europenne	EI	Aer Lingus P.L.C.
	DA	Air Georgia	EI★	Aer Lingus P.L.C. (Flight Numbers 400-401 Hamburg Airlines Luftfahrtgesellschaft (HX); 633-634, 638-639 Sabena Belgian World Airlines (SN))
	DB	Brit Air		
	DC	Golden Air Flyg AB		
	DE	CONDOR Flugdienst GmbH		
	DE★	CONDOR Flugdienst GmbH (Flight Numbers 1422-1423, 1978-1979, 2434-2435, 2718-2719, 3422-3435, 3524-3525, 4422-4435, 4784-4785, 4922-4923, 5726-5727, 5956-5957, 6410-6411, 6466-6467, 6826-6827, 7624-7625, 7728-7729, 7778-7779, 7788-7789, 7978-7979 Germania; 5828-5829, 6454-6455, 6508-6509, 6226-6527, 6632-6633, 6688-6689, 6744-6751, 6806-6807, 6842-6845, 6926-6947, 6972-6973, Lufthansa German Airlines (LH); 7566-7567, 7662-7663, 7878-7879 Lufthansa German Airlines (LH))	EJ	New England Airlines, Inc. ■
			EK	Emirates Airlines
			∞ EL	Air Nippon Co. Ltd.
			EL★	Air Nippon Co. Ltd. (Flight Numbers 2101-2102 EVA Airways Corporation (BR))
			EN	Air Dolomiti S.P.A.
			EO	Express City S.P.R.L.
		# EQ	Tame C.A.
			ES	Helicusco S.A.
			ET	Ethiopian Airlines
			EW	Eurowings Luftverkehrs AG
			∞ EZ	Sun-Air of Scandinavia A/S
	DF	New ACS Ltd.	E2	Everest Air
	DI	DEUTSCHE BA	E3	Domodedovo Airlines
#	DJ	Air Nordic Swe Aviation AB	E4	Aero Asia International (Pvt.) Ltd.
	DK	Eastland Air	E5	Samara Airlines
	DL	Delta Air Lines, Inc.	E6	Elf Air
	DL★	Delta Air Lines, Inc. (Flight Numbers 25-26 Singapore Airlines (SQ); 90-91 Malev-Hungarian Airlines (MA); 100-101, 110-111, 120-121, 2650-2681 Swissair (SR); 501-502, 2780-2789 Austrian Airlines (OS); 541, 548, 2700-2735 Sabena Belgian World Airlines (SN); 814-815, 818-819, 836-837, 855, 865, 2830-2864 Varig, S.A. (RG); 2600-2609 Aeromexico-Aerovias de Mexico S.A. de C.V. (AM); 2635-2636 Korean Air (KE); 2801-2820 Virgin Atlantic Airways Ltd. (VS); 2871-2872 Finnair (AY); 2896-2899 TAP Air Portugal (TP))	E7	Downeast Express ■
			# FA	Finnaviation
			FC	Berliner Spezial Flug
			FE	Eagle Canyon Airlines, Inc.
			FF	Tower Air, Inc.
			FI	Icelandair
			FJ	Air Pacific Ltd.
			FJ★	Air Pacific Ltd. (Flight Numbers 500-501 Solomon Airlines (IE))
			FK	Flamenco Airways, Inc. ■
			FL	AirTran Airways
	DL★	Delta Connection (Flight Numbers 3000-3904 Comair, Inc. (OH); 4301-4974 Business Express (HQ) ■; 5203-5212 Scenic Airlines, Inc. (YR) ■; 5215-5990 Skywest Airlines (OO); 7000-7998 Atlantic Southeast Airlines, Inc. (EV) ■)	# FN	F.S. Air Service, Inc.
			FQ	Air Aruba
			FQ★	Air Aruba (Flight Numbers 090-091 Avianca (AV); 504-511 Sociedad Aeronautica Medellin (MM))
			FR	Ryanair
	DM	Maersk Air	∞ FS	Missionary Aviation Fellowship
	DP	Air 2000 Ltd.	FT	Vancouver Island Air Ltd.
#	DQ	Coastal Air Transport ■	FU	Air Littoral
	DS	Air Senegal	FV	Viva Air
	DT	TAAG-Angola Airlines	FW	Isles of Scilly Skybus Ltd.
	DU	Hemus Air	FY	FFD Flugdienst Friedrichshafen GMBH
	DY	Alyemen-Airlines of Yemen	# FZ	Air Facilities
	D2	Damania Airways Ltd.	F3	Flying Enterprise AB
	D3	Daallo Airlines	F5	Archana Airways
	D5	NEPC Airlines	F9	Frontier Airlines, Inc.
	D6	Inter Air	GA	Garuda Indonesia

Airline Codes and Abbreviations, cont.

GA★	Garuda Indonesia (Flight Numbers 625-628 Korean Air (KE); 1930-1931 EVA Airways Corporation (BR))	HV	Transavia Airlines
∞ GB	Great Barrier Airlines Ltd.	HW	North-Wright Air Ltd.
∞ GC	Lina-Congo	HX	Hamburg Airlines Luftfahrtgesellschaft mbH
GD	TAESA-Transportes Aereos Ejecutivos S.A. de C.V.	HY	Uzbekistan Airways
GD★	TAESA-Transportes Aereos Ejecutivos S.A. de C.V. (Flight Numbers 611-612 Aviacion Del Noreste S.A. de C .V. (OC))	HY★	Uzbekistan Airways (Flight Numbers 901-952 European Airways Ltd. (L8))
		HZ	Euroflight Sweden AB
GE	TransAsia Airways	H2	SA Heli Inter Riviera Helicopters
GF	Gulf Air Company	H3	Harbour Air Ltd.
GF★	Gulf Air Company (Flight Numbers 1854-1857 Air Malta Company Ltd-Air Malta (KM))	H4	Hainan Airlines
		H5	Magadan Airlines
# GG	Tamair	IB	Iberia
GH	Ghana Airways	IB★	Iberia (Flight Numbers 6122-6123 Carnival Air Lines (KW); 6840-6853 Aerolineas Argentinas (AR); 7454-7464; 7550-7561 SAS-Scandinavian Airlines System (SK); 7500-7519 British Midland (BD); 7576-7577 Austrian Airlines (OS); 7995-7996 Ukraine International Airlines (PS))
GI	Air Guinee		
GJ	Air Sao Tome e Principe		
GK	Go One Airways		
# GL	Greenlandair, Inc.	IC	Indian Airlines
GN	Air Gagon	∞ ID	Air Normandie
GN★	Air Gabon (Flight Numbers 132-133 Air France (AF))	IE	Solomon Airlines
		IE★	Solomon Airlines (Flight Numbers 702-703 Air Nauru (ON); 706-707 Air Niugini (PX))
# GO	Air Stord A/S		
# GP	China General Aviation Corp.	IF	Great China Airlines
GQ	Big Sky Airlines	IG	Meridiana
GR	Aurigny Air Services Ltd.	∞ II	Business Air Ltd.
GU	Aviateca S.A.	II★	Business Air Ltd. (Flight Numbers 551-556 Air Kilroe)
GU★	Aviateca S.A. (Flight Numbers 110-111 TACA International Airlines, S.A. (TA); 690-691 LACSA (LR))		
		IJ	TAT European Airlines
		IK	Loken Aviation, Inc. ■
GV	Riga Airlines-Express	IM	Carib Express
GY	Guyana Airways	IN	MAT-Macedonian Airlines
# GZ	Air Rarotonga	# IP	Airlines of Tasmania
G4	Guizhou Airlines	IQ	Interot Airways
G5	Island Air Ltd.	IR	Iran Air
G7	Guinee Airlines	IT	Air Inter
G8	Air Great Wall	IT★	Air Inter (Flight Numbers 391-392, 491-492, 591, 691-692, 891-892, 7391-7392, 7491-7492, 7591-7592, 7691-7692, 7891-7892 Crossair A.G. (LX); 4308 Tunis Air (TU); 5095-5906, 5195-5198, 6095-6096, 6195-6198 Brit Air (DB); 5097-5098, 6098 Air Littoral (FU); 5497-5498, 5694, 6197, 6497, 6693 Regional Airlines (VM))
G9	Grant Aviation, Inc.		
HA	Hawaiian Airlines		
HC	Naske-Air		
HD	New York Helicopter Corporation ■		
HE	LGW Luftfahrtgesellschaft Walter mbH		
HI	Papillon Airways, Inc. ■		
∞ HJ	Holmstroem Flyg AB	IU	Air Straubing
∞ HK	Swan Airlines	IV	Fujian Airlines
HM	Air Seychelles Ltd.	IW	AOM French Airlines
HM★	Air Seychelles Ltd. (Flight Numbers 010-011 Air France (AF))	# IX	Flandre Air Airline
		IY	Yemenia Yemen Airways
HO	Airways International, Inc. ■	IZ	Arkia Israeli Airlines Ltd.
HP	America West Airlines, Inc.	JB	Helijet Airways
HP★	America West Airlines, Inc. (Flight Numbers 8265-8998 Continental Airlines (CO))	# JD	Japan Air System
		JE	Manx Airlines
HP★	America West Express (Flight Numbers 5000-5410 Mesa Airlines (YV) ■)	# JF	L.A.B. Flying Service, Inc.
		∞ JH	Nordeste-Linhas Aereas Regionals S.A.
HR	China United Airlines	JI	Midway Airlines
HS	Highland Air AB	JI★	Midway Airlines (Flight Numbers 1501-1559 Great Lakes Aviation)
# HT	Air Tchad		

Airline Codes and Abbreviations, cont.

# JJ	Brasil Central Linha Aerea Regional S.A.
JK	Spanair S.A.
JL	Japan Airlines
JL★	Japan Airlines (Flight Numbers 411-414 KLM-Royal Dutch Airlines (KL); 435-436 Air France (AF))
JM	Air Jamaica Ltd.
JM★	Air Jamaica Ltd. (Flight Numbers 982-985 Air Canada (AC))
NJ	Rich International Airways
JP	Adria Airways
JQ	Trans-Jamaican Airlines Ltd.
JR	Aero California
JS	Air Koryo
JU	Yugoslav Airlines (JAT)
JV	Bearskin Airlines
JY	Jersey European Airways Ltd.
# JZ	Skyways AB
J2	Azerbaijan Hava Yollary
J5	Aviaprima-Sochi Airlines
J7	Valujet Airlines
J8	Berjaya Air
KA	Dragonair-Hong Kong Dragon Airlines Ltd.
KB	Druk-Air
KC	Kiwi Travel International Airlines
# KD	Kendell Airlines
KE	Korean Air
KE★	Korean Air (Flight Numbers 952-953 Garuda Indonesia (GA))
KF	OY Air Botnia AB
KG	King Island Airlines
# KH	Kyrnair
# KI	Air Atlantique
KJ	British Mediterranean Airways
KK	Transportes Aereo Regionais S.A. (T.A.M.)
KK★	Transportes Aereo Regionais S.A. (T.A.M.) (Flight Numbers 002-063 ■)
KL	KLM-Royal Dutch Airlines
KL★	KLM-Royal Dutch Airlines (Flight Numbers 001-047, 050-062, 070-074, 079-098, 151-154, 176-181, 317-318, 381-388, 401-402, 407-490 KLM Cityhopper; 246, 257, 263, Austrian Airlines (OS); 531-532, 537-538 Cyprus Airways (CY); 720-729 Air Exel Netherlands b.v. (XT); 2002-2085 Eurowings Luftverkehrs AG (EW); 2150-2845 Air UK (UK); 8036-8056 Northwest Airlines, Inc. (NW))
KM	Air Malta Company Ltd-Air Malta
KM★	Air Malta Company Ltd-Air Malta (Flight Numbers 603-604 Balkan-Bulgarian Airlines (LZ); 900-911 Malta Air Charter (R5))
KP	KIWI International Air Lines, Inc.
KQ	Kenya Airways
KQ★	Kenya Airways (Flight Numbers 292-293 Swissair (SR))
∞ KR	Kar-Air
KS	Peninsula Airways, Inc.
# KT	Turtle Airways Ltd.
KU	Kuwait Airways
KV	Transkei Airways Corporation
KW	Carnival Air Lines
KX	Cayman Airways Ltd.
K2	Kyrghyzstan Airlines
K4	Kazakhstan Airlines
K7	Yakutaviatrans
K9	Skyward Aviation Ltd.
LA	Lan Chile S.A.
LB	Lloyd Aereo Boliviano
∞ LD	Lineas Aereas del Estado (LADE)
LF	JetTrain Corporation
LG	Luxair
LG★	Luxair (Flight Numbers 133-134 Conseta-Cirrus)
LH	Lufthansa German Airlines
LH★	Lufthansa German Airlines (Flight Numbers 1050-1080 Deutsche Bahn Rail (2A); 1130, 1143, 1308, 1311, 1624-1643, 1648-1649, 1723-1728, 4375, 4384, 6070-6149 Lufthansa CityLine GmbH (CL); 1507-1545, 6000-6058 Cimber Air (QI); 1646-1647, 1651-1660, 6160-6171 Eurowings Luftverkehrs AG (EW); 6200-6273, 6868-6869 Lauda Air (NG); 6290-6297 Aliadriatica (JP); 6301-6304 Luxair-Luxembourg Airlines (LG); 6350-6357 Business Air Ltd. (II); 6400-6562 United Air Lines, Inc. (UA); 6680-6685 Varig, S.A. (RG); 6744-6745 Thai Airways International Ltd. (TG); 6800-6806 Finnair (AY); 6816-6817 LOT Polish Airlines (LO); 6820-6849 Air Dolomiti S.P.A. (EN); 6850-6857 Canadian Airlines International Ltd. (CP))
LI	Liat (1974) Ltd.
LJ	Sierra National Airlines
LM	ALM-Antillean Airlines
LO	LOT-Polish Airlines
LO★	LOT-Polish Airlines (Flight Numbers 221-222, 229-230 Austrian Airlines (OS); 297-298 Swissair (SR))
LP	Euro City Line
LR	LACSA
LR★	LACSA (Flight Numbers 730-731 TACA International Airlines S.A. (TA); 970-971 Aviateca S.A. (GU); 1610-1651 SAN-Servicios Aereos Nacionales S.A. (WB))
∞ LS	Iliamna Air Taxi, Inc.
LT	LTU International Airways
LV	Albanian Airlines Mak S.H.P.K.
LW	Air Nevada
LX	Crossair A.G.
LX★	Crossair A.G. (Flight Numbers 721-726 Regional Airlines (VM))
LY	El Al Israel Airlines Ltd.
LZ	Balkan-Bulgarian Airlines
L2	Love Air
L2★	Love Air (Flight Numbers 901-926 Montserrat Airways)

Airline Codes and Abbreviations, cont.

	L3	Kaiken Linea Aereas	NK	Spirit Airlines
	L5	A.S. Luftransport	NL	Shaheen Air International
	L6	Air Maldives	NN	Cardinal Airlines Ltd.
	L9	Air Mali S.A.	NO	Aus Air Pty. Ltd.
	MA	Malev-Hungarian Airlines	# NP	Piccolo Airlines
	MA★	Malev-Hungarian Airlines (Flight Numbers 801-810 Austrian Airlines (OS); 822-823 Czechoslovak Airlines (OK))	NQ	Orbi Georgian Airways
			NR	Norontair
			NS	Cape York Air Services
#	MB	Western Airlines	# NU	Japan Transocean Air
	MD	Air Madagascar	NV	Northwest Territorial Airways Ltd.
	ME	Middle East Airlines	NV★	Northwest Territorial Airways Ltd. (Flight Numbers 168-172 Buffalo Airways; 200-209 Air Tindi; 503-519 Northwestern Air Lease (3E))
#	MF	Xiamen Airlines		
	MH	Malaysia Airlines		
	MH★	Malaysia Airlines (Flight Numbers 122-123, 9001-9045, 9069-9128 Ansett Australia (AN); 9052-9057 Ansett New Zealand (ZQ); 9271-9347 British Midland (BD))	NW	Northwest Airlines, Inc.
			NW★	Northwest Airlines, Inc. (Flight Numbers 2030-2762 Horizon Air (QX); 3800-3809 Pacific Island Aviation, Inc. (9J); 3901-3952 Asiana Airlines (OZ); 4748 Trans States Airlines, Inc. (9N); 6980-6985 Business Express (HQ) ■; 7085-7567 Alaska Airlines (AS); 8601-8665 KLM-Royal Dutch Airlines (KL))
	MI	SilkAir		
	MJ	Lineas Aereas Privadas Argentinas S.A. (LAPA)		
	MK	Air Mauritius		
	MK★	Air Mauritius (Flight Numbers 534-535 Air Austral (UU))		
			NW★	Northwest Airlink (Flight Numbers 3001-3499 Mesaba Aviation (XJ) ■; 5101-5898 Express Airlines I, Inc. (9E) ■)
	ML	Aero Costa Rica Acori S.A.		
#	MM	Sociedad Aeronautica de Medellin S.A.		
#	MN	Commercial Airways (Pty.) Ltd. (COMAIR)	NX	Air Macau Company Ltd.
	MP	Martinair Holland	NY	Norlandair (Iceland)
	MQ	Simmons Airlines	NZ	Air New Zealand Ltd.
	MR	Air Mauritanie	NZ★	Air New Zealand Ltd. (Flight Numbers 312-315 Polynesian Airlines, Ltd. (PH); 321-334 Canadian Airlines International Ltd. (CP); 340-343 Air Pacific Ltd. (FJ); 354-368 Qantas Airways Ltd. (QF); 373-378 Korean Air (KE); 2000-5995, 8040-8902 Air New Zealand Link)
	MS	Egyptair		
	MU	China Eastern Airlines		
	MV	Great American Airways		
	MW	Maya Airways		
	MX	Mexicana de Aviacion		
	MX★	Mexicana de Aviacion (Flight Numbers 1500-1501 Avensa (VE); 4300-4635 Aeromar Airines (VW); 7100-7933 Aero Caribe (QA); 8121-8739 Services Aer Litoral)	N2	Aerolineas Internacionales S.A. de C.V.
			N4	National Airlines Chile S.A.
			N5	Nations Air Express
			N6	Aero Continente
	MZ	Merpati Nusantara Airlines	N7	Nordic East Airways
	M8	Moscow Airways	N9	North Coast Aviation Pty. Ltd.
	M9	ModiLuft	OA	Olympic Airways
	NC	National Jet Systems Pty. Ltd.	OA★	Olympic Airways (Flight Numbers 8750-8751 VASP (VP))
	ND	Airlink Pty. Ltd.		
#	NE	Knight Air	OC	Aviacion del Noreste S.A. de C.V.
	NF	Air Vanuatu (Operations) Ltd.	OD	Zuliana de Aviacion C.A.
	NF★	Air Vanuatu (Operations) Ltd. (Flight Numbers 210-211 Air Pacific Ltd. (FJ); 500-521, 523-585 Vanair (V3); 704-711 Solomon Airlines (IE))	OF	Travaux Aeriens de Madagascar
			OI	Prestige Airways
			OJ	Air St. Barthelemy
			OK	Czech Airlines
	NG	Lauda Air	OK★	Czech Airlines (Flight Numbers 022-029 Air Ostrava (8K); 472-473 Luxair-Luxembourg Airlines (LG); 554-557 Lufthansa German Airlines (LH); 608-615 Tyrolean Airways (VO); 618-619 KLM-Royal Dutch Airlines (KL); 780-783 LOT Polish Airlines (LO); 786-787 Malev-Hungarian Airlines (MA))
	NH	All Nippon Airways Co. Ltd.		
	NH★	All Nippon Airways Co. Ltd. (Flight Numbers 555-556, 6555-6556 Austrian Airlines (OS))		
	NI	Portugalia-Companhia Portuguesa de Transportes Aereos SA		
	NI★	Portugalia-Companhia Portuguesa de Transportes Aereos SA (Flight Numbers 200 TAP Air Portugal (TP))		
			OL	OLT-Ostfriesische Lufttransport GmbH
	NJ	Vanguard Airlines	OM	MIAT-Mongolian Airlines

Airline Codes and Abbreviations, cont.

	ON	Air Nauru	P6	Trans Air
#	OP	Chalk's International Airlines ■	P7	East Line Aviation
	OR	Air Comores	P8	Pantanal Linhas Aereas Sul-Matogrossenses S/A
	OS	Austrian Airlines		
	OS★	Austrian Airlines (Flight Numbers 28-29, 33, 36, 37, 38 Crossair A.G. (LX); 33, 36, 37, 38-96, 153, 156, 286-287, 629-630, 639, 642-647, 650, Tyrolean Airways (VO); 801-810, 827-836, 847-848 Tyrolean Airways (VO); 251-252, 255-256 Iberia (IB); 482 KLM-Royal Dutch Airlines (KL); 488, 491-492, 495-496, 499 Sabena Belgian World Airlines (SN); 527-528 Swissair (SR); 539-540 Air Mauritius (MK); 623-628, 631-632 LOT Polish Airlines (LO); 640-641, 648-649 Czechoslovak Airlines (OK); 683-686 Finnair (AY))	QD	Grand Airways, Inc. ■
			QE	Air Moorea
			QF	Qantas Airways Ltd.
			QF★	Qantas Airways Ltd. (Flight Numbers 3-4; 309-310 Canadian Airlines International Ltd. (CP); 110-111, 150-151, 197-198 Air Caledonie International (SB); 135-138 Australia Asia Airlines; 270, 275-279 Air Vanuatu (Operations) Ltd. (NF); 271-272 Solomon Airlines (IE); 281-285 Air Niugini (PX); 289-298 Air Pacific Ltd. (FJ); 301-308, 323-324, 329-332, 341-344 American Airlines, Inc. (AA); 311-319, 326-328 USAir (US); 333-338, 345-358 Air New Zealand Ltd. (NZ); 570-599, 700-819 Eastern Australia Airlines; 650-689, 920-953 Australian Airlink; 690-698, 963-995 Southern Australia; 820-919 Sunstate Airlines)
	OT	Evergreen Alaska		
	OU	Croatia Airlines		
	OV	Estonian Air		
#	OW	Metavia Airlines (Pty.) Ltd.		
∞	OX	Orient Express Air		
	OZ	Asiana Airlines		
	PA	Pan Air Lineas Aereas S.A.	QH	Qwestair
	PB	Air Burundi	QI	Cimber Air
	PC	Air Fiji	QL	Lesotho Airways Corporation
	PD	Pem Air Ltd.	QM	Air Malawi
	PE	Pine State Airlines ■	QM★	Air Malawi (Flight Numbers 392-393 Air Zimbabwe (UM))
	PG	Bangkok Airways		
	PH	Polynesian Airlines Ltd.	QP	Airkenya Aviation Ltd.
	PH★	Polynesia Airlines Ltd. (Flight Numbers 356-357 Air New Zealand Ltd. (NZ); 565-566 Air Pacific Ltd. (FJ))	QQ	Reno Air, Inc.
#			QR	Air Satellite, Inc.
			QS	Tatra Air
	PI	Sunflower Airlines Ltd.	∞ QT	S.A.R. Avlons Taxis
	PK	Pakistan International	QU	Uganda Airlines
	PL	Aeroperu	QV	Lao Aviation
	PM	Tropic Air	QW	Turks and Caicos Airways Ltd.
	PN	S.N.A.M. (Societe Nouvelle Air Martinique)	Q4	Mustique Airways
#	PO	Aeropelican Air Services Pty. Ltd.	Q7	Qatar Airways
	PQ	Skipper Aviation Pty. Ltd.	Q9	Interbrasil Star S.A.
	PR	Philippine Airlines, Inc.	RA	Royal Nepal Airlines Corporation
	PR★	Philippine Airlines, Inc. (Flight Numbers 933-934 Vietnam Airlines (VN))	RB	Syrian Arab Airlines
			RC	Atlantic Airways Faroe Islands
	PS	Ukraine International Airlines	RD	Avianova
	PS★	Ukraine International Airlines (Flight Numbers 470-471 Swissair (SR); 615-620, 845-846 Austrian Airlines (OS); 995-996 Iberia (IB))	# RE	Aer Arann
			RG	Varig S.A.
			RG★	Varig S.A. (Flight Numbers 296-297 Transbrasil S/A Linhas Aereas (TR); 704-705, 776-789 TAP Air Portugal (TP); 770-773 Lufthansa German Airlines (LH); 876-877 LACSA (LR))
	PT	West Air Sweden AB		
	PU	Pluna		
	PW	Challeng'Air		
	PX	Air Niugini	RH	SAL Luftverkehrsgesellschaft
	PX★	Air Niugini (Flight Numbers 4393 Singapore Airlines (SQ))	∞ RI	P.T. Mandala Airlines
			RJ	Royal Jordanian
	PY	Surinam Airways Ltd.	RK	Air Afrique
	PY★	Surinam Airways Ltd. (Flight Numbers 4977-4978 ALM-Antillean Airlines (LM))	RL	Region Air (Caribbean) Ltd.
			RN	Euralair International
	PZ	LAPSA-Lineas Aereas Paraguayas S.A.	RO	Tarom-Romanian Air Transport
	P3	Promech, Inc.	RQ	Air Engiadina
	P5	AeroRepublica	RR	Royal Air Force-38 Transport Group

Airline Codes and Abbreviations, cont.

# RS	Intercontinental de Aviacion	
RT	Lincoln Airlines Pty. Ltd.	
RV	Reeve Aleutian Airways, Inc.	
RW	Rheinland Air Service GmbH	
RY	Air Rwanda	
R3	Armenian Airlines	
R7	Aeroservicios Carabobo C.A. (ASERCA)	
SA	South African Airways	
SA★	South African Airways (Flight Numbers 158-159 Emirates Airlines (EK); 1002-1399, 1602-1704 SA Express; 1501-1531 Zambian Express Airways (1995) Ltd. OQ))	
SB	Air Caledonie International	
SB★	Air Caledonie International (Flight Numbers 112-113, 154-155, Qantas Airways Ltd. (QF))	
SC	Shandong Airlines	
SD	Sudan Airways	
∞ SE	Wings of Alaska	
# SF	Shanghai Airlines	
SG	Sempati Air	
SH	Air Toulouse International	
SK	SAS-Scandinavian Airline	
SK★	SAS-Scandinavian Airline (Flight Numbers 3501-3536 British Midland (BD); 3581-3582 Spanair S.A. (JK); 3851-3866 Icelandair-Flugleidir (FI); 3953-3958 Varig, S.A. (RG))	
SL	Rio-Sul-Servicos Aereos Regionais	
SL★	Rio-Sul-Servicos Aereos Regionais (Flight Numbers 532-533 TABA-Transportes Aereos Reg. da Bacia (T2))	
SN	Sabena Belgian World Airlines	
SN★	Sabena Belgian World Airlines (Flight Numbers 124-125 Delta Air Lines, Inc. (DL); 341-342, 345-346, 349-350 Austrian Airlines (OS); 630-632, 635-637 Aer Lingus P.L.C. (EI); 793-798 Maersk Air (DM); 912, 915, 918-919, 922-923, 928-929 Air France (AF); 9351-9364 Swissair (SR))	
SO	Sunshine Airlines ■	
SP	SATA Air Acores	
SQ	Singapore Airlines	
SR	Swissair	
SR★	Swissair (Flight Numbers 22-24, 31, 116-117, 496-497, 4117 Austrian Airlines (OS); 28-29, 33, 36, 37, 38, 414-415, 891, 896, 3314-3971, 6406-6973 Crossair A.G. (LX); 33, 36, 37, 38-96 Tyrolean Airways (VO); 122-123 Delta Air Lines, Inc. (DL); 136-137 Air Canada (AC); 144-145 LADECO Airlines (UC); 9369-9382 Sabena Belgian World Airlines (SN))	
# SS	Shabair	
ST	Yanda Airlines	
SU	Aeroflot-Russian International Airlines	
SU★	Aeroflot-Russian International Airlines (Flight Numbers 007W-008W, 051W-054W, 091W, 092W-096W, 2211-2212, 651W-652W Domodedovo Airlines (E3); 1171-1196, 6111-6112 Joint Stock Aviation Company Donavia (D9); 147W-150W, 8485-8486 Krasnoyarsk Airlines (7B); 4105-4106 Magadan Airlines (H5))	
SV	Saudi Arabian Airlines	
SW	Air Namibia	
SX	Aeroejecutivo S.A. de C.V.	
SY	Sun Country Airlines, Inc.	
# SZ	China Southwest Airlines	
S2	Sahara India Airlines	
S5	Virginia Islands Airways Ltd.	
S6	Air Saint Martin	
S7	Siberia Airlines	
S8	Estonian Aviation Company ELK	
TA	TACA International	
TC	Air Tanzania Corporation	
TE	Lithuanian Airlines	
# TF	Air Transport Pyrenees	
TG	Thai Airways International Ltd.	
TG★	Thai Airways International Ltd. (Flight Numbers 7920-7952 Lufthansa German Airlines (LH))	
TK	Turk Hava Yollari	
∞ TL	Airnorth Regional	
TM	LAM-Linhas Aereas de Mocambique	
TM★	LAM-Linhas Aereas de Mocambique (Flight Numbers 708-709 TAP Air Portugal (TP))	
∞ TO	Alkan Air Ltd.	
TP	TAP Air Portugal	
TP★	TAP Air Portugal (Flight Numbers 226-227 LAM-Linhas Aereas de Mocambique (TM); 331-349 Varig, S.A. (RG); 801-851 Portugalia (NI); 862-895 Aerocondor)	
TQ	Transwede Airways AB	
TQ★	Transwede Airways AB (Flight Numbers 031-036 Finnair (AY))	
TR	Transbrasil S/A Linhas Aereas	
TR★	Transbrasil S/A Linhas Aereas (Flight Numbers 420-421 Varig, S.A. (RG))	
# TS	Samoa Air ■	
∞ TT	Air Lithuania	
TU	Tunis Air	
TV	Sierra Expressway ■	
TW	Trans World Airlines, Inc.	
TW★	Trans World Express (Flight Numbers 7001-7797 Trans State Airlines, Inc.)	
TX	Societe Nouvelle Air Guadeloupe	
∞ TY	Air Caledonie	
TZ	American Trans Air	
T2	TABA-Transportes Aereos Regionais de Bacia Amazonica S.A.	
T3	Tri Star Airlines, Inc.	
T4	Transeast Airlines	
T8	Transportes Aereos Neuquen Del Estado	
UA	United Airlines	
UA★	United Airlines (Flight Numbers 1932-1933 Emirates Airlines (EK); 3000-3207 Air Canada (AC); 3375-3495, 4153-4199 Gulfstream International Airlines, Inc. (3M) ■; 3500-3825	

Airline Codes and Abbreviations, cont.

	Lufthansa German Airlines (LH); 4033-4117, 4206-4288 Aloha Airlines Inc. (AQ); 4500-4515 Cayman Airways Ltd. (KX); 4571-4578 ALM-Antillean Airlines (LM); 4600-4648 Aeromar Airlines (VW); 4654-4797 Trans States Airlines, Inc. (9N); 4810-4849 British Midland (BD); 4903-4968 Ansett Australia (AN); 4970-4992 Ansett New Zealand; 8500-8515 Serendipity Bus)
UZ★	**United Express** (Flight Numbers 5002-5116, 5700-5763 United Express/UFS; 5256-5608 United Express/Air Wisconsin Airlines Corp; 5800-6145 United Express/Great Lakes; 6150-6599 United Express/Atlantic Coast Airlines; 6600-7394 Westair Airlines; 7450-7999 Mesa Airlines ■; 8400 Colorado Mountain Express)
UB	**Myanmar Airways International**
UC	**LADECO Airlines**
∞ UD	**Hex'Air**
UG	**Tuninter**
# UH	**Corporate Airlines Canberra**
# UJ	**Aerosanta Airlines**
UK	**Air UK**
UL	**Air Lanka Ltd.**
UL★	**Air Lanka Ltd.** (Flight Numbers 194-195 Royal Jordanian (RJ))
UM	**Air Zimbabwe**
UM★	**Air Zimbabwe** (Flight Numbers 023-064 Qantas Airways Ltd. (QF); 392-393 Air Malawi (QM); 601-624 United Air Charter)
UP	**Bahamasair**
UQ	**O'Connor-Mt. Gambiers Airline**
UR	**British International Helicopters**
US	**USAir**
US★	**USAir Express** (Flight Numbers 3001-5998 USAir Express ■)
US★	**USAir Shuttle, Inc.** (Flight Numbers 6001-6541 USAir Shuttle, Inc.)
UU	**Air Austral**
# UV	**Air Kangaroo Island**
# UW	**Perimeter Airlines (Inland) Ltd.**
UX	**Air Europa**
UY	**Cameroon Airlines**
UZ	**UP Air**
U5	**International Business Air**
VA	**Viasa**
VC	**Servivensa**
VD	**Air Liberte**
VE	**Avensa**
VG	**VLM Viaamse Luchttransportmaatschappij**
VH	**Air Burkina**
∞ VI	**Vieques Air Link, Inc.** ■
VJ	**Royal Air Cambodge**
∞ VK	**Air Tungaru Corporation**
# VL	**North Vancouver Air**
VM	**Regional Airlines**
VN	**Vietnam Airlines**
VN★	**Vietnam Airlines** (Flight Numbers 591-592

	Philippine Airlines, Inc. (PR); 766-769 Cathay Pacific Airways Ltd. (CX))
VO	**Tyrolean Airways**
VP	**VASP**
# VQ	**Impulse Airlines**
VR	**TACV-Cabo Verde Airlines**
VS	**Virgin Atlantic Airways Ltd.**
VS★	**Virgin Atlantic Airways Ltd.** (Flight Numbers 011-012 Midwest Express Airlines, Inc. (YX); 501-504 Malaysia Airlines (MH); 3200-3320 City Jet (WX); 4001-4417 British Midland (BD))
VT	**Air Tahiti**
VT★	**Air Tahiti** (Flight Numbers 010-091, 645, 845, 1015-1815 Air Moorea (QE))
VU	**Air Ivoire**
VV	**Aerosweet Airlines**
VW	**Aeromar Airlines**
VX	**ACES**
V2	**Associated Airlines Ltd.**
V4	**Venus Airlines**
V4★	**Venus Airlines** (Flight Numbers 700-761 Skybus)
V5	**Vnukovo Airlines**
V7	**Confortair, Inc.**
V9	**Bashkir Airlines**
WA	**Newair**
# WB	**SAN-Servicios Aereos Nacionales S.A.**
WC	**Islena Airlines**
WD	**Halisa Air**
∞ WE	**RHEINTALFLUG Seewald Gesellschaft mbH**
WF	**Wideroe's Flyveselskap**
WG	**Taiwan Airlines Company Ltd.**
WH	**China Northwest Airlines**
∞ WI	**Rottnest Airlines**
WJ	**Labrador Airways Ltd.**
WK	**Southern Air Ltd.**
# WL	**Aeroperlas**
WM	**Windward Island Airways International N.V.**
WN	**Southwest Airlines**
WO	**World Airways**
WP	**Aloha Islandair, Inc.** ■
WR	**Royal Tongan Airlines**
WR★	**Royal Tongan Airlines** (Flight Numbers 300-305 Air Pacific Ltd. (FJ); 351-359 Air New Zealand Ltd. (NZ))
WS	**Air Caraibes Exploitations**
WT	**Nigeria Airways Ltd.**
WU	**Wuhan Airlines**
WV	**Air South, Inc.**
# WW	**Whyalla Airlines Pty. Ltd.**
WY	**Oman Aviation**
W3	**Swiftair S.A.**
W5	**Tajikistan International Airlines**
W7	**Western Pacific Airlines, Inc.**
W8	**La Costena S.A.**
W9	**Eastwind Airlines, Inc.**
XF	**Vladivostok Air**
XK	**Compagnie Corse Mediterranee**

Airline Codes and Abbreviations, cont.

#	XL	Country Connection Airlines Pty. Ltd.		Z2	Zhong Yuan Airlines
#	XO	Xinjiang Airlines		Z7	Zimbabwe Express Airlines
	XP	Casino Express Airlines		Z9	Aero Zambia
#	XQ	Action Airlines ■		2F	Frontier Flying Service
	XT	Air Exel Netherlands b.v.		2L	Karlog Air
	XU	Link Airways		2M	Moldavian Airlines
	XV	Air Express I Norrkoping AB		2P	Air Saravi
#	XW	Walker's International ■		2S	Island Express ■
	XY	Ryan Air, Inc.		2U	Western Pacific Air Services
	XZ	Flugfelag Austurlands H.F.		2W	Wairarapa Airlines Ltd.
	X2	China Xinhua Airlines		2Y	Helenair Corporation Ltd.
	X4	Haiti Trans Air S.A.		2Z	Chang-An Airlines
	YC	Flight West Airlines		3C	Camai Air
	YH	Air Baffin Ltd.		3D	Palair Macedonian
#	YI	Air Sunshine Inc. ◀■		3E	Northwestern Air Lease
	YJ	National Airlines (Pty.) Ltd.		3J	Air Alliance
	YK	Cyprus Turkish Airlines Ltd. Co.		3J★	Air Alliance (Flight Numbers 205-226 Aviation Quebec Lab; 721-722 Air Shefferville)
	YL	Long Island Airlines ■			
	YN	Air Creebec (1994), Inc.		3K	Tatonduk Flying Service
	YO	Heli-Air-Monaco		3M	Gulfstream International Airlines, Inc. ■
	YP	Aero Lloyd		3P	Equator Airlines Ltd.
	YQ	Helikopterservice AB, Euro Air		3Q	Yunnan Airlines
	YR	Scenic Airlines, Inc. ◀■		3R	Air Moldova International S.A.
	YS	Proteus		3S	Shuswap Air
	YT	Skywest Airlines		3T	Contact Air
#	YU	Aerolineas Dominicans S.A.-Dominair		3U	Sichuan Airlines
	YV	Mesa Airlines ■		3W	Nanjing Airlines
	YW	Air Nostrum	#	3X	Japan Air Commuter Co. Ltd.
	YX	Midwest Express Airlines, Inc.		3Z	Necon Air Ltd.
	YX★	Midwest Express Connection/Skyway Airlines (Flight Numbers 1000-1978 Skyway Airlines)		4A	Thunderbird
				4B	Olson Air Service, Inc.
	YZ	Transportes Aereos de Guine-Bissau		4C	Aires
	Y2	Alliance Airlines		4D	Air Sinai
	Y5	Arax Airways		4E	Tanana Air Service
	ZB	Monarch Airlines		4G	Shenzhen Airlines
	ZC	Royal Swazi National Airways Corporation		4H	Hanna's Air Saltspring
	ZE	Arcus Air Logistic		4J	Transaero Airlines
	ZF	Airborne of Sweden AB		4K	Kenn Borek Air Ltd.
	ZG	Sabair Airlines Pty. Ltd.		4M	Island Air
	ZH	Air Truk (Lineas Aereas Navarras)		4N	Air North
	ZI	Aigle Azur		4R	Spurwing Air
#	ZJ	Teddy Air A/S		4S	East West Airlines
	ZK	Great Lakes Aviation Ltd.		4U	Dorado Air S.A.
	ZK★	Great Lakes Aviation Ltd. (Flight Numbers 5201, 5203-5206, 5209-5214, 5222-5311 Arizona Air Express/Great Lakes ■)		4V	Voyageur Airways
				4W	Warbelow's Air Ventures, Inc.
				4X	Fairlines
∞	ZL	Hazelton Airlines		4Y	Yute Air Alaska, Inc.
	ZM	Scibe-Airlift		5A	Alpine Aviation, Inc. ■
	ZN	Eagle Airlines		5B	Bellair, Inc.
	ZO	Southflight Aviation Ltd.		5C	Conquest Airlines Corporation ■
	ZP	Air St. Thomas ■		5E	BASE Regional Airlines
	ZQ	Ansett New Zealand		5F	Arctic Circle Air
	ZR	Muk Air		5G	Kieler Business Air
	ZT	Satena		5H	Odinair
∞	ZU	Freedom Air ■		5J	Cebu Pacific Air
	ZX	AirBC Ltd.		5K	Kenmore Air ■
	ZY	ADA Air		5L	AeroSur

Airline Codes and Abbreviations, cont.

	5M	Joint Stock Company Siat (SIBAVIATRANS)	8R	Avia Air NV
	5N	Aerotour Dominicano Airlines	8T	Travelair
	5P	Ptarmigan Airways Ltd.	8U	Dolphin Airlines ■
	5Q	Skargardsflyg AB	8V	Wright Air Service, Inc.
	5S	Airspeed Aviation, Inc.	8Y	Ecuato Guineana de Aviacion
#	5T	Airlink Airline (Pty.) Ltd.	9B	Intourtrans
	5U	Skagway Air Service, Inc.	# 9C	Gill Airways Ltd.
	5V	Community Express Airlines	9C★	Gill Airways Ltd. (Flight Numbers 550-553 Air UK (UK))
	5W	Interline Aviation		
	6A	Aviacsa-Consorcio Aviaxsa S.A. de C.V.	9D	Expresso Aereo
	6B	Baxter Aviation	9E	Express Airlines I, Inc. ■
	6C	Cape Smythe Air Service, Inc.	9G	Caribbean Air
	6D	Alaska Island Air, Inc.	9J	PACIFIC ISLAND AVIATION, Inc.
	6E	Malmo Aviation	9K	Cape Air ■
	6G	Las Vegas Airlines ■	9K★	Cape Air (Flight Numbers 98-124 Nantucket Airlines)
	6K	Korsar Airlines		
	6L	Aklak Air Ltd.	9L	COLGAN AIR ■
	6M	40-Mile Air, Inc.	9M	Central Mountain Air Ltd.
	6R	Air Affaires Afrique	9N	Trans States Airlines, Inc.
	6S	Ketchikan Air Service, Inc.	9P	Pelangi Air
	6T	Air Mandalay Ltd.	9Q	Taquan Air Service, Inc.
	6U	Air Ukraine	9S	Sabourin Lake Airways Ltd.
	6U★	Air Ukraine (Flight Numbers 193-194 LOT Polish Airlines (LO))	9T	Athabaska Airways Ltd.
			9U	Air Moldova
	6V	Air Vegas, Inc. ■	9V	Air Schefferville
	6W	Wilderness Airline (1975) Ltd.	9W	Jet Airways (India) Pvt. Ltd.
	6Y	Nicaraguense de Aviacion S.A. (NICA)		Alaska Central Express, Inc.
	7A	Haines Airways, Inc.		
	7B	Krasnoyarsk Airlines		
	7C	Columbia Pacific Airlines ■		
	7E	Nepal Airways Pvt. Ltd.		
	7F	First Air		
	7F★	First Air (Flight Numbers 400-431, 440-461 Air Inuit (1985) Ltd. (3H))		
	7H	ERA Aviation		
	7I	Imperial Air		
	7K	Larry's Flying Service, Inc.		
	7L	Air Belfast		
	7N	Air Manitoba		
	7P	APA International Air S.A.		
	7R	Redwing Airways, Inc.		
	7T	Trans Cote, Inc.		
	7U	Aviaenegro		
	7W	Air Sask Aviation 1991		
	7Z	Laker Airways (Bahamas) Ltd.		
	8A	Americana de Aviacion		
	8B	Baker Aviation, Inc.		
	8D	Awood Air Ltd.		
	8E	Bering Air, Inc.		
	8F	Haiti National Airlines (HANAIR)		
	8G	GP Express Airlines, Inc. ■		
	8H	Air South West		
	8K	Air Ostrava		
	8L	Grand International Airways, Inc.		
	8M	Mahalo Air, Inc.		
	8O	West Coast Air		
	8P	Pacific Coastal Airlines Ltd.		

Scheduled Intra-State Air Carriers

EX	Dallas Express Airlines, Inc.
H9	The Blade Helicopters
IS	Island Airlines, Inc.
3L	West Isle Air, Inc.
4Q	Trans North Aviation Ltd.

Other Codes

★ — (Following 2-character airline code) Code Sharing Carrier. Indicates a flight operated by a different airline from the airline whose code is shown.

★★ — Refer to carrier code and flight number on Airline Codes and Abbreviations to determine actual operating carrier.

■ — Indicates Part 204 Commuter Air Carrier: A Part 298 Commuter Air Carrier which has been found fit pursuant to Part 204 of the Economic Regulations of the United States Department of Transportation. Flight schedule listings for Part 204 Commuter Air Carriers are published in the Official Airline Guide chronologically with those of Certified Air Carriers.

◄ — National Air Transport Association, Inc.

♦ — Part 298 Non-certificated Air Taxi.

∞ — Duplicate Carrier Code.

— Non-scheduled Duplicate.

Appendix D

International Standard Time Chart

Standard Time: Legal time for each country fixed by law and based on the theoretical division of the world's surface into 24 zones each of 15° longitude with certain deviations due to frontiers or local option.

Daylight Savings Time (DST): Modified (advanced) legal time adopted by certain countries for part of the year, especially during local summer.

△—Arizona and parts of Indiana do not observe DST.
‡—Province of Saskatchewan and certain Canadian cities remain on Standard Time all year.
★—Except Broken Hill, N.S.W.; follows South Australia times.
■—Certain States of Brazil do not observe DST.
E —Estimated Date Based on Previous Year.
* —Listed are MAJOR cities for each zone.
▽—Serbia and Montenegro

	Standard Time		Daylight Savings Time	
Country	Hours from GMT	Time at 1200 hrs GMT	Hours from GMT	Effective Period (first and last day)
Afghanistan	+4 1/2	16 30		
Albania	+1	13 00	+2	Mar. 31, 1996E—Oct. 26, 1996E
Algeria	+1	13 00		
American Samoa	−11	01 00		
Andorra	+1	13 00	+2	Mar. 31, 1996E—Oct. 26, 1996E
Angola	+1	13 00		
Argentina	−3	09 00		
Armenia	+3	15 00		
Aruba	−4	08 00		
Australia				
Lord Howe Island	+10 1/2	22 30	+11	Oct. 29, 1995—Mar. 30, 1996
New South Wales, Australian Capitol Territory (A.C.T.)★	+10	22 00	+11	Oct. 29, 1995—Mar. 30, 1996

Reprinted by special permission from the February 1996 issue of the OAG Desktop Guide-Worldwide Edition. *All rights Reserved. Copyright 1996, Reed Travel Group.*

335

International Standard Time Chart, cont.

Country	Standard Time — Hours from GMT	Standard Time — Time at 1200 hrs GMT	Daylight Savings Time — Hours from GMT	Daylight Savings Time — Effective Period (first and last day)
Australia (cont.)				
Victoria	+10	22 00	+11	Oct. 29, 1995—Mar. 30, 1996
Northern Territory	+9 1/2	21 30		
Queensland	+10	22 00		
South Australia and Broken Hill	+9 1/2	21 30	+10 1/2	Oct. 29, 1995—Mar. 30, 1996
Tasmania	+10	22 00	+11	Oct. 01, 1995—Mar. 30, 1996
Western Australia	+8	20 00		
Austria	+1	13 00	+2	Mar. 31, 1996—Oct. 26, 1996
Azerbaijan	+3	15 00		
Bahamas (excluding Turks and Caicos Islands)	−5	07 00	−4	Apr. 07, 1996—Oct. 26, 1996
Bahrain Island	+3	15 00		
Bangladesh	+6	18 00		
Barbados	−4	08 00		
Belarus	+2	14 00	+3	Mar. 31, 1996E—Oct. 26, 1996E
Belgium	+1	13 00	+2	Mar. 31, 1996—Oct. 26, 1996
Belize	−6	06 00		
Benin Peoples Rep. (Dahomey)	+1	13 00		
Bermuda	−4	08 00	−3	Apr. 07, 1996—Oct. 26, 1996
Bhutan	+6	18 00		
Bolivia	−4	08 00		
Bosnia Herzegovina	+1	13 00	+2	Mar. 31, 1996E—Oct. 26, 1996E
Botswana	+2	14 00		
Brazil ■—East (including All Coast and Brasilia)	−3	09 00	−2	Oct. 15, 1995—Feb. 10, 1996
West	−4	08 00	−3	Oct. 15, 1995—Feb. 10, 1996
Territory of Acre	−5	07 00		
Fernando De Noronha	−2	10 00		
British Virgin Islands	−4	08 00		
Brunei Darussalam	+8	20 00		
Bulgaria	+2	14 00	+3	Mar. 31, 1996—Oct. 26, 1996
Burkina Faso	GMT	12 00		
Burundi	+2	14 00		
Cambodia	+7	19 00		
Cameroon, Republic of	+1	13 00		
Canada ‡—Newfoundland	−3 1/2	08 30	−2 1/2	Apr. 07, 1996—Oct. 26, 1996
Atlantic	−4	08 00	−3	Apr. 07, 1996—Oct. 26, 1996
Eastern	−5	07 00	−4	Apr. 07, 1996—Oct. 26, 1996
Central	−6	06 00	−5	Apr. 07, 1996—Oct. 26, 1996
Mountain	−7	05 00	−6	Apr. 07, 1996—Oct. 26, 1996
Pacific	−8	04 00	−7	Apr. 07, 1996—Oct. 26, 1996
Yukon Territory	−8	04 00	−7	Apr. 07, 1996—Oct. 26, 1996
Cape Verde Islands	−1	11 00		
Cayman Islands	−5	07 00		
Central African Republic	+1	13 00		
Chad	−1	13 00		

International Standard Time Chart, cont.

Country	Standard Time Hours from GMT	Standard Time Time at 1200 hrs GMT	Daylight Savings Time Hours from GMT	Daylight Savings Time Effective Period (first and last day)
Chile				
Continental	−4	08 00	−3	Oct. 15, 1995—Mar. 09, 1996
Easter Island	−6	06 00	−5	Oct. 15, 1995—Mar. 09, 1996
China, People's Republic of	+8	20 00		
Cocos (Keeling) Islands	+6 1/2	18 30		
Colombia	−5	07 00		
Comoros (see Mayotte)				
Congo	+1	13 00		
Cook Islands	−10	02 00		
Costa Rica	−6	06 00		
Cote d'Ivoire	GMT	12 00		
Croatia	+1	13 00	+2	Mar. 31, 1996E—Oct. 26, 1996E
Cuba	−5	07 00	−4	Apr. 07, 1996E—Oct. 05, 1996E
Cyprus	+2	14 00	+3	Mar. 31, 1996—Oct. 26, 1996
Czech Republic	+1	13 00	+2	Mar. 31, 1996—Oct. 26, 1996
Denmark	+1	13 00	+2	Mar. 31, 1996—Oct. 26, 1996
Djibouti	+3	15 00		
Dominican Republic	−4	08 00		
Ecuador				
Continental	−5	07 00		
Galapagos Islands	−6	06 00		
Egypt	+2	14 00	+3	Apr. 26, 1996—Sep. 26, 1996
El Salvador	−6	06 00		
Equatorial Guinea	+1	13 00		
Eritrea	+3	15 00		
Estonia	+2	14 00	+3	Mar. 31, 1996—Oct. 26, 1996
Ethiopia	+3	15 00		
Falkland Islands	−4	08 00	−3	Sep. 10, 1995E—Apr. 20, 1996E
Faroe Island	GMT	12 00	+1	Mar. 31, 1996—Oct. 26, 1996
Fiji	+12	23 59		
Finland	+2	14 00	+3	Mar. 31, 1996—Oct. 26, 1996
France	+1	13 00	+2	Mar. 31, 1996—Oct. 26, 1996
French Guiana	−3	09 00		
French Polynesia				
Gambier Island	−9	03 00		
Marquesas Island	−9 1/2	02 30		
Society Is., Tubual Is., Tuamotu Is., Tahiti	−10	02 00		
Gabon	+1	13 00		
Gambia	GMT	12 00		
Georgia	+4	16 00	+5	Mar. 31, 1996—Oct. 26, 1996
Germany	+1	13 00	+2	Mar. 31, 1996—Oct. 26, 1996
Ghana	GMT	12 00		
Gibraltar	+1	13 00	+2	Mar. 31, 1996—Oct. 26, 1996
Greece	+2	14 00	+3	Mar. 31, 1996—Oct. 26, 1996
Greenland				
Except Scoresbysund and Thule	−3	09 00	−2	Mar. 30, 1996—Oct. 25, 1996
Scoresbysund	−1	11 00	GMT	Mar. 31, 1996—Oct. 26, 1996

International Standard Time Chart, cont.

Country	Standard Time Hours from GMT	Standard Time Time at 1200 hrs GMT	Daylight Savings Time Hours from GMT	Daylight Savings Time Effective Period (first and last day)
Greenland (cont.)				
Thule	−4	08 00	−3	Apr. 07, 1996—Oct. 26, 1996
Guadeloupe (inc. St. Barthelemy, Northern St. Martin)	−4	08 00		
Guam	+10	22 00		
Guatemala	−6	06 00		
Guinea	GMT	12 00		
Guinea-Bissau	GMT	12 00		
Guyana	−4	08 00		
Haiti	−5	07 00	−4	Apr. 07, 1996E—Oct. 26, 1996E
Honduras	−6	06 00		
Hong Kong	+8	20 00		
Hungary	+1	13 00	+2	Mar. 31, 1996—Oct. 26, 1996
Iceland	GMT	12 00		
India (incl. Andaman Is.)	+5 1/2	17 30		
Indonesia				
Central	+8	20 00		
East	+9	21 00		
West (Jakarta)	+7	19 00		
Iran (The Islamic Rep. of)	+3 1/2	15 30	+4 1/2	Mar. 21, 1996—Sep. 21, 1996
Iraq	+3	15 00	+4	Apr. 01, 1996E—Sep. 30, 1996E
Ireland, Rep. of	GMT	12 00	+1	Mar. 31, 1996—Oct. 26, 1996
Israel	+2	14 00	+3	Mar. 29, 1996—Aug. 31, 1996
Italy	+1	13 00	+2	Mar. 31, 1996—Oct. 26, 1996
Jamaica	−5	07 00		
Japan	+9	21 00		
Johnston Island	−10	02 00		
Jordan	+2	14 00	+3	Apr. 05, 1996—Sep. 18, 1996
Kampuchea, Dem. (see Cambodia)				
Kazakhstan	+6	18 00	+7	Mar. 31, 1996E—Oct. 26, 1996E
Kenya	+3	15 00		
Kiribati, Rep. of	+12	23 59		
Canton, Enderbury Islands	−11	01 00		
Christmas Island	−10	02 00		
Korea, Democratic People's Republic of	+9	21 00		
Korea, Republic of	+9	21 00		
Kuwait	+3	15 00		
Kyrgyzstan	+5	17 00	+6	Apr. 14, 1996E—Sep. 28, 1996E
Laos	+7	19 00		
Latvia	+2	14 00	+3	Mar. 31, 1996E—Oct. 26, 1996E
Lebanon	+2	14 00	+3	Mar. 31, 1996E—Oct. 26, 1996E
Leeward Islands				
Antigua, Dominica, Montserrat, St. Christopher, St. Kitts, Nevis, Anguilla	−4	08 00		
Lesotho	+2	14 00		
Liberia	GMT	12 00		
Libyan Arab Jamahiriya	+1	13 00	+2	Mar. 30, 1996—Sep. 29, 1996
Lithuania	+2	14 00	+3	Mar. 31, 1996E—Oct. 26, 1996E

International Standard Time Chart, cont.

	Standard Time		Daylight Savings Time	
Country	Hours from GMT	Time at 1200 hrs GMT	Hours from GMT	Effective Period (first and last day)
Luxembourg	+1	13 00	+2	Mar. 31, 1996—Oct. 26, 1996
Macedonia	+1	13 00	+2	Mar. 31, 1996E—Oct. 26, 1996E
Madagascar	+3	15 00		
Malawi	+2	14 00		
Malaysia	+8	20 00		
Maldives	+5	17 00		
Mali	GMT	12 00		
Malta	+1	13 00	+2	Mar. 31, 1996—Oct. 26, 1996
Martinique	−4	08 00		
Mauritiania	GMT	12 00		
Mauritius	+4	16 00		
Mayotte	+3	15 00		
Mexico*				
Except Baja California Norte, Baja California Sur, Nayarit, Sinaloa, Sonora	−6	06 00		
Baja California Sur and N. Pacific Coast (states of Nayarit, Sinaloa and Sonora)—Culican, La Paz, Mazatlan	−7	05 00		
Baja California Norte (above 28th Parallel)—Mexacli, Tijuana	−8	04 00	−7	Apr. 07, 1996E—Oct. 2, 1996E
Midway Island	−11	01 00		
Moldova, Republic of	+2	14 00	+3	Mar. 31, 1996E—Oct. 26, 1996E
Monaco	+1	13 00	+2	Mar. 31, 1996E—Oct. 26, 1996E
Mongolia (Ulan Bator)	+8	20 00	+9	Mar. 31, 1996E—Oct. 26, 1996E
Morocco	GMT	12 00		
Mozambique	+2	14 00		
Myanmar	+6 1/2	18 30		
Namibia	+1	13 00	+2	Sep. 03, 1995—Mar. 31, 1996
Nauru, Republic Of	+12	23 59		
Nepal	+5 3/4	17 45		
Netherlands	+1	13 00	+2	Mar. 31, 1996—Oct. 26, 1996
Netherlands Antilles (incl. Southern St. Maarten)	−4	08 00		
New Caledonia	+11	23 00		
New Zealand (excluding Chatham Is.)	+12	23 59	+13	Oct. 01, 1995—Mar. 16, 1996
Chatham Island	+12 3/4	00 45	+13 3/4	Oct. 01, 1995—Mar. 16, 1996
Nicaragua	−6	06 00		
Niger	+1	13 00		
Nigeria	+1	13 00		
Niue Island	−11	01 00		
Norfolk Island	+11 1/2	23 30		
Norway	+1	13 00	+2	Mar. 31, 1996—Oct. 26, 1996
Oman	+4	16 00		
Pacific Islands Trust Territory				
Caroline Is. (excluding	+11	22 00		

International Standard Time Chart, cont.

Country	Standard Time Hours from GMT	Standard Time Time at 1200 hrs GMT	Daylight Savings Time Hours from GMT	Daylight Savings Time Effective Period (first and last day)
Pacific Islands Trust Territory (cont.)				
Ponape Is., Kusaie, and Pingelap)				
Kusaie, Pingelap, Marshall Is. (excluding Kwajalein)	+12	23 59		
Kwajalein	−12	00 01		
Mariana Island (excluding Guam)	+10	22 00		
Palau Island	+9	21 00		
Ponape Island	+11	23 00		
Pakistan	+5	17 00		
Panama	−5	07 00		
Papua New Guinea (and Bougainville Is.)	+10	22 00		
Paraguay	−4	08 00	−3	Oct. 01, 1995—Feb. 29, 1996
Peru	−5	07 00		
Phillippines, Republic of	+8	20 00		
Poland	+1	13 00	+2	Mar. 31, 1996E—Oct. 26, 1996E
Portugal				
Azores	−1	11 00	GMT	Mar. 31, 1996—Oct. 26, 1996
Madeira	GMT	12 00	+1	Mar. 31, 1996—Oct. 26, 1996
Mainland	+1	13 00	+2	Mar. 31, 1996—Oct. 26, 1996
Puerto Rico	−4	08 00		
Qatar	+3	15 00		
Reunion	+4	16 00		
Romania	+2	14 00	+3	Mar. 31, 1996—Oct. 26, 1996
Russian Federation*				
Zone 1 Kaliningrad	+2	14 00	+3	Mar. 31, 1996E—Oct. 26, 1996E
Zone 2 Moscow, St. Petersburg, Murmarsk, Astrakhan, Volrograd—(Moscow time)	+3	15 00	+4	Mar. 31, 1996E—Oct. 26, 1996E
Zone 3 Samara, Izhevsk	+4	16 00	+5	Mar. 31, 1996E—Oct. 26, 1996E
Zone 4 Chelyabinsk, Ekatrinburg, Perm, Nizhnevatovsk	+5	17 00	+6	Mar. 31, 1996E—Oct. 26, 1996E
Zone 5 Novosibirsk, Omsk	+6	18 00	+7	Mar. 31, 1996E—Oct. 26, 1996E
Zone 6 Krasnojarsk, Kyzyl, Norilsk	+7	19 00	+8	Mar. 31, 1996E—Oct. 26, 1996E
Zone 7 Irkutsk, Ulan-ude, Bratsk	+8	20 00	+9	Mar. 31, 1996E—Oct. 26, 1996E
Zone 8 Chita, Yakatsk	+9	21 00	+10	Mar. 31, 1996E—Oct. 26, 1996E
Zone 9 Khabarovsk, Vladivostok	+10	22 00	+11	Mar. 31, 1996E—Oct. 26, 1996E
Zone 10 Magadan	+11	23 00	+12	Mar. 31, 1996E—Oct. 26, 1996E
Zone 11 Petropavlovsk-Kamchatsky	+12	23 59	+13	Mar. 31, 1996E—Oct. 26, 1996E
Rwanda	+2	14 00		

International Standard Time Chart, cont.

	Standard Time		Daylight Savings Time	
Country	Hours from GMT	Time at 1200 hrs GMT	Hours from GMT	Effective Period (first and last day)
Saint Pierre and Miquelon	−3	09 00	−2	Apr. 07, 1996E—Oct. 26, 1996E
Saint Vincent and the Grenandines	−4	08 00		
Samoa	−11	01 00		
San Marino	+1	13 00	+2	Mar. 31, 1996E—Oct. 26, 1996E
Sao Tome Island and Principe Island	GMT	12 00		
Saudi Arabia	+3	15 00		
Senegal	GMT	12 00		
Seychelles	+4	16 00		
Sierra Leone	GMT	12 00		
Singapore	+8	20 00		
Slovakia	+1	13 00	+2	Mar. 31, 1996E—Oct. 26, 1996E
Slovenia	+1	13 00	+2	Mar. 31, 1996—Oct. 26, 1996
Solomon Islands (excluding Bougainville Is.)	+11	23 00		
Somalia	+3	15 00		
South Africa	+2	14 00		
Spain				
Canary Islands	GMT	12 00	+1	Mar. 31, 1996—Oct. 26, 1996
Continental, Belearic and Mallorca Islands	+1	13 00	+2	Mar. 31, 1996—Oct. 26, 1996
Melilla	+1	13 00	+2	Mar. 31, 1996—Oct. 26, 1996
Sri Lanka	+5 1/2	17 30		
St. Helena	GMT	12 00		
Sudan	+2	14 00		
Suriname, Republic of	−3	09 00		
Swaziland	+2	14 00		
Sweden	+1	13 00	+2	Mar. 31, 1996—Oct. 26, 1996
Switzerland	+1	13 00	+2	Mar. 31, 1996—Oct. 26, 1996
Syria	+2	14 00	+3	Apr. 01, 1996—Sep. 30, 1996
Taiwan	+8	20 00		
Tajikistan	+5	17 00		
Tanzania	+3	15 00		
Thailand	+7	19 00		
Togo	GMT	12 00		
Tonga	+13	01 00		
Trinidad and Tobago	−4	08 00		
Tunisia	+1	13 00		
Turkey	+2	14 00	+3	Mar. 31, 1996E—Oct. 26, 1996E
Turkmenistan	+5	17 00		
Turks and Caicos Islands	−5	07 00	−4	Apr. 07, 1996—Oct. 26, 1996
Tuvalu	+12	23 59		
Uganda	+3	15 00		
Ukraine (except Simferopol)	+2	14 00	+3	Mar. 31, 1996—Oct. 26, 1996
Simferopol	+3	15 00	+4	Mar. 31, 1996—Oct. 26, 1996
United Arab Emirates (Abu Dhabi, Dubai, Sharjah, Ras Al Khaimah)	+4	16 00		

International Standard Time Chart, cont.

Country	Standard Time: Hours from GMT	Standard Time: Time at 1200 hrs GMT	Daylight Savings Time: Hours from GMT	Daylight Savings Time: Effective Period (first and last day)
United Kingdom	GMT	12 00	+1	Mar. 31, 1996—Oct. 26, 1996
U.S.A.				
Eastern Time △	−5	07 00	−4	Apr. 07, 1996—Oct. 26, 1996
Central Time	−6	06 00	−5	Apr. 07, 1996—Oct. 26, 1996
Mountain Time △	−7	05 00	−6	Apr. 07, 1996—Oct. 26, 1996
Pacific Time	−8	04 00	−7	Apr. 07, 1996—Oct. 26, 1996
Alaska (except Aleutian Islands W. 169.30 Deg.)	−9	03 00	−8	Apr. 07, 1996—Oct. 26, 1996
Aleutian Islands 169.30 long. W. to Western tip	−10	02 00	−9	Apr. 07, 1996—Oct. 26, 1996
Arizona △	−7	05 00		
Hawaiian Islands	−10	02 00		
Indiana (East) △	−5	07 00		
U.S. Virgin Islands	−4	08 00		
Uruguay	−3	09 00		
Uzbekistan	+5	17 00		
Vanuatu	+11	23 00		
Venezuela	−4	08 00		
Vietnam, Socialist Rep. of	+7	19 00		
Wake Island	+12	23 59		
Wallis and Futuna Islands	+12	23 59		
Winward Islands				
Grenada, St. Lucia	−4	08 00		
Yemen, Republic of	+3	15 00		
Yugoslavia (Former) ▽	+1	13 00	+2	Mar. 31, 1996E—Oct. 26, 1996E
Zaire				
Kinshasa Mbandaka	+1	13 00		
Kasai, Kivu, Haut-Zaire, Shaba	+2	14 00		
Zambia	+2	14 00		
Zimbabwe	+2	14 00		

Glossary

Adult   Person who is 12 years or older when travel commences.

Adventure travel   Travel experience in which participants engage in personal challenges in outdoor settings.

Aeroflot   National airline of the former Soviet Union

Air tariff book   Publication containing comprehensive airfare information.

Airlines Reporting Corporation (ARC)   Organization that distributes ticket payments between member carriers.

Apex fare   Discounted economy airfare.

Banker's selling rate (BSR)   Rate at which a bank sells foreign currency.

Banknotes   Bank-issued promissory notes payable to the bearer on demand without interest; accepted as money.

Blue Train   Famous South African train between Cape Town and Pretoria.

Border   Line separating countries.

BritRail Pass   Rail pass needed for travel to, from, or within Great Britain.

Business visa   Visa required for business travel; *see Visa*.

Channel Tunnel A 31-mile long rail tunnel under the English Channel that connects France with Great Britain; sometimes called the "Eurotunnel" or the "Chunnel."

Child Person between 2 and 11 years of age when travel commences.

Cholera Disease state caused by contaminated food and drinking water; characterized by diarrhea and vomiting.

Commonwealth of Independent States (CIS) Treaty that established eleven of the independent Russian republics.

Connection Portion of a flight that does not interrupt the traveler's journey; also called a transfer.

Consul A government-appointed official who lives in a foreign country to serve, to represent and to protect the citizens of the appointing country.

Customs Declaration Form Document that details the retail value of all items acquired abroad.

Customs duties Taxes imposed on imported items.

Customs officers Officials charged with checking baggage for prohibited items in the customs control area.

Diplomatic passport Passport issued to a diplomat on government assignment; *see Passport*.

Duty-free State in which an item is not subject to sales tax in the country of purchase.

Earthwatch International program in which scientists, teachers, students, and artists are sponsored to research and document the changing world.

Eastern & Oriental Express Southeast Asia's first luxury train that traverses the Malay Peninsula between Singapore and Bangkok.

Economic and Monetary Union (EMU) Organization dedicated to establishing one stable and standard European currency; one goal of the Maastricht Treaty; *see Maastricht Treaty*.

Ecotourism Responsible travel that conserves environmental resources while supporting local people.

Eight Freedoms of the Air United Nations regulations governments must follow during air traffic negotiations.

Elapsed flying time Total time spent flying from the point of origin to the point of destination.

Embassy Body of diplomatic representatives appointed to protect the citizens of the appointing country.

Eurailpass Most popular European rail pass; *see Rail pass.*

Europass Rail pass offering unlimited rail travel in five of seventeen participating European countries; *see Rail pass.*

Europe Tax-Free Shopping (ETS) Tax refundable program in which participating European merchants refund the country's value-added tax (VAT) for items transported out of the country; *see Value-added tax (VAT).*

European Currency Unit (ECU) Standard European currency unit; goal of the Economic and Monetary Union (EMU); *see Economic and Monetary Union (EMU).*

European Economic Community (EEC) Political organization of twelve member countries that is based on the notion of free trade in Western Europe.

European Union (EU) Unified organization that developed when the twelve European Economic Community members (EEC) signed the Maastricht Treaty; groups later welcomed three additional member countries; *see European Economic Community (EEC) or Maastricht Treaty.*

Eurostar High-speed passenger train operating between London, Paris, and Brussels.

Excursion fare Discounted economy fare.

Fare calculation ladder A detailed breakdown of how the airfare was constructed.

Flag carriers Airlines that display their national colors.

Foreign Exchange Certificate (FEC) Only form in which travelers receive Chinese currency.

Game reserve Remote location that contains a variety of wildlife habitats.

Green card Document that verifies its holder has obtained permanent resident status in the issuing country.

Greenwich Mean Time (GMT) Mean solar time at the Greenwich meridian (0 degrees longitude) on which all time zones are based; also called Universal Time.

Hepatitis A Virus spread by contaminated food and water that is characterized early by fever, chills, fatigue, and aches and pains; later by loss of appetite, darkened urine, and yellowing of the whites of the eyes; treated effectively with gamma globulin.

Hepatitis B Virus spread through skin penetration that is characterized early by fever, chills, fatigue, and aches and pains; later by loss of appetite, darkened urine, and yellowing of the whites of the eyes; gamma globulin treatment is ineffective.

IATA Passenger Services Conference Resolutions International Air Transport Association (IATA) publication on which the IATA Ticketing Handbook is based; *see IATA Ticketing Handbook.*

IATA Ticketing Handbook Publication of the International Air Transport Association (IATA) that delivers detailed instructions on how to issue and reissue interline airline tickets; *see International Air Transport Association (IATA).*

Immigration and Naturalization Services (INS) Organization that functions mainly to control who enters and departs the United States.

Immigration officers Officials charged with checking travel documents immediately when travelers arrive; officers decide if travelers may enter their countries.

Immunizations Treatments administered to travelers to render them safe from disease.

Import permit Registration form for restricted items.

Infant Person under 2 years old when travel commences.

INSPASS New immigration system developed by Immigration and Naturalization Services (INS) that is designed to prevent long immigration checks for member citizens in the United

States, Canada, Bermuda, and the Visa Waiver Program; *see Immigration and Naturalization Services (INS).*

Interline agreement An understanding between two airlines to transport the other's passengers and to transfer those passengers' baggage at connecting points.

International Air Transport Association (IATA) Private organization of scheduled international airlines that regulates international air traffic.

International Airlines Travel Agency Network (IATAN) Organization whose main function is to serve United States travel agencies; services include authorizing American travel agencies to sell international tickets and setting travel industry standards.

International arrivals The number of visitor arrivals to a location, not the number of people arriving. The same person arriving numerous times would be counted each time as a visitor arrival.

International Date Line Imaginary line directly opposite Greenwich Mean Time (GMT) used to separate one day from the next; *see Greenwich Mean Time (GMT).*

International Organization for Standardization (ISO) Group that standardizes international commercial and industrial regulations and has established country codes.

International tourism receipts Revenue that results when international visitors pay for goods and services.

International tourist Any person who travels to a country in which he or she does not reside for at least 1 night.

International visitor Any person who travels to a country in which he or she does not reside for 1 year or under.

Jet lag Condition in which the body's internal clock becomes disturbed and disrupts such things as body temperature and sleep patterns.

Le Shuttle One-half hour train service that transports passengers and their vehicles through the Channel Tunnel; *see Channel Tunnel.*

Maastricht Treaty Agreement signed by twelve European Economic Community (EEC) members to form a united Europe with common foreign, defense, monetary, and immigration policies; also called the Treaty on European Union; *see European Economic Community (EEC)*.

Malaria Flu-like illness caused by the bite of an infected mosquito that is common in tropical and subtropical areas of India; characterized by fever and shivers lasting more than 2 days.

Meningococcal meningitis bacteria Bacteria that attacks the brain and manifests itself in severe headaches, neck stiffness, and light sensitivity; can be fatal if not immunized against.

Motion sickness Condition in which the body's senses of balance and movement are disturbed.

National Traveler who is a citizen of a country.

National Audubon Society Organization that works to conserve natural ecosystems, particularly those of birds and other wildlife.

Nonparticipating countries Countries that do not participate in Europe's Eurailpass program and charge rail travelers fees; *see Eurailpass*.

Normal fare Unrestricted and totally flexible airfare.

Norms Rules of socially acceptable behavior; sometimes unwritten.

Official passport Passport issued to all government workers except diplomats; *see Passport*.

Open-jaw air ticket Airline ticket with a portion of the trip that is not traveled by air.

Passport Government-issued document that identifies its bearer as a citizen of the issuing country or the country in which the bearer was naturalized.

Point of origin City in which a journey originates.

Point-to-point fares   Local currency fares quoted on through fares from the point of origin to the point of destination.

Rail pass   Ticket accepted for train travel; most economical and flexible means of travel.

Regular passport   Passport for business or vacation travelers; *see Passport.*

Reunification Express   Vietnamese nonluxury train between Ho Chi Minh City in the south and Hanoi in the north.

Stopover   Traveler's voluntary interruption of a flight for more than 6 hours between the point of origin and the point of destination.

Student visa   Visa required for student travel; *see Visa.*

Sustainable tourism   Form of tourism that supports the continued survival of indigenous cultures while having as little environmental impact as possible.

Tetanus   Germ that grows inside an infected wound; characterized by jaw and neck stiffening, leading to seizures throughout the body and possibly death if not treated.

Tourist card   Document that replaces the passport or visa; *see Passport or Visa.*

Tourist visa exempt   Classification in which the passport holder does not need a visa to visit foreign countries; *see Visa.*

Transit visa   Visa that is available upon arriving at the airport; *see Visa.*

Trans-Siberian Railroad   Railway that runs from Vladivostok to Moscow.

Travel agent identification card   Document that identifies a United States travel agent as a professional travel industry employee.

Traveler   A person who makes a journey of some length.

Traveler's checks   Drafts purchased from a lending agency to guard against forgery.

Traveler's diarrhea Abnormally frequent intestinal evacuations caused by bacteria ingested in food or water; commonly experienced by travelers to developing countries.

Typhoid fever Stomach infection caused by poor hygiene or contaminated food or water; characterized by diarrhea and fever.

Universal Time *See Greenwich Mean Time (GMT).*

Value-added tax (VAT) European equivalent to national sales tax; *see Europe Tax-Free Shopping (ETS).*

Visa Endorsement on one of the passport's blank pages that allows the holder to enter a foreign country; *see Passport.*

World Tourism Organization (WTO) Group that publishes current statistics on domestic and international travel and tourism and forecasts 10-year travel and tourism trends.

World Travel & Tourism Council (WTTC) Multinational organization whose goal is to show governments how travel and tourism benefits local and international economies.

Yellow fever Condition caused by a virus circulated among animals in certain tropical areas whose main symptom is high fever; common in wet tropical areas like Africa.

Index

A

Aborigines, 223, 275–78
Adventure travel, 262, 264, 267, 268–69
Adventure Travel Society, 264, 267
Aeroflot, 190–91
Africa, 5, 6, 11, 235
    and international tourist arrivals, 8, 10, 236
    rail travel in, 238–42
    South, 236–42
    See also Algeria, Egypt, Ethiopia, Morocco, Nile River, Sudan, Tanzania, Tunisia, Zambezi River Valley, Zambia, Zimbabwe
Air routes, 50–52
Air tariff book, 99, 100, 101
Air Tariff Worldwide Fares Book, 100, 101, 103, 104
Air traffic
    agreements, 34–35
    regulations, 41
Air travel geography, 34
Air routes, 50–52
Airfare, 92–99
    airline specific, 138
    apex, 107
    calculation ladder, 132, 133
    in European Union, 154–55
    excursion, high-season, 110
    lightly restricted, 106
    local currency, 132
    non-restricted, 110
    rule, 94
Airlines
    codes for, 47–50
    national, 41
Airlines Reporting Corporation (ARC), 42, 122, 123, 126, 128, 133, 134, 136, 137, 138, 139
Airspace, international, 34
Algeria, 10, 235
Altitude sickness, 18
Amazon, 270–73
    Center for Environmental Education and Research (ACEER), 273
Ambato, 250
American Airlines, 12
American Automobile Association, 12
American Express, 12
American Samoa, 227
Americas, the, 6, 10, 11
    and international tourist arrivals, 7, 8, 9
Animals
    endangered, 82
    and protecting habitats, 279–82

351

Animals *cont.*
   transportation of, 44
   unique, 194, 195, 213, 223
Antarctica, 253, 254–55
Apartheid, 237
Apex fares, 95–97, 107, 111, 113, 135
   displays, 102–04
Apollo Travel Services, 109, 110, 111, 112, 113
Archaeological attractions
   African, 242, 245
   Asian, 223
   European, 82, 167, 168
   Pacific, South, 226–27
Architectural attractions
   Asian, 213, 216, 219, 221
   European, 164–65, 166, 167–68, 172, 175, 176, 177
   Pacific, South, 225
   Russian, 180, 193–94, 196, 197
Arctic Circle, 178
Arctica, 198–201
Argentina, 251–54
Arrests, 71, 73, 81–82
Arrivals
   international tourist, 6–7, 8, 9, 14, 15, 209, 210, 211, 216, 236
   by region, 8
Art, 244
Asia, 208–10
   East, 6, 7, 8, 9
   and international tourist arrivals, 7, 8, 9, 209
   and rail travel, 210–16
   and tourism receipts, 11
   South, 9, 281
Australia, 9, 210, 220–24, 275–78, 281–82
Aviation code, 42–43

B

Baggage
   allowance, 124–27
   transfers, 44, 154
Bangkok, 215

Bank notes, 153
Banker's selling rate (BSR), 83
Blue Train, 238–42
Bolder Adventures, 267, 280
Bora Bora, 227
Border, 34
Brazil, 278–79
British Airways, 12
Bullet Train (Shinkansen), 197
Business travel, 5
   visa for, 71
Butterworth, 214

C

Cambodia, 9, 81
Cape Town, 238
Caribbean, 9
Castles, 166, 175, 176, 177, 197
Caves, 225
Channel Tunnel, 151, 159, 160, 161
Checks, 153
Children, 68, 69, 97–98
   fares for, 97–98, 132–35, 139, 157
   and proof of custody, 76
Chili, 251–54
China, 196, 210
Cholera, 19, 21, 22
Circle-trip, 94
Civilization, ancient, 242
Citizenship, 69, 73
   proof of, 76–77
Claim tags, 44
Climate, 3
Codes
   airline codes, 48–50
   aviation, 42–43
   baggage, free, 126
   city codes, 48–49
   excursion/apex fare basis, 96–97
   and global indicators, 50–52
   IATA, 47–50
   international tax and currency, 127
   passenger identification, 121, 123, 124
   sales indicator, 129–31

Commonwealth of Independent States, 187–89
Connection, 92–93
Consequential requirement, 120
Consulates, 71
Cook Islands, 227–28
Countries of the World and Their Leaders Yearbook, The, 237
Credit cards, 153
Crimes, 77
Cruises, 173–77, 199, 223, 242, 255, 268, 270–73
Cuenca, 251
Culture, 6, 180, 201, 211, 255, 263–64, 282
   adapting to, 263–64
   and diversity, 29, 237, 255
   preservation of, 262, 265, 273–79
   and Russia, 189
Currency, 81, 82, 83–84, 127
   codes, 84
   European, 151
Customs, 44, 77, 85, 154
   duties, 79, 81
   officers, 77
   procedures, 79–81
   and restricted items, 81–82

D

Da Nang, 219
Deportation, 73
Desert, 222–23, 237, 251
   Antarctic, 254
   Sahara, 242
Destinations
   choosing, 263–64
   most popular, 13–16
   See also Africa, Antarctica, Asia, Europe, Russia, South America, South Pacific
Detainment, 73
Developing nations
   and environmental concerns, 272
   preparations for traveling to, 234–35

Diamond mines, 240
Diplomatic passport, 68, 71
Diplomat's international ticket, 123
Drugs, illegal, 77, 81, 82
Duties, 79, 81

E

Earthwatch, 267–78
Easter Island, 226–27
Economic and Monetary Union (EMU), 151, 153–54
Economy fares, 95
Ecotourism, 262, 264–68
Ecuador, 248–51
Education, of travel professionals, 2–3
Egypt, 7, 242, 244–45
Eight Freedoms of the Air, 35–40, 155
Elapsed flying time, 58–60
Embassies, 71
Employment, 12–13
England. *See* Great Britain
Environmental concerns, 22, 265–66, 269–70, 279–82
Ethiopia, 246
Europe, 4, 6
   destinations, 162–73
   Eastern, 197–98
   and international tourist arrivals, 7, 8, 9–10
   and rail travel, 155–56
      passes for, 156–59
   Tax-Free Shopping (ETS), 84–85
   and tourism receipts, 10, 11
   travel, 154–55
   and value-added tax, 84–85
   See also France, Germany, Great Britain, Greece, Israel, Italy, the Mediterranean, Morocco, Scandinavia, Spain, Turkey
European Currency Unit (ECU), 151
European Economic Community (EEC), 150

European Union (EU), 13, 44, 150–54
   and financial concerns, 153–54
   member nations, 150–52, 153
Exchange rates, 83, 153
Excursion fares, 95–97, 107, 135
   and displays, 102–04
   high-season, 110

F

Fare displays, 99–104
   automated, 104, 107, 109
Fares, 50–52. *See also* Air fare
Fiji, 226
Five Freedoms of the Air, 35
Flag carriers, 41
Foreign Exchange Certificates (FEC), 84
France, 5, 10, 172–73
   and the Riviera, 162, 164

G

Game reserves. *See* Wilderness areas
Geography, 2–3
   IATA areas, 45–47
Germany, 10, 175, 197–98
Geysers, 228
Ghan, The, 22–23
Gold mines, 240
Great Britain, 4, 78, 79, 172
Greece, 167–68
Green card, 73
Greenwich Mean Time, 55
Guayaquil, 251

H

Hanoi, 220
Health issues, 16–17
   altitude and motion sickness, 18
   food and water, 18–19
   illnesses, 19–26
   jet lag, 17–18, 29
Heathrow Airport, 78
Helicopter
   shuttles, 94–97
   tours, 247

Hepatitis, 22, 24
Hertz Corporation, 12
Historical items, 82
History
   of travel, 4
Ho Chi Minh City, 217
Holiday Inn, 12
Hong Kong, 208, 210
Hue, 219

I

Illness. *See* Health issues *and* individual illnesses
Immigration, 77–79, 154
   control, 44
   inspectors, 73
   officers, 77
Immigration and Naturalization Services (INS), 78
Immunizations, 19, 22, 26
Import permits, 82
India, 9
Indian Pacific, 221–22
Indochina, 210
Indonesia, 9, 277, 280
Industry Agents' Handbook, 122, 126, 128, 133, 134, 136, 137, 138, 139
Infants, 68, 97–98
   fares for, 97–98, 135, 136
INSPASS, 79
Interline travel, 44
International Airlines Travel Agency Network, The (IATAN), 43–44
International Air Transport Association (IATA), 41–43
   agent responsibilities, 120–21
   airfares
     excursion and apex, 95–97
     infants and children's, 97–98
     normal, 94
     rule displays, 98–99
     stopovers and connections, 92–93
   codes, 47–50
   and geography, 45–47

Passenger Services Conference
  Resolutions, 120
Resolutions
  800b, 120
  830a, 120
Ticketing Handbook, 93, 120, 121
ticketing procedures, 132–39
International Date Line, 57–58, 225
International Expeditions, 273
International Organization for Standardization (ISO), 84
International tourism receipts, 10
International tourist
  defined, 3
International World Congress on Adventure Travel and Ecotourism, 264
Ipoh, 214
Iran, 9
Irkutsk, 194
Israel, 7, 77, 169
Italy, 10, 11, 173
  and the Riviera, 162, 164–65
Itineraries
  apex-fare, 135
  excursion-fare, 135
  fully packaged, 189–90
  international, 68
  normal-fare, 132, 134, 135

J

Japan, 196–97
Jet lag, 17–18, 29
Johannesburg, 240
John F. Kennedy Airport, 79
Jungle, 210, 213, 215, 216, 220, 224–28

K

Khabarovsk, 195
Kimberley, 240

L

Lake Baikal, 194
Language, 42
Laos, 9
Lapland, 178
Le Shuttle, 160, 162
Leisure travel, 5–6

M

Maastricht Treaty, 150–51
Macau, 208, 210
Malaria, 26, 28
Malaysia, 213–14
Mandela, Nelson, 236, 237, 238
Mediterranean, the, 9–10, 162, 163, 235, 244
Meningitis, 26, 27
Mexico, 76
Middle East, 6
  and international tourist arrivals, 7, 8
  and tourism receipts, 10, 11
Monaco, 164
Money
  currency codes, 84
  foreign currency, 82, 83–84
  value-added tax, 84–85
Money orders, 81, 153
Morocco, 10, 167, 235
Moscow, 191, 192
Motion sickness, 18
Mountainous destinations
  African, 235, 237, 238, 241
  Asian, 208, 210, 213, 214–15, 216, 217, 219, 220, 266
  Australian, 222, 223
  European, 162, 164, 165, 167, 175, 177
  Russian, 193–94, 196–97
  South American, 248–54
  South Pacific, 224–28
Museums, 164, 165, 166, 172, 240

N

National Audubon Society, 267, 268
Nepal, 9
New Zealand, 9, 228
Newark International Airport, 79
Nha Trang, 217, 219

Nile River, 242–46
Normal fare, 94, 99, 102, 104, 134, 135
North Pole, 199–201

O

OAG Desktop Guide—Worldwide Edition, 48–49, 51, 56
Official passport, 71
Open-jaw air ticket, 211
Orangutan Foundation, 280
Orient Express, 169–73
    Eastern &, 210–16

P

Passport, 68–71, 84, 154
    countries not requiring, 76
Pearson International Airport, 79
Philippines, 210
Point of origin, 99, 129
Point-to-point fares, 132
Portugal, 5
Proof of citizenship, 76–77
Proceedings of the 1994 World Congress on Adventure Travel and Ecotourism, 269
Protection, 68, 71
Puerto Montt, 254
Punta Arenas, 252–53
Pyramids, 244–45

Q

Queenslander, The, 223–24
Quito, 249–50

R

Racism, 237
Rail passes, 156–60
Rain forests, 210, 213, 214, 223, 224, 269, 270–73
    African, 247
    South American, 270–73
Reefs, coral, 223–24, 226, 269
Regulations, governmental, 34
Religious attractions, 165, 168, 172, 173, 175, 176, 177, 189, 193, 195, 198, 211–12, 213–14, 215, 219

Buddhist, 195, 213, 215, 216, 217, 219, 220
Christian, 165, 172, 173, 175, 176, 177, 189, 193, 198, 213
Egyptian, 244–45, 246
Greek, 168
Hindu, 211, 213, 214
Muslim, 168, 189, 213
Taoist, 213
Restricted route, 112
Reunification Express, 217–20
Riobamba, 250–51
River travel. *See* Waterways
Round-trip, 94, 95, 96
Rule, apex, 113
Rule E025, 103
Rule E687, 104
Rule N3615, 108
Russia, 186
    air travel in, 190–91
    destinations, 191–201
    rail travel in, 191
    See also Commonwealth of Independent States (CIS) *and* Arctica, China, Europe, Irkutsk, Khabarovsk, Lake Baikal, Moscow, Siberia, Ulan Ude, Vladivostok, Yaroslaw

S

Safari, 241, 242, 248, 264
Scandinavia, 177–80
Sea and ocean destinations
    African, 237, 238, 241
    Asian, 211, 214, 215, 216, 217
    Australian, 221–22, 223
    European, 162, 164, 165–66, 168, 177–80
    Russian, 196–97
    South American, 251–54
    South Pacific, 224–28
Seven Wonders of the World, 168, 245
Shopping, 244
    duty-free, 81
    and value-added tax, 84–85

Siberia, 193–94
Singapore, 211, 213
SITI (sold inside, ticketed inside), 130
SITO (sold inside, ticketed outside), 131
SOTI (sold outside, ticketed inside), 130
SOTO (sold outside, ticketed outside), 129, 131
South America, 248–54
South Pacific region, 6, 208, 224–28
   and international tourist arrivals, 7, 8, 9
   See also American Samoa, Bora Bora, Cook Islands, Easter Island, Fiji, New Zealand, Tahiti, Tonga
Souvenirs, 82
Soviet Union, 4
Spain, 165–67
Sphinx, 245
Sri Lanka, 9
Statistical information, 6
Stopover, 92–93, 94, 95, 102, 135, 136
   rule, 105, 111
Student visa, 71
Sudan, 245–46
Switzerland, 173, 175

T

Tahiti, 227
Tanzania, 241–42
Taxes
   departure, 129
   international, 127–29
Tetanus, 22, 25
Thailand, 9, 77, 214–16
Third World countries. *See* Developing nations
Ticketing procedures, 120
Tickets, 42, 43
   for extra seat, 124
   international airline, 121, 122
      and baggage allowance, 124–27
      diplomat's, 122
      passenger name, 121, 122, 123, 124
      sales indicator code, 131
      tax computation and currency code, 127–29
   one-way, 86
Tierra del Fuego, 252
Time
   elapsed flying time, 58
   International Date Line and, 57–58
   24-hour clock, 52–54
Time zones, 54–57, 199
Tonga, 225–26
Tour groups, 73
Tourism
   in developing nations, 234–36
   receipts, 10, 11, 12
   sustainable, 262–64
   trends in, 6–7
Tourist
   card, 76
   visa exempt, 73
Train travel, 155–56
   in Africa, 238–42
   Australian, 220–24
   and the Orient Express, 169–73
   passes for, 156–60, 220
   in Russia, 191, 192, 193–94, 195
   South American, 249, 250
   in Vietnam, 217–20
Trans-Siberian Railroad, 195
Trans World Airlines, 100, 101, 103, 104, 105, 107, 108
Transit visa, 73
Travel
   agencies, 42, 83
   agent identification cards, 43–44
   economic effect of, 12
   employment in, 12–13
   historical reasons for, 3–4
   interline, 44
   international, 5–6, 263–64
   professionals, 263–64
   socially responsible, 265–66
   trends, 6–7

Travel documents
   passport, 68–71
   proof of citizenship, 76–77
   tourist card, 76
   visa, 71–75
Travel Industry Yearbook: The Big Picture, The, 7, 208, 235
Travel tips, 26, 29
   and airline observation, 41
   on culture and customs, 180, 201, 255, 263–64, 282
   and flexible planning, 140
   and immigration laws, 78–79
   and luggage, 61
   and one-way tickets, 86
   and personal travelog, 114
   and photographs, 201
   and travel documents, 86
   U.S. State Department advisories, 228
Travel Weekly, 13, 210, 216
Traveler, 3, 262
   and adaptability, 263–64
Traveler's checks, 81, 83
Traveler's diarrhea, 18–19
Tunisia, 235
Turkey, 168

U

Ulan Ude, 195
United States, 13
   Department of State Advisory, 228
      (sample), 74–75
   departure tax, 129
Universal Time, 55
Ushuaia, 252

V

Value-added tax, 84–85
Vietnam, 9, 208, 210, 216–20
Visa, 71–75, 78, 154
   countries not requiring, 73, 187
Vladivostok, 195–96

Volcanoes, 224–28, 235, 241, 249, 250, 254

W

Walt Disney Company, 12
Water sports, 211, 247, 248, 251, 254
Waterfalls
   African, 235, 241, 245, 246, 247
   Asian, 214, 215
   Australian, 222
   European, 173, 178
   South American, 251, 252
   South Pacific, 224–28
Waterways
   Amazon, 270–73
   the Danube river, 176–77
   Nile River, 242–46
   the Rhine river, 173, 174, 175–76
Wilderness areas, 268
   African, 240, 241, 242, 248
   Antarctic, 254
   Arctic, 180
   Asian and Pacific, 213, 214, 215
   maintaining, 269–70, 273, 279–82
   Russian, 193, 194, 195
   South American, 252, 270–73
World Tourism Organization (WTO), 6, 8, 14, 15, 16
World Travel & Tourism Council (WTTC), 12, 13

Y

Yaroslaw, 193
Yellow fever, 19, 20

Z

Zambezi River Valley, 246–48
Zambia, 241, 246
Zimbabwe, 241, 246